BARBED-WIRE IMPERIALISM

BERKELEY SERIES IN BRITISH STUDIES

Edited by Mark Bevir and James Vernon

Aidan Forth   •   BARBED-WIRE
IMPERIALISM

Britain's Empire of Camps, 1876–1903

UNIVERSITY OF CALIFORNIA PRESS

University of California Press, one of the most distinguished university presses in the United States, enriches lives around the world by advancing scholarship in the humanities, social sciences, and natural sciences. Its activities are supported by the UC Press Foundation and by philanthropic contributions from individuals and institutions. For more information, visit www.ucpress.edu.

University of California Press
Oakland, California

Library of Congress Cataloging-in-Publication Data

Names: Forth, Aidan, author.
Title: Barbed-wire imperialism : Britain's empire of camps, 1876–1903 / Aidan Forth.
Description: Oakland, California : University of California Press, [2017] | Series: Berkeley series in British studies; 12
Identifiers: LCCN 2017010810 (print) | LCCN 2017021208 (ebook) | ISBN 9780520967267 (ebook) | ISBN 9780520293960 (cloth : alk. paper) | ISBN 9780520293977 (pbk. : alk. paper)
Subjects: LCSH: Concentration camps—Africa—19th century. | Great Britain—Colonies—Africa—19th century. | South African War, 1899–1902—Concentration camps. | Concentration camps—India—19th century. | Great Britain—Colonies—India—19th century.
Classification: LCC JV1027 (ebook) | LCC JV1027 .F65 2017 (print) | DDC 365/.34—dc23
LC record available at https://lccn.loc.gov/2017010810

Manufactured in the United States of America

25 24 23 22 21 20 19 18 17 16
10 9 8 7 6 5 4 3 2 1

For my parents

CONTENTS

FIGURES

ACKNOWLEDGMENTS

The research and writing of this book took place at libraries and archives in four continents and over a dozen countries. On this nearly decade-long journey, I learned a great deal about camps, liberalism, violence, and empire, but my most valuable lesson has been in the virtues of scholarly collaboration.

This book started its life as a PhD dissertation at Stanford University. Priya Satia was an ideal supervisor: creative, dynamic, and with a keen eye for the "big stakes" of a project. Her own scholarship has inspired me and many others to make history relevant to a global contemporary audience. Also at Stanford, J. P. Daughton, Amir Weiner, David Como, James Sheehan, Keith Baker, Paul Robinson, and Hal Kahn provided valuable guidance and support. James Vernon and Thomas Laqueur, meanwhile, welcomed me to their stimulating seminars across San Francisco Bay and to the Stanford-Berkeley British Studies reading group. Finally, Peter Stansky became a lasting friend who continues to inspire me as a model of humanity and scholarship.

As I traveled further abroad I benefited immensely from Elizabeth van Heyningen's mentorship. As the leading scholar of the Anglo-Boer War concentration camps, she was generous with her time and insights. Iain Smith at the University of Warwick has been a tireless supporter of my work; his conference on colonial concentration camps at All Souls College, Oxford, and the many hours I spent at his home in Leamington Spa discussing the South African War were formative in the generation of my argument, though he may (still!) not agree with everything I say.

Of the many archivists and librarians who have assisted in tracking down photographs, obscure diaries, or unfiled documents hidden in the depths of archival repositories, Jaya Ravindran at the National Archives of India stands out. Also in India, Radhika Singha, Dinyar Patel, Riyad Koya, Eesvan Krishnan, and Dwayne Menezes introduced me to warm and welcoming intellectual communities in Mumbai and Delhi. Jonas Kreienbaum, Christopher Holdridge, and Matthew Wm Kennedy have provided a stimulating cohort of young scholars working on colonial camps, and I have benefitted from collaborations with them at conferences from Oxford to Ghent to Rostock. After years of rewriting and refinement, the book has at last come to completion at Loyola University Chicago, where I have been surrounded by many supportive colleagues, friends, and students. Timothy Gilfoyle has been my advocate from the moment I started my career and has applied his keen editor's eye to the manuscript, which he carefully read in its entirety. Michael Khodarkovsky, Jo N. Hays, and Elliot Gorn also commented on the manuscript, while Suzanne Kaufman, Stephen Schloesser, Robert Bucholz, John Donoghue, Kyle Roberts, Edin Hajdarpasic, Alice Weinreb, Jane Currie, Patricia Clemente, and David Hays have been especially supportive. Among the many other scholars and friends who deserve credit are Clare Anderson, Jordanna Bailkin, Susan Bell, Jane Burbank, Anna Clark, Deborah Cohen, Nicholas Coetzer, Jane Currie, Sandra den Otter, Michael David-Fox, Kevin Grant, Peter Holquist, Deborah Hutton, Linda Huyhn, Fredrick Albritton Jonsson, Ben Kiernan, Katharina Matro, Katherine McDonough, Bill Meier, Noah Millstone, Kathyrn Müller, Bradley Naranch, Carl Nightingale, Panikos Panayi, Dean Pavlakis, Art Palmon, Susan Pedersen, Fransjohan Pretorius, Tehila Sasson, Ben Stone, Susan and Gordon Summers, Michelle Tusan, Jeanine Visser, and Lindsay Weiss. The participants of the SSRC-IDRF Fellows workshop in Portland; the "Colonial Concentration Camp" conference at All Souls College, Oxford; "The Soviet Gulag: New Research and New Interpretations" conference at Georgetown University; the "Imperial Cloud" conference at the University of Rostock; and the "Carceral Archipelago Conference" at the University of Leicester along with commentators at many other conferences, seminars, and workshops are too numerous to name, but they all deserve mention. The shortcomings of this book are, of course, entirely my own, the first of which is I have surely failed to name other important scholars who have contributed to my work.

This book would not have been possible without generous funding from a wide variety of institutions. These include the Department of History at Stanford University; the Social Sciences and Humanities Research Council of Canada; the

Council for European Studies Pre-Dissertation Fellowship; the Anglo-California Foundation; the Stanford Graduate Research Opportunities Grant for Research on Modern British History and Culture; an Andrew W. Mellon Dissertation Fellowship awarded by the Stanford Humanities Center; a generous grant from the James B. Weter Memorial Fund; and a monetary prize from the Pacific Coast Conference on British Studies. A grant from the Elliot School of International Affairs enabled me to attend the Summer Institute on Conducting Archival Research at George Washington University, thereby giving direction to my initial archival forays. An International Dissertation Research Fellowship from the Social Science Research Council (SSRC-IDRF) permitted me to travel to South Africa and India, thus facilitating a "transimperial" approach. While conducting research in Britain I benefited immensely from the rich social and academic atmosphere of London's Goodenough College, a stay made possible by an award from the London Goodenough Association of Canada, while residence at the Camargo Foundation in Cassis, France, offered a calm and reflective setting in which to write. Last but certainly not least, funding from the Department of History at Loyola University and a grant from the Loyola University Office of Research Services have permitted additional archival trips, while a generous research leave from Loyola in 2016 enabled me, at last, to complete the project.

At the University of California Press, Niels Hooper and James Vernon have been wonderful editors. As always, I trust James for his incisive advice and deeply appreciate his tireless efforts to go above and beyond the call of duty. Antoinette Burton and an anonymous peer reviewer provided helpful feedback that has sharpened the argument and organization of the book in meaningful ways. Bradley Depew, Sabrina Robleh, and Nicholle Robertson have been patient and understanding in their logistical guidance.

Above all, I am grateful to my family: my parents Drs. Christine Forth and Gregory Forth; my grandparents Leslie and Pretoria; and Kelly Summers, whose love and support has made an academic life exciting and worthwhile. Finally, Rupert and Beatrice have brought happiness in ways I had never imagined possible.

Aidan Forth, Chicago, Illinois

Britain's Empire of Camps

In the South African winter of 1900, the Strauss family lived on a farm on the out-skirts of Springfontein in the Orange Free State. Until then, their memories were happily carefree. In the garden, the children climbed a blue gum tree. Mr. Strauss tended horses with his older son, while his daughters modeled new bonnets on their farmhouse stoop. With the outbreak of war, however, global geopolitics descended on their doorstep. The family's domestic tranquility was punctuated when "a group of soldiers with fixed bayonets" searched the house for weapons and supplies. From then on, officious intrusions from khaki-clad officers—demanding answers in an alien language (English)—became more regular and more ominous. British soldiers soon requisitioned the farm itself and "in the depth of winter" the family, now destitute and homeless, slept on "the cold hard ground" in "two lonely tents in Block C" of a "concentration camp."[1]

An ocean away, but just a few months previously, a father and daughter endured a similar ordeal on the frontier of India's Bombay Presidency. They were also interned, this time in the thatch and iron huts of a "plague segregation camp." Two of countless thousands detained as suspected disease carriers, their story is known because they wrote a letter of protest to the British District Commissioner. The camp, they complained, was dirty, dark, and damp. Inmates were treated with dis-dain and had to follow orders, delivered in clipped English or broken Hindi, from an "insulting and sarcastic" superintendent.[2]

Meanwhile, on the Sholapur Road, sixteen miles from the Indian city of Poona, the *Manchester Guardian* correspondent Vaughan Nash saw "hundreds of people

. . . squatting on the ground, each man, woman, and child beside a heap of broken and unbroken stones." One girl was "vainly trying to break a small lump of stone" beneath the tropical sun. Without shade on a sunbaked plain, daytime temperatures exceeded 100°F but at night, the "refugees," as Nash called them, shivered under "threadbare *kamblis* [blankets]." They had no choice but to live in a "famine relief camp," where the Bombay Revenue Department enforced heavy labor but largely failed to provide suitable accommodation for the many thousands encamped.[3]

Vast cultural, linguistic, and geographic distances separate these distressed subjects. They were targets of different colonial policies and immersed within different social, political, and military milieus. Yet all found themselves inmates in Britain's nineteenth-century "empire of camps." Victims of famine, disease, or war, all were vulnerable and desperate, afflicted by circumstances beyond their control. But each represented a threat, in official minds, to the maintenance of British power. As a result, colonial policies demanded they be concentrated in camps. Between bramble and barbed wire, lodged in canvas tents or thatched huts, they would be counted and classified; fed and sheltered; disciplined and punished; and reformed or neglected.

This book examines, for the first time, the multiple camps that proliferated across Britain's Victorian Empire. It explores the dynamics that created them, the careers of those who administered them, and the experiences of those detained. In the final decades of the nineteenth century, Britain concentrated more than ten million men, women, and children in camps during a series of colonial crises. Yet this vast network of confinement is largely forgotten. Inmates—marginal, illiterate, and dead—were long ago hushed into subaltern silence. All that remain are the decomposing documents of British officials and the published observations of missionaries and travelers.

DISASTER IMPERIALISM: FAMINE, PLAGUE, AND WAR

Between 1876 and 1903, a convergence of subsistence, medical, and military catastrophes ravaged the British Empire. The economic policies of viceroys Lytton and Curzon created what Mike Davis has called Britain's "late-Victorian holocausts." Monsoonal failure caused drought, but cash cropping, escalating revenue demands, and the enlistment of subsistence farmers into a global capitalist economy turned local scarcities into widespread famines.[4] The Indian subcontinent's integration into a system of imperial trade, meanwhile, made it vulnerable to global pandemics. Plague microbes from Hong Kong, attached to circulating products and people, infected India in 1896, while troop movements during the Anglo-Boer War transported the disease to South Africa in 1900, presaging an international public health emergency.[5] And at the very moment famine afflicted South Asia and plague spread across the world, settler-colonial expansion—driven by the demands of gold magnates and finance capitalists in Johannesburg and London—triggered a devastating war between Britain and two diminutive Boer (or Afrikaner) states: the South African Republic (or Transvaal) and the Orange Free State. Destruction wrought by the twentieth century's first major conflict—an early example of "total war" in the dawning age of mechanized violence—bore heavily on civilians.

These three disasters—famine, plague, and war—had their own local causes, but they were not isolated events. Across the empire, colonial disasters and the responses to them were tied together by the mandates of imperial commerce, military expansion, and fiscal priorities that favored British interests over those of racially and socially marginalized subjects. And in a globalizing world, events on distant shores intersected in revealing ways. The economic historian and anti-imperial critic Romesh Chunder Dutt recognized as much when he complained that financial burdens related to the distant South African War diverted resources from India amid worsening hunger.[6] Meanwhile, poverty in South Africa, which pauperized many Boer farmers in the 1890s, augmenting wartime suffering, derived from the same global climatic events that triggered famine in India.[7] In sum, British imperialism gave rise to an interconnected series of crises, from South Asia to South Africa, which it tried to solve with mass encampment.

In response to the global and imperial emergencies of famine, plague, and war, camps, in their many permutations, operated according to distinct dynamics that demand attention to local contexts. Boer War concentration camps were products of military conflict, while famine and plague camps operated in ostensible times of peace. Boer farmers, of European and Christian heritage, along with native Africans (black workers on the Strausses' farm included) populated the former; Muslims and Hindus the latter. Hard labor defined camp life for famine-struck Indians and African war refugees, but less so for detained Afrikaner women and plague-stricken Brahmins. To reconcile political dissidents to British rule, meanwhile, Boer camps enforced a "hearts and minds" campaign, but "redemption" was rarely the agenda at Indian camps.

Whatever their differences, the camps of famine, plague, and war were also products of more general cultural proclivities and structural regularities. As kindred reactions to diverse crises, they operated according to deeply embedded imperial mentalities that tell us much about the contested priorities and constraints of Britain's late-Victorian empire. In each case, camps were responses to the tightly braided colonial politics of humanity and security.[8]

AN EMPIRE OF CAMPS

Barbed-Wire Imperialism is the first book to consider Britain's vast empire of camps as a product of more basic "governmentalities."[9] The sudden and almost simultaneous proliferation of camps in multiple imperial sites and contexts is more than mere coincidence. Rather, British camps emerged from evolving government rationales—an imperial complex of shared mindsets and mentalities—that circulated throughout the empires and cultures of Western civilization. As the world's leading industrial and imperial power, nineteenth-century Britain synthesized many of the "basic ingredients" that would generate camps throughout the twentieth century.

Though ostensibly driven by context and contingency, colonial camps were artifacts of a late-Victorian "episteme"[10] oriented around "curing" or "rehabilitating" diseased, destitute, and otherwise "dangerous" bodies. By treating camps in isolation and within their own historiographical silos, existing narratives miss the larger imperial forces that generated them. The extensive scholarship dedicated to Boer War concentration camps,[11] like histories of colonial famines[12] and plagues,[13] treat camps as epiphenomenal. Historians have henceforth ignored connections between related imperial practices and the broader developments in Western culture that rendered camps conceivable and feasible technologies in diverse but related circumstances.

The South African (or Anglo-Boer) War (1899–1902) generated the best-remembered system of British camps. At the dawn of the twentieth century, in a violent war of attrition, British forces under generals Frederick Roberts and Horatio Kitchener removed some quarter-million men, women, and children (including the Strausses) from their homes, corralled them into nearby towns, and eventually interned them in a network of almost one hundred camps. It was here the term *concentration camp* first entered our modern lexicon, though the phrase was originally more descriptive than pejorative, referring simply to the spatial concentration of scattered populations.

Military historians have recently emphasized the ways in which British practices in South Africa resembled the Spanish general Valeriano Weyler's earlier "recon-centration" campaign during a colonial uprising in Cuba (1896–97).[14] Indeed, the global development of counterinsurgency tactics provides one rubric for understanding the emergence of colonial camps in the early twentieth century. South African concentration camps accommodated civilians displaced by scorched-earth warfare, while the American and German militaries similarly placed rural populations in urban "concentration zones" during contemporary "small wars" in the

Philippines (1899–1902) and South-West Africa (1904–5). Irregular warfare, however, was only one of many contexts in which camps emerged, and the concentration of colonial populations was never limited to military arenas. In an important contrast to Britain (one often missed by existing literature), Spain and America did not erect a system of *camps* to control destitute and displaced populations: the goal was simply to evacuate the countryside and thus deny guerrillas the support of rural communities. Once concentrated, Cuban and Filipino peasants were not billeted in barracks or tents but were left on city streets to fend for themselves. Meanwhile, German camps in South-West Africa did not serve the purposes of anti-guerrilla war, but were erected at the conclusion of hostilities.[15]

By emphasizing the military function of camps, historians of the South African War likewise misunderstand the nature of institutions that were operated by civil authorities for the vast majority of their existence and in which the military took very little interest. Ultimately, Boer concentration camps were less instruments of military counterinsurgency than humanitarian responses to the hunger, disease, and social chaos unleashed by modern war. As technologies of emergency discipline and relief, they resembled famine camps in India, which sheltered and relieved those suffering from hunger in return for labor on public works, as well as plague segregation camps, which quarantined the "dirty" and "uncivilized" as a sanitary measure. As in Cuba, the essential counterinsurgency function of segregating rural populations from guerrillas could have been accomplished in South Africa without the use of camps.

In essence, Britain's wartime concentration camps, like famine and plague camps before them, were kindred products of an emerging emphasis on what Foucault called "biopolitics."[16] Their ostensible goal was to preserve health and well-being, while addressing imperial security concerns raised by destitute and displaced populations considered socially, racially, or politically suspect. Camps, then, emerged from practices of welfare and social control that oscillated between Britain and its colonial "periphery." The same forces that generated prisons, factories, and workhouses in nineteenth-century Britain created colonial camps (along with mining compounds, convict settlements, and other imperial enclosures). Like their metropolitan correlatives, famine, plague, and wartime concentration camps were disciplinary institutions that operated according to putatively humane principles of "poor relief" and "protective custody." Britain encamped populations "for their own good" and in the name of relief and humanity. Yet camps also responded to metaphors of social danger and contagion, which dehumanized those detained.

Amid the already autocratic circumstances of empire, camps often confined inmates against their will, depriving them of basic rights. In contrast to prisoners at metropolitan jails, inmates at famine, plague, and wartime concentration camps were not detained as guilty individuals but as members of broad population categories formulated by Victorian social science: "dangerous classes," uncivilized "savages," "disease carriers," and racial "degenerates." Inmates were both victims and villains—"at risk" and "a risk," in Ann Stoler's words.[17] Their care and control subsequently demanded strict security as much as cordial sympathy. In the official mind, camps showcased British reason and benevolent intent, but to those confined, they symbolized the coercion of a colonial state intent on exercising power over life and death. Characteristic of empire's "double edge," imperial exercises in humanitarian relief exhibited the violence and exploitation upon which British global supremacy depended.

In the context of colonial emergencies, camps enforced a preemptive and preventive logic: they confined "dangerous" categories, not for any crime, but for the potential threat they posed. "States of exception," Giorgio Agamben argues, have proven central prerogatives of modern liberal democracies: they are the hidden ground upon which naked, sovereign power is exercised.[18] Martial law and administrative decree facilitated arbitrary arrest, inaugurating an era in which colonial states—from French Algeria to America's Guantánamo Bay—exercised the prerogative of exception to detain "problem groups." Less a reversal of received forms of democracy, however, colonial camps represented an intensification of autocratic methods already inherent to imperial rule. Exemplars of what Partha Chatterjee terms "the rule of colonial difference,"[19] camps were deeply embedded in evolving imperial practices oriented around bodily coercion and the deferral of rights. Indeed, empire itself might be considered a more permanent state of exception in which liberal rights and self-determination were indefinitely suspended: without their own national sovereignty, colonial populations were, in a sense, "stateless."[20] These were conducive conditions for camps.

COLONIAL "LEGIBILITY"

Above all, camps reflected imperial Britain's habitual anxieties about "order." Whether in Bombay or Bloemfontein, the colonial world presented Europeans with the specter of unordered space: of teeming and potentially dangerous masses; of disorienting and unfamiliar environments; and above all, of dirt, degeneration, and disease. "Normative disorder" and perpetual discord characterized "the daily life of Empire," Antoinette Burton argues: far from stable and secure, dangers were forever "lurking at the edges."[21] Moments of crisis only intensified a chronic sense of unease. Crime and instability amid famine, plague, and war portended more serious insurgencies; unhygienic surroundings suggested moral contagion and political dissent; wandering populations challenged systems of state surveillance. In this context, spatial segregation reaffirmed comforting assertions of racial and cultural difference. In an imperial world already pattered by partition, camps were geometric responses to heightened chaos and dislocation. More than "rational" responses to social, medical, or military predicaments, camps mediated larger crises of signification between order and disorder, and purity and pollution.

As technologies designed to discipline unruly populations, camps controlled the movement of refugees, wanderers, and those deemed "out of place." Components of broader efforts to monitor colonial mobility, camps were outcomes of search and capture operations, whether in the context of famine, plague, or war, that concentrated the scattered, itinerant, and displaced. At their core, camps changed the relationship between populations and space: they relocated mobile bodies to fixed and observable sites. Once secured in narrowly contained enclosures, an effort to "know" colonial subjects—through classification, statistics, and standardized reports rather than the unreliable mediation of native informants—complemented the "biopolitical" project of regulating health and welfare.[22]

Above all, the logistical feat of accommodating hundreds of thousands in purpose-built camps depended on larger developments in government capacity. In accounting for the origin of colonial "concentration camps" in British South Africa (as well as in the Spanish, American, and German empires), Jonathan Hyslop has convincingly emphasized the development of professionalizing militaries as an essential ingredient that facilitated the organization of populations on a mass scale.[23] Added to this was the development of modern bureaucracy and an administrative machinery oriented around welfare and social control.[24] Developed in the context of new efforts at social governance, technologies of identification—numbers, passes, and most drastically, camps—helped the colonial state "see" previously inscrutable (and therefore suspect) collectivities. In the words of James Scott, camps rendered colonial society "legible" and amenable to control by outsiders, who often lacked cultural, linguistic, and personal connections with local communities.[25] An unhappy triumph of modern methods, camps addressed the central problem of imperial rule: the occupation and surveillance of immense landscapes and the effective management of distant "strangers" by a small contingent of reliable Europeans.[26] The suffering and violence that concentration often entailed also stemmed from bureaucratic maladies: the colonial state did not see inmates as human beings but as integers in larger fiscal, medical, and military calculations.

INTERIMPERIAL TRAJECTORIES

Apart from showcasing phenomenological affiliations between episodes of concentration normally considered in isolation, *Barbed-Wire Imperialism* traces the flow of information and personnel that linked famine, plague, and wartime camps in direct and concrete ways. Even the most marginalized members of colonial society recognized the global sinews stitched by British imperialism. Inmates at Indian famine camps were roused by "fantastic rumors" they would be shipped overseas as cannon fodder to the battlefields of South Africa.[27] As refugees fled the Transvaal warzone, meanwhile, some ended up destitute on the distant streets of Bombay, where Indian Revenue officers considered placing them on famine relief works; they had fled one system of camps for another.[28] If inmates made such connections, so, emphatically, did cosmopolitan officials, who developed a diverse repertoire honed across multiple imperial sites. By treating camps as elements of discrete national or postcolonial histories, existing scholarship is attuned to local complexities and contextual specificities, but has thus far ignored the tangible transfers of power and knowledge that united geographically disparate camps, from Springfontein to Sholapur, into a cohesive interimperial narrative.

Combining domestic and imperial modes of governance, camps were shaped by a wide cast of social reformers, journalists, soldiers, and officials who traveled between Britain and the multiple sites of empire. Yet it remains for historians—of British camps and of empire more generally—to explore interactions *between* different colonies. As Thomas Metcalf argues, India and South Africa were never hermetically sealed units "dangling separately at the end of [their] own string[s]." Rather, they existed in webs of connection and interchange, tied together by the lines of the telegraph, the movement of officials, and the transmission of ideas and experience from one imperial venue to another. And as the crown jewel of empire, India presented an important "nodal point" from which ideas and expertise radiated outward.[29] This was especially true during the Anglo-Boer War, when South Asia and South Africa constituted "interlocking worlds" bound together by the flow of troops, labor, and commodities, as well as by colonial officials with expertise managing displaced and destitute colonials.[30]

Interimperial connections, however, were not innate. They had to be actively forged. Perceptive observers recognized analogies between different camps from early on. Indian officials considered the management of plague and famine camps to be overlapping skillsets, while the Cape Colony government turned to advisors from India to monitor South African plague camps. But it was moments of crisis rather than quotidian practices of everyday governance that forged the strongest interimperial connections. In South Africa, it was not until mortality from camp diseases like measles and dysentery fomented a damaging political scandal that authorities actively solicited guidance from other colonies. Faced with growing public outrage, the Colonial Office consulted an imperial "archive of expertise"[31] to reform and normalize camp management. In doing so, it recruited officials from India versed in plague and famine camps (where epidemics similarly spread in crowded conditions) to revamp operations at South African concentration camps. Ultimately, the camp that interned the Strauss family was administered by officials seconded from South Asia. The journeys of these "imperial careerists"[32] across the Indian Ocean help us map intensified spatial connections between plague, famine, and wartime concentration camps at the dawn of the twentieth century.

Based on archival research on four continents, *Barbed-Wire Imperialism* traces the interimperial exchange of practices and personnel that forged and refashioned Britain's empire of camps. In doing so, it reorients imperial geographies by showcasing their interconnected and multidirectional natures. The narrative that follows exemplifies the extent to which the "Indian Ocean World"[33] transmitted not only commodities and capital, but state practices, sanitary and disciplinary ideals, and, most relevantly, expertise in the erection and management of camps. Ultimately, an interimperial "learning curve" facilitated a process of standardization in which the identification and replication of preferred disciplinary and sanitary arrangements consolidated an identifiably "British" approach to camps, and one that could be consulted by future regimes.

"LIBERAL EMPIRE"

The British Empire has left a divided legacy. For Rudyard Kipling, empire spread commerce, civilization, and Christianity. Niall Ferguson, empire's latter-day apostle, concurs: British imperialism was essentially a humane force that endowed the world with human rights, Westminster parliaments, and market capitalism.[34] For others, however, empire was an exercise in racism, violence, and economic exploitation—a jingoistic profit-making enterprise built on its victims' corpses.[35] Britain's empire of camps—with its simultaneous mandates to relieve and discipline the displaced and distressed—embodied these tensions. Inmates experienced them firsthand. Barbed-wire fences demarcated humanitarian relief zones; military search parties arrested "suspects" in order to "save" them; and racist mantras and repressive force accompanied "civilizing missions" and paternalistic concern.[36]

At first glance, camps fit awkwardly within concurrent developments in British liberalism, exposing what Homi Bhaba terms the "aporia" of liberal rule.[37] The mass, collective confinement of civilians violates a view of the inviolable self. The coercive arrest and detention of populations deemed collectively suspect contravenes basic precepts of individual rights and due process. In one sense, camps were the flipside of liberal inclusion: they suggested an "external limit," a constitutive "other" to liberal governance, drawing our attention to an illiberal history of the British Empire. And yet, camps were products of a putatively, even quintessentially, "liberal" power—one dedicated, in theory if not in practice, to free movement, laissez-faire politics, and the rule of law. How might these seeming inconsistencies be resolved?

The ubiquity of British camps reminds us that liberal rule was premised on the construction of a certain type of subject: trustworthy, self-governing, and hygienic. While free movement emerged as a fundamental right for model citizens in metropolitan Britain—respectable, industrious, and white—mobility augured danger and criminality for racial or social "inferiors." Camps contained the reprobate (and usually colonial) "other" of respectable liberal subjects. They remind us that securing liberal freedom in Britain depended on creating and ruling through self-acting individuals—a status categorically denied to the suspect collectivities of empire. As predominantly colonial phenomena, camps proliferated in the absence of liberty's basic preconditions. They thus reveal the internal contradictions—the constitutive tensions—of liberal empire: liberal rights (which in principle are innate and universal) could not be extended to subjects who (in practice) were considered illiberal.

Camps also highlight the temporal lag inherent to imperialism. According to the historical and evolutionary timescapes that informed British power, camps concentrated populations deemed not (yet) ready to exercise freedom. This was true both for refugees in the Orange Free State and for famine victims in Poona. Like their counterparts in future regimes—from America's "strategic hamlets" in Vietnam to French *camps de regroupement* and even the "special settlements" of the Soviet Union, which trained inmates for life in a socialist society—British camps were transformative technologies. The goal was to make inmates loyal, sanitary, orderly, and, above all, governable (though government rationales differed for Indians, black Africans, and Afrikaners: only the latter were trained to be self-acting, democratic subjects). Like metropolitan prisons and workhouses, camps rested on modernity's basic premise: that humanity is pliable. By transforming "barbarism" into civilization, moreover, camps accentuated an animating imperial logic. Although the conversion of abject colonials into liberal selves was rarely realized, the *promise* of transformation bestowed camps with sustaining legitimacy.

If camps proved compatible with Britain's larger imperial project, what difference did liberal political cultures make to those behind the wire? How might Britain's empire of camps be distinguished from the concentrations of more authoritarian regimes? The camps of totalitarian empires and those of liberal states like Britain, France, and America were not axiomatic opposites: indeed their family resemblances (albeit distant ones) unsettle conventional distinctions between liberalism and autocracy.[38] British camps were not immune to the prevailing tendencies of the age: impersonal forms of violence, denigration of broad categories of humanity, and erasure of individual dignity amid the mass organization of "problematic" crowds. Liberal and illiberal states alike policed social, racial, and political outsiders, while modern bureaucracies across the ideological spectrum empowered governments and militaries to manage populations on macro scales. And despite Kiplingesque odes to the contrary, there was nothing exceptional about the British character. Imperial agents were just as capable of cruelty as their counterparts elsewhere. Indeed, accounts that emphasize totalitarian violence as the teleological endpoint of world history overshadow the coercive practices of "liberal" polities like Britain, France, and America, which were longer lasting and more widespread.

Yet real differences remain. The radicalization of World War I and the revolutionary context of interwar Europe altered the form and function of totalitarian camps. Practices of "social uplift" were not absent from illiberal regimes—they were particularly pronounced in the Gulag[39]—but fears about traitors and internal enemies provided new impetus for forced detention in the twentieth century. Britain's nineteenth-century empire of camps primarily policed social deviance, but in the radical polities of World-War Europe, political fanaticism converted camps into genocidal instruments of racial and ideological purity. Such was a horrific extreme only dimly hinted at in the camps of India and South Africa. Moreover, British officials expressed genuine anxiety that extrajudicial detention during famine, plague, and war contravened the foundational principles of liberal politics, ensuring that camps were deconcentrated at the end of a crisis. In contrast, Nazi concentration camps and the Soviet Gulag rested on emergency measures that remained in place for the duration of their regimes.[40]

Finally, Britain's free press and lively civil society served as a brake on documented abuses.[41] Grim mortality, unforgiving superintendents, and shameful living conditions in India and South Africa provoked scandals, which could not be muted or contained. Herein laid an all-too-delicate distinction. Time and again, criticism and debate, along with protest from native communities, softened camp regimes and resulted in lasting and meaningful reforms. True to liberal narratives of progress, British camps were evolving institutions that responded to outside input. The health and welfare (if not the overall happiness) of inmates improved over time, while disciplinary and administrative procedures responded to dissent and dissatisfaction. Controversy and resulting reforms were therefore central to the history of British camps. Life behind the wire was fashioned by those who opposed or sought to reform camps as much as by those who created them.

TWENTIETH-CENTURY LEGACIES

How, ultimately, did Britain's empire of camps contribute to the modern world? First generated by a colonial culture of confinement and control that originated in the nineteenth century, camps have outlasted the world wars and the discredited Nazi and Soviet empires to remain integral features of our contemporary geopolitical landscape.[42] Only a decade after World War II, Britain detained an entire ethnic group—nearly 1.5 million Kikuyu—in a "pipeline" of "rehabilitative centers" in Kenya, while concentrating half a million ethnic Chinese in Malaya's "New Villages."[43] America, Canada, and Britain similarly interned German and Japanese "aliens" during both world wars in what contemporaries referred to as "concentration camps." And our world today maintains a global network of fenced camps used to resettle displaced civilians and detain so-called "undesirables." Britain's empire of camps anticipated future practices of military internment, political detention, and racial violence. But its most direct line of descent leads to contemporary shelters and detention centers housing refugees and displaced persons under international humanitarian management. Indeed, the proliferation of such enclosures in recent years, especially in the wake of the Syrian refugee crisis, has induced some scholars to lament the return of the camp.[44] Whether in transit centers at Lampedusa or Nauru, or in refugee camps organized by the Red Cross and the United Nations' High Commission for Refugees (UNHRC), camps remain integral features of our world. In these contemporary institutions may be found echoes of a British colonial past—and the dynamics of "liberal empire" with its dual emphasis on care and control—that first made camps a durable mode of population management.

Social scientists like Hannah Arendt and Wolfgang Sofsky define camps as typologies of terror that crystallize an ideal essence of inhumanity.[45] But as Mark Mazower points out, Nazi and Soviet brutality are neither typical nor illustrative of state violence in the modern world.[46] Primo Levi and Alexander Solzhenitsyn offer compelling elegies, but they are exceptional cases that fit uneasily within larger trajectories of modern statecraft.[47] Without attending to Britain's contribution to a larger transnational history, scholars risk missing crucial aspects of encampment overlooked in narratives of genocide and extermination.

Ultimately, British camps laid the foundations for Anglo-American political traditions that would remake the world in the wake of World War II. Examining the provenance of camps under British global supremacy helps us better understand their persistence and diversity as instruments for managing large populations—displaced, distressed, dangerous, and suspect—in the twentieth and twenty-first centuries. The chapters that follow highlight the violence and suffering entailed by an institution that continues to govern its inmates, both vulnerable and undesirable, with a condescending colonial attitude. Considering structural connections and concrete interchanges between the camps of famine, plague, and war, they also trace humanitarian motives and the dynamics of reform and amelioration that rendered camps a permissible (if problematic) instrument of discipline and relief. In doing so, *Barbed-Wire Imperialism* offers a genealogy of the present that accounts for the durability of camps in the world today in a way that narratives dominated by Nazi and Soviet atrocities cannot. Before considering this trajectory, however, we turn to the emerging material conditions and cultural dispositions of Victorian Britain, which offered fertile ground for the development of new techniques of social and spatial control. The Strauss family's encampment, like that of countless Indians, cannot be understood without this larger backdrop.

CHAPTER I · Concentrating the "Dangerous Classes"

The Cultural and Material Foundations of British Camps

Repression and relief, servitude and shelter: camps, historically, have performed an array of contrary functions. Medieval Sicily's Christian rulers concentrated the island's Muslim population in isolated settlements.[1] Jesuit "reductions" in eighteenth-century Latin America forcibly concentrated indigenous communities into "prayer villages" in the name of Christianity and taxation.[2] Catherine the Great established prison camps in the western reaches of the Russian Empire to punish rebels of the Polish Bar Confederation (1768–72).[3] French republicans used extrajudicial enclosures to concentrate counterrevolutionary forces in the Vendée (1793), while Napoleon interned suspect foreigners in wartime France.[4] Modern Britain did not "invent" camps. But the cultural and material foundations of Britain and its empire—the most influential global power of the late nineteenth century—offered important groundwork for the twentieth century's ubiquitous barracks and barbed wire.

British camps responded to contingent factors. But they also rested on deeper cultural transformations in both metropole and colony. As confinement emerged in the nineteenth century as the normative motif of modern discipline, the exclusionary practices of segregation and isolation proliferated. Britain's empire of camps was part of a worldwide "carceral archipelago" that sought to classify and control "problem populations" deemed dangerous or undesirable. Britain's counterinsurgency against its own poor relied on the concentration of "criminal classes" in workhouses, prisons, and suburban labor camps. In the empire, meanwhile, social and spatial control resulted in the mass concentration of native insurgents and "criminal tribes" in a network of enclosed settlements, which confined nomadic groups defined as a collective threat. In the context of professionalizing armies and emerging forms of medical expertise, these spaces operated according to strict military discipline and sanitary policing, suggesting templates for later and larger camps convened during famine, plague, and war. The essential preconditions for Britain's empire of camps were laid in the Victorian period.

URBAN CONCENTRATION

Nineteenth-century Britain was a society in motion. Rapid social and political change transformed a rural country into an urban and industrialized one; a "revolution in government" established mechanisms of universal education and modern administration; and mass democracy replaced earlier systems of aristocratic patronage, fortifying the rule of law and transforming subjects into rights-bearing citizens. According to Whiggish narratives, a series of legislative acts consolidated a constitutional system based on popular sovereignty and an ever-expanding franchise, while capitalist development and free market prosperity fortified Britain's stable constitutional monarchy. Yet liberty and progress were accompanied by the birth of new disciplines and coercive technologies. The "age of optimism" was also an age of camps.

The social dislocations and forced relocations of enclosure and urbanization are familiar stories. At times, industrial capitalism displaced peasant farmers as dramatically as famine, war, and disease. The ongoing fencing and privatization of common lands—a function, in turn, of market exchange and the cash nexus—uprooted vast and newly mobile masses, who were subsequently concentrated in urban centers like London and Manchester. Accompanying this dynamic was the compression of space and time facilitated by railways and the transportation revolution. Shrinking distances facilitated convergence and concentration at fixed points. Meanwhile, relaxation of the laws of settlement (1834)—legislation that once restrained the mobility of the poor at the parish level—along with calamities like the Irish Famine (1845–52), compelled thousands of destitute migrants to the center of burgeoning cities.[5] As Eric Lampard notes, the "level of [urban] concentration" underwent an exponential increase.[6] Elites, meanwhile, spread into spacious suburbs: nineteenth-century cities increasingly segregated inhabitants by class (as well as race and gender).[7]

FIGURE I.

"Tent cities": The early urban form of colonial towns like Johannesburg (above)
resembled camps like Springfontein in wartime South Africa (below). Johannesburg's
first land surveyor, Captain W. K. Tucker, later became the chief superintendent of
concentration camps during the Anglo-Boer War. [Credit: F. M. van der Waal, *From
Mining Camp to Metropolis: The Building of Johannesburg* (Pretoria: C. van Rensburg
Publications for the Human Sciences Research Council, 1987), 8; NAUK CO 1069/215,
Image 60, Entrance from the Railway Springfontein Camp.]

As temporary and sometimes mobile erections, camps suggest an antithesis to
fixed and permanent cities. At the same time, however, they evoke a primitive urban
form. In the nineteenth century, "tent cities" and mining camps developed on the
periphery of industrial "shock cities" and gold-rush towns.[8] In Johannesburg, once
a paltry collection of canvas, the land surveyor W. K. Tucker introduced a "rectilinear street plan," thereby establishing a "grid system . . . well suited to mechanisa-
tion and standardized building components."[9] The liminal shelter of tents and huts,
expedient and haphazard, eventually gave way to bleak workers' barracks or salubri-
ous model communities designed by industrial philanthropists. In microcosm,
Britain's empire of camps embodied the forces of urbanization—displacement,
concentration, and regulation.

The "mass society" of urban and industrial Britain engendered new spatial arrangements and the proliferation of standard serialized facilities. Whether in the service of regulation or recreation, Victorian Britain was a land of "camps." With uniform "living quarters . . . a camp store, always a hospital (the infirmary), and, of course, places to eat," a wide variety of institutions, from military barracks to outdoor summer camps conformed to basic templates for quartering mass populations.[10] Likewise, public schools, amusement parks, stadia, and even zoos, with their aggregated facilities, "crowd control," and surveillance techniques, were products of a shared historical moment.[11] These new urban arrangements exhibited standardized mass architecture, gesturing toward plague, famine, and Boer War concentration camps, which were "constructed in sections, bolted together and easily removable."[12]

Urban concentration posed serious social and sanitary challenges, however. As local face-to-face transactions dissolved amid the tide of mass society, the unprecedented scale of nineteenth-century cities demanded new institutions, bureaucracies, and anonymous methods of observation, classification, and control. The concentrated populations of industrial cities—and the spread of diseases like typhoid and cholera in particular—occasioned advances in sanitary management and new surveillance regimes.[13] At ground level, urban planning refurbished disorderly conglomerations according to the meticulous logic of right angles. Planners rendered space abstract: countable, interchangeable, and reduced to mathematical regularity. In contrast to Paris or Vienna, a liberal regard for property rights saved London's organic amalgam of winding streets from grandiose rationalization. But new industrial and colonial centers proved more conducive to disciplinary interventions—and to the fetish of the straight line. In the words of Paul Rabinow, the governable and geometric streets of New Delhi and Johannesburg suggested an "urban parallel to Bentham's panopticon," that utopian prison of utilitarian rationality.[14] Converting colonial chaos into Cartesian order, camps exemplified, in the words of Lewis Mumford, the "geometric clarification of the spirit" that the nineteenth century inherited from the Baroque. The perpendicular sightline of camps, with their uniform plots and interchangeable tents and huts reflected the bird's-eye view of the planner and the "mechanical pattern[s]" of the machine age.[15] Such was modernity's aspiration for order.

THE CARCERAL ARCHIPELAGO

Above all, camps emerged within a "carceral archipelago" of prisons, workhouses, factories, and hospitals that organized nineteenth-century people and places.

Incarceration was not exclusive to the Victorians: in the 1700s, for example, naval hulks on the River Thames—floating work camps, of a sort—accommodated criminals prior to their transportation overseas.[16] But as Michel Foucault and Michael Ignatieff confirm, confinement replaced banishment and execution as the Victorian era's standard strategy to regulate deviance.[17] No longer were convicts dispersed to remote Australian outposts: they were concentrated instead. New prisons like London's Pentonville effaced the premodern spectacle of the scaffold, concealing inmates in uniform, rectilinear cells, segregated from society. And the prisons filled. Fear of the rootless and mobile was deeply engrained in Western political culture, and a liberal equation of property with rights served to criminalize poverty over the course of the nineteenth century.[18] To this end, proliferating vagrancy laws reflected anxieties about the itinerant poor. In Britain but especially in the colonies, Julie Kimber argues, legislation remained flexible enough to endow magistrates with formidable powers of detention.[19]

To those incarcerated, prisons were sites of terror. Simultaneously, however, they attained symbolic status as technologies of Enlightenment. Apportioning a "just measure of pain," they represented a "humane" alternative to the archaic violence of execution.[20] In sum, they embodied a characteristic tension between coercion and care reproduced in Britain's empire of camps. Prisons and camps differed in logic and purpose: the former, in principle, were instruments of normal (though always contested) judicial procedure, detaining inmates convicted by established legal channels. Camps, meanwhile, were temporary, extrajudicial affairs—the impermanent products of emergency. Yet prisons and camps shared a fundamental emphasis on isolation, segregation, and (at times) rehabilitation. Each operated according to what Chris Otter calls the principle of "agglomeration": as in hospitals and asylums, formerly scattered inmates could be better identified, classified, and observed when organized within a single space.[21]

Prisons were also tools of imperial conquest, and as they proliferated globally, they served as conceptual and architectural precursors for imperial camps.[22] In contrast to those of metropolitan Britain, however, colonial prisons consisted of improvised huts and single-story outbuildings surrounded by fences and equipped with guardhouses and sentry posts. In Mauritius, for example, prisoners were lodged in old army barracks and "huts made out of dried grasses."[23] According to David Arnold, such arrangements reflected "a more relaxed principle of spatial separation," with inmates confined to "sheds or barracks divided by internal walls."[24] This relative laxity, however, gave way in the late nineteenth century to a period of systematic prison construction as the "total institution"—with common messing, scientific diets, and the close surveillance of work, behavior, and medical arrangements—spread to India and other imperial domains. Meanwhile, published manuals, starting in the 1870s, systematized penal procedures, inspiring future concentrations.[25]

Such developments intersected with metropolitan trends, though colonial prisons relied more heavily on physical force and arbitrary arrest. In the empire, assertions of European supremacy over denigrated racial collectivities took precedence over the production of improving, self-correcting individuals. Imperial Britain's most forbidding penal outpost—the convict settlement on the Andaman Islands—accentuates the exploitative nature and fiscal stringency of colonial rule. Here, some twenty thousand common criminals and political prisoners were banished "across the black waters" after the 1857–58 Indian "Mutiny," thereby "purifying" the subcontinent of social and political disorder. Even after the construction of a permanent prison—reserved for the worst of the "politicals"—the majority resided in provisional thatch-and-bamboo camps and labored on public works projects, a practice discontinued in Britain by the late eighteenth century.[26] The principles of confinement and the legitimizing cloak of the metropolitan penitentiary inspired arrangements throughout Britain's empire of camps; but so did practices (banishment, bodily coercion, extramural labor) deemed outmoded by the standards of metropolitan modernity. Like colonial prisons, Britain's empire of camps would synthesize practices old and new.

"MITIGATED PRISONS": FACTORIES AND LABOR COMPOUNDS

Just as prisons partitioned space according to new mandates of control, factories inaugurated new rhythms of work and a new regulation of the body. Karl Marx described British factories as "mitigated prisons," while Max Weber noted the "military discipline" typical of "big capitalist enterprises."[27] Industrial factories experimented with synchronized labor, panoptic surveillance, and rigid time discipline on mass scales—all practices that would feature in colonial camps.[28] Not only the means to some productive end but an expression of exalted virtue, work became an end in and of itself. Segmented task work and assembly-line production were as alien to Indian famine camp inmates and subsistence farmers in South Africa as they were to peasant cultivators and petty artisans in preindustrial Europe; in each case, however, factories and camps proved potent vehicles of social and industrial reform, inaugurating modern rhythms and ideologies of labor. Despite limits to enforcement in colonial settings, camps, like factories, were ancillary tools of modernization: the vehicles (in theory, at least) of ideal colonial societies accustomed to exacting discipline and productive labor.

As the first industrial nation and the world's foremost imperial power, Britain transported labor discipline abroad. Without cash economies or mobile workforces inured to factory regimens, however, material improvement in the colonies depended on unfree labor. The Atlantic slave trade refined longstanding practices of confinement at slave lodges and galleys. Indeed, slave ships were perhaps the world's first "concentration camps": these "floating prisons" applied the logistics of military planning to incarcerate human bodies in unspeakable concentrations.[29] As in future concentration camps, smallpox, malnutrition, and ill treatment flourished on overcrowded vessels, even if ships—"the first hygiene cit[ies] in miniature"[30]—also pioneered the sanitary management of concentrated humanity.

With slavery's abolition in 1833, chain gangs and indentured labor filled the void. Lacking the wage labor force predominant in Britain, the infrastructure projects of empire depended on penal labor.[31] Apart from colonial plantations manned by indentured laborers, imperial public works departments became centers of expertise in billeting and supervising workers. Its executives—Cape Colony's Lewis Mansergh in particular—later played central roles in the construction and management of famine, plague and wartime concentration camps, for they "thoroughly underst[ood] the management of native labor."[32]

Empire also organized a global system of migrant workers. Transit camps and coolie depots housed workers shipped to Mauritius, South Africa, and the Caribbean: like convict settlements, these spaces experimented with common messing and penal diets, bureaucratic systems of registration and surveillance, medical inspection, and reformative labor.[33] With the various imperial gold rushes of the nineteenth century, meanwhile, mining camps in South Africa concentrated native labor in tightly administered disciplinary regimes. Here the vast labor resources and mineral wealth of empire coincided. Consisting of enclosed barracks, compounds "facilitated [the] control and discipline of migrant male workers,"[34] achieving a "synthesis of penal and labor architecture." Such facilities recalled earlier modes of confining slaves, reviving residual practices of bygone eras. The link was especially clear in Kimberley, where enclosed compounds drew inspiration from Cape Town's eighteenth-century slave lodge.[35]

Surrounded by barbed-wire fences, South African mining facilities intersected with global networks of labor camps, extending from the *villes indigenes* in Belgian Congo to diamond-mine compounds in Brazil. Locally, they were direct and tangi-

FIGURE 2.

Ndabeni repurposed the former Uitvlugt plague camp. Cape Colony's director of Public Works, Lewis Mansergh, presided over the construction of both wartime concentration camps and Cape Town's native locations. With corrugated iron barracks, austere living, and lack of privacy, native housing, in Nicholas Coetzer's judgment, "resembled the architecture of the concentration and military camps of the South African War."[1] [Credit "Native Location: Ndabeni (The Main Thoroughfare)," *Cape Argus Weekly*, November 30, 1904.]

[1] Nicholas Coetzer, *Building Apartheid: On Architecture and Order in Imperial Cape Town* (Burlington, VT: Ashgate, 2013), 187. Rudolf Mrazek notes similarities between camps and worker housing in colonial Batavia: "service villages" for native workers were easily repurposed as Japanese concentration camps during World War II. *Engineers of Happy Land: Technology and Nationalism in a Colony* (Princeton, NJ: Princeton University Press, 2002), 60–73.

ble inspiration for British concentration camps in the Boer War, where "mine managers" were specified as model superintendents.[36] Mining compounds also intersected with South Africa's first native locations, like Uitvlugt (Ndabeni), built to concentrate and better manage segregated black African workers.

Through the manipulation of space, labor compounds would transform pre-industrial populations into disciplined capitalist workers. Yet minimal expenditure on housing, diets, and hospitals betrayed the limits of reform. And while communal bathing facilities and medical attendance introduced inmates to "sanitary civilization," administrative apathy and parsimony gave rise to "distinctive patterns of disease" that foreshadowed horrific epidemics at future concentrations.[37] Balance between human life and economic exploitation was not always achieved, as empire synthesized forms of bodily coercion deemed too drastic for the metropole but which formed the cultural and material bedrock of future colonial camps.

MEDICAL DETENTION

Modern medicine offered important foundations for Britain's empire of camps, both legally and ideologically. By isolating dangerous groups suspected of carrying disease, camps emerged not only as instruments of social control but of sanitary surveillance. Speaking of modern refugee shelters, Michel Agier notes "there is nothing more practical than a camp for carrying out a medical screening."[38] More ominously, Alison Bashford and Carolyn Strange point to "quarantine-detention" as a "historic precedent for the current detention of asylum seekers."[39] Conversely, recent efforts to police Ebola have invoked emergency legislation first drafted to detain terrorists.[40] The incarceration of Haitian refugees at Guantánamo Bay in the 1990s on suspicion they carried AIDS highlights congruencies between medical and military policing, as does the seamless apartheid-era conversion of Robben Island off the coast of South Africa from a leper colony to a political prisoner camp.[41] The quarantine of plague suspects in India likewise set logistical (and in some cases juridical) precedents for famine and wartime camps.

Medicine, moreover, governed the cultural representations that facilitated mass detention. Camps involved the segregation of outcast populations denigrated according to discourses of purity and pollution: they enforced what Judy Whitehead has termed a "cosmic dualism" between clean and unclean, civilized and barbaric, industrious and idle, and healthy and diseased.[42] As organic and bodily metaphors for society gained prevalence in the Victorian era,[43] encampment became a surgical procedure: policy makers imagined "criminal classes" to be "parasites" or "social pathogens" that needed to be "healed," physically isolated, or else excised completely.

But while fears of moral and physical contagion governed Victorian statecraft, they were especially powerful in the colonies. Visualized as disease-rich environments infested with unwashed "hordes," colonies were like "populous cit[ies] where signs of the plague have appeared." Spaces of moral and racial decay, they "crie[d] out loudly for a Lazaretto."[44] Such statements underscore the sociologist Zygmunt Bauman's observation that medicine, along with "gardening" and its practices of cultivation, fencing, and pruning, became a defining allegory of modern government.[45] Camps emerged, accordingly, from social languages of "plague," "pestilence," and "contagion" that have patterned segregation throughout the twentieth century.[46] The result, to quote Frantz Fanon, was a "world divided into compartments."[47]

Practices of "quarantine" or "protective custody" informed the development of camps in more tangible ways as well. If the chaotic peoples and places of empire could not be remade, they could at least be concealed at a distance. Plague camps responded to specific medical concerns, but discourses of dirt and disease also framed "urban cleansing operations" against refugees "littering" city streets. Meanwhile, "sweeping drives" cleansed the battlefield during colonial "dirty wars" in South Africa and elsewhere.

Famously, the Contagious Diseases Act (1868) combined medical and moral policing. In India, the police concentrated prostitutes "scattered around the bazars" in hygienic sites of "confinement and punishment."[48] The legislation sparked libertarian protest, but "lock houses" offered ideological foundations for the forced concentration of marginalized disease carriers in times of plague and famine. Likewise, Britain's Public Health Act (1875) mandated forced hospitalization for anyone "suffering from [a] dangerous infectious disorder" and who, tellingly, did not reside in "proper lodging or accommodation."[49] In this context, public hospitals complemented prisons and factories as sites of terror and confinement, especially for the poor. Regulated institutions replaced the home as the locus of death or convalescence, while medical knowledge was concentrated in the hands of "professionals."

In contrast to Britain's brick-and-mortar hospitals, colonial public health initiatives, though in some ways more urgent, were also more provisional. In Europe, cholera epidemics in the 1850s promoted permanent infrastructure—sewers and running water—and the emergence of sanitary science as a discrete discipline. By cleaning and controlling the "unwashed masses," sanitation was a potent political tool that could transform the metropolitan poor into respectable and responsible subjects.[50] In the colonial world, however, where mass democracy was never an objective, disease suspects were instead segregated in tents and huts. The Indian army regularly moved cholera-stricken prisoners and soldiers from permanent barracks into tented camps,[51] while rows of canvas huts accommodated tuberculosis "suspects." Finally, the Indian Medical Service (IMS) detained religious pilgrims—suspected sources of medical contagion and political unrest—at Haridwar's Kumb Mela festival. Sanitary Commissioner S. J. Thomson "compelled [pilgrims] to live in a camp set apart for the purpose."[52] "Concentration camps," as they were called, also helped contain and monitor sleeping sickness in twentieth-century Africa.[53] Such practices offered models for future medical policing, as well as guidelines for the siting and management of plague, famine, and wartime concentration camps.

MILITARY DISCIPLINE

The military provided both a vehicle for sanitary reform and a receptacle for Britain's "dangerous classes." Army barracks were important disciplinary innovations—laboratories par excellence, in Patrick Joyce's words, for "creating spaces around and between bodies."[54] With their geometric tents and huts, fortified and enclosed, army camps offered early lessons in the social and sanitary control of mass populations via the built environment. Like medieval monasteries before them, military barracks were conspicuous sites of discipline, drilling, and parading, "one of the great mass spectacles [of an] increasingly servile populace," in Lewis Mumford's judgment.[55] Military culture was never confined to the army or navy, however; its proclivity for discipline and regulation offered a model for nineteenth-century society writ large, and for prisons and workhouses particularly.[56] Western civilization's first cities were themselves glorified military outposts. Indeed, the military camps of ancient Rome developed from "outposts of control and colonization" into full-fledged "urban centers like Vienna, Prague, Barcelona, and Manchester."[57] In a nineteenth-century variation of this primal transition, European capitals were redesigned as "army camps," replete with wide and straight boulevards amenable to military parades. And by century's end, public housing projects relegated the outcast to "civic barracks" on monotonous and uniform grids.

The evolving form and function of British army camps accompanied shifts in Europe's broader culture of war. Early modern army camps functioned as trifling venues of aristocratic and theatrical display;[58] but with the advent of mass national armies, professional command structures, and the increasing militarization of society during the French Revolutionary Wars (1792–1815), barracks became sites for converting raw bodies of men into disciplined mass armies. Because Britain, unlike its continental rivals, habitually spurned standing armies and hence the permanent barracks to maintain them, its military gained much experience building temporary tented erections in moments of perceived emergency. As liberal proclivities mitigated against permanent garrisons or billeting soldiers in private homes (a practice largely extinguished after the Seven Years' War, 1756–63), the development of temporary camps "resolved the problem . . . of accommodating a large army" and

FIGURE 3.

Family quarters, Aldershot, 1884 (left) and an army field camp (right). In her quixotic 1897 novel *On the Face of the Waters*, the Anglo-Indian novelist Flora Steel described a military "camping ground [as] white as a poppy field with tents." Four years later, an observer noted the "weird whiteness" of tents at Heidelburg concentration camp in South Africa. The silvery way in which they shine" recalled, for her, one of "Flora A. Steel['s]. . .Indian books."[2] [Credit: "'Tommy Atkins' Married – Past and Present," *The Graphic: an illustrated weekly newspaper*, 12 January 1884, issue 737, 44; "The Nile Expedition for the Relief of General Gordon: The Iroquois Pitches His Tent in the Land of the Pharaohs," from Sketches by our special Artist, Mr. F. Villiers, *The Graphic*, November 22, 1884, issue 782, 532.]

[2] Flora A. Steel, *On the Face of the Waters: A Tale of the Mutiny* (New York: Macmillan, 1897), 302; Deane/Streatfield Papers 2/11, Transcripts of letters from Lucy Streatfield to her sister, 91.

proved "less objectionable," Gordon Bannerman notes, "than impositions on local communities."[59]

With the army's growing size and the professionalization and centralization of command, temporary and diminutive camps became larger and more permanent. First erected during the Crimean War (1853–56), Aldershot in rural Hampshire recycled buildings from an existing workhouse and went on to serve as a model military camp. Before Aldershot, its historian remarks, "no . . . camp existed in the whole of the country for the concentration or training of troops on a large scale." Reflecting the more general spatial dynamics of the age, Aldershot "concentrat[ed] troops, brought in from old and unsuitable garrisons and stations elsewhere in the United Kingdom, in a unified and organized command."[60] As with urbanization, modernity demanded concentration.

Aldershot's serried grids implied order and regimentation, though messier realities existed on the ground. Drafty tents and "dingy huts" were, for an 1858 observer, more reminiscent of a "colonial settlement . . . than a military station in our mother country."[61] Camp life proved especially hard for wives and children. Indeed, Aldershot's family quarters foreshadowed hardships at future civilian concentrations in Africa and India. As many as ten families were allocated single barracks with nothing but a "rug, rough blanket or ragged sheet" to divide them; in other cases, they slept on the ground in circular bell tents designed for soldiers in battle rather than families at home. Military wives and children lived communal lives under conditions which "by modern standards are indescribable"; such were the prevailing conditions at home as Britain forcibly concentrated suspect colonials overseas. Yet conditions were no worse, apologists remarked, than "in the crowded cottages and terraced rows of dwellings in the mean streets clustered around the factories of the then new industrial centers."[62] The comparison between industrial housing and camp life proved a common refrain—a fitting parallel given that camps were enmeshed within wider cultures of concentration and confinement.

The collection of soldiers in camps complemented their dispersal overseas. Tented outposts of empire, in Sudan and Afghanistan, Bombay and Bengal, facilitated the global expansion of British power and the subsequent spread of camp culture. So central were camps to British imperium that Delhi's Red Fort, that symbolic cradle of displaced Mughal power, was converted into a British garrison after the 1857–58 Rebellion. Other colonial cities were themselves sometimes little more than army cantonments populated by military men. Traveling judges and revenue officials likewise spent much of their year "in camp," albeit in surroundings more lavish than the average soldier (or concentration camp inmate) could hope for.[63]

Not only did army camps project physical power, they enforced the social and spatial distancing of colonizer and colonized. Following the 1857–58 Rebellion, the army removed its camps from Indian towns, shifting them to urban peripheries according to mounting imperial anxieties. As an earlier age of cosmopolitan "boundary crossing," described by Maya Jasanoff, gave way to more rigid racial and cultural distinctions, camps enforced new spatial partitions.[64] The military thus established a suburban camp topography that the enclosures of famine, plague, and war would later replicate. In their new sterile milieu, camps would be "oases of purity"[65] and "pockets of orderliness and tidiness."[66] In the words of the Anglo-Indian novelist Flora Steel, the tidy appearance of British army camps in 1897 "stood out in keen contrast with the sordid savagery" of a "wretched [native] hamlet" nearby.[67]

The internal geography of camps also reflected Victorian convictions about unhealthy colonial environs. Sanitary officials pitched rows of tents perpendicular to nearby indigenous settlements, while more spacious barracks, paved cantonment roads, plumbing, and latrines served to ward off native "miasmas." Sanitation was as much a vehicle of class and racial supremacy as an objective science, and it developed a coercive edge. The Indian Cantonment Act of 1864 endowed European magistrates with discretionary or even "despotic" powers to enforce sanitary regulations at army camps, and in the name of health, cantonment superintendents regulated the mobility of native interlopers with passes.[68] In the case of vagrants and venereal disease carriers, meanwhile, regular inspection and confinement awaited. Perimeter walls and cordons sanitaires between European cantonments and native cities were material incarnations of military sanitation and of the racial and cultural conceits that colonial rule laid bare.[69]

POW CAMPS

Experience disciplining British and colonial subalterns was readily adapted to control prisoners of war. With the mass conscript armies born of nationalism and political modernity, nineteenth-century POW camps reflected new scales of population management. Emerging from a continuum of disciplinary enclosures, like convict stations and disused prison hulks, early POW shelters were improvised and ad hoc. In 1792, for example, a converted workhouse at Stapleton, Gloucestershire, housed prisoners from the American War of Independence.[70]

Erected in 1797 to concentrate French Revolutionary troops—the soldiers of what David Bell deems "the first total war"[71]—Norman Cross in Cambridgeshire represented the world's first purpose-built POW camp. Its layout experimented with the utilitarian architecture of Benthamite prisons—oriented toward panoptic surveillance—and camp officials made major advances controlling disease among concentrated populations. After typhoid ravaged the camp in 1800–1801, regular medical inspections, a segregated hospital ward, and the demarcation of clean water supplies reduced mortality, offering guidelines for the sanitary management of POWs and other displaced populations for generations to come.[72] But as the enduring and tragic history of camp epidemics suggests, such arrangements were rarely followed until too late.

With the French Revolutionary Wars a distant memory, the Confederate prison camp at Andersonville during the American Civil War (1861–65) offered a new spectacle of internment—and one that photography and mass media rendered visible to British and global audiences. Here the suffering of concentrated inmates—28 percent of whom died from exposure and malnutrition—highlighted the perils of encampment.[73] Three decades later, the British Army hoped to avoid Anderson-ville's infamy with thoughtful geometric barracks for POWs during the Anglo-Boer War. Ironically, these facilities provided better living conditions than hastily erected concentration camps for unarmed civilians.

In both the American Civil and South African conflicts, the precociously modern, totalizing nature of war dissolved boundaries between soldier and civilian, though existing patterns of racial segregation also determined the demography of encamp-ment.[74] In this vein, tented "contraband camps" concentrating African American refugees from the South heralded the ways in which civilians would be embroiled in future wars. Like inmates in Britain's looming colonial camps, the contrabands' plight evoked humanitarian sympathy and activity by Quaker relief committees. But like African and Afrikaner refugees in the Boer War, inmates were threatening enough—as disease carriers, potential criminals, and racial outcasts—to be segre-gated from nearby towns and put to hard labor.[75] On both sides of the Atlantic, nineteenth-century camps simultaneously exhibited a humane and repressive edge decades before the terms "refugee camp" and "concentration camp" were concep-tually differentiated.

CONFINEMENT AND CLASS WAR

Above all, metropolitan workhouses embodied the ideological foundations of Brit-ain's empire of camps.[76] Concentration camps were tools of military conquest and confinement during the Anglo-Boer War, but workhouses were instruments of a prior and more ancient counterinsurgency—one waged against Britain's own vagrant poor. As they expanded, cities became "virtual combat zone[s]" as "danger-ous classes," concealed in hidden rookeries like Whitechapel in London's East End, launched raids against bourgeois property owners.[77] Class warfare was a low-intensity, asymmetric conflict, its dynamic more akin to guerrilla skirmishes than to formal combat among uniformed armies; it was patterned less by decisive battles than by methodical policing and the detention of "troublemakers." But as strategic instruments of class war, workhouses were military sites: ex-army officers with their "ability to control large numbers of barely subordinate paupers," were favored candidates for workhouse masters.[78]

Bridewell was London's oldest and most imitated workhouse. As a technology of class warfare that immobilized urban transients, it presaged the enclosures that proliferated after the 1834 Poor Law. Victorian commentators defended workhouses as preemptive measures that protected the supposedly peaceful and productive by segregating criminality and disease. Targeting "the criminal classes" as a social rather than juridical category, workhouses, like many future camps, curtailed freedom of movement in order to filter respectable from potentially dangerous elements. To this end, Britain's 1869 *Habitual Criminals Act* complemented existing vagrancy legislation with permits and police registration that further monitored the movement of "dangerous classes."

Social control was spatial control, but so too was it sanitary control; cleanliness, for the Victorians, was next to Godliness. Hygiene's talismanic power did not simply pattern life inside the workhouse—it justified confinement in the first place. Workhouse walls were metropolitan equivalents of the cordons sanitaires surrounding military cantonments in India. Pervading metaphors of disease, galvanized by the ascendant authority of professional medicine, helped contemporaries conceive workhouse confinement as a "social cleansing" operation. Oliver Twist and the soot-encrusted protagonist of Charles Kingsley's *The Waterbabies* made explicit the connection between social and sanitary policing. Institutes of social hygiene, workhouses offered a baptism and moral cleansing.[79]

Apart from sanitation, the workhouse's emphasis on labor and bare-subsistence rations conformed to doctrinaire free market ideologies that elevated political economy above the comfort and health of inmates and militated against supposed pauperization. Workhouse conditions were harsh by conscious design. Enforced with military discipline—the workhouse was to be a "well-oiled military machine,"[80] its governors urged—labor assumed a more punitive and didactic function than it did in factories. The infamous workhouse treadmill—work for work's sake—would find its colonial correlative in the senseless shifting of stones, from one pile to another, at Indian famine camps. At the same time, workhouses, like prisons, represented an ostensibly more rational and enlightened alternative to previous practices of discipline and punishment, like flogging and transportation. Workhouses aimed, in theory, to reform and rehabilitate, excluding inmates temporarily in the name of (eventually) incorporating them as respectable members of society. As instruments of Zygmunt Bauman's "gardening state," the animating logic was "cultivation" rather than "extermination."[81] In reformer Robert Pearson's strident language, however, the goal was to "tame the most savage of animals."[82]

BRITAIN'S "WANDERING TRIBES"

Prisons, workhouses, and military camps were building blocks of a new society. But social reformers encountered the limits of liberal rehabilitation at the fin de siècle.

By the 1880s, a climate of pessimism descended in the face of a "dangerous residuum" seemingly beyond the pale of reform. "Degenerate" and "rootless" vagrants, many of them economic refugees displaced from Ireland, seemed ever more menacing and an increasing threat to law and order. In the face of social crisis, temporary work camps supplemented Britain's permanent workhouse infrastructure to impound "undesirables." In the words of George Bernard Shaw, the Fabian playwright and normally a critic of such schemes, camps would "tak[e] off the insurrectionary edge of poverty."[83]

At the high noon of empire—during the "scramble for Africa" and its Boer War pinnacle—Victorian social commentators imagined London's East End as a colonial space. Conflating race and class, the capital's urban jungle was analogous, for commentators like the Salvation Army general William Booth, to the "dark continent" and the wilds of sub-Saharan Africa. "Primitive" and "savage" "tribes"—"nomads" and "street arabs"—inhabited its confounding rookeries.[84] Informed by social Darwinism, the emerging social sciences identified the "wandering tribes" of London as recognizable (and thus understandable) collectivities with their own dress, language, and physiognomy.[85] A class apart, the poor were also a degenerate race. Echoing Cesare Lombroso's biological theory of "born criminals," the pioneering social reformer Henry Mayhew spoke of "criminal races" with large muscles and defective intelligence, who were promiscuous, irreligious, and lazy.[86]

In the wake of the Irish famine, such descriptions often pertained to Irish migrants depicted as an inferior and uncivilized "race." Even those who blamed poverty on underemployment and low wages rather than genetic deficiency grouped the destitute into subhuman categories. Mayhew's contemporary Charles Booth, among the most sympathetic late-Victorian commentators, believed the "lowest categories" of criminal poor presented a hopeless and "intolerable drain." Others deployed the language of disease. Herbert Gladstone, the Liberal member of Parliament and son of the famous prime minister, lamented that "some criminals [were] irreclaimable, just as some diseases are incurable."[87] At a moment when medical science achieved new levels of cultural authority, commentators turned to epidemiological strategies of isolation and quarantine to prevent the figurative contagion of the social body by a pathological other. Viewed in categorical terms, the "criminal classes" were objects of compassion, certainly, but they were also sources of fear and loathing that needed to be excluded, "amputated" from society, or "fenced off."

Chronic angst about social "others" turned acute during moments of crisis. The summer of 1887 was a highpoint of class warfare as the "denizens" of "darkest

FIGURE 4.

Hadleigh labor colony, Essex, administered by the Salvation Army. Similar arrangements emerged in the settler colonial world. The "unemployment camp" at Braamfontein, South Africa, housed "poor whites" in bell and marquee tents recycled from the Anglo-Boer War.[3] [Credit: Unattributed photograph on a postcard, Mary Evans/Peter Higginbotham Collection, No. 1041620.]

[3] Peter Kallaway and Patrick Pearson, *Johannesburg: Images and Continuities, A History of Working Class Life through Pictures, 1885–1935* (Braamfontein, South Africa Ravan Press, 1986), 82–83.

England" "invaded" the West End.[88] Desperate times called for desperate measures. Charles Booth even proposed a scheme for the mass removal of Britain's racial and biological "degenerates" to overseas labor camps, where some 345,000 "dangerous" social elements could be segregated; the empire seemed an appropriate dumping ground for the metropole's human refuse.[89] With its combination of impracticality and stoic authoritarianism, Booth's system was never fully implemented—not least because colonial governments proved unwilling receptacles. But amid currents of eugenicist thought, which recast the "criminal classes" as an abnormal human type, calls for the erection of overseas "penal camps" remained popular throughout the 1890s. These camps, according to the Bethnal Green preacher Osborn Jay, would house a "peculiar," "separate class" of the metropolitan poor, a category of humanity that was born lazy, immoral, and deficient in intellect.

As advocates of overseas labor camps maintained, "not all men can be treated as equal."[90] Even progressives like William Beveridge, architect of Britain's post–World War II social democracy, favored the creation in 1909 of compulsory colonies for the "unemployable" that would provide "a lower standard of living, a lower scale of relief and a rougher kind of work."[91] As a preventive measure, spatial exclusion would purify society by removing populations for the *potential* threat they posed. Such was the logic of the camp.

Though Charles Booth's ambitious system of overseas camps was never made a reality, a more modest network of "industrial settlements" and "farm colonies" emerged in the 1890s under the supervision of (the unrelated) General William Booth's Salvation Army and the London Central Committee for the Unemployed. Located at Hadleigh, Laindon, Hollesley Bay, and other sites outside London, these camps provided shelter and work—breaking stones, digging ditches, and preparing rough roads—for the unemployed up until World War II and the installation of the welfare state. Acting as temporary open-air workhouses, each camp contained several hundred inmates housed in tents and huts for three months' training. Fences and security personnel regulated egress and ingress, and the threat of denied benefits compelled inmates into camp. In this way, work camps segregated the "submerged residuum" at a safe distance. At the same time, however, they upheld the promise, however remote, of rehabilitation. While inmates constituted a "residuum of unhelpables," camps did not entail a permanent exile from the social body. The stated goal, according to the historian John Field, was to "harden young men through heavy manual labour" and "recondition them" for the workforce.[92] In sterner tones, however, the Victorian economist Alfred Marshall urged that "descendants of the dissolute" be segregated in order to preserve "living room" for the more "legitimate" working classes.[93]

IMPERIAL EXPANSION, NATIVE CONCENTRATION

The enclosure and spatial reorganization of land and people had a long history in metropolitan Britain, but such efforts intensified in the empire. Just as workhouses and work camps offered confined sites to control the socially "suspect," settlements, reserves, and guarded villages concentrated indigenous populations in South Asia, Australia, and the Americas.

Particularly in its settler form, colonialism involved "the displacement of people from their land and its repossession by others."[94] Like the "wild Irish" consigned beyond the pale, the empire's natives were inveterate "wanderers" with "no attachment to place."[95] In this vein, the Enlightenment notions of Locke and Mill—who agreed that those who failed to "settle" or cultivate the land could be legitimately displaced—helped justify the often-violent removal and concentration of scattered or nomadic populations behind barbed-wire fences. America's Indian Removal Act (1830) and the forced marches, hunger, and disease suffered by native populations in the American South during the "Trail of Tears" were only the most violent chapters in a larger process reenacted across the settler colonies of the Western world.[96] Whether for the purposes of extermination (as at Wybalenna off the shores of Tasmania[97]), or in the name of "containing, controlling and segregating" natives from "a civilization . . . they [did] not understand and from which they need[ed] protection" (as at Australia's Kahlin Compound[98]), European expansion mandated native concentration. Delineated with wire fences and "arranged in a manner conducive to order and regularity of appearance," native "settlements" helped transform nomadic populations into sedentary cultivators.[99] By transforming colonial space into a knowable *place*, moreover, these institutions facilitated the collection of data—both statistical and ethnographic—about tribal groups. Reservations were the information technology of the settler-colonial age.

As in other episodes of encampment, the language of Christian uplift lent legitimacy to these efforts. Organized by missionaries, many native settlements resembled labor colonies run by the Salvation Army. Across Britain's settler domains, R. J. Surtees suggests, a liberal philanthropic impulse coalesced in the 1830s to collect and settle natives in "protective reserves," which, in theory, would transform inmates into prosperous and civilized subjects.[100] But reserves were never simply humanitarian. Security and sympathy were tightly intertwined. Analogous to the workhouse's pacifying role in Britain's "war" against "criminal classes," reserves for "Red Indians" functioned, Laleh Khalili notes, as "militarily useful spaces for concentrating and monitoring native fighters."[101] The aim was to empty colonial landscapes of their troublesome human content and provide "living room" for European settlers. The pacification of imperial hinterlands—and the use of native reserves—rested on developing theories and practices of "asymmetric warfare" and a global strategic reservoir of "small war" counterinsurgency.[102] Collective punishment, forced relocation, scorched-earth warfare and an impulse to "civilize" and "settle" by fixing natives to sedentary sites accompanied the spatial expansion of empire. A "sinister and impersonal" aesthetic of "barbed-wire fence[s] and . . . bark and iron huts" aptly befitted the brutal process this entailed.[103]

INDIA'S "CRIMINAL TRIBES"

The global reach of British power extended the practices of concentration and segregation across the world, but it was India that emerged as the primary arena of British camps. Starting in the 1830s—and thus converging with policies in the Americas—efforts to compel the nomadic tribes of upland South Asia into a sedentary and "civilized" existence generated a system of "guarded villages," "schools of industry," and "penal residences."[104] Primary targets were populations like the Bhils, who represented an insurgent threat in Bombay, "attacking towns" and "carrying off cattle and hostages."[105] The concentration of these groups was the colonial correlative of Britain's efforts to immobilize East London's "wandering tribes" in work camps and prisons.

In India, "increased product competition and cyclical weather instabilities" in the 1830s resulted in famine and a larger crisis of political economy. The result, Sandria Freitag notes, was a "watershed decade" in which organized crime, or at least the perception thereof, rose dramatically.[106] Anxieties about rootless masses in Britain, which coalesced around the 1834 Poor Law, proved even starker in the empire as roving dacoits (professional criminals) and organized "thugs" suddenly occupied the official mind. Steeped in a waning Romanticism, an earlier appreciation for the "dignity and manliness," "heroic postures," and "nobility and chivalrous instincts"[107] of daring *thugee* raids gave way to more menacing representations of vicious plunder and savage bloodshed. Such discursive shifts accompanied Britain's nineteenth-century transition in South Asia from a mobile commercial empire to a landed imperium encompassing vast swathes of newly conquered territory. The guerrilla instincts of "wandering gangs" were no longer compatible with revenue collection and the sedentary agrarian base upon which a territorial empire depended. Outside state control, wandering populations could no longer be tolerated.

Sporadic efforts to concentrate and settle South Asia's tribal population intensified with the passage of the Criminal Tribes Act (1871), which legalized existing efforts to pacify dacoits and thugs and to settle nomadic groups like the Bhils.[108] In the judgment of General Booth of the Salvation Army, the new policies also resembled American measures "adopted with great success in dealing with the Red Indians" and in "wean[ing] [them] from their evil and lawless habits."[109] As policy developed in decades to come, it also followed the pattern of labor colonies laid down by Booth for the English poor.[110] Drawing from analogous practices controlling Irish travelers and Britain's "wandering tribes," the legislation adapted Britain's Habitual Criminals Act (1869) and its workhouse infrastructure to a colonial context, empowering officials to confine vagrant and outcast (literally out-*caste*) groups in purpose-built settlements under police control. In the image of British labor colonies, many of these settlements eventually came under the dual public-private administration of the colonial police and the Salvation Army.

The Indian legislation defined "notified criminal tribes" like the Bawarias, Minas, and Sanorias as criminal by virtue of their heredity and tribal membership: they were the "born criminals" of India.[111] As Sanjay Nigam points out, the "criminal tribe" category was an invention of colonial ethnography, emerging from contemporary misgivings about India's unruly inhabitants.[112] A component of Britain's global culture of confinement, the legislation facilitated the round up and detention, David Arnold notes, of a widening array of "wandering groups," including "nomadic petty traders and pastoralists, gypsy types, hill-and-forest-dwelling tribals" and "a wide variety of marginals who did not conform to the colonial pattern of settled agricultural and wage labor."[113] (Later on, the act would be used in spurious fashion against nationalist agitators in the interwar period: thus can the genealogical foundations of state-sponsored political repression in India be traced to earlier practices of social control.[114]) In total, some 3.5 million were criminalized—1 percent of South Asia's total population—though the number actually placed under surveillance was much smaller.[115]

Apart from passports and police checkpoints, criminal tribes were "concentrated in camps or settlements where," the Salvation Army officer Frederick Booth-Tucker noted, they could "be supervised, sifted, sorted, dealt with, reformed, and above all suitably employed."[116] Such efforts aimed to maintain Victorian distinctions between the respectable and irredeemable poor. In India, however, the fight against crime called for special measures. In contrast to England, where there was "some chance," magistrate James Monro maintained, "of crime not being concealed [and] of criminals being informed against,"[117] India presented a vast and dangerous domain populated by the untrustworthy and unknown. Criminal elements might be "concealed" within the jungles, and other inhabitants "connived at their concealment."[118] The problem was one of legibility: "born criminals" invented fictitious identities and they skillfully "camouflaged [themselves] as local peasants."[119] "From ages past," the Berar police official Major Gunthorpe complained, criminal tribes had "assimilated themselves to the common . . . dress" and often their "disguises are extremely well got up." They "learn so well the prayers, sayings and doings of religious mendicants," he continued, that it is "next to impossible . . . to see through their artifice."[120] Four months a year, dacoits would "gather together in gangs to roam across . . . the subcontinent," but they "spent the balance of the year in their home villages, appearing to the outside world as ordinary peasants."[121]

Even at its height, the British Raj was beset by anxiety. Danger lurked in hidden quarters: mild and passive peasants might transform into menacing gangs; religious mendicants might be political subversives. Nothing was secure, nothing reliable, nothing entirely predictable: such was the lesson of the shock "Mutiny" of 1857–58. The "regular codes of signals," inscrutable to outsiders, that gangs like the Bowriahs used to communicate secret messages portended especial danger.[122] Officials faced a semiotic crisis as they tried, often vainly, to disassociate the threatening tribal, mired in an exotic fury, from the "moral" agrarian peasant, upon whom British power depended.

The encounter between a territorial and bureaucratic state and an itinerant "horde" entailed a "clash of spatial cultures" that anticipated future episodes of encampment. Ostensibly genetic traits aside, "born criminals" were defined by their relationship to space. Instinct and intuition were the dacoits' habitus, speed and stealth their modus operandi. British prejudice marked "absolute nomads" as dangerous and suspect.[123] Criminal conspiracies could not be contained, Booth-Tucker complained: they "overspread the entire country."[124] "Like the Red Indians of the American continent," he continued—and in some senses, like the Boers of South Africa—they "roamed at will over the land" eluding the grasp of modern political society.[125] Major Gunthorpe expressed similar frustrations: "gangs consisting of 40, 50, or even 150 well-armed men would go long distances . . . for the purposes of attacking houses . . . or wealthy travelers on the highroads." The Bowriahs were "known to break into a house" with lighting speed and vanish unseen, "put[ting] 30 miles between it and their halting-place the same night."[126] Inspired by the game of chess—a metaphor, Gilles Deleuze and Felix Guattari note, for "institutionalized, regulated, coded war"[127]—the colonial police hoped concentration and detention would "checkmate [criminal tribes] to the benefit of the state and the welfare of the public."[128] Preventing born criminals from freely roaming over the country was to reproduce Indian space in the interests of British administration. Colonial police divided "infected" districts into "police circles," which they swept with regular search-and-capture patrols. "The scattered members of these castes" were then "collected together" in settlements.[129]

Such a project entailed substantial coercion. To "pacify" the countryside would be to "wage continual warfare" against those who existed "in enmity with . . . society," Inspector General C. P. Carmichael lamented.[130] Like class war in Britain, however, this was an irregular and asymmetric conflict, a lingering policing operation without heroic battles. For Booth-Tucker, writing in 1911, the decades-long struggle was reminiscent of the recent Anglo-Boer War: "inured to hardship" and "adept in every artifice," the criminal tribes "carr[ied] on guerrilla warfare which defies the combined efforts of an army of 150000 . . . to repress." They "meet power with cunning" and "move rapidly from point to point unencumbered by weapons, ammunition, or commissariat."[131] Faced with a "vast fugitive army of bandits,"[132] civilian concentration emerged in India, as it would in South Africa, as a military strategy. Victory depended on collecting suspect populations, including women and children, and segregating insurgents from the terrain and population that gave them succor.

If some turned to the language of guerrilla war, others described India's "predatory tribes" with dehumanizing hunting-and-trapping metaphors: as "wild animals," they would have to be "[broken]. . . into harness."[133] Thus did agriculture and counterinsurgency share a disciplinary logic. Turning hunters into prey, the colonial state would "round them up" and "herd" them into barbed-wire pens, though once domesticated, tribesmen appeared to one British official as "cattle, just cattle."[134] Ultimately, the concentration of scattered tribes within the fenced grids of government settlements would offer traction to the flailing Raj by enabling the colonial state to "get a hold" of these "savage and turbulent people."[135]

Predictably, medical metaphors complemented military language as conceptual inspiration for concentration. "Eaters of vermin,"[136] or else vermin themselves who "infested" the country, criminal tribes were often likened to plague and other infectious diseases.[137] Not for the last time, outcast groups associated with pestilence, locusts, and rats were segregated in camps. Using metaphors of contagion, the framers of the 1871 Act turned to "quarantine" to prevent tribes from "infect[ing] the social body."[138] Like the carriers of "cholera, plague, or smallpox," those "beyond the pale" would be segregated from the mainstream. In Booth-Tucker's more strident language, "segregation was . . . the most effective means of combating epidemics of crime" and the tribesmen "ought to be . . . made to spend their time under the yellow [quarantine] flag." A great deal of crime was "curable," the Salvation Army spokesman added, but only if appropriate hygienic measures were taken.[139] As a code for "civilization," sanitation dominated the governance of workhouses, military camps, and criminal tribe settlements alike. But sanitary language also framed colonial policing operations. From the long battle against tribal criminality to twentieth-century guerrilla counterinsurgency, mass detention became a common tool of colonial war and social hygiene.

"THE NICETIES OF CIVIL RIGHTS"

Amid the authoritarian policing of colonial "undesirables," the sensational language of war and disease facilitated measures that fit awkwardly within Britain's liberal culture of due process and individual rights. Like future camps, whether in the British empire or in Nazi Germany and the Soviet Union, criminal tribe settlements confined categories of people designated potential threats by virtue of their ethnicity and communal membership. Critics voiced concerns that indiscriminate internment differed little from slavery. Later, the settlements offered fodder for interwar Indian nationalists critical of British liberalism.[140] Faced with the supposedly "peculiar or hereditary nature" of colonial crime, however, British observers deemed ordinary laws "deficient" and dealt with criminal tribes "as a whole, and under "special rules."[141] Habitual criminals were "enemies of us all," the Amritsar commissioner P. H. Egerton concurred, and they required special treatment outside existing jurisprudence.[142]

Detention was at once collective and preventive. If a wolf wandered into a flock of sheep, the official logic decreed, the shepherd "would not wait until there was *tangible proof* that his flock was in danger."[143] With a "guilt by association" mentality, Britain detained India's "wolves" (including women and children) as a dangerous species rather than as guilty individuals. Criminal tribes legislation provided more sweeping powers of summary arrest and detention than any English legislation. Indeed, the more liberal-minded police inspector C. P. Carmichael conceded, "in our own country . . . such measures of vexatious surveillance" have been "repudiated and held up to reprobation in the dramas of the country." If enacted in Europe, they would meet with the "universal condemnation" of both Britain and France, "two of the most civilized nations in the world."[144] But while British law books "proceeded on the principle that no man is guilty until he has been convicted [of a crime]," the situation in India called for extraordinary measures of collective punishment.[145] Criminalized by fiat and detained indefinitely, criminal tribes were denied the benefit of a trial. Inevitably, the colonial government conceded, "so sweeping an Act of class legislation" would involve "very many innocent persons and families in penal disabilities, extending to the deprivation of their natural liberty and degrading whole classes under one common law of reprobation."[146] Particularly egregious were the innocent women and children concentrated alongside their suspect male relations. Yet in India, the question of women's confinement rarely raised controversy.[147] In a land where security trumped liberty, and where governance operated through collectivities rather than individuals, "repressive measures towards the whole tribe" were justified as practical necessities. "Something more . . . is wanted in India," officials concurred.[148]

India, apparently, was no place for "the niceties of civil rights."[149] According to developing languages of "protective custody," mass confinement "protected" a settled and respectable agricultural class from hereditary criminals. Often the mere fact they wandered was proof of the menace they posed. Evidence against them, in Sanjay Nigam's judgement, was "of a general descriptive nature that constantly slipped into stereotypical and discursive accounts of the criminality of criminal tribes."[150] As if combatting a cryptic plot, colonial police officers relied less on detective work and sober forensics than on "informers" and "approvers." Mass confinement without trial was of "extremely doubtful authority," they conceded: it was "curiously hazy" and "palpably illegal." Yet the Raj was anxious not to eschew legal frameworks entirely. Instead of operating outside the law, the colonial state developed new laws—what the legal scholar Sandria Freitag terms an "alternate legal structure"—that retained the rudimentary trappings of due process and the rule of law.[151] As the political scientist Laleh Khalili argues, liberal "states of exception" do not necessarily indicate the complete absence or rejection of law, but are products of a deliberate legal process of delineating a new body of law—whether martial law or other emergency legislation—that replaces or exists alongside a suspended but eventually restored legal code.[152] Far from a legal void, colonial policing relied on a multiplying corpus of coercive statutes—or, in the words of Radhika Singha, "a despotism of law."[153]

"A STOUT BARBED-WIRE FENCE"

What became of criminal tribes once concentrated? Enclosed settlements were not the only option. A magistrate in the North-Western Provinces "desired to get rid of these people, root and branch, by having them transported to some isolated island," though banishment "to remote Himalaya valleys" was also considered.[154] Conforming to Britain's developing culture of confinement, however, "walled settlements" were the preferred solution.[155]

Much like workhouses and mining compounds, the paradox of work—as a punitive and civilizing force—dominated life inside the settlements. Some inmates performed heavy labor on nearby canals and railways, while others worked on agricultural settlements tilling the soil: to cultivate an untamed landscape was to cultivate themselves.[156] In still other cases, small-scale intramural work prevailed. Modeled explicitly on labor colonies like Hadleigh as well as prisons and workhouses, inmates manufactured bricks, carpets, and army tents (some of which were shipped, incidentally, to South Africa to shelter concentration camp inmates).[157]

The settlements thus displayed continuity with other outposts in Britain's carceral archipelago. At Bidauli, a government spokesman noted the "settlement must in fact be a prison" if wandering tribes were ever to "settle down to hard but honest industry."[158] In other cases, an "ordinary factory could be declared a settlement, and the factory manager appointed the manager of the settlement." In principle, labor was curative and enforced for the benefit of those confined, though in practice, unfree labor remained central to colonial economies. The police thus became labor procurers for private industries requiring compliant workers and during World War I the settlements functioned primarily as labor depots for the army.[159]

In theory, criminal tribe settlements enforced an absolute division between outside and inside: they were isolated and insulated. Police guards and government passes regulated egress and ingress, and according to C. A. Elliot, an administrator in the North-Western Provinces, superintendents enforced nothing less than "open prison discipline."[160] Within the settlement walls, meanwhile, separate "undesirable wards" detained the especially incorrigible according to developing gradients of perceived danger. The worst offenders were banished to the Andaman Islands, where the Indian Ocean itself would act as a cordon sanitaire saving the subcontinent from criminal contagion.[161] In other cases, barbed wire sufficed. In 1896, the settlement at Bitragunta "was fenced in with a stout barbed-wire fence on steel rail posts and reinforced with a thorn hedge, the exit being under control of a watchman the whole of the day and night."[162] Some decades later, the settlement, still in existence after colonial independence, reminded an investigative committee of "a Nazi concentration camp." The "children being bred behind barbed wire as though they are very dangerous animals was a very tragic sight," the committee concluded.[163] Such arrangements, however, were far from universal, especially in the nineteenth century, when official apathy, corruption, and disorder marked many of the settlements. The system of roll calls was frequently a farce, superintendents were often absent, and settlement walls did not always pose a barrier for those determined to abscond.[164]

Meanwhile, the emphasis on curative labor competed with financial constraints and penal objectives. In Bombay, Governor Richard Temple, a man who would soon gain infamy for austerity measures in the 1876–77 famine, was especially keen to curtail government expense. Resulting conditions, though punishing, were rarely conducive to rehabilitation. "Nothing short of starvation [would] induce [inmates] to undertake labor of an arduous nature," Inspector General of Police Lieutenant-Colonel A. H. Paterson maintained.[165] But high death rates at settlements like Bhiwani (22%) and Dhariwal (12%) could not be squared with humane or rehabilitative agendas, and as sanitary inspectors like S. J. Thomson in the North-Western Provinces discovered, epidemic diseases spread rapidly among concentrated

FIGURE 5.
"Barbed-wire imperialism" at the
Bitragunta Criminal Tribes Settlement.
[Credit: A. Aiyappan, *Report on the
Socio-Economic Conditions of the
Aboriginal Tribes of the Province of
Madras* (Madras: Government Press,
1948), 169.]

populations. The settlements, like Britain's empire of camps to come, offered ambiguous legacies: a sustaining language of "civilization" coupled with substantial coercion and repressive conditions; labor as a moral imperative but also an economic necessity; official apathy and incompetence that proved counterproductive to the original goals of concentration; the simultaneous rehabilitation and discursive marginalization of inmates; and a pattern of mortality and disease that would recur in future concentrations.

CULTURAL AND MATERIAL FOUNDATIONS

For all their controversy and coercion, camps concentrating "criminal tribes" were relatively small affairs. The tens of thousands they contained paled in comparison to the hundreds of thousands in wartime concentration camps and the millions in Indian famine and plague camps. New scales of concentration accompanied the colonial disasters of the late nineteenth century as the concomitant need for surveillance and security (as well as relief and rehabilitation) spread ever wider. Yet while they emerged in visibly distinct contexts from future camps, criminal tribe settlements and other related enclosures drew together Victorian Britain's developing practices of social and spatial segregation and the medical and military discourses that informed them.

There developed in Britain and the empire over the course of the nineteenth century a climate conducive to the concentration of "dangerous" or marginal populations in demarcated enclosures. In its projects of domestic reform and imperial expansion, Britain assembled the cultural and material foundations for its empire of camps. Prisons reflected a new emphasis on confinement as a disciplinary technology, while workhouses and labor colonies stemmed from developing attitudes that linked poverty with moral decay and "criminal classes" with biological inferiority. Industrialization demanded increasing magnitudes of population management and inaugurated new patterns of arranging bodies over space. Factories initiated new rhythms and ideologies of work as both exalted and punitive, while the military epitomized many of these trends and disseminated them abroad. Concurrent with the development of liberal democracy in Britain was the expansion of imperial rule over populations marked by cultural and racial difference and denied political rights. Native reservations and criminal tribe settlements were colonial derivatives of Britain's late-Victorian impulse to discipline, order, classify, and control. Like their domestic counterparts, imperial concentrations spotlight intersections between humane and coercive impulses and between the intrusive social engineering and laissez-faire sentiments that would animate the history of British camps—and of liberal empire more broadly—into the twentieth century.

As Britain strived for an inclusive social body at home, it amputated dangerous elements. To cultivate its garden was to eliminate, or at least to "fence off," weeds. But imperial and Victorian Britain's disciplinary enclosures offered more than a cultural backdrop. In response to mounting crises, colonial governments drew from established repertoires. Inspectors at South African concentration camps drew from personal experience as factory inspectors and poor law guardians. The deputy administrator of the Orange River Colony, Major Goold-Adams, specified factory foremen as ideal superintendents at wartime concentration camps.[166] The sanitary commissioner of Allahabad, Charles Planck, noted that Indian famine camps reproduced the disciplinary techniques of workhouses—the segregation of sexes, the enforcement of manual labor, and a regime of silence at "feeding" times.[167] J. S. Wilkins, an IMS officer active in plague and famine camps, started his career in 1874 inspecting British army camps.[168] Workhouses and prisons provided templates for forced labor; military barracks provided blueprints for exacting hygiene and discipline; and the policing of criminal tribes rehearsed counterinsurgency measures later implemented during the Anglo-Boer War. Britain's empire of camps drew from the nineteenth century's disciplinary landscape in conscious and concrete ways. The relationship was more than structural: it was genealogical.

CHAPTER 2

"Barbed-Wire Deterrents"

*Detention and Relief at Indian Famine
Camps, 1876–1901*

Famine in India was the context for the concentration of colonial populations on unprecedented scales. In the 1890s, the American missionary Reverend Jefferson Scott described a typical scene. Travelling as chairman of the Methodist Episcopal Relief Committee, he saw "forty dead bodies on the road" who had evidently "tried to reach a relief camp but had waited too long before setting out."[1] The camps to which Scott referred were centers of labor and relief, another missionary continued, and they collected all the "waifs and strays of the district"—the "superfluous" and itinerant poor who "wandered about wearily."[2] Some hapless "refugees" traveled from town to town, while others congregated in cities like Bombay and Madras where their emaciated frames presented pitiable specters of suffering, but also social and sanitary hazards. Many were harmless and vulnerable. Others, however, were suspected dacoits, members of the "criminal classes" who warranted careful surveillance. In a colonial crisis as cataclysmic as a great famine, security competed with sympathy as animus behind British camps.

As Scott continued his travels, he encountered another, larger, camp where "more than seven thousand people" carried earth "like a colony of ants." The workers were "busy removing a sand-bank by filling caskets and carrying them on their heads across a narrow valley, which was to be leveled."[3] "Formed into gangs, sixty, eighty, a hundred in each"[4] with a "head ganger" and Public Works Department supervisor, inmates comprised "all sorts": "men and women, boys and girls, children and babies." At night, they slept in 400 huts "covered with thatch, each designed for twenty." The camp was a complete but makeshift village for the dissolute: there was a hospital (accommodating 450), a storehouse, an orphanage (accommodating 114), and "on the outskirts, places for the disposal of the dead." And despite its putatively humane purpose, fences regulated egress and ingress, along with police and military guards.[5]

Before Britain coined the term "concentration camp" during the Anglo-Boer War (1899–1902), the British Raj erected a vast system of camps to combat the suffering and social upheavals of hunger. The camps Scott described were only a few of thousands. In 1900, the *Manchester Guardian* correspondent and social reformer Vaughan Nash counted "nearly five million people camped out on famine works" across the subcontinent.[6] Government statistics confirm Nash's numbers: in Bombay and the Central Provinces, the worst-affected districts, 1,017,965 and 1,252,474 were counted respectively; other provinces pushed total camp inmates above four million. Though statistics are less reliable for earlier famines, ten million famished Indians likely found themselves in camps over the course of the 1870s and 1890s.[7] Only "those who have seen or personally known these things" could truly grasp the scale, the Bombay governor Sir Richard Temple reflected.[8]

In the midst of crisis, famine camps performed multiple functions. Detention centers or "relief camps" proliferated in famine's early stages to contain the "wandering classes" deemed most likely to perish or commit crime on city streets. Meanwhile, dormitory camps attached to large public works projects accommodated starving peasants, who received subsistence wages in return for heavy labor. Like workhouses and other enclosures for the poor, famine camps emerged from shared attitudes assembled over the course of the nineteenth century. Inheriting the army's veneration for tidy geometric lines and its emphasis on social and sanitary discipline, famine officials engaged in widespread practices of confinement, isolation, and partition: such were the ingredients of British famine camps.

"THE WORST INDIA HAD SEEN"

Famine was a quotidian feature of British India. Exacerbated by the East India Company's increasing revenue demands, the catastrophic Bengal famine of 1770 killed ten million and subsequently dominated collective memory. But India's late-Victorian famines were even worse. At a time when British rule had "narrowed . . . the sources of national wealth," the "extent and intensity" of famine was "unexampled . . . in either ancient or modern times." Such was the judgement of the economic historian and Indian nationalist Romesh Dutt.[9] Vaughan Nash concurred:

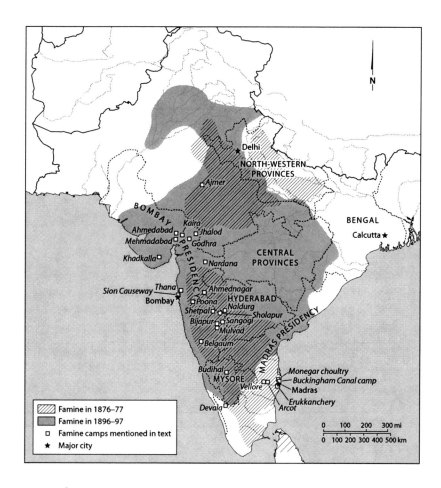

FIGURE 6.

The Great Famine of 1876–77 afflicted approximately fifty million people, mostly in Bombay and Madras Presidencies. The end of the American Civil War contributed to a slump in cotton prices, making matters worse in southern regions. The 1896–97 famine also originated in Bombay and Madras, but spread north in its second year, afflicting fifty-eight million. [Credit: Map by Bill Nelson.]

by 1900 "the state of affairs" was "the worst India ha[d] seen."[10] Many considered the "Great Famine" of 1876–77 the worst in living memory. But it was eclipsed in 1896–97 and 1899–1901 as a constellation of climatic, epidemiological, and economic disasters descended upon India. The outbreak of plague in 1896, during which "whole villages had to leave their home and camp in huts,"[11] made matters considerably worse, as did the financial strain of world events. The concurrence of India's final nineteenth-century famine with the Anglo-Boer War was also not entirely coincidental. Though a continent away, the escalating expenses of a prolonged conflict—and later, the considerable costs of maintaining a quarter million South Africans in concentration camps—drained the colonial treasury and diverted resources from famine relief.[12] Such were the connections between two systems of camps on opposite sides of the Indian Ocean.

On the surface, famine was a natural disaster—the result of drought and a failed monsoon. But it also stemmed from "entitlement failures" fostered by imperial ideology and political economy. Famine was thus a register of human action rather than divine sanction. Cash-cropping, spiraling revenue demands, and the conscription of peasant cultivators "into a London-centered world economy" all fostered conditions conducive to famine. So too did India's deindustrialization under British rule and its growing dependence on European goods in return for agricultural produce.[13] Viceroys Lytton (1876–1880) Elgin (1894–99) and Curzon (1899–1905) were not only the architects of British famine relief; their policies manufactured hunger in the first place. Nash noted as much in 1900 when he defined famine as the "logical outcome of the British revenue system" and the "iron law of wages."[14] The economist Amartya Sen's Nobel Prize–winning work confirms what contemporaries already knew: famine was not the result of absolute food shortage—indeed, grain exports from India to Britain continued unabated—but of meager wages, dwindling savings, and failures in the mechanisms of supply.[15]

THE "SCIENCE" OF RELIEF: FROM IRELAND TO INDIA

Just as famine emerged from colonial constellations of political and economic inequality, Britain's response derived from a self-same imperial dynamic. In precolonial India, free kitchens and the distribution of alms in villages and religious rest houses alleviated hunger. "Traditional" charity, inscribed within patterns of patronage and "custom," operated according to established moral economies, though ones Britain derided as "demoralizing" and corrupt.[16] Replacing the "Orient's" "irrational" and "indiscriminate" charity with "system" and "science" was a primary justification for colonial rule, Viceroy Curzon believed.[17] Britain would replace the "temporary impulse of sympathy," Finance Minister John Strachey added, with "that real benevolence which is founded on sound principles [and] dispassionate intelligence."[18] Yet British famine relief fell lamentably short. In the new age of "biopolitics,"[19] which saw health and welfare supplant brazen territorial conquest as government's guiding rationale, Indians died in the millions of hunger and disease.[20]

Colonial famine policy emerged from long-term developments in state capacity and the economics of Adam Smith. In the wake of Britain's newly minted Poor Law (1834), scarcities in Rajasthan in 1837–38 offered early opportunities for state-sponsored relief: in return for wages, famine victims replaced convict laborers (who were shipped further afield to Mauritius and the Andaman Islands) in the construction of roads, canals, and irrigation tanks.[21] Above all, however, the Great Irish Famine (1845–51) framed agendas in India, highlighting the degree to which colonial practices emerged within larger frameworks of interimperial exchange.[22]

Many analogies existed between Britain's oldest colony and its largest. Both realms experienced the tensions of liberal empire in stark relief: the classical-liberal economic injunction to prevent "extravagant spending" and "enormous losses to the British Exchequer" competed with a humane impulse to sustain life.[23] India and Ireland also shared analogous cultural representations. In the language of social-scientific racism, the famished of both colonies were suspect ethnic "others." Lazy, improvident, and adherents of a "superstitious" religion, the Irish, like their Indian counterparts, were "born and bred . . . from time immemorial in inveterate indolence . . . disorder and consequent destitution," a *Times* article maintained.[24] They were never blameless victims.

At the helm of Irish (and later, Indian) policy, Treasury Secretary Charles Trevelyan exhibited a fanatical faith in laissez-faire ideology and a determination to resist "pauperization" through government relief. Famine, he believed, was a providential judgment and moment for moral instruction. Officials in India repeated this mantra when they proclaimed that famine victims must learn the "hard lesson of self-dependence."[25] Motivated to save expense and reduce taxes for landholders, officials in Ireland adopted stern attitudes about "dependence." The Whig government reversed Robert Peel's earlier policy of importing food, and Trevelyan's work-or-starve policy erected nominal relief works, which complemented Ireland's overburdened workhouses. But "the sad truth," James Donnelly writes, was "too many earned too little to enable them to ward off starvation."[26] In Ireland as in

India, Victorian racism colluded with the despotism of the "free market" as "hundreds of thousands . . . died from disease, starvation, exposure or exhaustion."[27]

Though Irish policies supposedly fostered individual responsibility, they also enshrined famine relief as a public imperative, laying the groundwork for more systematic Indian policies under viceroys Lytton and Curzon. With moral dogma came state planning. Trevelyan ironically oversaw a dramatic expansion of government intervention. Though meant to curb charitable spending, relief works were remarkably expensive and entailed substantial administrative machinery, including a new twelve-thousand-member Board of Works. And while Trevelyan's disciples feared the "disturbing influence . . . [of] public opinion,"[28] they conceded "the State [could not] divest itself . . . of the responsibility of providing necessary relief [to] . . . a famine-stricken population."[29] Humanitarian action was now on the table. Rigid economic restraints remained, but were tempered by emerging views, expressed by S. J. Thomson, an official in India's North-Western Provinces, that the "state [had] to think of the greatest good of the greatest number."[30] In the wake of Ireland and amid the rise of Gladstonian liberalism, the "civilizing missions" that accompanied the "new imperialism" recalibrated empire as an arena of humane intervention.

Irish efforts marked an exemplary distinction, in official circles, between professional famine management—British, rational, modern—and supposedly "irrational" premodern practices. In his defense, Trevelyan contended Ireland had permitted "extensive experiments in the science . . . of relieving the destitute,"[31] and when famine next struck India, his example loomed large. In his later career, Trevelyan served as governor of Madras and finance minister to the government of India, where he directly influenced officials like Sir Richard Temple, who personified the tensions of Britain's response in India. As governor of Bombay in 1876–77 and special famine advisor in Madras, Temple was adamant that saving lives should not undermine colonial revenue collection. But at the same time, he believed "the welfare of the [Indian] peasant [was] the primary justification of British rule . . . and the foundation of economic and social progress."[32] Under Temple and his successors, Indian famine policy would oscillate between these competing mandates for decades to come.

Local considerations also shaped Indian policy. The subcontinent, after all, was not Ireland. A vast and distant terrain with only a tenuous European presence, India was populated with less familiar, and by many accounts more menacing, inhabitants. India also lacked a colonial Poor Law or Ireland's permanent system of workhouses,[33] which had accommodated a million Irish famine victims between

1847–49.[34] New techniques and institutions therefore developed as prevalent attitudes about colonial poverty were translated into an Indian context. Above all, famine camps emerged to distribute relief and discipline India's poor, performing similar functions to more enduring welfare and penal infrastructure in Britain and Ireland. With their cheap and rudimentary facilities, camps forestalled the assembly of a more permanent (and expensive) colonial welfare state, even as famine became a recurring feature of British rule.

"WALKING SKELETONS"

Fiscal ideologies set the parameters of social intervention, but fear and anxiety also shaped Britain's response. Famine generated apocalyptic scenes, and its response was driven by security concerns as much as by sympathy. Even more than in Ireland, Indian famine victims were foreign and disturbing sights. Reverend Scott noted the "gaunt refugees" who "fill our streets," releasing "piteous cries." The "rivers were dried up," he lamented, and "along their sunbaked, kiln-dried beds, countless thousands of ragged, haggard, foot-sore beggars wandered aimlessly."[35] In Bombay, Nash similarly observed ten thousand "refugees wandering about the [city's] streets by day, and camping out on open spaces." When they "first began to appear, the police collected them and sent them back in boatloads to their own parts." But "groups of stolid men and tired women" appeared again and again.[36]

British spokesmen identified the "evil of wandering" as a principle concern, and the Famine Commission president Antony MacDonnell pointed to itinerant refugees as the most challenging aspect of famine management.[37] "A love of liberty" combined with a dislike of regular work and a passion for begging induced "hundreds of emaciated and half-starved wanderers to cling to the streets," officials complained, and it was "only by the most strenuous efforts" that they "could be collected and removed."[38] "Walking skeletons" and "emaciated strangers" emerged as potent symbols of desperation but also of danger. Earlier famines fomented social disruption and a "country . . . infested by bands of marauders."[39] But the scale in 1876–77 was greater. In the worst-affected districts, a quarter of the population left their farms for canal-irrigated tracts or nearby towns. Many "aimless wanderers" were members of traditionally nomadic groups, who persisted in itinerant lifestyles despite intensifying efforts starting in the 1830s to "settle" them at monitored sites. Analogous to "gypsy tribes" and criminal gangs, they occupied the margins of colonial society: "beggars, unprovided widows, and the criminal classes," as one observer grouped them.[40] Distinct from *ryot* cultivators (tenant farmers) upon whom the stability of British governance depended, wanderers represented a restless ethnographic specter. The distinction—so clear in colonial anthropology—was not as obvious in practice, however. As crops failed and drought intensified, more sedentary peasants, artisans, and landless laborers lost their traditional "ties to the land" and transformed into a rootless population.[41]

Migration was long an accepted and logical response to hunger. "Just as the Irish troop over to England at particular seasons,"[42] authorities noted, India witnessed "many . . . mass migrations away from barren, drought-baked plains." But officials viewed "aimless wandering" as an irrational flight emanating from "the blind instincts of the wild animal."[43] Genuine compassion motivated observers, but the reduction of the famished to "helpless and hopeless automata" guided "only by [an] instinctive craving for food"[44] dehumanized the target of British operations. According to General Sir Michael Kennedy, advisor to the Madras government, famine victims suffered from "the mental imbecility which attends starvation."[45] Reduced to the merely physical, they lost any status as rational, rights-bearing agents. They were bodies first and foremost.[46]

Even sympathetic observers relegated famine wanderers to subhuman status. In a poignant portrait of humanity on the edge of ruination, Vaughan Nash wrote of the "lines of long-suffering endurance," the faces "dulled into stupor," and "the large glassy eyes" of emaciated wanderers, which "stare straight in front" in "perpetual and hopeless misery."[47] The visual correlative of Nash's written testimony was a growing genre of "famine photographs." The commercially profitable images of Captain W. W. Hooper, a British army officer and amateur photographer in Madras, elicited humanitarian comment, but they also underscored the helplessness and dependency of impassive bodies. Prostrate, agentless, and discursively stripped of intellect or volition, such images recall Primo Levi's "Muselmann" or the "naked man" described by Hannah Arendt: the senseless and homogenous creatures that populated the extermination camps of wartime Europe.[48] In this sense, at least, the victims of nineteenth-century imperialism prefigured those of twentieth-century totalitarianism.

However disturbing Hooper's images, it proved hard for British observers to recognize famished wanderers as fully rounded human beings. If empathy depends on the recognition of one's self in the "other," then emaciated strangers presented an alien specter. It is hard for the well-fed to sympathize with the hungry, the photography critic Zahid Chaudhary notes, "because we 'do not grow hungry' in reaction to such a scene;" "we cannot properly . . . be said to sympathize with their hunger." Instead, famine, and the visualizations it elicited, augured contra-

FIGURE 7.

Famine wanderers detained in a Madras relief camp, W. W. Hooper, 1877. [Credit: ©
Royal Geographical Society Picture Library (with IBG), S0002006 "Objects deserving of
gratuitous aid in Madras (during the famine 1876–1878) – Tamil Nadu – South India."]

dictory responses: such scenes "satisf[ied] a latent sadistic desire even as they
provide[d] the basis for sympathy that could lead to altruism."[49] Many articulated
humane concern for India's most marginal. More often than not, however, the
skeletal "living corpse"—the human body in grotesque form—provoked fear and
disdain.

Less amiable versions of dehumanization rendered famine refugees "intolerable
pests." Many were like "beasts of the field": "hardy" and "primitive," they "set no
value on human life."[50] Some were even covered in "soft-looking black fur" (a
downy hair produced by prolonged starvation), giving them "a more simian look
than ever," the *Reuters* correspondent Francis Merewether observed.[51] Others,
Temple's auxiliaries noted, displayed a "constitutional inability to bear the strain
of any prolonged effort" and were "designed by nature" to perish.[52] Despite odes
to humanity, famine could still be understood as the catalyst of a Darwinian struggle or Malthusian correction among beings less-than-human.[53]

Colonial officers routinely described famine wanderers as superfluous forms of
life—as "utterly useless and worthless members of the community" and the "most

abject scum of the country."[54] Whether callous or caring, such commentary reduced the famished to a state of corporal materiality described by Giorgio Agamben as "bare life."[55] Famine wanderers emerge from official records as anonymous and undifferentiated bodies: stripped of worldly goods and any means of self-support, they are discursively deprived any psychological depth, social life, or politico-legal existence.

Such representations had not always been dominant: they were products of historical change. At one time, wandering vagrants presented stock images of pity and compassion. William Wordsworth's Cumberland beggar was a bucolic installation of village life: a gentle figure of early Romanticism who compelled the human heart to acts of charity and love. So too, in early nineteenth-century India, the wandering vagrant might pass gently by with "charity and without censure"—an exotic curiosity of the tropical pastoral.[56] As hardened attitudes toward poverty and race fostered more menacing representations, the cadaverous wanderers of the 1870s and 1890s were different. No longer vulnerable wayfarers, these threatening apparitions were foreigners undeserving of help. "Innocent victims" and the "deserving poor" transformed, in British eyes, into "lazy" and "worthless" transients, just as dacoits and criminal tribes transitioned, in popular imaginaries, from daring and heroic highwaymen into enemies of civilization. At best, famine wanderers were obstinate simpletons who made "slovenly and unscientific cultivator[s]."[57] At worst, they were "able-bodied parasites," "reservoirs of contagion," "squatters polluting the city," and a law and order problem.[58]

"THE CRIMINAL CLASSES"

Above all, famine victims suggested danger and unrest. Victorian equations of poverty and sin legitimized coercive measures against wandering, as did associations between rootless mobility and delinquent criminality. Even in its opening stages, famine represented a threat to public order. Authorities recognized "a great increase in violent crime"[59]—"panics in the bazaars" and the plundering of grain[60]—as "early warning indicators."[61] Crime was most serious, Bombay's official famine commission reported, among "Bhils, Mangs, Kolis, Thakurs and members of other similar classes, who are generally averse to continuous labor and take to pilfering and housebreaking when they are short of food."[62] The crisis renewed fears about "criminal classes," as the famished plundered grain shops.[63] Looting, robberies, and riots (150 in August–September 1877 in the North-Western Provinces alone) were quelled at the point of the bayonet, and in some districts, police opened fire on rioters.[64] In the most lawless districts, where Temple recorded "daring and frequent" robberies, the crime rate surged sixfold.[65] Some famine-related crime was "chiefly of a petty nature," but more serious disorder prevailed.[66] "Dacoity, robbery, burglary and theft" became "very serious features of the famine," the 1880 Famine Commission recorded, and at hunger's height, "lawlessness and insecurity of life prevailed to such an extent that whole hamlets were deserted, and the inhabitants flocked into the larger villages for security."[67] Escalating crime placed existing penal infrastructure under tremendous strain: though India had no workhouses, its prison population more than doubled.[68]

Mobile masses had long provoked unease within British political culture. But associations between wandering and organized crime took on special import in India. The dislocations of famine only intensified existing fears of "criminal tribes" and "wandering gangs," who symbolized the untamed violence of a fearsome colonial landscape. The political agent of Mahi Kantha highlighted the "great feeling of unrest and anxiety" that famine produced among "criminal classes" whose "civilization [was] only skin deep." In the Central Provinces, dacoities quadrupled, and one gang of criminal tribesmen committed a "series of depredations" with "matchlocks, swords and axes" before "a special officer with 40 armed police . . . hunt[ed] them down."[69] Few wanderers had any formal association with notified "criminal tribes," but the upheavals of famine cast suspicion over ever-widening groups. In more aggressive tones, Mr. A. Colvin, the collector of Bijnor, equated famine refugees with "criminal lunatics" who had to be arrested and confined "by force."[70] Security, as much as compassion, governed the turn to camps.

Political anxiety accompanied India's insurgency of the hungry. With this great movement and mixing of populations, Richard Temple predicted famine would generate "political excitement," and officials worried hunger would unleash members of "semi-political criminal bands."[71] Their concerns were not unfounded: as the famous Russian-American sociologist Pitirim Sorokin confirmed, apart from crime, famine "on a massive scale" often resulted in "insurrection, social uprising, and [even] revolution."[72] Indeed, famine incited radicals like Vasudev Balwant Phadke—the "Robin Hood of the Deccan" and the "father of Indian armed rebellion"—to raid government treasuries and redistribute money to the famine-stricken poor. More ominously, Temple feared populist uprisings in the Bombay Deccan, the lawless and mountainous "heart of the country," would "assume a political significance," for it was here "the Mahrattas of old encountered their Muhammedan conquerors." And this was where "they would encounter the British tomorrow, if they had the chance." With memory of the 1857–58 rebellions still fresh, and with Britain's ever-tenuous hold on the subcontinent continually under strain,[73] the political ramifications of hungry, mobile masses excited special apprehension.[74] If history were not to repeat, the "restless, ambitious, [and] discontented" demanded special vigilance.[75] Whatever the political peril, however, emaciated strangers were easy scapegoats. Many were "illegal immigrants" from semiautonomous Native States like Mysore and Hyderabad who had "invaded" British territory and threatened to spread trouble. As low-caste pariahs, their appearance was an omen; Britons and Indians alike blamed these "bands of foreigners"[76] if not for famine itself, then for the failure of relief to reach a district's "actual residents."[77]

Public health authorities also warned that famine wanderers posed considerable danger as a "class of people . . . most likely to catch and spread disease."[78] Homeless and desperate, they congregated on the streets. Specters of pollution, they were "matter out of place,"[79] the displaced "dregs" of colonial society. At Nashirabad army base, the provost marshal expressed concern about "famine refugees just outside cantonment limits" and the "risk to the garrison from smallpox" that "these wandering *Marwaris*" posed.[80] The same held true for towns and cities. Dr. Cornish, the sanitary commissioner of Madras, pointed to the epidemiological threat of "destitute wanderers" who were "picking up a precarious living by begging in the streets."[81] Cholera and smallpox were traditional threats, though medical anxiety also mapped onto gendered tropes, and officials quickly associated wandering women with venereal disease. Some were destined for colonial lock hospitals, but the numbers involved overwhelmed existing facilities. Bubonic plague also emerged as a new menace in 1896, and the emergency regulations of the Epidemic Diseases Act (1897) empowered the summary arrest of famine refugees, who "tend[ed] in a serious degree to promote the said disease."[82] It was thus that famine and plague operations intersected at the junction of social control and medical policing.

In reality, the vast majority of famine victims were innocuous; but representations proved more powerful than reality. The famished were not on the whole disloyal, Temple conceded. But as hunger progressed, the distinction between bona fide victims and dangerous criminals or disease carriers came under increasing strain. For his part, Temple's telling slippage confounding the terms "victim" and "offender" in public testimony before the Indian Famine Commission offers insight into the mindset of officials tasked with relieving and controlling wanderers conceived simultaneously as harmless and harmful. Discussing measures to "summarily stop famished wanderers," he noted the importance of "catch[ing] offenders," before hastening to clarify: "not that these poor people are offenders, but . . . they bed about the streets, preferring a precarious subsistence of this kind to the steady discipline and subsistence," he went on to add, of a government relief camp.[83]

BEHIND BRAMBLE AND BARBED WIRE

Authorities cited the "round up" and "concentration" of famine wanderers as "the first object of famine administration." The means to achieve this was to "keep up . . . temporary camps" for "collecting and relieving" the displaced.[84] Whether victims or "offenders," famished bodies proved offensive to humanitarian and commercial sentiments alike. Phrases like "the evil of wandering" described refugees' distressing circumstances but they were also moral judgements. Reduced to alimentary reflexes, "aimless wanderers" had lost the ability "to exercise[e] intelligent volition," British commentators warned.[85] "Trapping" subhuman animals against their (nonexistent) will could be cast as a necessary policing operation.

In both the 1876–77 and 1890s famines, a network of regulated detention centers—"relief camps" or "poorhouses" in officialdom's euphemistic terms—concentrated mobile masses at "central spots where high roads converge."[86] Such enclosures, a Central Provinces publication indicated, were "refuge[s] for infirm and diseased paupers and vagrants, and . . . penitentiar[ies] for . . . persons who contumaciously refuse to work."[87] In large cities, operations transformed into systematic "urban cleansing" campaigns. As the task of "picking up all the emaciated persons"[88] scattered across the country gained momentum, a system of police and military patrols "visit[ed] the lanes and byeways of towns, and the roads principally traversed by travelers, in order to bring such persons in."[89] As Sorokin warned, the "intensive social struggle" that famine invariably portended resulted in the "strengthening of police force[s]" and "colossal increases in punishment [and] repression."[90]

Richard Temple set a precedent in 1876 by establishing suburban collecting camps on principal roads leading into the city of Bombay "at which all these miserable people [could be] stopped and taken care of."[91] Located along the Sion Causeway, these camps detained wanderers found congregating on city streets. Amid a crime wave in Ahmednagar, meanwhile, police did "good work" against nomadic Bhils by "gather[ing] them together and carr[ying] them off" to camps,[92] while Ahmedabad police devised similar schemes of "capture and deportation."[93] Likewise, Madras erected a "cordon . . . round . . . the town"[94] with guards "posted at all tollgates and roads" to turn people back or send them by force to camps organized by the commissioner of police. In the "interests of public health and safety," refugees "squatting" or "swarming" on city streets were "taken into custody." A "total clearance of the city" was thus effected by detaining wanderers "*nolens volens.*"[95]

As famine revisited Bombay's sprawling conurbation in the 1890s, suburban camps accommodated refugees from Gujarat and Kathiawar.[96] The police coordinated periodic raids, sweeping the city block-by-block, collecting more than eight thousand wanderers. Recognizing the importance of "rid[ding] the streets . . . of the mendicants and refugees that have *infested* them for months past," police forces marched those they captured to two camps eight miles from the train station. While the raid succeeded in "clearing the riffraff" from Bombay streets, authorities noted the difficulty of distinguishing between genuine refugees and habitual beggars residing in the city, thus highlighting the way famine relief merged into more general policing operations against the "dangerous classes."[97]

Whatever the case, the forced concentration of wanderers in camps indicates the degree of mistrust that existed between the Raj and its subjects. According to Thana officials, the "mere preservation of order among such a mob of people representing . . . the scum of the Bombay population" did not prove "an easy matter" and inmates had to be "retained . . . practically against their will." For their part, the famished mistrusted British police and many fled the camps, fearing "it was the intention of Government to have them drowned . . . or put an end to in some other way."[98] With rumors circulating that famine victims would "be deported or shipped as emigrants, or . . . murdered *en masse*," it was "found almost impossible" to get inmates "to remain in camp."[99] By no means were British camps the staging posts for genocide, but those detained sometimes feared otherwise.

"SALUS POPULI SUPREMA LEX"

Though putatively humane, British relief operated according to "military metaphor[s]."[100] Temple himself was "a skillful General commanding in battle,"[101] while camps in "key positions" offered one "tactic" in a larger "campaign" to relieve those "beleaguered" by the forces of hunger. Sadly, however, India remained "a battlefield . . . strewn with the dead [and] dying."[102] An exercise in both humanitarian care and military coercion, camps encapsulated the animating tensions of British imperialism: mass detention quickly compromised the cherished liberal tenets of free movement and rule of law.

Famine (and the camps it entailed) involved a ready suspension of civil liberties—already tenuous in colonial contexts—and a strengthening of executive authority. According to Lieutenant-Colonel S. J. Thomson, all consideration of "'rights' . . . disappear[ed] in a conflict [as] cataclysmic as a great famine." Executive orders could not be questioned nor "brought before a legal tribunal, as they would very likely be in England." On the contrary, Thomson continued, an effective "campaign" demanded "a leader—a Dictator," whose "summary words" would "sharply punish" offenses against government proclamations. In militaristic language, Thomson concluded all normal administration "must be subordinated to the task of beating the enemy."[103] This was a conviction shared by the Indian government's famine undersecretary S. C. Bayle, who declared that "in times of famine as of war, all ordinary administration must give way to the one main object of the campaign."[104]

Many wanderers entered camps voluntarily. Some were willing and even eager to accept confinement as a condition of relief: to the hungry, food trumps liberty. But others, a *Times* correspondent complained, "prefer[ed] freedom and starvation to confinement and a sufficiency of wholesome food."[105] Fearful of British intentions, many "persist[ed] in their obstinate refusal and continue[d] to reject the proffered aid." According to W. S. Whiteside, the collector of Arcot, a grave moral responsibility descended on officials who "allow[ed] deaths to occur" by respecting the "perverse and foolish scruples" of ignorant "natives."[106] Whiteside counseled "kind encouragement and persuasion." But others favored coercion. C. T. Langley, a collector in Madras, held that "*all* wandering emaciates should be *compelled* . . . to go to a relief camp,"[107] while Gerard Norman in Poona urged famine wanderers "be stopped by the police, and as far as possible, forced to go to relief [camps]."[108] Whiteside counseled similarly: famine wanderers should be "saved in spite of themselves."[109] Forced marches and the steel of the bayonet at times compelled famine refugees into British detention facilities.

Relief camps, the collector of Dharwar conceded, amounted to "practically illegal confinement."[110] How, then, were they justified? Famine, for British officials, was a self-evident crisis—a moment epistemologically detached from regular scarcity.[111] This was a posture that conveniently obscured long-term structural inequalities and the violence of ordinary poverty.[112] Worried "the ordinary peace establishment of the country [would] not bear the strain of the campaign,"[113] the government authorized the temporary employment of extra soldiers and police, and Temple invested subordinates with "summary power to enforce obedience."[114] With a declaration of "emergency," the man on the spot, from deputy collectors to subordinate judges and camp superintendents, received "first class magisterial powers"[115] to "seize and confine" the famished without recourse to courts of law.[116]

Governor Temple's approach stemmed from the emergency mindsets that governed famine. Although he articulated a customary respect for the rule of law, he admitted many famine operations were "of doubtful legality." While "anxious to live under a reign of law," officials "should be obliged," under exceptional conditions, "to do that which we know to be beyond the law."[117] Whether invested with special powers or not, many officials conceded it was "impossible to legally carry out the orders of Government." And yet, the "absence of legal authority" did not significantly hamper them from "doing what they felt to be the wisest and most humane thing."[118] "If the evil [of wandering] became so great," Temple continued, "we should be obliged to act, whether the law supported us or whether it did not."[119] A belief that "strolling beggars" were "not likely to bring an action for false confinement" facilitated arbitrary arrest and other departures from liberal precepts.[120] So too did Temple's proclamation "Salus populi suprema lex" [Let the people's welfare be the supreme law], an aphorism coined by Cicero and cited by John Locke.[121]

The rights and volition of colonial subjects hardly mattered in the face of mass displacement and destitution. But when officials did operate within legal frameworks, their actions only demonstrated the degree to which law served rather than limited colonial power. Following the 1876–77 famine, authorities proposed new "legal powers of compulsion" that would facilitate detention and confinement "without straining the law," though nothing so comprehensive as the Criminal Tribes Act was formulated.[122] Instead, future officials applied, in often dubious ways, a series of vagrancy acts (such as section 109 of Bombay's Code of Criminal Procedure) to justify coercion: wanderers were "dealt with according to law" and "rigorously imprisoned" as "vagabonds . . . with criminal intent."[123] In the 1890s, meanwhile, the spurious application of the 1897 Epidemic Diseases Act permitted forced detention under the pretense that famine wanderers harbored disease.

In sum, famine laid bare the coercive apparatus of the colonial state, with its selective application of emergency decrees and existing statutes. Far from a suspension of "normal" administration, however, recourse to executive power and brazen disregard for the rights of the governed only amplified the authoritarian tendencies of colonial rule. Carl Schmitt and Giorgio Agamben's "state of exception" paradigm applies problematically to colonial India because imperial rule already rested on powers exceptional to the liberal democracy and constitutions of Europe.[124] Famine camps were products of a crisis mentality, exceptional only to the extent that repressive measures during famine were more prevalent than usual.

"A VAST RING FENCE"

Famine administration proved especially challenging in remote and "lawless" landscapes. In a letter to Florence Nightingale, Temple attributed the Raj's unprecedented reliance on camps in 1876–77 to the uncultivated wilderness of southwestern India. Temple contrasted his experience as governor of Bengal during a lesser famine in 1873–74, where he claimed wandering and subsequent encampment were "for the most part prevented," with his provision of numerous camps in Bombay and Madras three years later. Temple's disparate response to the two events is normally attributed to a return to laissez-faire fundamentals after biting criticism about "extravagant spending" in 1873–74: encampment would save expense by curbing the generous "outdoor relief" provided in Bengal.[125] Yet camps were never simply instruments of fiscal restraint or humanitarian relief. They were technologies of spatial surveillance and social control.

Camps, according to Temple, were conducive to particular colonial topographies, and the differing environments of Bengal and the remoter tracts of Bombay and Madras were partially to blame for their proliferation in 1876–77. In settled and manageable Bengal—the oldest and most familiar region of British India—"the villages [were so] close together," Temple recounted, that "on looking around one sees the whole horizon dotted with clumps of trees, and each one . . . indicates a village." Bengal's densely settled inhabitants existed, for Temple, as fixed and "legible" entities that could be easily observed and relieved in their villages: they were already "enclosed as it were in a vast ring-fence," and during periods of famine it was "practically impossible for any man, woman, or child to wander about in a famished state." The peasants of Bengal were also of a "remarkably tractable and stay-at-home disposition," Temple maintained. Through frequent inspections and a considerable official presence, the government "place[d] the whole tract from beginning to end" under a figurative "state of siege." Because they were "situated in a comparatively concentrated area admitting of supervision," there was accordingly little need to collect or detain the famished of Bengal.[126]

Two years later, however, the organization and occupation of space in Bombay and Madras provided greater scope for wandering, making confinement more pressing. Here, the population was "interspersed among hills, valleys, and areas partly uncultivated and uninhabited." Supervision was "consequently much more difficult" and it "became very hard to prevent the people from wandering hither and thither." The principles of political economy remained unchanged between 1873–74 and 1876–77, Temple continued: "whatever variations existed in practice arose from [a] diversity of circumstances in provinces widely apart," he insisted.[127] In Bombay's remote Deccan, where hills and jungles abounded, it was "impossible to keep inhabitants at home" or in fixed settlements, and there was never "the same proportion of European supervision as in some other parts of the empire."[128]

Wherever British agents were stretched thin, or where jungles concealed transients from official observation, it proved difficult to keep inhabitants under surveillance or organize relief in homes and villages. Camps, then, proved especially appropriate for sparse populations accustomed to uninhibited movement—for those who practiced "the art of not being governed," in the words of the political scientist James Scott.[129]

Spatial control was thus an important component of famine operations, as it had been for "criminal tribes" and other "nomads" corralled into settlements and reserves. In some ways, famine operations resembled the "mapping out" of "vast tracts of working-class housing" by Victorian social investigators in the "wilds" of London's East End,[130] though in India, operations were more tentative and relied on coercion more than consent. Military counterinsurgency and colonial policing operations also offered prototypes. Inspired by "police beats," famine officials, like their counterparts combatting "criminal tribes," divided famine districts into circular surveillance units and located camps at "suitable central positions . . . where wanderers could be controlled."[131] More metaphorically, Temple described the dislocations of famine with medical imagery. Like a "plague," he warned, famine wanderers would "spread indefinitely" if the government did not "avail itself of many means of repression."[132]

The best prevention of wandering, Temple continued, was the "plotting out [of] distressed territories into groups or sub-circles of villages," which could be searched by a "trustworthy supervisor."[133] In this way, famine officials imposed a geometric matrix to convert amorphous landscapes into intelligible units, and illegible, nomadic terrain into an orderly network navigable by the modern state.[134] At "a central place in each circle," inspectors erected a "closed camp."[135] Marked by red or blue dots on official maps,[136] these centers functioned, like police headquarters, as central operations bases. Meanwhile, patrolling "circle officers," often drawn from the military, colonial police, or survey department—whose geometric precision and "intimate knowledge of the people and of the country" were deemed especially useful[137]—conducted weekly inspection tours. A "dragnet" of surveillance could thus identify and arrest emaciated wanderers and concentrate them within the enclosed ring-fence of a government detention camp. Though jungles and mountain landscapes, often occupied by aboriginal tribes, presented further challenges, Temple successfully concentrated tens of thousands of wanderers and "got a quantity of good honest work" from them—an undertaking praised by Vaughan Nash as "a splendid achievement."[138] Camps thereby rendered large and largely unknown populations visible to British officialdom. The micro space of the camp provided the means for macro-spatial control, detaining treacherous itinerants and bringing expansive landscapes under observation. Famine operations therefore satisfied more general ambitions to "know" the Indian landscape and the people who inhabited it.

"THE BACKBONE OF RELIEF"

Camps detaining famished wanderers embodied the tensions of British imperialism: security, sociospatial control, and paternalistic sympathy. Reserved for "moribund immigrants . . . [and] inveterate cripples,"[139] however, these enclosures were neither the largest nor most enduring system of British famine camps. With the failure of the spring harvest, millions of more sedentary *ryots* balanced a precarious line between subsistence and starvation. In an act of desperation that only amplified their vulnerability, peasants sold tools and family heirlooms in exchange for food; others benefitted from local charity or loans to weavers and artisans; still more clung to their homes, dying out of sight. But as hunger extended beyond the vagrant and criminal classes to India's vast agricultural population, Temple and his successors turned to large public works projects on canals, roads, and railways to exact work in exchange for subsistence wages. Departing from tried-and-tested tactics like cash advances, revenue remittance, or the government distribution of grain, the "concentration of labor on large [relief] works" and the confinement of workers in attached dormitory camps emerged as the undisputed "backbone of relief" in the 1870s and 1890s.[140] From camps detaining wanderers in the hundreds of thousands, public relief works encamped Indians by the *millions*.[141]

Relief work camps were tentative and distinctly colonial derivatives of Victorian workhouses. Observers like the journalist and humanitarian critic William Digby immediately recognized the continuities, noting that Indians of the "better sort" felt the same "repugnance for relief camps which the respectable poor in England have to the Union Workhouse." The "degradation of living at a relief [camp],"[142] Digby continued, "offered some test in preventing the better classes from partaking of the charity of Government."[143] Manifesting a habitual aversion to "outdoor" relief propagated by Britain and Ireland's New Poor Law, dormitory work camps operated according to "the theory . . . that the genuinely destitute" would accept onerous conditions of confinement while "others would go back to their villages and live on their own resources."[144] Although life had to be saved "at any cost," the government maintained simultaneously that relief "should impose as little cost as possible."[145] Dormitory camps presented a means to rationalize relief, applying a formula designed to maximize efficiency while minimizing expense. They filled the space, in other words, between the competing demands of economy and humanity: they fed and sheltered the destitute as cheaply as possible while avoiding the ideologically suspect distribution of gratuitous charity via government-purchased grain. Further, the Bombay famine official Benjamin Robertson added, the severity of camp life disabused Indians of the notion that "relief was a matter of right."[146]

Security and suspicion motivated relief work camps as well as detention centers for wanderers. But if the latter functioned as "nets" trapping dehumanized mendicants within barbed-wire snares, new and larger work camps functioned as "filters," sorting inmates according to social need while "weeding out" potential malingerers.[147] In contrast to detention centers, which forced wanderers into camp, enclosures attached to relief works existed to deter all but the most desperate from seeking government assistance. They facilitated what Madras officials called a "double process of 'weeding' and concentration." But despite their differences, detention centers and dormitory work camps operated in tandem: the eventual induction of emaciated wanderers into the steady labor and discipline of relief works remained an abiding goal. After medical inspection, authorities selected the physically fit—and socially obedient—to move "up" Britain's network of relief institutions and labor on public works. Healthier and more trustworthy wanderers received "food enough for the journey" and traveled under supervision to a nearby worksite—a move that reflected a welcome improvement in physical condition but portended heavier labor, along with residence in a larger and more rudimentary, albeit less tightly regulated, camp.[148]

"AUTOMATIC TESTS"

Anyone applying to government relief works in 1876–77 or 1896–1902 was admitted, but only on the onerous conditions of mandatory confinement and exacting physical labor. Temple chastised India's poor for its "infatuation" with "eating the bread of idleness."[149] Now that an appetite for leisure had apparently driven countless millions into destitution, camps were his moral and logistical solution. By applying a series of "automatic tests," dormitory camps would select the genuinely needy from the swarms of "sham applicants" feared to be seeking easy handouts.

To combat "demoralization," the "workhouse" principles of mandatory confinement demanded a "residence test." In place of brick-and-mortar workhouses, however, Temple erected thatch-and-bamboo camps. According to the Indian

Famine Commission, camps offered a "proper [e]nclosed place of residence" that enabled "systematic control."[150] By depriving liberty—conceived in Victorian India as a privilege of affluence rather than a basic human right—camps made relief as unattractive as possible. They constituted "an uncomfortable prison or workhouse" for inmates, but they were "the form [of relief] most convenient for the Government to give."[151]

Like Union workhouses, famine camps were uncomfortable by conscious design. They existed to administer what the historian Michael Ignatieff terms a "just measure of pain."[152] "Life in camp," one commissioner confirmed, "involve[d] certain restraints and sacrifices which men not absolutely in distress are not likely to face."[153] In a colonial context, however, the threshold of suffering was higher and cost-cutting measures more severe. Victorian views about poverty and public welfare were accentuated in India, David Hall-Matthews notes, by a "denial of [government] responsibility for the normal condition of the peasantry and what amounted to racist perceptions of India as 'the land of famine.'"[154] In particular, an abiding reluctance to remit revenue collection or to interfere with the market price of grain (two potential alternatives to camps) coincided with the conceptualization of India as a vast plantation colony. Colonial odes to humanity routinely competed with lyric exaltations of economy. The £7 million spent in 1876–77 and similar sums in the 1890s therefore paled against England's annual poor relief budget of £21 million in the same period, for a population of only twenty million.[155]

In some districts, camps also enforced a "distance test," which denied famine sufferers relief close to their own homes. Instead, they had to travel ten or fifteen miles to camp. Many, Temple noted, exhibited "a dread of marching on command at any distance,"[156] especially peasants whose winter crop demanded substantial preparation in anticipation of future rains. In such cases, the ideology from which camps stemmed undermined the agricultural output India so desperately needed. In the Bijapur district it proved almost impossible to draft laborers to distant Belgaum tank works, and authorities finally relented by opening relief camps closer to home as "many appeared to be falling into a bad condition."[157] Where it was enforced, however, the distance test attached an extra deterrent to public relief and was thus deemed "effective in getting rid of people not in real need."[158] In this way, camps reoriented the locus of relief away from the home and toward a regulated site under government observation.

Distance tests inscribed workers into a larger imperial space connected by roads, railways, and the material infrastructure of capitalist modernity. While detention camps arrested wanderers, the distance test forced sedentary peasants into new and unfamiliar spatial relations. As deputy secretary of the Public Works Department, Thomas Higham noted the "extension of the railway system" offered "great facilities for deporting labourers to large works at great distances from their homes."[159] Relief camps along Buckingham Canal, for instance, removed workers hundreds of miles from their homes,[160] placing them in surroundings "as unknown to many of them as Caithness Moor to a Cornish Miner."[161] The distance test thus facilitated new patterns of movement and interpersonal relations, providing the underpinnings of anonymous capitalist exchange. Removing famine victims to distant works connected with larger efforts to create and control a mobile South Asian wage-labor force, albeit on a temporary basis and under significant duress. At the same time, however, the existence of "fantastic rumors" (in 1900, for example) that British officials would "ship [relief workers] to the Transvaal where they would be put in front of the British firing line"[162] indicates the degree to which Indian peasants continued to harbor strong connections to place. Moreover, it suggests the extent to which the famished experienced camps as acts of terror comparable to Britain's infamous military aggression in South Africa.

"THE LABOR OF LARGE BODIES OF MEN"

Above all, relief works enforced rigid "labor tests" that imposed onerous burdens on anyone seeking government assistance. Camps, Digby observed, were spaces in which "the labor of large bodies of men" could be "advantageously concentrated"[163]—though women and children often comprised the majority of workers.[164] Once registered and organized into gangs, inmates marched to nearby worksites supervised by the Public Works Department. Common tasks included stone or metal breaking and earthwork on roads, railways, and canals. At Mehmadabad, for example, work consisted of drawing hand-carts filled with stones one-and-a-half miles, four times a day, a task described by inspector Benjamin Robertson as "very heavy," especially over the "sandy Kaira lanes."[165] At another camp in Khadkalla, "the attractions of stone-breaking [were] not obvious," Vaughan Nash noted in understatement. The "people [were] unused to the work," and "the stones [were] hard and difficult to crack." Nash "took the hammer from a little girl who was vainly trying to break a small lump of stone, but after thirty blows, directed, as [he] thought, with judgment, [he] gave it up and handed it to the ganger," who took "another dozen strokes to split the stone into two or three bits, and these bits had

FIGURE 8.

Women and children at an earthwork (1899–1900). Each worker was divided "into units according to how much work they could perform," with a working child comprising "1 unit, an adult man 4 units, [and] a woman 2 units." A "unit of child" was distinguished from an infant once "it [*sic*] ha[d] teeth in both jaws." It was difficult to establish the age of minors, but children over seven were expected to work.[4] [Credit: © British Library, IOR/Photo 430/25(25) Curzon Collection: Views of Bikaner, "Railway diversion through Palana Collieries. Earthwork."]

[4] T. Higham, *Report on the Management of Famine Relief Works and Notes on Famine Relief Works in Madras, Bombay, Bengal, North-Western Provinces and Oudh, Punjab, and the Central Provinces.* (Simla: Government Central Printing Office, 1897), 11, 5. Public Works officials found young children could not perform set tasks and interfered with supervision. The collector of Ahmednagar admonished the engineer in charge of the Kowadi relief work for "personally order[ing the] remov[al of] older children from the work and class[ing] them as under 7 owing to the small amount of work" they could perform. The collector continued: "this may be sensible from the point of view of obtaining a fair amount of work for the money spent but it is entirely opposed to the code and Government are now finding ... fault with the high percentage of non-working children." MSA Revenue Department (Famine), 1897, Vol. 10, Classification of certain children from 7 up to 12 years of age as non-working children.

again to be severally assailed before they would pass through the two-inch ring" and be accepted by a supervisor.[166] And yet, metal breaking was a preferred form of labor, perhaps, officials speculated, because it was an individual rather than communal pursuit.[167]

Relief works offered some return on British financial outlays, but they were rarely profitable. Famished bodies made inefficient workers; a shortage of tools hampered progress; and in many cases, it was difficult to find projects of real utility.

Famine labor was thus only a fraction as productive as regular skilled labor. Nonetheless, the building of roads, railways, and canals—symbols of the "expert knowledge and science of the West"[168]—offered some validation to British policy. More important than functional utility, however, was labor's moral impact. Though temporary and expedient circumstances limited comprehensive "social engineering," labor was nonetheless valorized as a vehicle of inner transformation and civilizational uplift, much like at criminal tribe settlements.[169] Even humanitarians like Digby and Florence Nightingale—who advocated a "civilizing" as opposed to "imperial" strategy[170]—approved of the "labor test" in theory, though they criticized its inhuman execution. Indiscriminate almsgiving "represse[d] individuality, cramp[ed] personal effort and [was] suited only for a backward state of civilization," they maintained.[171]

Relief work, then, was not only productive but didactic: it was enforced even when there was "no means of employing people in a really useful manner." Forced labor existed "not for its own sake," the Indian Famine Commission concluded, "but for the sake of the people employed."[172] As such, activities like metal breaking were sometimes imposed for purely ideological reasons as inmates moved stones from one pile to the next, and back again.[173]

ONE POUND A DAY

What was life like for relief workers themselves? Destitution and illiteracy have largely obscured their voices, while official records are full of abstract entities and faceless automata rather than actual human beings. But whatever its moral lessons, labor must have tolled heavily. After a day of inspection, but before an evening at the Madras philharmonic orchestra, Richard Temple reported "feeling rather knocked up by the sun."[174] For famished workers, the heat must have been unbearable. Already weakened by hunger, many further deteriorated in bodily condition. Sojourn at a work camp only "prolong[ed] a man's death . . . instead of cutting his misery short," one critic maintained.[175] Often workers fell sick, only to be replaced by others. Dr. Cornish, the Madras Sanitary Commissioner, witnessed "work attempted when the ground was as hard as iron, and with tools much too heavy for the strength of those who had to wield them." The "bodily wear and tear of moving half a cubic yard of material . . . [was] considerable" he concluded.[176] Yet an uncompromising logic demanded relief work "*at all times*" be that "which no person would willingly perform . . . unless impelled thereto by want."[177]

Marked by the blowing of a horn, work began at sunrise, and it was not until sunset that workers returned to camp for "feedings." According to Sanitary Commissioner S. J. Thomson, however, the "enormous population" at many camps made it "an obvious impossibility to see to the actual distribution of [cooked] food [to] each family."[178] With the exception of milk and soup kitchens for children, camps distributed monetary wages pegged to the market price of grain, or in some cases "zinc tickets," which "could only be cashed in the camp."[179] Logistical concerns aside, cash payments preserved a "free market" designed to "foster . . . a spirit of independence and self-reliance amongst the people," who purchased their food from merchants operating in camp.[180] In reality, however, bare subsistence wages rarely translated into sufficient nutritional intake. And a lack of kitchens meant grain sometimes had to be eaten raw.

Though camps did not ration inmates directly, they were laboratories for pinpointing an "optimal" famine diet—one that approached the minimal threshold "necessary for the preservation of human life," but which was "so low," a government communication instructed, "that people [could] not live on it without some suffering."[181] As noted previously, famished India never suffered from an absolute food shortage; hunger outside the camps was a function of market failure, while minimal diets inside were outcomes of ideological dogma rather than deficits in supply.

Computing the caloric value of human life satisfied larger ambitions to quantify the social world. Diets at Bombay prisons and shipboard rations for emigrant coolies offered explicit models,[182] though recommended diets for working men in British factories were deemed inapplicable to the divergent physiques of India.[183] The nascent tenets of nutritional science offered loose guidelines, but their application was selective and contested. Dr. Cornish recommended eighteen to twenty-four ounces of grain daily, along with vegetables and condiments. Guided by economic calculus rather than medical expertise, however, Temple reduced diets in Bombay camps to a single pound (sixteen ounces) of grain, in the process impelling one hundred thousand workers to leave the relief camps (a move, Temple noted with satisfaction, that saved significant expense). Yet nutritional experts agreed: the notorious "Temple wage" would "not even replace the nitrogenous waste of a resting Indian,"[184] and mounting evidence of physiological decline resulted in a return to eighteen ounces for the duration of 1876–77.[185] Even spokesmen like Famine Secretary Sir Thomas Holderness conceded "lower grades of the wage scale were insufficient to keep workers in good health."[186]

More than a form of relief, food was a disciplinary device. Deterrence aside, reduced rations punished "willful idleness" and other violations against camp regulations. In doing so, they compromised humanitarian mandates. In a cruel bureaucratic logic, those in most desperate need suffered most from so-called "penal rations:" the weak and emaciated who were unable to perform prescribed tasks and were "fined" accordingly. In camps like Nardana in Khandesh, meanwhile, mandated taskwork was unrealistic: authorities limited every single worker to a "penal minimum" that sanitary officials deemed "inadequate to sustain life."[187] Despite drawbacks and controversy over "penal wages," however, Temple insisted that camps kept those in absolute need in "fair health and strength . . . prolong[ing] . . . life beyond the period of famine."[188] Willingness to accept a "starvation diet" was thus an additional test of destitution.

"LIKE A GREAT MACHINE"

Ultimately, Reverend Scott concluded, camps enabled a small number of trusted officials to care for and control "masses of struggling humanity" seemingly infinite in extent.[189] But Temple and his colleagues remained wary of the "chicanery and deceit" they associated with the colonial poor. Observers complained that children of nine or ten were pretending to be six or seven to avoid work, while wealthy minors "pos[ed] as dependents" in order to claim rations (and their mothers apparently concealed "ornaments" and "jewellery" when applying for relief).[190] Inmates were "not likely to tell tales" when they were "all adopting the same stratagem," the collector of Khandesh feared, and he noted it was "difficult, if not impossible, to detect the sham dependants."[191]

Authorities even charged that Indian women were starving their own children in order to gain sympathy. There is "reason to believe," F. K. H. Sharp, the acting collector of South Arcot maintained, "that mothers recognise in a half-starved infant a potent pass for relief and are glad to [turn] their babies [into] skeletons to secure their own interests."[192] Portraying Indian women as bad mothers cast the colonial state as benevolent and paternalistic by contrast.[193] S. J. Thomson claimed to witness "the deadening of even maternal instincts by the craving for food,"[194] and the normally sympathetic Digby observed "that though the mother had an animal affection for her child . . . she loved tobacco and betel nut [a mild narcotic] more."[195] Such charges strain credulity and are contradicted by other witnesses testifying to the great privations suffered by parents for their children. But the ubiquity of such statements reflects the degree of mistrust between Britain and her Indian subjects. Nash sardonically paraphrased the government's attitude: "Yes, your need is great . . . but there are really so many of you, that we shall be bound to deal with you on the assumption that you are tricking us."[196] Famine victims, in sum, were guilty until proven innocent. Effective relief demanded effective "sorting mechanisms."

Normally, Temple maintained, "the personal knowledge of some proper authority"[197] might have distinguished real famine sufferers from simulated victims.[198] But "inquiry into the circumstances of each individual of the vast hordes of people" was quite "out of the question."[199] Digby noted similarly: though "house-to-house visitation" and "the preparation of correct lists may be feasible in a small country" like England, personal inquiry proved beyond the "limits [of] human power" in the "gigantic operation" of famine relief, where "recipients [were] counted by thousands, over thousands of square miles."[200] In the emergency context of rural India, where knowledge of colonial subjects was tenuous at best, the filtering of those in real need depended on other mechanisms.

For his part, Temple believed successful relief demanded "the highest national qualities of the English people."[201] But critics like Nash doubted whether "a little band of Englishmen" could ever grapple with so intense and widespread a crisis.[202] And while British rule inevitably relied on local collaborators, European officials associated "native management" with "fraud, favouritism and oppression."[203] Complaints about the venality and corruption of "ill-paid and untrained, undisciplined, unprincipled Native subordinates" became common currency, with Temple even alleging that native functionaries "positively thrive[d] on the continuance of distress," deriving "therefrom a motive to bring about mortality in order that relief operations [and hence their own positions] may be kept up and extended." Whatever the validity of such statements, Temple widely mistrusted native agents as repositories of local knowledge, fearing they would "embezzle . . . public funds" or "stint the poor people of their . . . doles" in order to divert resources to those with money and personal influence.[204]

In the face of dire personnel shortages, British camps existed to distribute relief in a "regular and impersonal" manner.[205] Relief camps, according to Benjamin Robertson, were "orderly and methodical arrangements" that accommodated "an undisciplined crowd."[206] They offered what Nash called "cheap and automatic substitution[s] for a well-considered organisation."[207] Conceding it was "hopeless . . . to cover the length and breadth of the land . . . with an intelligent and more especially with a trustworthy agency," officials relied instead on "self-acting" tests that did not "depend on the judgment and honesty of employees" to distinguish the needy from those "not

FIGURE 9.

Camps rendered the famished visible to colonial bureaucracy: counted, measured, and observed, relief applicants became "docile bodies" amenable to social control. Such at least was the ideal. Composed for metropolitan audiences, *The Graphic*'s idealized image of a Madras famine camp depicts British officials in calm and authoritative postures, while humble famine sufferers are prostrate and receptive to British benevolence— grateful applicants rather than arrested suspects. [Credit: "The Famine in India— Distribution of Relief to the Sufferers at Bellary, Madras Presidency," *The Graphic*, October 20, 1877, 368–69.]

really in want."[208] Camps operated "automatically," Viceroy Lytton argued, and thus avoided the pitfalls of fallible natives and scarce Europeans.[209]

Ultimately, camps represented economical exercises in colonial "crowd control." "Like a great machine" they applied "automatic methods" to classify inmates in legible environments.[210] Their provenance in the industrial age was thus no coincidence: camps subsumed human agency and human value into a mechanical system. Further, they embodied the rise of an impersonal bureaucratic state organized along the "rational" principles demanded by utilitarian rhetorics of "reform" and "modernization." At the very moment that Max Weber developed his theory of bureaucratic rationality, British camps purportedly eliminated "all those emotional and irrational manifestations" that had governed premodern and precolonial charity.[211]

They replaced sympathy with system, and personalities with procedures. Anonymous and instrumental, they were also ethically blind.

"BARBED-WIRE DETERRENTS"

Despite their professed utility, camps were contested institutions, both within official circles and the larger Indian public. Proponents heralded camps as economic and logistical successes. But dissenters criticized them as expensive, repressive, and ultimately ineffective. Following the 1876–77 famine, agricultural economists James Caird and H. E. Sullivan, both members of the Indian Famine Commission, wrote a minority dissent advocating gratuitous charity and small relief works run by local village headmen rather than large, centralized dormitory camps.[212] Others, especially officials in Bengal who remembered the more successful, albeit costly, operations of 1873–74, condemned the "monstrous doctrine" that "relief should be accompanied by terms . . . so humiliating" to respectable families.[213] Further, they complained of the costs of "locating many thousands of distressed persons in pauper villages."[214] Meanwhile, prominent Indians like Syed Ahmed Khan noted that camps violated caste boundaries. Britain remained wary of disrupting the traditional hierarchies and confessional divisions that facilitated colonial rule,[215] but the new social and spatial proximities of concentrated camps proved offensive to higher-caste natives, who often preferred the physical death of starvation to the social and spiritual "death" of encampment. The thrust of the Commission's 1880 report, however, was to vindicate government policies and enshrine famine camps as pivotal mechanisms of security and relief.[216]

Critics renewed their attack in the 1890s, with Vaughan Nash at the *Manchester Guardian* disparaging camps as "deterrents of the barbed-wire order."[217] The voices of inmates themselves are harder to recover. Subaltern protests manifested in sweat and tears, but rarely in writing. Low wages and rations led to numerous strikes, however. The largest involved over a hundred thousand inmates organized by the Poona Sarvajanik Sabha, a moderate nationalist organization.[218] But hunger and exhaustion often muted resistance. A demonstration at a camp in Bijapur in 1897 against heavy labor and meager rations was soon broken. The petitioners refused work for several days, but in response, Commissioner Spence quoted "the ancient proverb makers" that "half a loaf is better than no bread."[219] The government refused to ameliorate conditions, and inmates had no choice but to submit.

Literate Indians were more vocal and perhaps more successful than their powerless inmate brethren. At stake was a discursive contest between British and Indian elites over the proper care and control of the native poor. As anticolonial sentiment coalesced in the 1890s, Romesh Dutt and Dadabhai Naoroji, leader of the Indian National Congress (INC), harnessed the repressive symbolism of famine camps to criticize Viceroy Curzon and the priorities of British rule. "Tens of thousands were still in relief camps when the Delhi Durbar was held in January 1903," they charged.[220] More drastically, Britain's merciless approach to famine provided impetus for Bal Gangadhar Tilak, leader of the INC's radical wing, to pursue "Irish methods" of direct action—riots, looting, assassinations—against British tax collection.[221]

Back in Britain, critical assessments also intersected with debates over poor relief in Britain and doubts about workhouses as an institution. Figures like the future colonial secretary Joseph Chamberlain had already softened workhouse regimes in Britain by reintroducing outdoor relief and improving accommodation at existing facilities. Channeling these developments, critics condemned the "obsolete formulas of the English Poor Law" that continued to operate in India. For the left-leaning Nash, famine camps were "fetish[es] of pauperism" and he argued that Victorian doctrines of poor relief bore "no earthly relation to the facts of Indian life."[222] By distinguishing pauperism in England from the pervasive poverty of India, Nash and likeminded commentators articulated a new fin-de-siècle understanding of poverty as a systemic product of employment cycles and the boom-and-bust rhythms of capitalism.

The detention of wanderers remained a central component of famine management, but British spokesmen eventually conceded that compulsory residence at relief works was counterproductive. Led by the Irish civil servant Antony MacDonnell, the 1901 Famine Commission at last concluded that "neither a distance test nor compulsory residence should be imposed." The forced encampment of relief workers was "difficult to justify," and it was "unreasonable to expect people to travel great distances in order to obtain relief." With an eye on disease and the destruction of fragile village economies, meanwhile, the Commission further highlighted the "risks involved in moving large bodies of men great distances away from their homes."[223] By suspending the distance and residence tests, and by introducing more liberal wages and gratuitous relief, the new policy substantially curtailed encampment in future famines.

Yet camps continued as optional rather than compulsory sites of relief, leaving lasting legacies into the twentieth century. Benjamin Robertson, a Bombay famine official who went on to supervise international relief efforts after World War I, argued that "well-constructed and laid out" camps were effective technologies of humanitarian management.[224] Wherever "the spirit of humanity and pity" presided, relief camps were effective tools, Sir Claude Hill, secretary to the Bombay governor, concurred.[225] British famine policy even provided a template for relief (or the lack thereof) in the postcolonial period, including the use of camps during the "Great Bengal Famine" of 1973 and the 1983–85 famine in Ethiopia.[226] For their part, British authorities gained unprecedented experience controlling colonial masses and managing concentrated spaces. And while major droughts and famines were mercifully absent from South Asia until 1943, camps were cemented as a new colonial technology applicable to other instances of social danger and distress. Bramble fences and bamboo huts were by no means obsolete.

CHAPTER 3

· "A Source of Horror and Dread"

Plague Camps in India and South Africa,
1896–1901

The tenure of Lord Curzon—India's last and perhaps most controversial viceroy—was marked not only by famine but by the catastrophe of plague. From an endemic center in upland southeast China, plague traveled to Canton on the bodies and belongings of political refugees before following the canals of the Pearl River delta, where it invaded Hong Kong in 1894. Despite quarantine aboard the vessel *Hygeia*—a "floating camp" of sorts—contagion could not be contained.[1] Carried by the steam ships of modern empire, the outbreak reached the Indian port of Bombay in August 1896.

Pestilence had a classical pedigree. For Dr. William J. Simpson, a Calcutta medical officer and global plague authority, the epidemic recalled mythic scenes from "grand Cairo" and ancient Constantinople. A disease of Eastern provenance, mysterious and malevolent, it triggered a heightened sense of alarm. But despite its classical lineage, the "third global pandemic" was a modern event: the outcome of advanced trade networks and capital flows, transportation technology, and the web of social, political, and military relations that connected a globalizing world. As the "secondary hub" of Britain's interconnected empire, Bombay was a key center of water and rail transportation that attracted two hundred thousand merchants and travelers every month. While fueling the global circulation of labor and goods, imperialism also facilitated the transmission of microorganisms, escalating the speed and scope of epidemics and the concomitant urgency of disease control. Ironically, it was the railroad—that vaunted symbol of free trade and British beneficence—that

FIGURE 10.

Urban cleansing, Bombay. Suspect cases were transported via military escort to fenced segregation camps. [Credit: "The Plague in Bombay: The President of the Local Committee and an Indian Doctor on Their Daily Round in the Native Quarter," *Illustrated London News*, February 5, 1898. Drawing by Melton Prior.]

facilitated plague's rapid transmission across India. The disease spread to Calcutta, Delhi, and the Punjab in 1897.

And while plague was a disease of trade, it was also a disease of war. The movement of troops and equipment from India to southern Africa (via Patagonia and other imperial way-stations) during the Anglo-Boer War (1899–1902) served as an additional vector of contagion. Cape Town was infected in 1900, and the disease reached Transvaal in 1904, further complicating hunger and displacement in a war-torn society. Microbes likely attached themselves to Indian "coolies" travelling to Johannesburg for postwar rebuilding, while imperial troops returning home at war's end spread plague to Australia and other outposts.[2]

As plague spread horror and dread across the globe, Britain's militarized turn-of-the-century campaign to arrest and detain suspected plague carriers offered a new context for the proliferation of barbed wire. "Plague camps" operated under the dual auspices of segregating the "dangerous classes"—deemed most likely to carry disease—and accommodating homeless "refugees" evicted from unsanitary areas. As preemptive measures, "detention camps" (variously known as "segregation," "contact," and "observation" camps) detained supposedly contagious "suspects" arrested at rail stations, ports, or caught in urban cleansing operations. Surrounded by barbed-wire or bramble fences, they represented the most tightly regulated containment site Britain had yet devised. Larger "evacuation camps," meanwhile, accommodated less dangerous categories evicted from inner-city slums and relocated to supposedly hygienic living environments. Camps thus detained not only those infected with plague but broad categories of humanity considered dangerous for a variety of social and cultural reasons. They were artifacts of colonial anxiety and social-military control as much as rational responses to disease.

All told, plague camps were significant points of contact between the British state and sizable colonial populations. Between October 1898, when it started keeping records, and May 1901, when the Bombay epidemic subsided (though it continued in other parts of India), the Municipal Commissioner of Bombay recorded 131,264 inmates passing through the city's segregation camps, while permanent evacuation camps to the city's north accommodated a peak of 47,939. India-wide, over a million found themselves in camps, while tens of thousands of black and colored Africans were detained in South Africa. Many—the poor, the listless, the mobile—were even encamped twice, first for famine, then for plague.[3]

"A FOREIGN AND ABSOLUTE EXPEDIENT"

Plague, Dr. Simpson recognized, was a seemingly timeless affliction. But it elicited different responses in varying historical contexts. Medical internment, in other words, was not a natural or necessary response to plague, but the product of particular historical and cultural configurations. In his global history of the disease, Simpson located forced encampment within venerable Western traditions of quarantine. Representing a departure from fatalistic medieval worldviews, pesthouses in Quattrocento city-states detained foreign travelers and social outsiders: Renaissance lazarettos, Simpson suggested, were the first plague camps.[4] In this way, British spokesmen wed coercive medical interventions to the reputed birth of Western "rationality." Coercive detention was an apparently tried and tested—and subsequently legitimate—response to plague.

Yet Simpson ignored more recent and relevant traditions that were fiercely inimical to camps. The 1890s pandemic never reached British shores, but earlier outbreaks highlight a liberal wariness of authoritarian measures within Britain. In 1720, for example, when plague threatened Europe for the last time, authorities in London made plans to "move the infected by force to pest houses." One proposal even called for troops to surround London and "shoot anyone who escaped." Bishop Edmund Gibson emerged as a forceful advocate for coercion: there was no sense in dwelling "upon rights and liberties and the ease and convenience" of mankind, he argued, when "plague [was] hanging over our heads." The citizens of London responded, however, with a language of constitutional rights that cast medical detention as "totally unsuited to the 'free constitution' of Britain." Conceding the unsuitability of "foreign expedient[s]" more appropriate to "absolute government in France," authorities subsequently relented. London was not to become a colossal detention camp.[5]

Britons continued to denounce quarantine in the eighteenth and nineteenth centuries as an "instrument of continental despotism inimical to free commerce," and unlike European rivals, English ports rarely detained merchant marines.[6] British seafarers derided the "Turkish cruelty" of an Ottoman quarantine station in the Red Sea where ship passengers "were turned onto a desert island" and humiliated by "violent and abusive camp guards."[7] In India, too, a prevailing emphasis on cultural "difference," and a comparative disinterest in the health of racial "others" had habitually curbed direct interventions in colonial health. Though army barracks and prisons were "enclaves" of sanitary surveillance, colonial medicine was limited to institutional venues and rarely "touched" the Indian body, David Arnold notes.[8]

Britain's forceful response to plague in the 1890s thus represented a substantial break from earlier norms. With a liberal dose of "Russian Tyranny," the British Empire detained and encamped plague suspects by the millions. In the words of the Poona plague commissioner Charles Rand, British measures to combat plague were "the most drastic that had ever been taken to stamp out an epidemic."[10] After decades of cautious nonintervention and financial noncommitment the plague panic catalyzed a new coercive ethic in which the rights of colonial people—from India to Africa—were readily violated.

In both India and South Africa, a number of cultural, economic, and geopolitical concerns converged to launch a campaign of unbridled coercion—a "war of extermination"—against disease. "Suspects" were detained and neighborhoods were "cleared" with methods that were previously inconceivable, both financially and politically. The epidemic, to be sure, was deadly. In the city of Bombay, 86,000 people—some 8 percent of the population—perished in the first two years, while another 250,000 died in the presidency as a whole. This was a staggering figure, though one surpassed by 370,000 cholera deaths in the same period, not to mention malarial fevers that killed even more but rarely evinced comment.[9] In contrast to more quotidian ailments, however, plague carried significant cultural weight. As fear of the disease spread through literature and historical writing, nineteenth-century epidemiologists branded it "the black death," imbuing plague with medieval shock value.

Colonial settings, moreover, augmented authoritarian responses. Like their counterparts during famine, medical practitioners construed target populations as dirty, dangerous, and in need of British intervention—a suspect and untrustworthy collectivity devoid of civil rights. Even more than Bourbon France or Romanov Russia, India and South Africa were congenial settings for camps. As Partha Chatterjee writes, colonial government "was at core absolutist and authoritarian." As such, "English principles of liberty would always have to seek grounds for exception in India."[11] Yet the response to plague was not determined by cultural or political factors alone. Ultimately, the disease posed an existential threat to imperial commerce, prompting unprecedented interventions. Crippling embargoes on Indian goods levied by France, Germany, and other powers motivated authorities to take vigorous action—a "pre-emptive strike"—to reassure investors the disease was under control.[12] Imperial profit spurred new possibilities.

"THE WAR ON PLAGUE"

In the empire, medicine and military power were tightly interwoven. It was thus that health authorities declared a "War on Plague." Bombay's surgeon-general George Bainbridge labeled plague "the greatest and most important event India has had to face since the Mutiny."[13] No expenditure was considered "too great to defeat and get rid of an invading army," Simpson added, since an "attack [of plague] is likely to be more serious and destructive than that of any army if not resolutely met at the beginning."[14] Bainbridge called, accordingly, for reinforcements to be "obtained at any cost," even at the price of deflecting troops from the Afghan borderlands. "The whole of India must help us in Bombay, where the struggle on behalf of the whole of India is at present going on," he concluded.[15]

Like martial law, plague operations rested on emergency powers. Military language yielded military solutions. Plague camps thus emerged as expedients of war—they were "immediate and essential necessit[ies]," Surgeon-Major Richard Baker maintained.[16] In particular, the far-reaching powers of India's Epidemic Diseases Act (1897) warranted "the segregation, in . . . temporary accommodation or otherwise, of persons suspected . . . of being infected [with] disease."[17] One of the most "draconian pieces of sanitary legislation ever adopted in colonial India," according to David Arnold, the act sanctioned substantial military violence and the forced detention of entire populations.[18] For its proponents, though, such legislation offered an opportunity to demonstrate the ascendency of Western methods, uplifting a superstitious and unhygienic population.

Discursively, the battle against plague (like that against famine) operated according to "assaults," "invasions," and "offensives." "Combat" was "the *mot juste*" to describe efforts to curb the "onward march of pestilence," secretary to the Bombay governor Claude Hill remarked.[19] It is no coincidence that a "military model" of public health prevailed in the nineteenth century. Though military metaphors may have reached their apogee in World War I, Susan Sontag remarks,[20] they first proliferated in the age of empire, when, as Philip Curtin demonstrates, military expansion depended on medical advance.[21] As in concurrent outbreaks of war across the globe—in Sudan, the North-West Frontier, and South Africa—"invasive organisms" were to be attacked by "campaigns," "corps" and "flying columns" of medical experts and military troops.[22] Once suspected plague carriers were associated with the enemies of war, militarized camps proved fitting technologies of disease control.[23]

The plague campaign was warfare materially as well as metaphorically. Even more than in famine, British sanitary measures mobilized soldiers and military officers, who conducted the struggle like a counterinsurgency operation over a vast and perilous terrain. At the helm was James Cleghorn, the Indian government's surgeon-general and Bainbridge's superior at the Indian Medical Service (IMS)—an organization, Mark Harrison notes, that was "predominantly military in orientation."[24] At a time when maneuvers on the North-West Frontier preoccupied India's military establishment, the surgeon-general requested the Army "give . . . as many Medical Officers and subordinates as they can spare for plague duty," urging that "every available officer—civilian or commissioned, medical or combatant—be placed at the disposal of Government." "If six or more regiments . . . are [put] on plague duty," Bainbridge calculated, "and every regiment in India [were] to lend an officer, it will not be too much trouble or expense if we can . . . stop the spread of plague."[25] Officers like Colonel James S. Wilkins (IMS) and Captain A. F. W. King (IMS) were thus transferred from active service in Afghanistan to conduct plague operations in Bombay, while Lieutenant-Colonel S. J. Thomson (IMS), already familiar with famine camps as a sanitary commissioner, turned to plague control in the North-Western Provinces. In supporting roles were Staff Corps officers and Indian soldiers themselves: Wilkins, for example, travelled with an entourage of sepoys and lance corporals from the 21st Bombay Infantry.[26]

As in famine, however, plague operations suffered from a shortage of trusted personnel. In a retrospective analysis, the Bombay Plague Committee imagined an "ideal form" of surveillance that would have obviated the need for camps. Information concerning the outbreak of disease would be provided early on by European officers who "know [their] beat and . . . people so thoroughly that [they] at once hear of any case of suspicious sickness."[27] But the asymmetric ratio of Indians to Europeans did not permit such scrutiny. Great recruitment drives aside, the "supply of commissioned officers . . . and medical subordinates" was "almost exhausted [by 1899] and [would] remain so for as long as the Frontier Wars continue."[28] And while the "influence of the European Gentleman" was almost always preferred to qualified natives with local knowhow, those transferred from Britain or other colonies often lacked the language skills and cultural awareness to build relationships of trust and understanding with locals.[29]

In these circumstances, camps, in the wake of famine, offered familiar and affordable technologies that permitted inexperienced officers to control large numbers. Like their famine counterparts, plague camps were impersonal and "automatic" mechanisms that addressed a perennial problem of empire: the control of mass populations by a small corpus of Europeans. Plague camps thus represented a formidable monopoly of violence in the form of barbed wire and armed soldiers, as well as the colonial state's incapacity or unwillingness to connect with native society on an equal footing.

"FLEEING PESTIFIERS"

To British doctors, medical detention camps were objective instruments of science. Yet the science was divided. Influenced by "germ theory," colonial medical teams isolated plague bacteria under a microscope in 1897, though they were unsure whether *Yersina pestis* microbes were causal agents or symptomatic side effects. The means of transmission were also unclear. Local populations had long identified the die-off of rats as a harbinger, and scientists identified fleas as possible vectors in 1898. But the contested discipline of bacteriology did not gain traction for another decade, and in India it competed with outdated miasmic theories, which privileged environmental approaches that conveniently associated disease with the putatively dirty and uncivilized conditions of Indian life.[30]

As officers rounded up "suspects," the "unclean" environs of native quarters did potent symbolic work. In her seminal study *Purity and Danger*, the anthropologist Mary Douglas argues ideas about cleanliness and disease map onto larger systems of sociopolitical relations.[31] Symbolic ecologies of purity and pollution intersected with racial and class discourse, as colonial dirt suggested the more general and "sometimes hidden dangers, political and corporeal, moral and cultural," of colonial landscapes.[32] The otherness of "dirty natives" was counterpoised against colonial officers bedecked in white. And apart from obvious health risks, plague, like famine, portended social unrest and even political danger in post-Mutiny India. Indeed, the upheavals of plague, following on the heels of famine, crystallized fears about Britain's hold on empire and its ability to maintain order. "All the consequences of bad times" could be observed in plague-and-famine-stricken India, Claude Hill lamented, including "political unrest" and "excessive crime."[33] But fear motivated authorities more than any reasoned assessment. "Plague," Rajnarayan Chandvarkar points out, "became the focus of the most terrible anxieties which India evoked in the British imagination."[34]

Whatever the medical threat, the response to plague stemmed from the sustaining mythologies of empire. As in famine, common slippages in official discourse cast native populations simultaneously as victims and offenders. "The move from the demonization of the illness to the attribution of fault to the patient is an inevitable one," Susan Sontag notes, "no matter if patients are thought of as victims."[35] A sympathetic appreciation for the human tragedy of the pandemic was never entirely absent, but images of impoverished Indians as "dangerous persons," "suspects," "fugitives," and "fleeing pestifiers" framed Britain's approach.[36] As in war, the campaign against an invisible enemy targeted segments of the population for visible social and racial markers.

British officers believed that native populations in general and the lower orders in particular were primary repositories of contagion. In Simpson's words, plague was "essentially a disease of the poor, attaching itself to the poorest, most crowded and filthiest localities of a town."[37] If not the wholesale "segregation of the poor," the crisis generated "special measures" and a "careful watch" of specific groups.[38] As in famine and the policing of criminal tribes, anxieties about marginal and evasive populations provoked coercive measures. The internment of plague "suspects," then, reflected not only an epidemiological effort to isolate microbes, but a physical and symbolic distancing of the colonial poor from the privileged European community.

Disease, above all, was associated less with fleas and microbes than with mobile Indian bodies. "Certain classes of people, such as gipsies and vagabonds," who "as a rule are dirty in their habits," posed "a special danger in conveying disease," Simpson continued. "Waifs, strays, migratory people . . . and low-class natives, over whom very little control can be exercised,"[39] were also threats, along with "pilgrims and other travelling . . . parties" who were "frequently dirty" and had no "fixed place of residence."[40] Like petty thieves or guerrilla combatants, they could "shift at any moment" down unseen alleyways.[41] Habitually suspected of crime and social unrest, such groups could not be accorded "the same liberty" as the general population, Simpson maintained. Plague therefore mobilized preventive, protective, and extrajudicial logics. Camps, in Simpson's words, were "of an anticipatory character."[42]

"THE DOUBLE NET"

Plague resulted from microorganic processes, but Cleghorn and Bainbridge conducted their campaign at a macro spatial level. The police and army established checkpoints and sanitary cordons along certain roads, while port authorities erected quarantine camps to detain ship passengers. But railroads proved indispensable axes of operation. A considerable network of detention camps located at rail stations arrested suspects in the hundreds of thousands fleeing infected regions or traveling for other purposes.

The iron lines of the railroad developed in post-Mutiny India to expedite commercial exchange and the movement of troops. In the context of plague, however, they facilitated the spread of microbes *and* concentrated motion along certain vectors, channeling passengers to points at which movement could be monitored. While the government pressured rail companies to close down key lines at crucial moments, an economy and ideology of unhindered commercial exchange precluded an entire transportation shutdown. Instead, the surgeon-general prohibited travel between smaller stations, siphoning passengers to major junctions. At these strategic points a system of surveillance and detention emerged as a compromise to permit the circulation of unobjectionable goods and people while segregating suspects according to contagionist views of disease. Ultimately, Bombay authorities identified railroad detention as the surest way to "keep the plague from straying beyond the borders of the area it has presently affected."[43] Cleghorn thus implemented a system of incoming and outgoing "land quarantine" to protect cleared areas and place infected areas in "a state of isolation."[44]

The geography of camps corresponded to the lines of the railroad. In infected cities like Bombay, "everyone leaving . . . [would, in theory] pass through a [screening] camp . . . remaining therein 7–10 days." The Modikhana and Wari Bunder camps opposite Bombay's Victoria Terminus detained passengers for a week or more before issuing passes to leave the city, as did suburban camps at Kalyan and Bandra. Meanwhile, Cleghorn and Bainbridge directed, "every place in communication by rail, road, or water with an infected area should have a camp through which all [non-European] travelers . . . should pass." The result, in Bainbridge's words, was "a double net spread to catch the fleeing pestifer."[45] Many suspects traveling by road or footpaths could still slip through the holes, but Bainbridge's net was designed to catch a large percentage of suspects, while deterring others from traveling in the first place.

"All travelers must be considered suspicious," Bainbridge maintained,[46] but the "lower castes" had "a special claim for camp accommodation."[47] Bacilli themselves, of course, did not distinguish between skin color or social origin. Indeed, "individuals of pure European parentage living under the best sanitary conditions"[48] contracted the disease and perished alongside their native counterparts. These included the president of the Bombay Plague Committee, Surgeon-Major Manser, and the daughter of Major General C. J. Burnett, commander of the Poona military district.[49] Above all, however, authorities targeted what the Bombay Plague Committee labeled "persons of the unsafe classes."[50] "It [was] better," Bainbridge asserted, "to ask no questions [and] treat all travelers alike." But in reality, British plague policy was highly discriminating.[51]

As with criminal tribe legislation and its "graduated scheme of . . . registration, reporting and restrictions of movements,"[52] plague detention operated within a hierarchy of surveillance measures. Europeans remained categorically beyond the pale of suspicion, and first-class native passengers were rarely detained, not only because they were apparently "little likely to be infected" but because they were "as a rule . . . persons of sufficient education and intelligence" to be trusted to take "the same precautions that a camp . . . is designed to secure."[53] Travelers holding written certificates or "passports" testifying to their health were also granted reprieve: "under no circumstances," Cleghorn insisted, would "any respectable healthy person who could give a reference letter . . . be detained."[54] Such exceptions, however, were reserved for elites and those who lived in a world of literacy and paper—and they were to be made "sparingly and only in cases where the traveler is known to live in a style of superior civilization."[55] In other cases, meanwhile, natives who displayed plague symptoms but who presented a "cleanly disposition" could be released after paying bail, calculated to be "beyond the power of persons of the unsafe classes to pay."[56] They were photographed and registered with police, but monitored outside camp. Travelers "should not be segregated if they can be trusted not to abscond," Lieutenant-Colonel King confirmed.[57] But in the cultural framework of colonial India, few could be trusted.

Statistics demonstrate the extent to which detention was founded on mistrust and social discrimination rather than medical evidence. Race and class habitually proved more powerful markers of contagion than actual symptoms like elevated fever and visible buboes. At rail stations, inspectors deemed passengers suspect if they appeared dirty, regardless of any symptoms they may have displayed. They were "suspicious," the government maintained, "by reason of their appearance" or "the dirty condition of their clothes or effects."[58] At Jalarpat, for example, Dr. J. S. Low noted that only 0.57 percent of the total 11,500 detained went on to develop plague. More than 99 percent of inmates were therefore disease free. Low was clear about the criteria for detention: "all dirty persons, and those who do not appear trustworthy, are detained." Those who "are 'suspicious' by reason of fever" or other confirmed medical ailment, meanwhile, formed "only a small proportion of detentions."[59] Comportment and trustworthiness were the determining factors.

How did travelers experience detention? Upon arrival at a station, carriage doors were locked to prevent escape, and passengers were "immediately handed over to the police." Military guards regulated egress from the station, while soldiers searched carriages "for anyone in hiding."[60] Nonetheless, Low reported, many practiced "highly ingenious . . . methods of evasion," and he estimated that between 3–10 percent of travelers ultimately avoided inspection.[61] Those caught in Britain's "double net" of inspection and detention, however, entered a highly regulated platform segmented with bamboo fences and organized with military precision, though "an appearance of confusion and want of system" characterized some operations, especially when panicked urban dwellers tried to flee infected cities.[62]

As passengers alighted, medical officials "invested with the widest discretionary powers of exemption or detention" inspected them. Those deemed safe for travel were issued passes. But persons of the "dangerous classes," who could not "be traced . . . or depended on to report themselves for surveillance," were subject to detention and disinfection. Authorities provided cloths for detainees to cover themselves while their clothing was soaked in lime or placed in a steam disinfection chamber, though tellingly, silk and other fine fabrics were exempt. Once the process was complete, they were then marched to camp by a police or military escort for a full observation period.[63]

Railroad detention was genuinely temporary, rarely lasting more than ten days (thought to be plague's maximum incubation period). But camps still proved frustrating and unpleasant. The vast majority of detainees could not record their experience in writing, though Bhikajo Agashe's letter protesting his treatment at Bhusawal on Bombay Presidency's northeastern frontier is a valuable exception. Though his experience was unusual—he was a literate first-class traveler detained because he had actual medical symptoms, and possibly because he was insolent—his letters offer insight into Britain's world of camps. Agashe and his eleven-year-old daughter carried passes from the uninfected Central Provinces, but they had visited the infected city of Poona and after registering fevers of 99.4°F, they were detained for observation. The camp was over a mile and a half from the station according to Agashe, who refused to carry his luggage or "allow the sick girl to go on foot to the Hospital like all other persons detained." Inside, an uncomfortable bamboo-and-tin shelter was "awfully dirty," offered little privacy, and had no cots or "proper light." The camp master, a Mr. Aquino, "used insulting and sarcastic remarks," Agashe complained, and ordered him to clean the camp "with sacred cow dung." The fact, moreover, that "different castes [were forced to] . . . huddle up together" in the same cold and unfurnished huts only augmented Agashe's humiliation. Though detention targeted the poor, there was an inescapable democracy inherent to germ transmission, and the mixing of castes became a major point of contention among the likes of Agashe, who were atypical inmates but the only ones literate enough to submit written complaints.

In their defense, British authorities passionately defended the camp's cleanliness, noting "it [was] in excellent repair and ha[d] only recently been strengthened for the monsoon." The observation ward, they maintained, was 50 by 18 feet (not the 15 feet square Agashe claimed) and was "divided into two parts, one for men and one for women," though admittedly no separate ward accommodated high-caste Hindus. A sweeper cleaned the camp daily and "portions of the floor [were] built up as in jail hospitals to serve as cots," which Agashe apparently refused to use. Even if he exaggerated some of his claims, there remains little doubt that plague camps were sites of discomfort, pollution, and humiliation for those interned. By the time of Agashe's detention, Bhusawal camp had operated for two years and was, according to British spokesmen, "the best in the Presidency in point of situation, dryness and comfort."[64] Yet Agashe's experience complicates visions of orderly and hygienic spaces depicted in official accounts. It offers insight into how limited resources and inexperienced or apathetic officials hampered even the best camps.

URBAN CLEANSING

The capture of suspected disease carriers was not the only practice leading to plague camps. Bolstered by a still controversial germ theory, contagionist views of disease competed with more deeply entrenched beliefs that associated plague less with transmittable microbes than with unhealthy localities—usually the crowded and chaotic dwellings of the poor. To this end, slum clearance and urban cleansing produced another type of enclosure for those removed from their homes and towns: "evacuation camps." Analogous to detention centers for famine wanderers, railroad camps represented the colonial state's assault on transient bodies. Evacuation camps, meanwhile, facilitated an offensive against India's built environment.

In military terms, the plague campaign was less a series of pitched battles than a guerrilla counterinsurgency. Plague bacilli were mobile, invisible foes; with even greater stealth than the celebrated commandos of the concurrent South African War, they occupied extensive landscapes and routinely evaded efforts to locate or arrest them. The "invasion of a locality by the plague bacillus," Simpson noted, differed from that of a regular army "in that the movements of the former are less discoverable . . . and it is only recognized by its effects."[65] The "filth, darkness" and "narrow and tortuous lanes" of Indian cities, Colonel J. S. Wilkins added, provided plague bacilli with a perfect "haven of rest."[66] As in guerrilla war, Surgeon-General Cleghorn targeted not only "enemy" bacilli but the surrounding population suspected of giving them sustenance.

Plague operations employed the spatial tactics of divide and rule. Conceiving the subcontinent as a vast battlefield, authorities divided districts and cities into discrete and manageable units, a task that contributed to the larger projects of demarcating exotic and seemingly chaotic spaces and gaining knowledge over the populations inhabiting them. In Bombay Presidency, Bainbridge ordered every city and town to be mapped and divided into divisions and wards. Each ward was further "divided into a number of blocks, of about 100 houses each" and patrolled by "flying columns"—a military formation borrowed from colonial counterinsurgency doctrine—of army and medical personnel.[67] As Andrew Wingate of the Bombay Plague Department explained: "the backbone of successful plague management is division of the town into as many sub-divisions as there are European officials or native officers of sufficient rank available."[68] Infected towns were then assigned superintendents, usually commissioned medical or military officers, to coordinate surveillance. In Bombay itself, the city's seven wards were each assigned a senior official—like Wilkins in the challenging and populous ward 5—who appointed military search parties to inspect "unwholesome" houses.

Rural districts underwent similar spatial partition as officials divided land into circles much as they did during famine operations. In the North-Western Provinces Lieutenant-Colonel Thomson divided a four-hundred-square-mile tract "into five divisions, each under a European officer [and] a native medical subordinate." Divisions were further segmented into surveillance circles in which "each village . . . was visited every three days, and every inhabitant of the area was examined every eight days." A similar system prevailed along the frontier between Bombay Presidency and the native states of Hyderabad and Mysore, where "a double row of circles with a diameter of 10 miles" was patrolled "so that a strip 20 miles broad all along the border" could be placed under surveillance by a sanitary inspector,[69] "whose duty [was] to patrol his circle systematically."[70] Although surveillance was less intensive in remote regions and native states, Colonel Wilkins disseminated favored methods of inspection and segregation during a travelling tour to the north, where he visited towns like Mandvi and Salaya at the invitation of the Rao of Kutch.[71]

In Bombay, operations commenced at 7 A.M. and search parties visited each neighborhood weekly or biweekly. "Flying columns" typically consisted of commissioned medical officers like Wilkins, armed soldiers, nurses and native assistants, and locksmiths to force entry. In some ways, search parties appropriated the techniques of metropolitan social investigation; Claude Hill, secretary to Bombay's governor, even observed prominent "English women," including the governor's wife, "visiting the worst slums in the city."[72] "Health visits," however, were often conducted at the point of a bayonet; endemic violence and mistrust framed efforts to close the information gap between ruler and ruled. At times, inhabitants cooperated, but for the "ignorant and . . . fanatical," steeped in "stupid prejudices," "sheer compulsion" was often necessary, Wilkins reported.[73] Hill himself referred to the "*invasion* of . . . dwelling-houses" by British soldiers.[74]

For buildings deemed infected or insanitary—and in violation of bourgeois domestic norms—the next step was evacuation. Surgeon-General Cleghorn ordered the "removal of the inmates from houses in which cases of plague occurred," though in practice, inhabitants of any of the city's "unhygienic" dwellings were subject to relocation. Cleghorn further arranged for "suitable huts [to] be provided, free of rent, for the accommodation of evicted residents."[75] It was thus that evacuation camps were born. Sprawling enclosures to the city's north sheltered forty thousand evacuees from Bombay's most impoverished *chawls*, while less expansive "tent cities" proliferated on the outskirts of other towns, as India's cities were forcibly suburbanized. In Mandvi, for example, Wilkins erected "long row[s] of comfortable sheds," though many evacuees preferred camping in "various gardens" on the outskirts of town. "Every endeavor short of actual force was employed," he reported, to move them to "segregation huts, where a better watch could have been kept."[76]

FIGURE 11.

Different levels of security awaited those displaced. Fenced "segregation camps" or "contact camps" (above), interned those residing in the same building as a plague patient or who were otherwise "suspect"—a vague, catch-all category—due to dirty habits or surroundings. Other "refugees" were turned out in blocks to open evacuation camps (below), where they lived for months at a time. [Credit: © British Library IOR/ Photo 806/8 Hogg Collection: Album of miscellaneous views in India and England, Image 43 "Segregation Camp for relatives of plague-stricken people, Palanpur"; Wellcome Library V0029291, ICV No. 29767, "A camp of wigwams for Mekranis, during the outbreak of bubonic plague in Karachi, India, 1897."]

In evacuated inner cities, meanwhile, disinfection squads, consisting mostly of convicts or coolies, washed the walls and floors of insanitary houses with lime and conducted other measures like separating latrines from living spaces with "an air space made by cutting walls or floors."[77] Often, "sanitary improvements" involved the wholesale demolition of houses and neighborhoods. According to Simpson, "the only remedy [was] pulling down every other house."[78] The Bombay Plague Department bulldozed entire city blocks, while in the countryside Commissioner G. R. C. Williams maintained "it would decidedly be a good thing to burn down [entire] village[s] bodily."[79] At times, plague operations resembled scorched-earth warfare. Often plans for house entry were kept secret, and armed soldiers conducted searches like "surprise military raids."[80] Houses were searched down both sides of the street, "the party dividing into two for the purpose," and on entering a dwelling, "sepoys were stationed at the doors to prevent [residents from] leaving until the search was completed. Each room was looked into, and if necessary, entered, and all the occupants scrutinized."[81]

Ultimately, decision makers concurred, concentrating suspects in camps would prevent them from "scattering and spreading . . . infection in the neighborhood."[82] The stated strategy was "to pass through the camps the greatest possible number of the poorer classes who live in insanitary houses."[83] In many smaller towns, and even larger centers like Ahmednagar and Sholapur, the entire native population was evacuated and encamped. But in Bombay, a city of nearly a million that lacked open sites for camping, it proved impossible to remove and encamp the entire population.[84] "As a rule," authorities focused instead on "inferior chawls and tenements"[85] and on evacuating "particular classes of people"[86]—amounting to a third of the city's total population. Coordinated police raids also rounded up famine wanderers, whom authorities considered especially dangerous as carriers of plague and cholera.[87] As Brigadier-General Gatacre noted, many suspects were "from famine districts" and those in an "emaciated condition" were "detained mainly to improve their condition by feeding them up."[88] Famine and plague operations dovetailed in their dual concern for the welfare and discipline of mobile bodies.

"CONSIDERABLE INGENUITY"

As in any "dirty war," the civilian population's loyalty and cooperation could rarely be assured. Dr. Low complained of natives' "utter disregard for the truth" and the false statements they made "with a view to throw the examiner off the scent."[89] Like criminology, colonial medicine depended on detective work. An article in the *British Medical Journal* confirmed that plague operations "called for many of the qualities of Sherlock Holmes."[90] The analogy at once spoke to widespread practices of deception attributed to Indians and highlighted the extent to which British authorities considered plague control a police matter. In general, officials perceived natives as obstacles rather than partners—the objects of colonial policing rather than trusted collaborators. The Bombay Plague Committee echoed these sentiments: "the people proved themselves alike agents in the dissemination of Plague and obstructive to remedial measures."[91] Convinced of the "gross ignorance . . . [and] unwillingness [of Indians] to submit to . . . preventive measures"[92] or else to "prevent evasion of the scheme by persons of the lower classes," British officials promptly embraced coercion.[93] All suspects must be "compelled to live in a camp set apart for the purpose," Thomson concluded.[94]

Despite the assumed ignorance of the unclean, however, officials credited "the subtle oriental mind"[95] with "considerable ingenuity" for their "systematic hiding of the sick" in closets, under beds and stacks of clothing, or in "lofts, privies and unoccupied rooms"—anywhere their presence was least likely to be detected.[96] As in other episodes of encampment, problems of visibility and camouflage preoccupied authorities. In Karachi, for example, a search party reported a "ghastly story" (possibly apocryphal) of its encounter with a native man at a card table who presented a "stolid appearance." As a member of the search party placed his hand on the man's shoulder "the figure swayed, and fell over prone on the floor." Upon examination it was "found the man had been dead some time, but to avoid the house being branded plague-stricken, [his] friends . . . had hastily propped him up and stuck some cards in his hand on the news that the search party was approaching."[97] J. S. Wilkins was horrified by such reports, and felt the "feeling of humanity . . . [was] blunted" among those attempting to evade scrutiny.[98] S. J. Thomson complained similarly that "a careful and systematic search" of the town of Kankhal "led to the discovery of no less than 39 bricked-up rooms . . . covered with mud plaster" concealing "articles of clothing, bedding, cooking utensils, and jewellery."[99] To counteract such initiatives, some districts appeased locals by assigning native gentlemen to accompany search parties. Another strategy, however, was the tightening of police coercion. In Bombay and Poona, authorities erected military perimeters around suspect neighborhoods "at an early hour of the morning" to prevent the smuggling of concealed bodies and other contraband. Sanitary cordons suppressed "communications from house to house," though they also escalated measures of evasion.[100]

Combatting plague also demanded a command of information. The campaign mobilized extensive intelligence networks and rested on the use of "paid spies or informers" to report on cases of plague and those suspected of carrying it. In this "information war," authorities highlighted the ability to "obtain early information" as most important. Yet reliable intelligence proved difficult. The absence of any effective registration of vital statistics demanded a different approach, the Indian Plague Commission observed, from what might have prevailed in Great Britain, "where 98 per cent of the deaths are certified either by registered medical practitioners or by coroners."[101] In the empire, plague demanded more direct means of gaining knowledge. As Simpson noted, colonial disease control was "not a question of notification of the sick by medical men, but of finding out the sick and dead," "cleansing and disinfecting" native dwellings, and ultimately, detaining the (potentially) diseased in camps for the purposes of observation, registration, and control.[102] By concentrating the transient and marginal, hitherto concealed within remote villages or in the narrow mazes of urban alleys, camps ultimately enabled Britain to gain vital statistics and epidemiological knowledge about previously inscrutable demographics.

In retrospect, the Indian Plague Commission noted, more effective arrangements for tracking disease might have rested on "the active and intelligent co-operation of the people themselves."[103] Though authorities in seventeenth-century England had detained homeless vagrants in pesthouses, house arrest in townhomes marked with red crosses sufficed for the majority (much as it did for Bombay's Anglo-Indians).[104] But the relative liberality of English measures depended on qualities that were absent in India: a (relative) nexus of trust between ruler and ruled, or at the least, a thick surveillance apparatus and a more intimate familiarity with London rookeries than Bombay *chawls*. From widespread complaints about native subterfuge, it was clear to Cleghorn and Bainbridge that Indians could not be trusted to isolate themselves responsibly or to report for regular inspections. Plague camps, like their famine counterparts, were calibrated to specific colonial conditions.

"ILLEGAL AFRICANS": PLAGUE IN THE SOUTHERN HEMISPHERE

As plague spread globally, camps offered widely applicable technologies of disease control. But they did not prevail everywhere. The varying response to disease at different colonial ports reflects the diversity of the British Empire and the degree to which camps emerged from specific racial and cultural contexts. In Australia, where the population was overwhelmingly British in origin, a liberal wariness of authoritarian measures framed attitudes, much as they had in eighteenth-century England. When the disease reached antipodean shores, Sydney's plague campaign was directed more at rats than human beings, and mass detention was mostly avoided, though tented camps detained Chinese migrants.[105] Authorities largely trusted citizens to report sickness, and comfortable hotels rather than makeshift camps accommodated candidates for quarantine.[106] In contrast to India, Australia's elected government fostered the civic institutions and "soft power"—schools, hospitals, and community centers—necessary to promote active cooperation from a newly enfranchised working class (itself a criminal stratum only a few generations previously).

South Africa, infected in 1900, was a hybrid case: part European settlement and part sub-Saharan colony. Ecological and climatic conditions meant that plague never reached Bombay's epic proportions—the epidemic lasted only one season in Cape Town and its victims numbered in the hundreds rather than hundred thousands. Yet disease served as a pretext for camps nonetheless. As in Australia, white settler society provided more European manpower than in India, and in normal times, if not amid the dislocations of the ongoing Anglo-Boer War, the colony boasted more substantial Western medical infrastructure. Nonetheless, sharp racial binaries and segregationist proclivities fostered the wholesale detention of native classes while permitting more liberal regimes of self-surveillance among middle-class Europeans.

South Africa's racial miscellany was every bit as complex as that of India. Indeed, the sizable white community only magnified the rubrics of purity and pollution that generated camps. Municipal politics self-consciously organized around hygienic tropes in the 1880s when the aptly named "Clean Party" emerged as a force in civic politics, promoting white British ideals of urban purity. Early on, visions of racial health and fears of native contagion framed segregationist movements, and South Africa's burgeoning cities reproduced implacable versions of India's segregated cantonments. When plague broke out, activities focused, unsurprisingly, on the "crowded, dirty, and ill-ventilated dwellings of poorer colored folk,"[107] which harbored conditions similar to Bombay *chawls* and were "unfit for human habitation," Cape Colony medical officer George Turner maintained.[108]

Fears of native evasion also spanned the Indian Ocean. "In spite of the vigilance exercised," one observer complained, "at least half a dozen colored people who were undoubtedly plague-stricken managed, aided by their friends, to dodge the searchers. Covered in their flight by the maze of narrow and filthy lanes with which the locality abounds and with the topography of which they are familiar, [they] speedily made good their escape."[109] Inscrutable colonial habitats and patterns of movement were another common complaint. As in India, Simpson reserved special scrutiny for "the migratory class of people," including "tramps, beggars, coolies, emigrants and pilgrims" who were "as a rule . . . dirty in their habits."[110]

Apart from their similar cultural structures, South Africa's plague campaign drew directly from Indian precedents. Cape Colony's health department reached across the ocean to recruit familiar figures like J. S. Low and W. J. Simpson, who served as Cape Colony's chief medical advisor. Indian experience, a South African historian confirms, had "serious implications for control of the disease at the Cape."[111] In language honed in Bombay and Calcutta, Simpson noted plague in South Africa was "largely a disease of the poor," and the "large proportion of filthy slums" occupied by "natives, colored people [and] Indians" were its primary breeding grounds. And yet Simpson failed to identify as a threat the many impoverished refugees (mostly white Britons) living in makeshift tents and shanties who had fled war-ravaged Transvaal in 1900. The only Europeans destined for camps, he noted, were Jews and "poor whites" of a "low racial type," usually dock laborers from southern Europe and occasional Afrikaans-speaking Boers. "The majority of the whites attacked were foreigners," Simpson emphasized, and "respectable" Britons were categorically exempt from segregation and evacuation.[112]

Statistically, Europeans suffered from plague in great numbers,[113] but camps were reserved for South Africa's "lowest and most drunken colored classes."[114] Racist tropes conceiving Africans as "uncivilized, impermanent immigrants" who formed "no real part of the city"[115] and who were, in Simpson's words, "unused to town life," justified camps as much as any medical principle.[116] The segregation of black Africans, another observer noted, prevented "contamination [of the city] with the Hottentot"—a prospect considered "as undesirable as [it was] dangerous."[117] Medical policing thus flowed into broader campaigns of racial distancing, leaving lasting scars on South Africa's urban landscape. "It was the merest step of logic," Maynard Swanson argued in a seminal article, "to proceed from the isolation of plague victims to the creation of a permanent location for the black laboring class."[118] In this way, South African plague camps united the "political and medical threads [of] racial segregation."[119]

South Africa's Indian diaspora was also destined for detention. Though British troop movements spread the disease, contemporaries blamed plague on the migrant voyages of indentured laborers, particularly in Natal, where officials arrested coolie laborers en masse. Johannesburg's *Rand Daily Mail* deplored the "filthy habits" of South Asians and their "gross perversion of the most elementary sanitary rules."[120] Dr. Jane Waterston, Cape Colony's first female doctor, confirmed that "the class of Indians . . . we have to put in tents" was an "ever present danger."[121] As plague reached the interior in 1903, newspapers urged authorities to "keep . . . coolies as far away as possible from the centers of [white] population."[122] The police accordingly cordoned off Johannesburg's entire "coolie location" and forcibly removed Indians and Africans to fenced segregation camps. The "agitation," one critical journalist noted, was "more anti-Coolie than anti-plague."[123]

As in India, operations were substantially militarized. Modeled on Indian methods, Simpson erected camps at Rosemead Junction (on Cape Colony's frontier) and other rail stations. And since many "natives [were] of a truculent disposition," soldiers and noncommissioned officers with "some knowledge of the Kaffir" were appointed to maintain order.[124] Meanwhile, Simpson orchestrated targeted roundups of "illegal Africans" in Cape Town, who were segregated in camps at Maitland, Ebenezer Road, and the massive Uitvlugt (Ndabeni) complex under the emergency provisions of Cape Colony's 1897 Public Health Act. The soldiers deployed "had fixed bayonets," one journalist observed, "and the mass of aborigines, numbering nearly a thousand, was soon closely fringed by the glitter of steel."[125] Inhabitants were "hurried out of their homes, in many cases . . . without being allowed to [collect] . . . their valuables, [or] secure a change of clothing"[126] and their houses were "demolished . . . *in toto*."[127] As the Cape Town resident Sam Ntungwana recalled, soldiers forbade him from entering his house to retrieve his belongings, which he had already packed in anticipation of removal, and when he later returned, his property had been incinerated. Foreshadowing famous forced removals under South Africa's apartheid government, Cape Town's District Six was almost entirely depopulated as a result of British plague operations.[128] "In a short time," Simpson noted, "all the natives . . . were removed . . . and placed under sanitary supervision in comfortable huts made of corrugated iron."[129]

Despite the substantial Indian influence, South African camps also reflected local conditions. With the outbreak of the Anglo-Boer War, plague operations intersected with a more general climate of surveillance and the military partition of people and space. The army enacted its own quarantine measures for traveling troops, but plague spread inland to Johannesburg nevertheless. In the early postwar years, meanwhile, officials with experience supervising camps erected to house civilians displaced by guerrilla war turned their energies to the related task of plague segregation as the disease travelled inland. The Johannesburg city councilor and former land surveyor Captain W. K. Tucker mobilized his experience as chief superintendent of wartime concentration camps in Transvaal when he organized Johannesburg's first plague camp at Klipspruit. The complex consisted of used tents and corrugated-iron huts recycled from the war and was located, appropriately enough, on a former sewage dump—a site that formed the nucleus of the infamous Southwestern Townships (Soweto) in the twentieth century.[130] In Cape Colony, meanwhile, Public Works Director Lewis Mansergh approached the simultaneous construction of both plague and wartime concentration camps as related endeavors. Along with Simpson, such figures highlight interconnections between the entwined projects of military and medical policing across Britain's sprawling empire of camps.

"A SOURCE OF HORROR AND DREAD"

Camps emerged on both sides of the Indian Ocean as contested symbols, whether scientific instruments calculated to save lives or artifacts of imperial overstep. Although British disease control was fortified by scientific authority and executed with military precision, plague officials failed to factor the human element into their equations. Madhava Rao, the plague commissioner of Bangalore and one of the few Indians to occupy a high-level post in the war on plague, complained: "in spite of every effort to popularize [the camps, they] were and are a source of horror and dread to the people . . . [who] manifested the utmost abhorrence to compulsory segregation" and convened "numerous meetings protesting against it." The Indian Plague Commission confirmed: the removal of suspects to segregation camps was "invariably resented" and "popular feeling against it [was] very deep-rooted."[131]

Colonial populations actively protested British plague measures. Africans organized dock strikes and open-air demonstrations, initiating a long century of struggle against racial discrimination and unequal treatment.[132] In India, meanwhile, the militant National Congress leader B. G. Tilak, already emboldened by his opposition to British famine policies, oversaw the assassination of Charles Rand, the plague commissioner of Poona. At his public trial, Tilak condemned camps as embodiments of foreign rule. Britain's ensuing "reign of terror" in reaction to Rand's death in turn prompted native newspapers to question the "boasted enlightenment and sympathy" of British administration. An article from the *Mahratta*, Tilak's English-language weekly, highlighted the gulf between the colonial government and its native subjects, commenting, "the plague authority who sits in his office and issues his mandates in the light of theory cannot see all [the] misery much less appreciate it." While blaming the bureaucratic anonymity that facilitated coercive measures, the article went on to suggest "a far wiser method" would be to "learn from . . . respectable native gentlemen" and "consult a few prominent and well-informed natives before . . . orders are issued."[133]

Popular hostility toward camps mapped onto protest against police coercion and the racism it laid bare. It also emerged from a "clash of medical cultures" accentuated by colonial rule. As S. J. Thomson observed, "rustics looked upon admission into a plague [camp] as equivalent to a sentence of death."[134] For Indians and Africans, who recognized the home as the proper locus of medical care, camps represented a grievous violation that removed the sick from the sanctity of their families. For inmates, camps were "less . . . a refuge from the ravages of plague," Rajnarayan Chandavarkar confirms, than "a potent and destructive instrument of terror."[135]

Inmates at Bandra camp "thought they were going to be poisoned" and "in many instances not only refused to take medicine, but refused to take even food and drink." The belief that inmates "were all operated on during life and dissected after death" was almost "universal," the Indian Plague Commission added.[136] Britain dismissed these "wild" and gruesome rumors as emanations of native unreason, but they reflected a genuine cultural disconnect between ruler and ruled. If British medicine was framed by a mistrust of natives, the feeling was more than mutual.

Others objected to perceived religious violations. Britain maintained a tactical awareness of caste and confessional divisions and at times provided segregated camps for various Hindu castes and for Muslim women in purdah. But arrangements were far from satisfactory. Apart from Hindu concerns about caste mixing articulated by the Bhusawal inmate Bhikajo Agashe, petitioners in Bombay complained of the "great grief and hardship" endured by "every Mohammedan family." Camps, they charged, caused "such severe pain and shock to those who are removed, and such violation of all the precepts of the Mohammedan religion," that forced removal "should not be persevered in even if it . . . proved . . . most useful for checking the progress of the disease." Many Muslims objected to the violation of purdah entailed by British soldiers invading private homes. Perceiving British measures as a foreign challenge to community rights over the female body, moreover, they levied a petition (signed only by men) asserting that "every Mohammedan woman would rather die" than "expose themselves to the *gaze*" of outsiders; "their husbands and fathers would rather see them dead," the petition added, "than polluted by the touch of strangers."[137] "Literally," Lord Curzon reflected, Indians "would rather die than be saved against their will."[138]

Locals also expressed disdain in judicial terms more familiar to British audiences. For leaders in Bombay, segregation camps constituted a grave "interference with the liberty of the individual."[139] The *Mahratta* agreed: "wrongful segregation, when converted into its legal equivalent, is nothing less than unlawful imprisonment."[140] Future leaders of the South African National Congress like Alfred Mangena also turned to legal arguments, using the courts to challenge forced encampment, though with little success. Another critical figure was the young Mohandas Gandhi. Living in South Africa, his firsthand observation of racist plague measures and the forced encampment of Indians in Natal helped launch his famed anticolonial career, which built on and superseded Tilak's agitation in Poona.[141] British camps, by the negative example they set, helped instantiate liberal discourses of individual freedom and political rights into communities across the Empire, nourishing early home rule and civil rights movements in both India and South Africa.

At times, however, reasoned debate descended into spirals of popular violence. "Policemen were murdered" and "medical officers were burned alive," Viceroy Curzon lamented.[142] Camps themselves were often rallying points of unrest. In Bombay, a serious riot in 1898 spread with "oriental rapidity" among an apparently "uneducated, bigoted and fanatical" substratum, who targeted Europeans identified with plague camps.[143] In Cawnpore, meanwhile, "fifteen hundred people, armed with *laithis* and hatchets . . . attacke[d] the camp," killed five camp guards, and set huts on fire.[144] And in Nasik, a crowd of seven hundred released inmates from two camps, burned down huts, destroyed the medical officer's tents and belongings, and "beat and struck . . . with axes" an assistant "who had been very energetic in plague measures." The crowd then marched to "the detention camp [at the rail station] about a mile from the town," which they burned before "brutally murdering" a member of the local plague committee. Yet however terrifying the unrest, a moral economy channeled violence towards specific ends. According to the local district magistrate, the rioters carefully avoided collateral damage and refrained from plunder to focus their efforts solely on demanding an end to forced detention.[145] Ultimately, authorities realized, camps had unsettled the composure of British rule.

"MORE HARM THAN GOOD"

Responding to local pushback, Britain substantially relaxed its disciplinary regime in 1898 after two years of coercion. More native doctors were employed and the "segregation of contacts" was "greatly reduced in strictness." Meanwhile, residents of infected houses who voluntarily reported disease were given "liberty throughout the day" and detained only at night.[146] To a certain extent, such changes reflected ambivalent attitudes among Britons themselves, who remained committed to liberal precepts of nonintervention and free movement despite the proliferation of camps. New policies also reflected the inefficacies of the former system. As IMS officers testified, coercion did "more harm than good." The "dread of the government segregation camp" was ironically the occasion for suspects to flee British patrols and "scatter like rabbits," further spreading disease rather than concentrating it at manageable sites.[147] Force, it seemed, was futile. "Venality on the part of guards" permitted inmates to bribe their way out, and J. S. Wilkins "found it difficult to get [people] to go into segregation camps" in the first place or to keep them there: inmates were "constantly leaving" and "spread[ing] plague all over the place."[148] Ultimately, however, it was protesting inmates themselves who forced the Indian Plague Commission to realize "no system of plague administration [could] be successful which does not carry the people with it."[149] Gradually, cooperation replaced coercion: Wilkins, for one, decided he would "act differently" in future by "calling the headman of each caste . . . to select a spot for a camp."[150]

Concentration was sometimes undermined. But despite—or rather because of—this tactical softening, plague camps remained lasting features of colonial rule. In 1900 the Plague Department recognized inmates should "be under no restraint whatsoever," but it affirmed evacuation as an "effectual measure."[151] With a combination of compromise and persuasion, voluntary evacuation camps (if not fenced detention centers) became legitimate and standardized tools of British plague policy. In a sign of changing attitudes, the Indian Plague Commission even rooted evacuation in ancient Hindu scripture (now apparently compatible with Western science) by citing the *Bhagavata Purana*'s injunction for people to abandon their homes when "rats fell from the roof above, jump about and die."[152]

With the normalization of camps, plague infrastructure became more permanent. In consultation with J. S. Wilkins, Mr. Playford Reynolds of the Bombay Improvement Trust designed mobile huts of a "strong" and "durable" nature that would "last for years." Gradually, "permanent weatherproof evacuation camps of corrugated iron" replaced interim canvas and thatch. As instruments of state planning and mass production—constructed "on a uniform pattern and with parts interchangeable"—these modular structures ensured that camps would endure as technologies of social and sanitary policing for decades to come. With an eye to future outbreaks and other colonial emergencies, the government kept these huts "at convenient centres, ready to be transported and put up at a day's notice."[153]

In some cases, plague camps even outlasted the epidemic to become integral components of urbanization and industrialization. In South Africa, where coercion against Africans and Indians continued long after plague subsided, camps formed the nucleus of permanent "locations" that lasted into the apartheid era. Similarly, Bombay's network of evacuation camps survived well into the twentieth century as suburban housing projects for the urban poor. With their straight and simple lines that could be cheaply reproduced, they even inspired some of India's first modernist architecture.

Wholesale clearances of inner city slums offered blank slates for urban planners, and by providing "abundant and comfortable camp accommodation," officials hoped not only to control plague but to "encourage a permanent movement from the overcrowded city to the open north." In contrast to earlier slum clearances in London or Haussmann's Paris, which "caused serious distress because those in charge failed to provide lodgings for the unhoused," Bombay authorities noted congenially that camps facilitated the work of "clear[ing] evil houses and open[ing] streets and spaces." The unclean classes, it concluded with satisfaction, "settled quietly, lived happily [and] gained health and strength" at suburban campsites.[154] In South Africa, too, a humane gloss legitimized "the new locations," which one superintendent believed "should form the greatest attraction to the people." At Uitvlugt on the Cape Flats, "the provision of a thoroughly equipped hospital, with excellent staff and cleanly surroundings" helped stem inmate protest. And with facilities more comfortable than the average African kraal, one official "wonder[ed] why, aside perhaps from the question of distance to and from their places of work, every native should not avail himself of the excellent accommodations provided."[155]

The large-scale restructuring of towns was only possible because authoritarian plague legislation sanctioned British planners to manipulate the built environment at will. But did camps succeed in suppressing plague? In 1907 the private secretary to Viceroy Lord Minto lamented, "the history of the efforts made by the Government to combat the plague is a melancholy one. These have lasted for over ten years and have produced practically no results."[156] In Bombay, Private Secretary Claude Hill concurred: "plague operations were not only ineffective," they "created an undercurrent of discontent most favorable for the dissemination of political disaffection."[157] Vaccinations and rat extermination offered some reprieve in the years before World War I, but the detention of suspects made little positive impact, and it was not until selective forces had rendered Indian rat populations immune in the 1920s that the pandemic came to an end. By this time, however, camps were cemented as lasting features of British colonialism.

CHAPTER 4 · Concentrated Humanity

The Management and Anatomy of Colonial Camps, c. 1900

The British Empire was made of canvas and thatch. Army barracks and the tented abodes of traveling administrators complemented outdoor prisons and criminal tribe settlements. But hunger and disease generated new and important "tools of empire." By the late nineteenth century, plague and famine camps emerged as discrete colonial instruments, recognizable to British observers and the many millions detained. Bird's-eye views of colonial camps in Victorian photo albums attest to their newfound ubiquity; and yet, the tidy geometries they depicted belied diversity and disorder on the ground.

Often, Viceroy Curzon noted, "camps were hurriedly improvised."[1] Consisting of bamboo barracks and army-issued tents, wattle-and-daub huts and reed fences, they came in many shapes and sizes. But whatever their cause or context—famine or plague, India or South Africa—camps posed technical problems common to each colonial crisis: the care and control of "concentrated humanity." Bramble and barbed-wire enclosures offered venues for medical, military, and civil administrators to care for and control unhealthy conglomerations of men, women, and children. But camps proved unpopular among inmates, especially when epidemics swept through their crowded confines. "When many people are congregated in a certain space," William Digby noted of famine camps, sanitation was a "great difficulty."[2] Apart from plague, cholera and smallpox were ubiquitous specters that killed many thousands. But if disease was "the inevitable result of massing people in unusual crowds,"[3] experience with plague and famine camps proffered lessons in hygienic and disciplinary management.

By the 1890s, government reports and published "Blue Books" circulated "standard pattern[s] upon which all camps should be constructed."[4] Meanwhile, a cosmopolitan array of "experts" conducted travelling inspections across the empire, enforcing a process of standardization by ensuring camps replicated favored layouts. This chapter examines an emerging typology of famine and plague camps—from detention centers for wanderers to evacuation camps for plague suspects—in order to reveal the recurring challenges camps posed, along with the growing experience in camp construction and administration British officials accumulated. And while inmate voices are hard to recover, exploration of the developing management and anatomy of British camps offers some insight into life behind the wire.

"AN ENCLOSURE NOT EASY TO SURMOUNT": CAMPS FOR FAMINE WANDERERS

Starting in the 1870s, camps detaining famine wanderers set an early template for the management of concentrated humanity. Situated at strategic junctures, proximity to settled populations facilitated easier police control along with access to established water supplies, local food markets, and medical facilities. Suburban milieus, in particular, proved convenient for concentrating vagrants caught in urban sweeps. When available, famine officials requisitioned hostels, religious *dharmasalas*, jailhouses, plantation compounds, and pilgrim transit depots: an existing culture of confinement was readily appropriated. In an effort to "control and systematize" operations, for example, the Madras government converted the Monegar Choultry, an institution founded by native gentlemen in 1782 to feed the hungry,[5] into a detention camp with "double fencing," mounted police, and medical surveillance.[6] Philanthropic organizations like the Society of Friends and the Salvation Army also accommodated wanderers at mission stations and "industrial schools," though most camps operated under government oversight.[7] Wherever it proved necessary to construct camps from scratch, however, "care [was] taken," the Bombay government recorded, "that expensive structures" were not "erected until there was a reasonable probability that so much accommodation . . . would be needed."[8]

The camp's paramount feature was its fence. Security, after all, vied with relief as a primary motive. Camps, Digby instructed, "must be enclosed and admission or exit" should "only be possible by a gate at which a guard is constantly posted."[9] Though "very expensive," the Madras police commissioner found it necessary to erect "double fencing . . . all round some camps to prevent escapes."[10] The

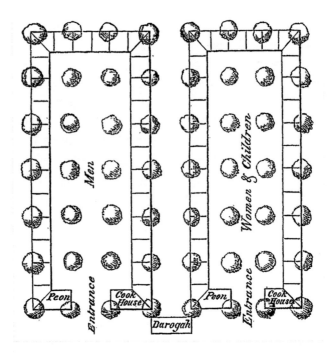

FIGURE 12.

Camps were "like industrial establishments" consisting of "enclosed sheds for residence, sanitary arrangements, dispensaries, kitchens and other necessary buildings."[5] The model camp prescribed in the North-Western Provinces segregated sexes in long barracks enclosing a central courtyard shaded by trees. [Credit: C.3086, *Report of the Indian Famine Commission, Vol. IV, "Evidence in Reply to Inquiries of the Commission"* (London: Her Majesty's Stationary Office, 1885), 229.]

[5] Srivastava, *History of Indian Famines*, 40.

North-Western Provinces likewise recommended that camps be "surrounded by an enclosure such as not to be easy to surmount, but not so formidable as to make it resemble a jail."[11] Without fences and guards, Temple concurred, inmates would "decamp . . . [and] once more . . . become wanderers."[12] Not only did "locked enclosures" prevent escape,[13] they kept "impostors" out, though William Digby observed that some "sham applicants for relief" proved adept at "creeping through . . . fence[s]" and guards were necessary to stop them from entering.[14] In theory, fences maintained discrete boundaries between camps and the outside world, though in practice, police patrols often had to "catch and bring back [escaped] wanderers and beggars."[15] "Idleness, love of home, [and] separation from relatives" were principle reasons for desertion along with the "discomforts inseparable from camp life."[16]

The physical layout of camps further regulated egress and ingress. Reverend Scott described a common format in Ajmer, a semiautonomous Native State that followed British precedents. "A mile out of town," the camp consisted of "a large square, walled in" and "internally divided into other smaller squares for the various classes of paupers."[17] Similar to workhouses and coolie compounds, central courtyards facilitated supervision and minimized points of entry. Further, they offered space for inmates to work. Although emaciated wanderers did not conduct heavy tasks like "able-bodied" relief workers, officials concurred that the "orderly management of the inmates" depended "in great measure upon their employment in some useful way."[18] Even "the feeblest old woman [could] spin a little thread," Digby affirmed, and "for the sake of [inmates'] health and spirits and self-respect, it [was] better they should do this than that they should sit idle all day."[19] In contrast to relief workers, however, detainees performed their labor—manufacturing textiles, repairing huts, sinking wells—within fenced enclosures, hidden from public scrutiny. As Major Baynes explained, the "effect on outsiders" of seeing inmates "working under strong guards like prisoners" would be "very bad." Furthermore, the "guard that could be supplied [was] not strong enough" to prevent them from "deserting."[20]

In contrast to the layout described by Scott, the Monegar Choultry camp in Madras erected labyrinthine entries and exits to prevent escape, along with fenced perimeters. Such barriers should not be exaggerated, however. In some cases, barbed wire was necessary to keep inmates in, though fences often consisted of inexpensive local products, particularly bamboo and grass mats combined with thorns, hedges of prickly pear, and five-foot trenches lined with brambles. These were detention camps, but primitive ones that lacked the security apparatus of twentieth-century sites of confinement. Inmates desperate to leave could and did escape.

What of life behind the fence? Food, above all, was the camps' humanitarian raison d'être, and onsite kitchens cooked and distributed rations. Serial numbers imprinted on color-coded tin or wooden tickets, worn around the neck, classified inmates, who were arranged in rows in the feeding sheds.[21] According to Surgeon Henry Gray, who volunteered in Madras after gaining experience at convict settlements in the Andaman Islands, "great discipline" was "essential" in the distribution of food.[22] Mealtimes—or "feedings" in the impersonal terms of officialdom— proved volatile moments among the desperately hungry. Many had "lost all the

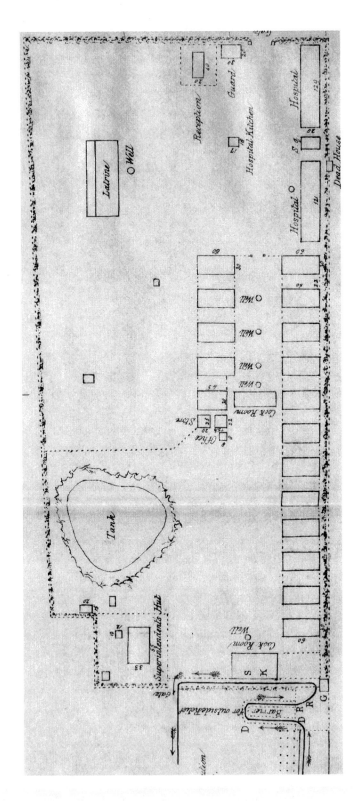

FIGURE 13.

Monegar Choultry camp in Madras detained wanderers after a "total clearance of the city." The huts were 60′ × 30′ and held 60–75 inmates each. Additional lean-to huts were erected when the camp became "alarmingly overcrowded."[6] [Credit: © British Library, Temple Papers, IOR/F86/183, Madras Town Famine Relief 1877. Report by Colonel W. S. Drever, Appendix H.]

6 Temple Papers, IOR/F86/183, Madras Town Famine Relief 1877. Report by Colonel W. S. Drever, 6–7.

better feelings of mankind,"[23] and without strict management, Reverend Scott concurred, the "whole miserable crowd" were likely to spring "like a pack of hungry wolves" at the first scent of food; once again, even sympathetic observers dehumanized the famished.[24] Feeding sheds were "strongly protected enclosures" with "different doors for ingress and egress."[25] Ultimately, however, superintendents recognized the "fullness, careful preparation, and orderly distribution of the diet" as "*the* essential elements" upon which "orderly behavior" depended.[26] Yet if satisfactory rations facilitated control, a "bare subsistence diet" often undermined the endeavor.

Camp life was simple and austere, designed to punish as much as to relieve. In line with individuating spaces at jails, six-inch mud ridges partitioned sleeping berths to prevent the "immoral" huddling of bodies.[27] String cots or piles of straw served as beds, along with simple pieces of *chittai* (cloth). As in metropolitan workhouses, the sexes were segregated as a necessary condition of relief, though mothers were rarely separated from young children. For males "physically capable of standing it," meanwhile, a "slight [corporal] castigation" helped enforce rules and regulations,[28] though Commissioner A.D. Younghusband was more strident when he recommended "the punishment of whipping, judiciously and vigorously applied," as being "generally appropriate."[29] Given that "deaths [were] likely to be numerous amongst the inmates," meanwhile, open "wasteland" accommodated those who reached the "vanishing point" of concentration.[30] India today is littered with anonymous mass graves, like the one at Jhalod, where 50 percent of inmates died; "eight or ten bodies at a time" were buried on the outskirts of the camp.[31] Vaughan Nash similarly witnessed "eleven corpses, desperately emaciated," along with "a sack of babies" disposed of at a camp in Godhra.[32]

"PAUPER VILLAGES": DORMITORY RELIEF CAMPS

Camps attached to relief works were usually larger than those detaining wanderers, though facilities were rarely "so lofty or substantial."[33] The Indian Famine Code mandated hut accommodation be organized before the opening of any work, though in practice, it was "seldom if ever" possible "to have huts ready," and in many cases, inmates spent their first nights at barren and unequipped sites that often proved detrimental to discipline and health.[34] At Mulvad, for example, the lack of accommodation induced arriving inmates to "herd together in the jungle, which [was] highly favorable to the development of disease."[35] Yet since many famine victims were "inured to a lower standard of living," it was no hardship, officials believed, to enforce compulsory camp residence, "even if huts [were] not provided."[36] As a compromise, Bombay authorities instructed that "immediate arrangements should . . . be made . . . for the proper hutting of weakly people and those with small children."[37] And "where camps [were] in very much exposed bleak spots . . . hutting for all" was required.[38]

Upon arrival, it was inmates' first task to erect their own shelter. Despite direction from Public Works officials and the demarcation of campsites by sanitary commissioners like S. J. Thomson, the reliance on inmate labor resulted in significant local variation, and in some cases inmates used branches and brambles "to run up any wigwams they pleased." Insubstantial "leaf huts" provided rudimentary shelter, but instructions in the Central and North-Western Provinces recommended sturdy huts "plastered with mud on the inside" and "white washed both inside and out."[39] In colder climates, "brick buildings" with "enclosed verandahs" sometimes prevailed.[40] On an inspection tour of Madras and Bombay, Richard Temple observed relief work camps as varied as the people and places of the subcontinent. He saw long barrack-like rows of huts at Erukkanchery, but elsewhere described "small structures capable of accommodating about 10 people" or "separate huts for each family."[41] The former proved "repugnant to those who wished to preserve self-respect,"[42] while the latter allowed "an air of cheerfulness [among] the inmates."[43] Whatever the case, military-style barracks were favored for sanitary and disciplinary purposes. It was "not possible to give separate spaces to each family without stopping ventilation and accumulating filth,"[44] sanitary officials concurred, and individual huts were "prone to filthiness" and "impede[d] conservancy."[45]

Nonetheless, small moveable huts, "such as the Wuddahs [an aboriginal south-Indian tribe] use in camping out" were often more practical.[46] The camps at Shetpal Tank, for instance, were necessarily mobile, shifting with the course of canal excavation. Accommodation consisted, accordingly, of "semi-cylindrical bamboo-frame tents" made of "khadi" cloth. These had the added benefit of providing employment to distressed weavers, and the fabric was more portable and "probably a better defense against rain and wind" than bamboo matting,[47] though army tents served similar purposes. Camps also varied by size. One "camp" Temple observed was "merely a small hut" for forty inmates. By contrast, facilities at Arcot contained "substantially built . . . coolie sheds . . . placed on high ground" accommodating upwards of three thousand.[48] Even larger was the Budihal Tank complex accommodating nineteen thousand across several satellite camps.[49]

FIGURE 14.
Uniform huts at Shetpal camp (above) suggest planning and official control, but their shoddy construction indicates their mobile nature. Other camps used canvas and khadi-cloth tents like in Naldurg (below). [Credit: © British Library, IOR/Photo 940/1, Album of Famine Camp views in the Poona District and Canal Construction Scenes in Sindh, image 6; Raja Deen Dayal and Sons, *Famine Relief: H. H. Niẓam's Dominions, Hyderabad (Deccan), 1899–1900*, 95, "Distribution of Wages, Dharaseo relief Camp, Naldurg District," Andhra Pradesh State Archives, Hyderabad, India. Photograph courtesy of Deborah Hutton.]

Whatever their individual characteristics, camps normally included a settlement of huts described by Antony MacDonnell's 1901 Famine Commission as a "pauper village."[50] Such a model was easy to erect, could be expanded in stages, and could accommodate large numbers at minimal cost. Accompanying Temple on his inspection tours, Bombay's sanitary commissioner T. G. Hewlett circulated early blueprints recommending shelters 30' × 10' accommodating twenty inmates each,[51] along with grain bazars and cooking sheds, though later camps added smaller 9' × 6' sheds for families along with "large shelters . . . for the nursing mothers to work under" and "shelters . . . for babies near where their mothers work."[52] The camp at Vellore was typical: it contained a "hospital, kitchen, [and] latrines" as well as "28 well-built huts . . . calculated to hold about 3000 persons," of whom "400–500 [were] employed in digging a trench and fencing the enclosure of [the] camp."[53] Sanitary Commissioner S. J. Thomson, meanwhile, recommended fences and "enclosure walls" with "broad entrances and exits every 50 yards to allow of air flushing the enclosed area." But with multiple points of entry and exit, such sites proved more difficult to police than smaller detention centers. Guards and fences facilitated "discipline and control" and prevented "workers [from] returning to their villages at night."[54] But often, Benjamin Robertson observed, compulsory residence was enforced with simple roll calls.[55]

For disciplinary purposes, camps were located a significant distance from local villages and in proximity to worksites. Though it was "difficult to keep the people in camp," authorities found that inmates "resided there readily enough when there was no village near and the camp arrangements . . . made it more convenient to live in camp than in the village."[56] Spatial distancing also prevented cholera and other "camp diseases" from spreading to nearby settlements, thereby intersecting with larger projects of social policing and disease control.[57] Nonetheless, when camps failed to provide adequate hutting (as they often did) local authorities quietly tolerated workers returning to villages at night (much to the Indian Famine Commission's dismay). Even when compulsory residence was enforced, remnants of village life survived: rows of huts were often organized in lines according to villages of origin and named as such—an arrangement popular with inmates and one that fostered labor cohesion.

Above all, cost-cutting measures limited camp construction. Although sanitary experts like J. S. Wilkins advocated watertight, "pucca-built" structures, the Bombay government mandated that huts be "light, inexpensive . . . and of a character that would admit of easy and rapid extension to meet emergencies."[58] More substantial marquee tents and "Swiss cottages" served as hospitals and accommodated British officials resident on the works, though the Revenue Department complained that such materials "involve[d] quite unnecessary expenditure" when bamboo and palm leaves were available for free.[59] Camps open during monsoons, meanwhile, demanded improved shelters plastered with mud and other waterproof agents, though the "prohibitive cost and expenditure on materials" made it "impossible to render all workers' huts perfectly watertight,"[60] and it became necessary, one Poona official lamented, "to keep people in their miserable wet damp huts" as long as relief continued."[61]

Ultimately, public works camps opened tensions within the overall strategy of famine relief. Although mandatory camp residence was intended to minimize costs by deterring relief applicants, the expense of providing adequate facilities often proved prohibitive.[62] And while sanitary and medical officials remained advocates for healthy campsites, their plans conflicted with the interests of a Revenue Department intent on reducing expenditure. Thus, while model camp designs emerged in the course of famine operations, comprehensive and methodical camps were rarely a reality. In Bijapur, an extreme example, only one out of twenty-nine camps met the provisions of the Bombay Famine Code. More vividly, a *Times* correspondent described a camp in Kaira in which "all but thirty" inmates "had died . . . out of 3334 . . . admitted." There "was stench and filth, the air was microbe-laden. . . .and outside, in the sun, lying on the ground, was a stark-naked woman in the last throes of cholera."[63] Failure was not total, however. Traveling through the Deccan highlands, the Public Works secretary Thomas Higham noted the "complete arrangement of the camps," which conformed closely to the Famine Code and consisted of "huts . . . of very ample size and substantial character," which were "laid out in streets with great regularity, so that the encampment has the appearance of a well-ordered village."[64] Colonial chaos could give way to Cartesian regularity, at least to outside observers.

"HOTBEDS OF DISEASE"?

Among the most challenging aspects of concentrating the famished in camps was the outbreak of disease. More than ten million Indians died of famine in the nineteenth century. Yet incredibly, the 1897 Bombay Famine Commission counted only eleven deaths from outright "starvation" in the entire Presidency.[65] Instead, it attributed the drastic rise in mortality to disease. "It is a well-ascertained law," Deputy Famine Secretary Thomas Holderness remarked, "that pestilence accompanies famine and that the two are the twin-offspring of drought."[66] Spokesmen remained adamant that government relief camps saved millions. But amid an already disease-rich environment, the health impact of camps was double-edged. By concentrating already weak and sickly inmates in crowded and unhygienic conditions, a government publication conceded, camps became "ready-made hot-beds for the development of epidemic disease."[67] In such cases, camps belied the biopolitical purposes for which they were first built.

Whenever large populations congregate together, epidemics follow: this was as true for famine camps as it was for the industrial cities of the nineteenth century. The "housing, food and water supply, sanitation, [and] policing . . . of thousands of people collected together in some out-of-the-way place" was no easy matter, the Society of Friends observer Joseph Taylor recorded.[68] "It goes without saying," British spokesmen concurred, "that the larger the aggregation of human beings and the more limited the area on which they are collected, the greater becomes the difficulty of successfully guarding them against sanitary . . . dangers." This was especially "the case when the community consists of persons . . . already in a debilitated state" whose "ignorance and prejudice renders them entirely apathetic to any efforts made for their welfare."[69] Many inmates who died in camps might have succumbed to hunger and disease regardless of their internment. But famine camps gained special reputations as "notorious centers of disease."[70] "There is no wonder that the camps were regarded with suspicion," William Digby confirmed, for "the death-rate in them was appalling."[71]

Unreliable water supplies at makeshift camps made ready mediums for gastrointestinal ailments, the "invariable accompaniments of famine."[72] "Almost all" the inmates of the relief camp visited by Joseph Taylor were "suffering from famine diarrhea or dysentery."[73] At Monegar Choultry, likewise, "mortality was very high and almost entirely due to diarrhea and dysentery."[74] *Cancrum oris*, a gangrenous growth around the mouth and genitals, broke out among camp children, the Society of Friends reported, and guinea worm was prevalent.[75] Contagious diseases also spread in crowded camp conditions. Along with measles,[76] Thomas Holderness identified smallpox as a disease that "require[ed] attention in managing a famine camp," though vaccination and the segregation of new arrivals curbed mortality in the 1890s.[77] More moralistically, officials observed symptoms of opium withdrawal, noting the drug was unobtainable in camp.[78] Finally, haphazard shelters portended "pestilential influences" and "unwholesome social relations."[79] Cold and wet conditions "inevitably tell on the large crowds encamped on relief works," a North-Western Provinces spokesman noted, and while a drought-stricken country welcomed rain, wet weather killed thousands from "pneumonia and allied diseases."[80] Whatever the ailment, children and the elderly were the first to succumb. In some camps, the collector of Ahmednagar reported, "much more than half the young children have died."[81] Such patterns foreshadowed similar tragedies in twentieth-century concentration camps.

Above all, cholera struck numerous camps causing panic and unrest. "In South Africa men exposed themselves to Boer bullets and unflinchingly face a hidden foe," Reverend Scott observed, "but in India, without the 'pomp of glorious war,'" the famished faced cholera: "a foe so wide-spread that fifty-million people feel its power, and so entrenched that there is but little hope of speedy conquest."[82] The "blue death" proved "practically impossible to prevent . . . when large masses of men [were] collected together . . . under famine conditions," the Indian Famine Commission conceded.[83] Observing a "raging visitation" at a camp in Gujarat, Vaughan Nash noted that inmates were "dying faster than they can be burned or buried," while "kites and jackals . . . gorg[ed] themselves" on dead bodies. Such apocalyptic scenes were repeated in Godhra, where sweepers "pick[ed] up some twenty dead bodies about the camp every day" and "a handful of Englishmen . . . had to collect and burn nearly a thousand bodies with their own hands."[84] Cholera also broke out in Khandesh: "all parts of the [Devala] camp were strewn with bodies of the dead and dying," a distraught medical officer reported, and "the stream that runs through the camp" was awash with "the bodies of those who . . . crawled down to die in it."[85] For his part, the local revenue collector attributed such scenes to "unusually dirty . . . habits"[86] among "ignorant and uncivilized" Bhils.[87] Blaming the victim was standard practice throughout Britain's empire of camps.

Famine officials insisted the "vast number of lives saved" by relief camps outweighed the "smaller number lost."[88] Yet famine camps, the historian Mike Davis charges, "may have killed more with microbes than they saved with grain."[89] Contemporaries certainly recognized the hazards of large camps. Temple conceded the "dreaded sanitary effect" of large concentrations,[90] while the collector of Poona confirmed "the collection of large numbers . . . in great discomfort . . . may lead to the outbreak of disease."[91] In Bombay, which recorded some of the highest cholera rates in India, the 1901 Famine Commission highlighted the connection between camps and disease, citing "the outbreak of epidemic[s]" as one reason to abandon the use of camps and shift toward a policy of local village relief in future famines.[92] "Cholera mortality would have been avoided," it concluded, had "large works" been "split up" and the people "return[ed] to their homes."[93] But while concentration clearly caused avoidable deaths, official mortality rates were consistently lower among camp inmates than the general population. The Bombay government, for example, recorded a province-wide mortality of 6.28 percent in the worst month of 1897 (compared to a decennial monthly average below 0.25%) but only 4.28 percent in relief camps. Yet statistics, though dutifully recorded, were imperfect because "panic-stricken" inmates routinely fled relief camps on the outbreak of cholera, despite efforts to forcibly detain them; and when they died, they were rarely recorded as camp inmates. Doubting its own numbers, the Bombay Famine Commission recognized the official camp mortality was "so small" that "it [could] not be supposed to include all the deaths of people who were employed on relief works."[94]

Despite harrowing local reports of corpse-laden enclosures, officials remained upbeat. The Famine Commission lauded the "strenuous . . . exertions . . . to combat disease," which reduced mortality at the best camps and rendered "the health of the people employed on the works . . . generally very satisfactory."[95] Captain King, a protégé of J. S. Wilkins in Bombay, noted that many camps were free from epidemics,[96] while Sanitary Commissioner S. J. Thomson drew attention to the comparatively small mortality from cholera in camps under his purview in the North-Western Provinces.[97] "The vigilance with which sanitary precautions were carried out" was largely responsible for "the comparative immunity enjoyed by the famine-relief camps," another report concluded.[98] For inmates and their advocates, camps developed stigmas as concentrations of pollution and disease. For the likes of Thomson, however, camps, when properly administered, could be healthy enclaves that facilitated hygienic discipline and medical surveillance, at least when guidelines were followed. Though actual camps rarely adhered to Thomson's instructions, famine provided training ground for sanitary experts who would go on to administer future camps in the twentieth century. Before that, however, the outbreak of plague provided a new and urgent impetus to refine the sanitary management of "concentrated humanity."

"A SHORT IMPRISONMENT": PLAGUE SEGREGATION CAMPS

With hunger came pestilence, and although outbreaks of bubonic plague were surprisingly rare at famine relief camps, the control of infectious disease was a challenge shared by plague and famine operations alike. Plague segregation camps demanded overlapping skillsets with famine relief, but as spaces operated primarily by public health officials, the purposeful concentration of plague suspects facilitated new medical and sanitary refinements in the 1890s. If camps challenged famine officials to prevent the spread of cholera and smallpox, plague authorities, usually civil doctors or members of the militarized Indian Medical Service (IMS), approached camp management as an exercise in sanitary discipline and medical surveillance. With disease control the chief priority, plague camps remained reasonably free from epidemic outbreaks, though they posed logistical and disciplinary challenges familiar from famine.

Printed under Professor W. J. Simpson's direction, the plan of Khana Junction detention camp in India circulated as a model for detaining plague suspects arrested at railway stations. Located in western Bengal on the main route to infected districts in Bombay, the camp was conveniently situated next to the railway inspection station. It was also close to a substantial water tank guarded by barbed wire to prevent fouling and subsequent outbreaks of cholera, dysentery, and other waterborne illnesses. The complex constituted three separate enclosures for some eight hundred inmates:

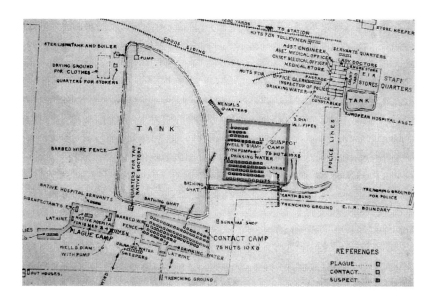

FIGURE 15.
The blueprint of Khana Junction Plague Detention Camp was circulated in Bombay as a model layout. It informed similar arrangements in South Africa once Simpson was seconded to Cape Town.[7] [Credit: MSA General Department (Plague), 1897, Vol, 69, Railway disinfection and detention camps.]

[7] Modern satellite imagery of the site is available at: https://www.google.ca/maps/place/Khana+Junction/@23.3159685,87.7768527,719m/data=!3m1!1e3!4m2!3m1!1s0x0:0x73da2cfd96f57677!6m1!1e1. Apart from the distinctive water tank, the camp has left little trace.

a hospital (or "plague camp") for those displaying actual symptoms; another "contact camp" for those suspected of having been in proximity to actual plague cases; and a third, much larger "suspect camp" for those in a generally "unsanitary state."

With the militarization of plague operations, it is unsurprising that segregation complexes—replete with watchtowers and guard-houses—sometimes resembled prisoner-of-war camps. In theory, each enclosure was hermetically sealed. "Segregation must be absolute," authorities in Bombay directed, and the "camp should be as self-contained and as self-supporting as possible."[99] Though illicit escapes sometimes occurred, "persons detained in quarantine [could] not leave camp without a written certificate from the Plague Authority," and "a Camp Inspector" kept "register[s] of all arrivals and departures" ensuring that "no person under observation leaves the camp."[100] As with famine, however, the Bombay Plague Committee

FIGURE 16.
Detention camp from the road, Poona, India. [Credit: © British Library, IOR/Photo 578/4, Lieut-Colonel John Lloyd Thomas Jones (Indian Medical Service) Collection, Album of miscellaneous views including the Plague Hospital at Poona, image 40.]

noted "difficulty. . . in preventing [inmates] from escaping at night" when there were "no walls or fences round the sheds, and the guard was not strong enough." Soon, however, "the fencing . . . was increased, and guards strengthened," and "every effort was made to reconcile the people to their short imprisonment."[101] Barbed wire was preferred for fences, though in some cases, as in the detention camp at Poona (above), hedges of prickly pear cactus demarcated camps as discrete disciplinary units.

Rituals of admission further delineated camp boundaries. Upon arrival, inmates underwent routine bathing and disinfection: a baptism into a sanitized and regulated environment, though carbolic acid substituted for holy water. Bathing and laundry facilities were at times rudimentary—a barrel and a hose—though some camps included state-of-the-art equipment like Equifax and Thresh disinfection chambers, which used pressurized superheated steam as a germicide. A regular cleaning routine continued inside the camp, where perchloride washed latrines and huts. In Bombay, the IMS officer J. S. Wilkins instructed a "special gang" to visit each camp "once a day . . . to disinfect all huts that had been vacated on the discharge of their occupants."[102] Encampment, it was hoped, would initiate inmates into a new life of cleanliness and order. However short, a sojourn in camp would offer healthy respite from "the hard work and unwholesome surroundings of a Bombay laborer."[103]

Apart from demarcating boundaries, British authorities closely regulated space and time within camps. Medical inspectors and superintendents, often borrowed from famine works, "went round the camp, morning, noon and night every day to see that everything was in order."[104] Meanwhile, the "Police Officer in command of the Camp guard . . . ascertain[ed] by inspection at 8am and 6pm that all inmates of the camp are present."[105] Sepoy gatekeepers proved ubiquitous in India, though personnel shortages sometimes necessitated the employment of low-ranking natives who were "giv[en] badges and allowances,"[106] a practice also common at famine camps, which "enlist[ed] a posse of quasi-constables" to enforce regulations.[107] In South Africa, meanwhile, the concurrent Anglo-Boer War taxed military resources, and regular colonial police performed the duties of camp guards. Assuming personnel were available, however, morning and evening roll calls complemented daily hut-to-hut inspections, further accentuating the intersections between medical and military policy. Such, at least, was the ideal. In practice, an article in the *British Medical Journal* complained, "intelligent and energetic supervision [was often] wanting."[108] And with the eventual relaxation of regulations in India, Wilkins lamented in 1901 that an inmate was practically "a free man . . . allowed to do exactly as he likes, as long as he comes back at night and sleeps there."[109]

Inmate populations varied according to the virulence of the epidemic. In Bombay, camps were closed and reassembled each year as new outbreaks occurred. Repurposed "huts, temporary sheds and other matting material formerly used for famine relief" afforded cheap mobile shelters,[110] which were easy to erect and dismantle, though corrugated iron prevailed at camps open during the monsoon. Tents were also common. Army-issued "bell tents" sheltered suspect families, while larger marquees "brigaded together" provided barrack accommodation.[111] In South Africa, meanwhile, Cape Colony's less verdant landscapes mandated tents rather than thatch and palm, though the Public Works director Lewis Mansergh later erected wood and iron barracks modeled after contemporary army accommodation—specifically, "military type 'A' and 'B' huts" that had proliferated across South Africa as a result of the upcountry war. In general, these shelters, while well ventilated, offered only rudimentary comforts, especially for women and children. Bedding was the inmates' responsibility, though local charities distributed blankets to those in "poor circumstances," and cots to the elderly.[112]

Segregation camps recycled existing disciplinary and industrial infrastructure as well. In Bombay, the camp at Kalyan was located on a military training ground, where two hundred huts accommodated five inmates each, while camps at Wari Bunder and Gokuldas Tejpal occupied existing hospitals.[113] In South Africa, meanwhile, Port Elizabeth camp was originally "an old convict station"[114] and in Cape Town, a disused lobster factory consisting of "two substantially brick-built warehouses, roofed with corrugated iron," served as a segregation camp.[115] Africans were usually accommodated in spartan canvas, but white townsmen were "anxious that every provision should be made" for the occasional European suspect.[116] In response, Lewis Mansergh erected spacious huts that conformed to metropolitan tenement regulations, and which provided for the privileged European more "pure [air] than in any building in England" for which such legislation was framed.[117] Not everyone was as fortunate, however: at a detention camp in Bombay an elderly Muslim woman, dying underneath a tree, was provided with no shelter but was "kept in the open air, on a mattress, the ground underneath which was all wet with rain."[118]

Racial and logistical considerations aside, overall camp comfort balanced a fine line between deterring travel and preventing escape. Financial considerations also loomed, though less so than in famine. The Bombay plague secretary directed that camps should be as "secure and as comfortable as possible for those detained," though others voiced concern that camps were becoming too "luxurious."[119] The collector of Satara C. B. Winchester argued, for example, that "it is better that persons who have passed through [camps] should not write to others 'all the arrangements are delightful and there is nothing [in detention] to prevent your following me' but rather that 'the Experience was most unpleasant and if you are a wise man you will stay where you are.'" It was therefore important, Surgeon-General Bainbridge concurred, that "camps should not be too comfortable."[120] Accordingly, camp rations, modeled on prison diets, offered only the merest subsistence, though with a pound of grain and six ounces of vegetables along with dhal and ghee, they were more generous than Richard Temple's notorious famine diet.[121] Moreover, inmates did not suffer the additional hardship of heavy labor: with standard quarantines of ten days, detention was too short for make-work projects to be feasible.

Just as camps marked preliminary divides between clean and unclean, they also reinforced social and racial distinctions. Portable bamboo screens compartmentalized the internal space of camps: "airtight" partitions, like those in East London, divided "the infected from the disinfected," but as W. J. Simpson pointed out, "special accommodation [was also] necessary for different classes."[122] Britons professed themselves aware that "many intricate questions relating to caste and race habits, food [and] religious scruples . . . require . . . careful treatment" when "dealing with Orientals."[123] When possible, suspects were detained in "different wards (males and females separately) . . . according to their . . . caste or community."[124] This was a practice initiated during famine, when Richard Temple recommended "the internal arrangement of [relief] camps" be adapted "as much as possible to the caste feelings and other social habits of the people."[125] Occasional high-caste Hindus complained that concentration placed them in proximity to untouchables. But at the very moment Viceroy Curzon was preparing to partition Bengal into Hindu and Muslim territories, camps proved effective at policing caste, class, and communal boundaries. They were thus compatible with British practices of "divide and rule."

The cultural preconceptions of Western sanitation often coincided with native views on the impurity of low-caste Hindus, and official communications instructed that special "care . . . be taken to separate their huts, their water, and their latrines from the rest of the camp." Meanwhile, provision of "special low-caste blocks" alongside "luxury" shelters and even separate "private camps" for wealthier rent-paying inmates of "superior civilization" reified caste distinctions, forging lasting legacies of communal division across South Asia.[126] Native philanthropists in large centers like Bombay also funded private hospitals and camps for separate Parsee, Muslim, and Hindu communities.[127] The appropriation of camps by native intermediaries did much to facilitate their proliferation across the subcontinent.

South African racial mentalities also demanded segregated camps. Separate wards, medical facilities, and bathing and dining spaces thus divided Europeans, "coloreds," and native Africans. "Location camps" or designated enclosures in larger compounds accommodated the latter, usually in tents rather than more comfortable huts. In Johannesburg, the Rand Plague Committee led by W. K. Tucker detained Africans and Indians at Klipsruit, eleven miles from the European town center. Meanwhile, the camp at Uitvlugt segregated Africans on the Cape Flats, billeting them in tents during the chilly rainy season. Public Works Director Lewis Mansergh arranged accommodation "so . . . that the Europeans are clearly separated from the Coloreds and Malays, not only practically but in such a manner as to obviate sentimental objections." Europeans (mostly "poor whites") were only a minority in camps, but they received twice the dining and kitchen facilities as the darker-skinned majority.[128] Such was the price of racial supremacy.

"TRANSPLANTED FROM CROWDED SLUMS": EVACUATION CAMPS

In both India and South Africa, plague segregation camps, with their attentive carceral architecture, were complemented by larger and less tightly regulated evacuation camps for inmates who were "cleansed" from select neighborhoods or else were "refugees" made homeless by sanitary clearances. Located on urban fringes, evacuation camps offered more liberal spaces of egress and ingress than segregation centers, permitting interaction with the social and economic life of nearby towns.[129] Wire or bamboo fences still demarcated them, but these camps imposed less formidable barriers: government-issued passes allowed inmates to travel outside for work, though inmates reported their movements and slept in designated huts. As developing suburban communities, moreover, evacuation camps erected schools, temples, churches, or mosques—rudimentary as they were, like the "prayer shed" at Byculla—as inmates stayed, unexpectedly, for months or even years following the destruction or condemnation of their homes. Many Bombay residents were "more or less permanently accommodated in . . . hutments in the North of the island,"[130] and over time they developed distinct camp economies. As in famine relief camps, merchants operated in allocated spaces to sell food and other goods, and while evacuation camps did not organize hard labor, they offered convenient sites for the recruitment of cheap workers by private corporations.

Nonetheless, by "transplanting people from the crowded slums of Bombay," evacuation camps afforded effective receptacles to control the colonial poor.[131] Camp masters, ideally trained European medical men but often native civil servants, resided in camp to oversee sanitary and disciplinary arrangements, while police patrolled "unruly sections" to keep "the hut population . . . under some supervision."[132] At Ebenezer Road in Cape Town, police arrested "inmates of the camp for creating a disturbance" or "using abusive and obscene language,"[133] while in Surat, India they "strictly prohibited . . . liquor and toddy shops in or near camps" following disturbances by "a dirty drunken set."[134] The same standard of supervision was not maintained everywhere, however. In many rural areas of South Asia, "control over the people was slight." "Camps" in these remote regions consisted of informal hutments erected by inmates themselves, who "were practically at liberty to scatter themselves over the country, and to carry plague about with them."[135] At a minimum, however, sanitary officials like S. J. Thomson marked out campsites in healthy locales.

The architecture and physical layout of evacuation centers facilitated medical policing as well as supervisory visits from sanitary inspectors and resident superintendents. The geometric lines at Dadar in Bombay's northern suburbs fostered a culture of discipline and surveillance hardly conceivable when inmates were "scattered in all directions."[136] Regular lines, with numbered streets and shelters, permit-

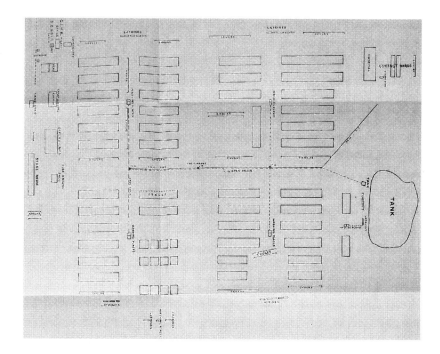

FIGURE 17.
Dadar Evacuation Camp, Bombay, 1898. The complex consisted of two separate camps accommodating 4,900 each. A military guard (1 havildar and 15 sepoys, 8th Bombay Infantry) was placed in charge, along with a camp master, a doctor, 14 subordinate inspectors and clerks, and 51 sweepers and sanitary laborers. [Credit: *Report of the Bombay Plague Committee* (Bombay: 'Times of India' Steam Press, 1898), 229.]

ted efficient inspection of the nine or ten thousand inmates. Camps also featured gas lamps and authorities experimented with electric lighting, which "enable[d] the night watchman to exercise more vigilance." Some considered such amenities a frivolous expense. But electricity carried the advantage, Lewis Mansergh concluded, of being "conducive to cleanliness on the part of the occupants of the camp." Further, they facilitated "the maintenance of order and discipline at night."[137] The mobilization of modern visual technologies thus secured scrutiny over the spaces and inhabitants of camps, facilitating surveillance and perhaps even promoting circumspection among inmates themselves. With camps, Britain replaced the dark and fetid alleys of South Asia and South Africa with the "bourgeois sensory environment" that municipal agencies had earlier brought to the rookeries of industrial

Manchester and London's East End.[138] As in Britain, the built environment would remake India's human materiel.

"EDUCATION IN THE MANAGEMENT OF VAST NUMBERS"

Plague and famine camps varied across time and space, but whatever their apparent function, they offered a general "education in the management of . . . vast numbers."[139] Regular inspections and bureaucratic centralization generated a "uniformity of procedure:"[140] architectural blueprints outlined a "usual design" for huts and hospitals,[141] while printed instructions "to be hung up in every Relief Camp Hospital" circulated guidelines for controlling epidemics.[142] The army had long experimented with orderly and hygienic camps for its troops,[143] especially after Florence Nightingale condemned cholera outbreaks in British barracks during the Crimean War.[144] As "sanitary enclaves," prisons and lock hospitals were also "exceptional sites of medical observation and control," David Arnold notes.[145] But by confining diseased and famished bodies on unprecedented scales—including large numbers of women and children supposedly less hygienic or disciplined than soldiers—plague and famine camps assembled important lessons in the management of concentrated humanity. In the process, inspectors synthesized broadly applicable guidelines—an "archive of experience"—that could be consulted in the future.

Above all, the health and well-being of inmates depended on a clean water supply—one, Thomas Holderness urged, that "must be kept pure at all costs."[146] Revenue officers in charge of famine relief often displayed a "laissez-faire" attitude toward matters of hygiene, but sanitary experts like S. J. Thomson outlined step-by-step procedures for guarding and disinfecting water sources and for assembling search parties to locate backup water supplies in case of sickness. Hospitals, in particular, were to have water supplies independent from the rest of camp, Thomson emphasized.[147] Such recommendations were then codified in government publications like "Hints for the Information and Guidance of those entrusted with the Management of Famine Camps" appended to Provincial Famine Codes.[148] Plague officials like James Cleghorn instructed similarly: "the best arrangements should be made for a plentiful supply of water to the different camps."[149] And vitally, it would have to be protected. Barbed-wire fences enclosing wells and tanks (a prominent feature at Simpson's plague camp in Khana) quickly became as important as fences demarcating camps themselves. "Guards [should be] mounted over every source of drinking water," Thomson continued, and "disinfection

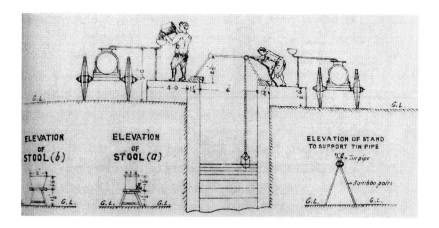

FIGURE 18.
Illustrated guidelines instructed designated "watermen" to draw water (after "wash[ing] [their] hands with . . . permanganate") using sterilized iron drums. Water was then funneled into a cart and delivered to enclosed "piaos" or watersheds, where pipes distributed it into inmates' vessels.[8] [Credit: "Water Supply for Famine Relief Camps: Plan Showing Arrangement at Wells." *Report on the Famine in the Central Provinces,* vol. III (Nagpur: Secretariat Press, 1901), 29.]

[8] *Report on the Famine in the Central Provinces,* vol. III, 21.

regularly practiced in every case where doubt as to the quality exists, even if no disease is present."[150] Chemical purification with permanganate of potassium and porcelain "Berkeland" filters gradually became common at both famine and plague camps, along with "a standard plan of water cart and water distributing appliances."[151] Should sickness break out, Thomson concluded, "foul wells [should be] absolutely closed."[152]

Protecting water supplies revolved around hygienic waste disposal, a subject upon which authorities exchanged long missives. For latrines, officials usually preferred the "trench system"—as opposed to the "bucket system"—and in a gesture to dignity (or to Victorian propriety) they provided inmates with grass privacy screens. Sanitary officials recommended "fenced paths" to purpose-built outhouses with attached washing and bathing facilities, but in practice, latrines remained haphazard, especially at famine camps located along shifting road, rail, and canal works. In such cases, Thomson recommended "a line of flags and posts" be "placed all round each relief work, and 300 yards from the same."[153] Sanitary assistants in "old red jackets, or other distinctive garments"[154] would enforce these boundaries and inmates "who do not ease themselves inside the boundary flags" would "at once be brought . . . for punishment."[155]

The threat of disease also generated debate concerning the position of camps. The "points requiring attention in the selection of a site for a relief camp" were "much the same as for a military encampment," Surgeon McNally noted in Madras, and arrangements at army barracks offered practical guides.[156] Drawing from military field manuals, Thomson, as sanitary commissioner in the North-Western Provinces, located camps in "healthy situations" and "broadside onto the prevailing wind."[157] Bombay's sanitary commissioner similarly advocated long huts "laid out in regular lines" and arranged in military echelon formation.[158] Like army cantonments, plague and famine camps were to be situated "distant from or windward of any likely sources of infectious disease" and preferably on high ground. With this in mind, W. J. Simpson erected Khana downwind from nearby settlements, and when such orientation was not possible, as at East London in South Africa, a "7ft galvanized corrugated iron" fence served to block wind from spreading airborne infection—a maneuver that reflected obsolete fixations with miasma, but which concealed unsightly camps from European townsfolk.[159]

Size also mattered. Recognizing the value of spatial concentration, Revenue officers recommended "large numbers" be "concentrated in as few centers as possible," and they complained when camps were "too scattered."[160] And yet, the "responsibilities involved in collecting large numbers of human beings into a limited area"—especially relating to health and hygiene—required limits on the numbers interned.[161] Less concerned with expense than with overcrowding and disease, Sanitary Commissioner Hewlett recommended streets 100 feet wide with 50-foot spaces between huts or tents, though Thomson felt a minimum of 30 feet was sufficient.[162] Following cholera outbreaks at large famine camps—where populations were normally "not under 4000 people"—authorities "reduce[d] numbers within manageable limits" by dividing larger concentrations into smaller units.[163] Plague regulations further underlined the pitfalls of aggregating "large numbers of [potential] plague cases in a limited area."[164] Cleghorn therefore confirmed that "camps should be greatly reduced in size,"[165] and Wilkins subsequently divided huge evacuation complexes like Dadar into more manageable blocks.

Smaller and less crowded camps were thus preferable from the perspective of health and hygiene. But economies of scale meant the "costs of guarding, cleaning and supplies" were excessive unless camps "accommodate[d] 5000 souls and upwards."[166] Though overcrowding could compromise control, others stressed that large camps were "more easily supervised" by the limited establishments available.[167] In formulating preferred dimensions, officials navigated between sanitary priorities and practical realities, striking compromise between the concentration conducive to economy and the open spaces necessary to prevent disease and overcrowding. Camps that took up "too much room" were a waste of public money, the Revenue Department feared.[168] Clear consensus was rarely achieved, but Famine Secretary Holderness settled on a maximum figure of five thousand as a "safe population." If camps were larger, he concluded, they should at least be subdivided into smaller sections "with a subordinate in charge as far as sanitary arrangements and [the] reporting of sickness are concerned." At the very least, medical assistants should have no more than 500–1000 inmates to supervise, he maintained.[169]

Growing experience facilitated greater planning. With "large numbers of distressed people . . . collected together," foresight was essential "if complete chaos was to be avoided," officials concurred.[170] "Regular streets . . . should be laid out in advance," the government publication "Notes on the Formation of a Famine Relief Camp" instructed, and if huts could not be ready, then "a supply of grass or matting" could be gathered in advance.[171] "In building a camp," the Bombay Sanitary Department continued, again with an eye on disease, "the first building erected should be quarters for the Medical Stores and Medical Officer and then the hospital buildings."[172] Thomson went further, noting "a spare hospital ahead of the one in use" should "be ready for an epidemic"[173] along with "segregation and observation huts" to quarantine suspects. Such arrangements were futile, he added, without the advance employment of hospital assistants and trained medical inspectors.[174]

Most importantly, plague and famine camps developed standard operating procedures to combat epidemic disease. Through trial and error, famine officers realized the importance of isolating infected populations. But the ascendency of sanitary experts like Thomson, Simpson, and Wilkins to positions of authority during plague enshrined medical arrangements as a chief priority. With fenced enclosures for contacts, "suspects," and those with actual symptoms, plague segregation camps refined medical quarantine to a science. Further, the Bombay Plague Committee determined, arriving inmates should "not be sent at once to the huts," but segregated "in a block specially reserved for all new comers."[175] Such guidelines met success: although medical detention did little to curb the pandemic itself, plague camps in Bombay were much healthier than their famine counterparts, recording an annual mortality of just 1.46 percent in 1899–1900.[176] When cholera or smallpox did break out, they were usually contained.

With frequent personnel transfers between plague and famine operations, famine camps benefited from a rich cross-fertilization of ideas. Increasingly, they erected their own quarantine wards: "all cases of infectious disease, or of dysentery and diarrhea, as well as cholera and smallpox should be segregated in separate shelters," a 1901 famine report instructed.[177] And "refugees from an infected camp arriving at a non-infected camp" were to be kept "separate for five days."[178] To this end, "a fence of thorn" quarantined emaciated wanderers arriving from plague-infected districts like Poona.[179] Conversely, J. S. Wilkins adapted famine camp procedures by erecting isolation sheds for smallpox and cholera at plague segregation camps. Apathy and administrative incapacity meant that many camps were chaotic and disease-ridden. But others, like a model famine relief camp at Sangogi, erected a "segregation camp" and imposed "quarantine against cholera" on all newcomers. Healthy and commodious, the "camp [was] well patrolled, water [was] well protected . . . [and] small-pox and cholera huts [were] satisfactory."[180] Increasingly, plague and famine camps resembled one another in their emphasis on disease control.

Finally, contingency plans developed for abandoning camps ravaged by disease. Whenever cholera, plague, or smallpox appeared, Thomson noted, it was crucial to enforce compulsory residence in segregated hospitals to prevent panicked inmates from spreading infection. But if disease continued, a controlled evacuation was necessary. Contagious disease hospitals (preferably constructed of grass huts) should be burned down and abandoned for new ones, Thomson directed. Infected plague huts, similarly, were to be "burnt at once" and the site disinfected and left unoccupied.[181] Further, the Bombay Famine Code instructed, if "more than three cases" of cholera occur, the entire camp "must be abandoned": inmates "must march, at right angles to the wind, to a fresh camp . . . prepared to leeward of the other camps."[182] To this end, prisons and army camps offered some precedent. Upon the outbreak of cholera, troops routinely vacated their barracks for tented camps, while prisoners in Agra jail found themselves "camping in the spacious and elegant gardens of the Taj Mahal and Akbar's mausoleum during [the] cholera outbreak of 1856."[183] Noting that plague was "judged and measured by what was known of cholera," Simpson reiterated that "fresh ground" must also be found for infected plague camps.[184] Meanwhile, areas of camps "polluted with excreta" were to be "disinfected with a solution of copper sulphate" and the site "pegged out and not used again for a month."[185] Last but not least, the "speedy . . . and careful disposal of the dead" in deep pits or supervised funeral pyres, and away from waterways or villages, was essential.[186]

"THE DIFFERENCE BETWEEN ORDER AND PANIC"

Officials like Thomson and Wilkins quickly realized that good sanitation among "unruly crowds" was inextricably linked to firm discipline. Though camps were not always the panoptic spaces imagined by Jeremy Bentham, they incorporated a broader set of techniques—the mustering, roll call, and inspection of inmates—associated with factories, prisons, and other penal institutions. The military, again, provided inspiration. Major C. D. Baynes, of the Madras Staff Corps, noted "the same principle which regulates the economy of a regiment appears to me applicable to any mass of men," with the first object being to arrange inmates "into conveniently sized parties for supervision and control."[187] Famine camps divided inmates, accordingly, into units or "gangs" analogous to military divisions. A model camp, in Vaughan Nash's description, was one where "huts are dug out and solidly thatched . . . gangs of workers know exactly what is the daily task and do it . . . orphans, clad in surprising jackets of yellow, are governed by five orphan corporals . . . and depots for the collection of the sick and starving are run with military precision."[188] Military continuities were also evident in the officials employed. The Poona district experimented with the complete militarization of operations by placing famine camps "as an experiment altogether in military hands."[189] Colonel Wilkins similarly militarized operations when he recruited Staff Corps officers like Captains Brackenbury and French to enforce discipline at Bombay plague camps. The Indian army thus offered a peripatetic reserve of manpower with growing expertise in camp management. Nash noted approvingly that "half a dozen cheery, competent soldiers in every camp . . . made all the difference between order and panic."[190]

As laboratories of colonial discipline, camps enacted alternating measures of compulsion and consent. The "state of exception" that generated camps fostered coercive tactics, but at times, the management of populations who lacked military discipline or obedience proved "a delicate" matter and one that called for "tact and temper."[191] Following riots and unrest, the Bombay plague department lauded the "great . . . courtesy of manner" that experienced Europeans claimed to profess.[192] Yet the economy of tact had limits, especially regarding sanitation. Though Britain ultimately retreated from the uncompromising measures that first fostered mandatory plague segregation, a coercive ethic still dominated the internal management of camps. Imagining themselves warriors in a contest between ignorance and science, officials doubled down with hardened conviction whenever they encountered "habits and customs . . . opposed to recognized sanitary principles." The abiding lesson, for S. J. Thomson, was that sanitary regulations should be enforced by persuasion when possible but "by force if necessary."[193] As Cleghorn concluded: inmates should be "compelled to wash if dirty" and "should be sent into hospital when ill [and] treated 'nolenas volentas' as modern science prescribes."[194]

Surveillance was also fundamental. "Evasive" and "untrustworthy," inmates were to be carefully watched. Roll calls were conducted morning and night, and doctors often had to "hunt about the camp . . . for patients and compel them" into fenced hospitals.[195] The camp itself should be constantly patrolled to ensure cleanliness and to detect the appearance of disease, Thomson directed, and inmates should "be regularly examined night and morning by a medical subordinate."[196] A printed list of "camp rules" at Ahmednagar confirmed: "all inmates . . . shall be examined by the camp hospital assistant every morning and evening."[197] Medicine, moreover, was to be the preserve of trained experts: access to camp hospitals, Thomson noted, must be strictly regulated to prevent "relatives of patients" from "swarm[ing] around."[198] Hygienic spaces of order and discipline would thus be carefully delineated from the dirty hordes outside. In this endeavor, police power underwrote medical authority. At Ahmednagar, "the Police Officer in charge of the camp guard" was to "ascertain by inspection at 8am and 6pm that all inmates of the [plague] camp are present,"[199] while Thomson appointed Police Superintendent C. E. W. Sands to enforce regulations in a camp at Haridwar.[200]

The control of concentrated inmates rested upon a parallel concentration of officials. Increasingly, famine codes and plague reports decreed that staff reside onsite in designated quarters, transforming camps into self-contained sanitary and disciplinary units. According to Famine Secretary and later Plague Commissioner Andrew Wingate, every camp "should be a complete center for relief, embracing hospital, feeding, nursing and working arrangements."[201] Simpson's model camp at Khana, for example, included separate onsite quarters for the superintendent and chief medical officers (ideally Europeans) and their assistants (usually natives), and for police constables and menial servants. And as camp procedures were formalized and bureaucratized, official conduct came under the scrutiny of senior inspectors who visited the camps. These included district collectors, sanitary commissioners like Thomson and Wilkins, and figures like Governor Richard Temple and Viceroy Curzon himself, who took special interest in plague and famine arrangements. Fences enclosed inmates, but they simultaneously demarcated cohesive units of management and control, with their own internal command structures.

Ultimately, "camp experts" concluded, effective discipline depended on the appointment of superintendents who exuded authority and "enforced on the inmates the necessity of carrying out sanitary rules."[202] Camps were less democracies than dictatorships, and by the end of the century, internal camp management—and the planning and construction of facilities—was concentrated in the hands of a single official. Provincial famine departments appointed "special civil officers" to conduct "the entire management of [famine] camps," including internal discipline, cleanliness, and sanitary arrangements; the provision of latrines, food, and fuel; and the "disposal of corpses."[203] Public Works engineers, however, supervised labor tasks on canal and road works. This system of "dual control" sometimes generated conflict, Benjamin Robertson recorded, but special civil officers' duties became clearer by the late 1890s. They assembled men for "digging trenches, cleaning camps," and performing the duties of "watchmen [and] well guards," and they presided over the "entire management of . . . arrangements connected with non-working children and adult dependents," mustering them "or feeding them as the case may be."[204] "Camp masters" at plague camps similarly emerged as central figures of internal discipline, though civil surgeons and sanitary commissioners monitored medical decisions. "Responsible European[s]" like Staff Corps officers (seconded in 1899–1901 from the Boxer Rebellion in China) were preferred superintendents,[205] though camps often had to settle for "Mamlatdars" (native officials in charge of district subdivisions) and a variety of clerks, schoolteachers, and police officers. Nonetheless, camp management emerged as a recognized skill, and one that was increasingly in demand.

"A STANDING INSTITUTION"

By the turn of the century, Britain consolidated the idea of the camp as a distinct technology with its own internal rules of management and anatomy. Famine codes and plague reports codified generic designs, and camps erected according to official templates became recognizable entities across South Asia and Southern Africa. And with bureaucracy and standardization came new forms of expertise. By 1900, on the eve of a twentieth century in which camps proliferated globally, there emerged a group of "camp experts" who had honed their skills in the disciplinary and sanitary management of plague and famine camps. Apart from numerous camp masters and special civil officers, these included prominent figures like W. J. Simpson, S. J. Thomson, J. S. Wilkins, T. W. Holderness, and James Cleghorn, who enforced a growing uniformity of design during traveling inspections. They would go on to advise future colonial regimes faced with the challenges of concentrated camps.

In reality, plague and famine camps varied greatly in layout and administration, but the challenges and pitfalls they posed fostered more general lessons in the "sanitary management called for by the concentration of large bodies of people."[206] Over the course of the 1890s, Thomas Holderness observed, the "supervising establishments became more expert" and officials "gained . . . experience in the management of large bodies" of men, women, and children.[207] Principles did not always align with practice. Inmates rebelled and at times epidemic disease threatened the very viability of civilian encampment. Ultimately, however, sanitary and disciplinary refinements served to vindicate well-managed, well-planned camps as legitimate venues for controlling displaced colonials.[208] As Vaughan Nash remarked, "if the . . . camp, in one shape or another, is to become a standing institution, as I fear it must be for a time, we shall have to scrutinize it well."[209] Thomson agreed, and with a growing air of confidence, he lauded the "extraordinary attention paid to sanitation" at camps across India. "Far from these congregations of people proving centers for disease," he added, "it was often found that disease originated in the villages."[210] At plague camps, especially, "crammed as they were with people from the most highly infected locations," inmates remained relatively healthy.[211] They enjoyed "pure air, sound treatment, and stimulating sustenance," Lord Curzon claimed,[212] and even critical observers like Nash exonerated model camps, conceding they "without doubt save[d] many lives."[213] None of this assured that future camps would be healthy or well run. It did mean, however, that camps, not yet discredited, would have a future in the twentieth century as instruments of liberal empire. War in South Africa, and the camps it generated, would soon put the lessons of plague and famine to the test.

CHAPTER 5 · Camps in a Time of War

*Civilian Concentration in Southern Africa,
1900–1901*

> I will make them a terror and an evil . . . I will *scat-
> ter* them. I will send war, famine and plague against
> them until they are destroyed from the land. (*Jeremiah*
> 24:9–10)

In the closing months of 1900, the inhabitants of southern Africa endured a great
and traumatic uprooting. War complemented hunger and disease in a triumvirate
of colonial catastrophe and as the context for a new system of camps. Recalling
scenes from India's great famines and from the plagues of biblical times, itinerant
droves of displaced Africans and Dutch-speaking Afrikaners (or Boers) wound their
way across a now-barren landscape. Starving and sickly, they were victims of Britain's latest colonial crisis: the Anglo-Boer or South African War (1899–1902). "At
most little stations one sees them," a sympathetic observer recorded,

> sitting, always the same, a little group of perhaps two old men, three women
> and three or four children, huddled on the platform or on a heap of sand with
> their "luggage" which is always the same, a tin box . . . a huge heap of
> perfectly filthy feather bedding, and an odd chair or old table, a pet goat or
> sheep, very starved.[1]

Displaced from their farms by "scorched-earth warfare," some followed a nomadic
existence, wandering destitute and emaciated across barren terrain. Fugitives in
mountains, caves, and reed-covered rivers, they desperately evaded the grasp of
British columns. Others congregated voluntarily in nearby towns seeking shelter in
churches, schools, and abandoned townhomes. Still others remained defiant, staying
on the veld or in burned-out farms until the British military collected and forcibly

FIGURE 19.

The collection, transportation, and concentration of civilians. For the first time, Britain pursued mass concentration against a "white" population. [Credit: "Burning the farm of a treacherous Burgher during the second Boer War," Louis Creswicke, *South Africa and the Transvaal War, vol. IV* (Edinburgh: T. C. & E. C. Jack, 1901), 128. Drawing by R. Caton Woodville, from a Sketch by Melton Prior.]

evacuated them. After long and arduous journeys, in wagons and open railcars, they found shelter in Britain's newest system of colonial camps.

At the juncture of modern warfare and modern humanitarianism, Britain's wartime "concentration camps" facilitated two separate but connected agendas: the coercive military concentration of scattered civilians and the care and control of these selfsame populations. Military historians often compare British policy with the Spanish general Valeriano Weyler's infamous pacification (or "reconcentration") campaign in Cuba (1896–97). The brutal efforts of Lords Roberts and Kitchener, Britain's commanding officers, to drive Boer and African civilians from the countryside and thus prevent them from aiding guerrilla fighters did indeed resemble earlier military actions.[2] But camps themselves (if not the policies that led to them) were more than instruments of security or antiguerrilla strategy: they were humanitarian reactions to the chaos and suffering of war. As implements of refuge and relief, Britain's wartime camps resembled earlier shelters in famine-and-plague-stricken India. They provided shelter, rations, and medical care to some quarter million white and black civilians.

Famine, plague, and wartime concentration camps were thus expressions of a shared culture of encampment spanning the British Empire. Henceforth the domain of nationalist South African historiographies, Boer War camps cannot be understood outside larger imperial trajectories. Fears about illusive guerrilla raids—and subsequent measures to "trap" an evasive population behind barbed wire—replicated similar dynamics witnessed in the policing of "criminal tribes" and earlier native insurgencies. By accommodating the displaced in camps, moreover, authorities drew from and contributed to existing traditions of colonial discipline and welfare. As with famine and disease, the tragedies of war facilitated the development of camps as economical exercises in social control and humanitarian relief. Though South African camps exhibited important differences from their counterparts in India—they concentrated populations of European ancestry in the context of an active rather than figurative war—structural similarities remain. Wartime concentration camps reflected analogous anxieties about colonial mobility, fiscal economy, and the control of mass populations cast simultaneously as destitute and dangerous. Like plague and famine camps, they embodied the repressive and humanitarian vagaries of the British Empire—the Jekyll and Hyde of Britain's fin-de-siècle imperial venture.

"THE WAR AGAINST THE FLEA"

Southern Africa was a prime economic and geopolitical prize. Located at the confluence of the Indian and Atlantic oceans, the British provinces of Cape Colony and Natal were crucial naval and commercial outposts. But the discovery of gold on the Witwatersrand in 1886 triggered a tectonic political and economic shift as British migrants flocked inland to the mines and fledgling industries of Johannesburg. Conflict over voting rights and access to resources animated relations with Afrikaners (or Boers), who had migrated inland in the 1840s during the fabled "Great Trek" to establish the independent South African Republic (or Transvaal) and Orange Free State. The result, in 1899, was war.[3] The goal, according to commentators like J. A. Hobson, an early critic of imperialism, was to bring mineral resources into the London-centered orbit of global capitalism.[4] High Commissioner Alfred Milner, however, articulated grander visions. For him, the war was a romantic contest between a modern, democratic, and industrial state (represented by its urban, English-speaking economic elite) and an uncivilized, illiberal republic of seminomadic cattle herders (represented by Boer ranchers inhabiting the veld).[5]

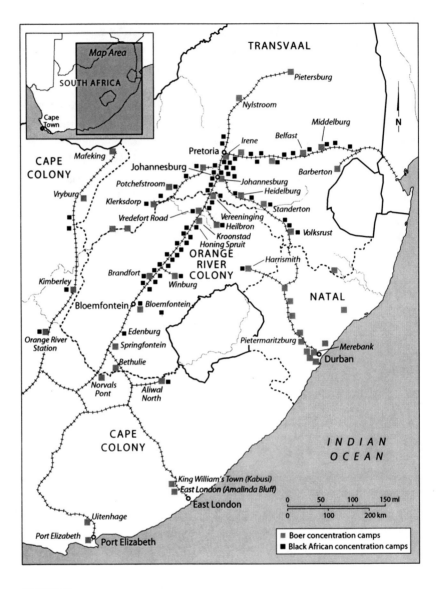

TRANSVAAL

Pietersburg

Nylstroom

Middelburg

Irene   Belfast
Pretoria ○

CAPE   Mafeking
COLONY   Barberton
        Johannesburg

        Potchefstroom   Johannesburg
Vryburg   Heidelburg
        Klerksdorp
                                            Standerton
        Vredefort Road   Vereeniging
                          Heilbron
                          Kroonstad   Volksrust
                          Honing Spruit
                          ORANGE
                          RIVER   Harrismith
Kimberley   Brandfort   COLONY
                          Winburg   NATAL

Bloemfontein ○ Bloemfontein

                Edenburg   Pietermaritzburg
Orange River   Springfontein   Merebank
Station   Durban
                Bethulie

        Norvals
        Pont   Aliwal
                North   INDIAN
                                          OCEAN
        CAPE
        COLONY

                            King William's Town (Kabusi)
                            East London (Amalinda Bluff)
                            East London   0   50   100   150 mi
                Uitenhage   0   100   200 km
Port Elizabeth
            Port Elizabeth   ▨ Boer concentration camps
                                        ■ Black African concentration camps

Map Area
SOUTH AFRICA
Cape
Town

N

FIGURE 20.

Map of South Africa. Camps mentioned in the text are labeled [Credit: Map by Bill
Nelson]

Whatever its causes, the culmination of nineteenth-century developments in military technology and political culture determined how the war was fought. Many expected an easy British triumph over the diminutive Boer Republics. But the conflict soon turned into a "national war": a contest not merely between governments and armies but between entire peoples. The same dynamic that generated a mass volunteer army in Britain and its settler colonies (abetted by 18,534 troops from India) also created an Afrikaner "nation in arms." Boer commandos were talented riders and riflemen, whose surprise, lightning raids confounded British soldiers. But their most potent resource was the civilians who harbored them: ideologically mobilized, and willing to sacrifice for the cause of independence. Britain was not fighting an army but a people.[6]

In its first phase, the war consisted of "regular" set piece battles fought for the control of towns and strategic points. After the famous relief of Mafeking and Ladysmith, Britain's commander-in-chief Lord Roberts captured the capitals of Bloemfontein and Pretoria and annexed the Boer Republics in May and October 1900. The streets of London celebrated "mission accomplished." But no clear delineation between war and peace existed on the battlefield. Roberts's march to Pretoria and Bloemfontein provided a definite territorial objective. "Like taking a queen at chess," the soldier-cum-writer Major Lisle Phillipps remarked, it was "rather a coup . . . to take the enemy's capital." And yet, he lamented, "I can't say it seems to make much difference. The Boers set no store by them apparently . . . and go on fighting after their loss just as if nothing had happened."[7] Divesting their cities of tactical significance, Boer commandos scattered across the open veld, where they pursued an insurgent guerrilla campaign that persisted until the signing of the Peace of Vereeniging on May 31, 1902.

In the latter, guerrilla phase of war, Boer forces pursued what the military theorist Robert Taber described as "the war of the flea."[8] With pinpointed strikes against telegraphs, rail transports, and supply depots, mounted guerrillas exacerbated the economic and political perseverance of their larger and more powerful enemy, slowly sucking the lifeblood of British occupation.[9] In this way, they established a conscious and strategic mode of resistance that would inspire future guerrilla fighters from Algeria to the Philippines. British troops, as the occupying power, suffered the "dog's disadvantage." There was "too much to defend [and] too small, ubiquitous and agile an enemy to come to grips with."[10] With the ability to strike and vanish before Britain could respond, guerrilla "fleas" proved a persistent irritant: a nagging pestilence that denied Roberts his desired victory.

The "true spirit" of the Boer nation, historian Thomas Pakenham writes, resided not in the city (where British interests dominated) but on "the illimitable veld."[11]

Immersed in vast and lonely expanses, British forces faced an enemy they could neither see nor confront. "Now we are fighting shadows," Major Phillipps remarked: "our columns march through the country and see no enemy," but "invisible eyes watch us all the time . . . we are teased and annoyed, but never definitely engaged."[12] Long before irrigation transformed South Africa with cultivated fields and rectilinear eucalyptus plantations, the "veld" presented a stark and barren landscape that filled British imaginations with illusion and mirage.[13] Technological advances, especially the use of smokeless gunpowder (which rendered "invisible . . . the man who uses it"[14]) contributed to British frustrations, while mounted Boer guerrillas, agile and ubiquitous, proved able to strike and retreat with astonishing rapidity. More than anything, British troops yearned for direct and visible confrontation; but an invisible "war of the flea" was all South Africa would yield. "This vagrant form of war is more formidable than it sounds," Phillipps warned: we "sit still waiting for an enemy who may be a hundred miles off or behind the next hill." But the enemy is "watching us . . . they are all round and about us like water round a ship, parting before our bows and reuniting round our stern."[15]

Many attributed Boer stealth to some mystic capacity for camouflage—a talent honed by centuries of "nomadic" life in the "dark continent." The Boers' uncanny capacity for deception (a trait they shared with Indian plague suspects) "worked upon the nerves" and kept British soldiers "under such a strain as no armies have ever suffered elsewhere or before."[16] Endowed with indigenous guile, the Boer commando was "a man of ambushes [and] the trickeries of war as formerly was the Sioux Indian," the German military expert Count Sternberg observed.[17] Lord Roberts certainly felt so, for he recruited as his chief scout a Minnesotan man (Frederick Burnham) who was raised on a Sioux Reserve. But in contrast to earlier foes, like American aboriginals and the tribal insurgents of India, Boer commandos were "armed with excellent firearms," and many of them "were educated and . . . led by men of knowledge and repute."[18] A chastened Winston Churchill, then a *Morning Post* correspondent, confirmed that Boer artillery was "inferior in numbers, but in nothing else, to ours." Suddenly, the young Churchill lamented, the "pom-pom" and the "15-pounder" were no longer guarantees of victory.[19]

The almost mythic figure of Christiaan de Wet, the esteemed Boer general, exemplified the cunning of the "flea." A master of evasion famed for his agility and craft, he displayed an unearthly ability to be at all or any place at once.[20] As the Colonial Office complained, "de Wet continues to be reported in six different places every day, places at impossible distances from one another."[21] Contrary to the assumptions of some military historians, the business of soldiering was never a

Nebelspalter.] [Zurich.

" Ah, whatever can I do to catch you ? I'd ike t·have you in my net,
indeed I would."

FIGURE 21.

Kitchener's wire net. Boer commandos like General de Wet often appeared to British soldiers as elusive tricksters with supernatural powers. Turning from magic to science, others compared them to "rays of Rontgen light, or the bodiless, unseen currents of the wireless telegraph."[9] [Credit: "Current History in Caricature," *Review of Reviews* 25, no. 148 (1902).]

[9] Ralph, *An American with Lord Roberts*, 28.

solely rational endeavor, and in the absence of direct and tangible confrontation, imaginations ran wild. Many confessed the "aching solitude" of the veld drove them "almost mad." Others "felt [they were] going out of [their] mind[s] with loneliness and lack of employment."[22] Depicted as elusive and ephemeral—imbued with magical powers to appear and disappear at will—de Wet epitomized wartime discourses that attributed Boer guerrillas with a transcendent and even magical omnipresence. Though commentators disparaged the Boers as primitive and unrefined, their escape from European decadence infused them, in British eyes, with rustic courage and the endurance of a martial race, replete with dexterous tracking and marksmanship skills.[23]

It remained unclear to British troops exactly who or where the enemy was. Insurgents' "instinctive" ability to hide from British view remained a constant concern.[24] It proved "almost impossible," Kitchener complained, "to surround or catch" them: the "country was so big" that insurgents could "always evade us and find a place of safety."[25] With daring and dramatic raids, Boer tactics resembled those of "criminal tribes" in India—and before they elicited terror and dread, Boer guerrillas evoked the same romantic interest as the dacoits and thugs. In other ways, they resembled plague suspects, who "infested" darkened alleys and hidden courtyards. Commando "fleas" could slip away into unseen quarters and unknown locales. The Boers had honed such vanishing acts "from primeval Asian wanderings," John Buchan, the prolific novelist and private secretary to High Commissioner Alfred Milner, believed. "Orientalized" as evasive and inscrutable, they were a lost tribe of Israel, he claimed.[26] "The Orient" thus provided a set of associations to describe and explain Britain's newest colony and the people that inhabited it.

"THE LAST OF THE GENTLEMEN'S WARS?"

As in previous episodes of encampment, legibility was a primary concern. Boer commandos replaced confrontation with camouflage as the new stratagem of war.[27] "The Boers are constantly found with swords at one moment and plough-shares the next," Under-Secretary of State Lord Onslow complained.[28] One day a civilian farmer, the next day the commando, still in civilian dress, would arm himself from a hidden weapons cache and leave his ranch for war. British officers imagined "each homestead [to be] a commissariat department and an arsenal."[29] Every farmhouse was "an intelligence agency and supply depot," Roberts's incoming replacement Lord Kitchener feared.[30] As commando "fleas" concealed themselves among civilians, a cloud of suspicion loomed over the population writ large—untrustworthy and evasive, and conceived as a collective threat. "Our columns are continually moving about trying to [capture] small bands of the enemy," Kitchener complained, "but the local support given the Boers enables them to evade our troops, and no decisive action is possible."[31] The population harboring guerrilla "fleas"—like the population harboring plague bacilli in India—became the principle target of operations.

To British generals, the Boers dissolved distinctions between soldier and civilian previously enshrined by the laws of war and civilization. As a result, British officers discursively criminalized Boer warfare and targeted a vastly expanded population as potential suspects. For Kitchener, Boer guerrillas were comparable to "Greek or Italian bandits."[32] They were "irregular and irresponsible" foes, Roberts complained.[33] Others recalled Britain's earlier campaign to round up "criminal tribes" in South Asia. Colonel Henry Rawlinson made the connection explicit when he declared: "this war is fast degenerating into the same kind of dacoit hunt we used to have in [India]."[34] Indeed, adjectives like "brigands," "dacoits," "marauders," "ruffians," "banditti," and "mobs of desperadoes"[35] populated British diaries. Such language reflected widespread convictions that the Boers' continued insurgency was unlawful and uncivilized: the act of terrorists rather than an honorable, uniformed army.

As earlier expectations of a "gentleman's war" dissolved, so too did respect for the Boers as a civilized foe. A white and respectable European diaspora discursively transformed into an untrustworthy and conniving colonial race. While British observers associated the Boers with superhuman abilities—including "supernatural" strength, "superior eyesight," and "mysterious" night vision[36]—they also dehumanized their enemy. In the language of social Darwinism, the Boers suggested a counterpoint to Western progress. Observing the war from Calcutta, Viceroy Curzon compared them to India's Eurasians: both were "treacherous" and "not to be trusted."[36] A "half caste race," as Rudyard Kipling called them, they embodied "the vices of both the black and white races."[38] Fought against "the lowest stock of European humanity"[39] and against an enemy tainted with a strong "infusion of the negro,"[40] the war was increasingly justified as a bid to populate South Africa with "a better type of European"—British and Dominion colonists who would retain "civilized" traits.[41]

Employing racial and evolutionary tropes, others considered Boers "nothing more nor less than a low type of the *genus homo*."[42] "There always appeared something intensely animal about these people," the military theorist and future luminary of the British Fascist Party Major-General J. F. C. Fuller proclaimed.[43] The more liberal-minded Alfred Milner agreed: commando "fleas" were a "low type of animal organism" that could "survive injuries, which would kill others of higher type outright."[44] Citing the "natural savagery" of upcountry Boers as justification for escalating violence against them, Kitchener similarly described the enemy as "uncivilized Afrikaner savages with only a thin white veneer."[45] More outspoken commentators even recommended that "verminous" Boers be "exterminated" with "the same ruthlessness that they slay a plague-infected rat."[46] Such rhetoric derived from yellow-press journalists or subaltern soldiers rather than senior military figures, but it demarcated an extreme against which the forced removal and concentration of Boer civilians seemed a mild and moderate alternative.

The discursive transformation of Boers from virile Anglo-Saxons to degenerate "organisms" reminds us of the flexibility of race as a category and the continued influence of the environment (rather than fixed biology) as a determining factor of racial ideology.[47] Early in the war, the Boers offered racially wholesome counterpoints to sickly volunteers from Britain's decadent industrial centers; but in the war's guerrilla phase, new anti-Boer perspectives dominated. "Primitive in the extreme," the Boers were a "dark race"—their skin blackened by dirt and the African sun. Sojourning on the "dark continent," they also inhabited the "dark ages."[48] They were a "medieval race oligarchy," Milner maintained; having left Europe before the Enlightenment, Boer culture was incompatible with "modern industrial society."[49] Their fighting consequently defied European "rationality." Though evasive and deceitful, Boers possessed inner instinct and natural ability. What they lacked was a fully developed human interiority. Mentally sluggish with "meagre imagination[s]," a dawn to the Boer was "only the beginning of the day," John Buchan wrote. And "a mellow veld sunset merely a sign to outspan."[50] Did Boers (any more than diseased and famished Indians) possess inner complexity? Depth of character? A soul? Such questions were open to debate among the military and civil authorities ultimately responsible for the development of wartime camps.

"METHODS OF BARBARISM"

Unable to capture or even confront roving commandos, Roberts and Kitchener turned instead to civilians suspected of harboring insurgents and providing them with material, logistical, and ideological support. These included male farmers, ranchers, and occasional urban burghers, but as in earlier operations against "criminal tribes," it also included women and children who bore the brunt of the war. It was "the women [who were] keeping up the war," Lord Kitchener complained, and they were "far more bitter than the men."[51] "Women are our principal enemies,"

Captain Applin concurred, for they prompted their men to action.[52] Some, rumor had it, even went on commando themselves.[53] Hardy and hostile, with sharp tongues and "uncompromising fighting conviction," the "unnatural" women of the veld suggested legitimate military targets.[54] So too did black Africans, many of whom remained loyal to Boer commandos as spies and scouts, assisting them "in many ways [and] at considerable risk."[55] If British troops could not catch or detain Christiaan de Wet and other guerrillas, they could at least target their wives, children, and African servants. Such was the genesis of collective punishment and "scorched-earth warfare": what Liberal Opposition leader Henry Campbell-Bannerman famously condemned as Britain's "methods of barbarism."

In April 1900, the British army started burning farms and destroying livestock and food supplies in regions "infested" with guerrilla "fleas."[56] In a "dirty war," "sanitary" measures would prove necessary. The goal was to cleanse the battlefield and deny commandos any safe haven, though in the event, civilian suffering likely only fortified Boer resolve. British violence was both punitive and performative: a demonstration of imperial might and a warning to Boer civilians of the consequences of aiding the insurgency. Early on, Roberts proclaimed his "intention to conduct this war with as little injury as possible to peaceable inhabitants and to private property."[57] But innocence was quickly lost. "Unless the people are generally made to suffer for the misdeeds of those in arms against us," he later maintained, "the war will never end."[58] The violence thus recalled Roberts's campaigns on India's North-West Frontier, where he razed Afghan villages in exemplary fashion. The burning of farms and destruction of villages also replicated scorched-earth tactics in Cape Colony's frontier wars against the Xhosa in the 1840s. Vengeance against colonial populations was longstanding. But the Anglo-Boer conflict offered an important rupture in the history of war, and one that presaged a future of total conflict in Europe itself: this was an early application of colonial methods to a putatively "European" people. Britain's discursive racialization of the enemy facilitated the pivot.[59]

As in plague and famine, emergency measures depended on a ready suspension of legal norms. Whatever the ethical objections to British practices, martial law sanctioned Roberts and Kitchener to unleash "all possible means" to end the war. The "general delegation of authority," a Colonial Office memo asserted, "empower[ed] any officer to do anything," and in Roberts's opinion, martial law did not set limits on military power. Rather, it consecrated the "will of the General who commands the army." In effect, Roberts concluded, it "meant no law at all."[60] This was a "state of exception" that endowed British soldiers with even greater powers than the emergency legislation of plague and famine.[61]

FIGURE 22.

British troops burned houses in India's "war against plague" (above) and as part of a guerrilla counterinsurgency in South Africa (below). In both cases, inhabitants were evacuated to camps. [Credit: © British Library, IOR/Photo 578/4(61), Lieut-Colonel John Lloyd Thomas Jones (Indian Medical Service) Collection, "Burning a badly-infected quarter"; War Museum of the Boer Republics, OM01673, "Scorched Earth."]

In the absence of legislative checks, civilians faced escalating outbreaks of collective violence. In October 1900, Lieutenant-General Hunter "burnt many farms and supplies . . . on account of occupants harboring the enemy and withholding information from us." Turning from rural districts to urban areas, Hunter razed the entire town of Bothaville sparing only the church,[62] while the "whole neighborhood . . . [of] Ventersburg town" was "denuded of supplies to prevent the enemy coming there again."[63] Frankfort was similarly destroyed and evacuated block by block: "not a roof nor a stick of wood [was] left in it,"[64] a Society of Friends observer reported. "We have to aim at the Boers where they are most vulnerable," Kitchener proclaimed: "their farms must be burnt down, [and] their wives and children separated from the men."[65] The scorched-earth clearances were more dramatic and less discriminate than those conducted by flying columns in the *chawls* of Bombay. As in plague, however, operations were preemptive in nature. "I do not gather that any special reason or cause is alleged or proved against the farms burnt," Major Phillipps confided, but "we find that one reason or other generally covers pretty nearly every farm we come to, and so to save trouble we burn the lot without inquiry."[66] Farms were burned not because they harbored guerrilla "fleas" but because they were *suspected* of doing so.

Some targets of British operations *had* harbored guerrillas or provided logistical support. But as Heibelberg's district commissioner confirmed, many victims were guiltless farmers who "did nothing to aid the raiders."[67] But as the line between terrorists and partisan warriors grew thin, Britain's army claimed a monopoly not only of violence but of legitimacy: "however severe on individuals," the military insisted, "we should be justified in taking any measures which . . . would put an end to the continued useless loss of life."[68] The ends justified the means: Boers would be saved in spite of themselves. In an early illustration of that animating paradox of modern war, violence was justified in the name of bringing peace.[69]

"A CHESS BOARD TO MATE DE WET"

To British minds, the Boers' guerrilla tactics mirrored their seemingly primeval "production of space."[70] In contrast to British outposts in Cape Colony, Boer settlements presented "none of the usual signs of a neighbourhood: no visible roads lead to [them]," Major Phillipps remarked, "no fertile and cultivated land surrounds [them]; no trees or parks or pleasure grounds are near [them]." Rather, the "barren, treeless veld" carried "these little unexpected towns on its breast with the same ease and unconsciousness that the sea carries its fleets of ships; surrounding and lapping at their very hulls" but "not changed itself nor influenced by their presence."[71] For the British writer Olive Schreiner, whose novel High Commissioner Milner read on his first voyage to South Africa, the Boers built "neither walls nor established cities" but "dwelt in . . . huge canvas-sailed wagons," which they "pilot[ed] . . . across infinite expanses of sand and rock."[72] "Half savage" and with "gypsy blood in their veins," John Buchan added, the Boers possessed an "undying vagabondage behind all their sleepy contentment." Like "any gipsy [sic]," he continued, the Boer "was a wanderer from his birth" and "trekking . . . was an incident of his common life."[73] The trope of the wandering Boer provoked familiar and deep-seated anxieties about scattered and itinerant populations. Ultimately, these cultural discourses would intersect with military efforts to rationalize colonial space and concentrate evasive "wanderers" at fixed and legible sites.

In contrast to images of the country as primeval and unsettled, pro-Boer advocates countered that Afrikaners had "from a desert . . . made . . . a prosperous agricultural state" connected with "telegraphs and railways" that offered "proof of a high order of civilization."[74] The landscape itself was thus a text that yielded multiple, competing interpretations. But as war lingered, the Boers conjured images of lawlessness and sedition. Whether in South Asia or South Africa, a nomadic existence "was the very embodiment of barbarity,"[75] and in the conflict's latter stages, Kitchener's troops associated the mobility and craft of enemy guerrillas with their "rootless" and "uncultivated" lifestyle. Like their counterparts in plague and famine, the Boers were not the first "transient" or supposedly "nomadic" people to be concentrated in camps—and they emphatically were not the last.[76]

Unable to locate evasive guerrillas, Kitchener turned, instead, to the physical environment. Hoping to bring symmetry to an asymmetric war, his forces pursued an ambitious project to "striate" the open veld on a macro scale. In essence, the goal was to impose Euclidean order onto a trackless "nomadic space," rendering it navigable to the forces of a modern state.[77] Combining methodical and impersonal forms of violence with geographic precision—an inclination honed in his youth by mapping colonial terrain as a military surveyor in Palestine[78]—Kitchener carved the battlefield into a matrix of fortified lookout posts—or "blockhouses"—connected with barbed wire. As in earlier episodes of encampment, Britain mapped and patrolled geometric units in an effort to gain leverage over an "illusive" and "inscrutable" population. But in contrast to the Indian famine's "circle patrols," Kitchener opted for squares. Like a "chess-board designed to mate De Wet" (the words are intelligence officer Lionel James's[79]) the system offered a spatial adaptation of the imperial mantra "divide and rule," parceling the veld into regular grids and clearing the way for "the gradual and systematic occupation of district after district of the Orange River Colony and Transvaal."[80]

Kitchener's methods helped establish a new optics over the battlefield. Designed to maximize panoptic surveillance, blockhouses provided British troops with a new visual (ad)vantage. Concrete anchors amid a seemingly fluid environment, they presented a linear system of orientation that reasserted the primacy of fixed points. As punctuation marks delineating a previously illegible terrain, Kitchener's block-houses "reproduced" South African space and reoriented the British soldier. Mean-while, barbed-wire fences linking each blockhouse functioned as cages that trapped a population imbued with animalistic qualities. "Like wild animals," Kitchener commented, the Boers "have to be got into enclosures before they can be cap-tured."[81] The system offered a massive barbed-wire dragnet to catch commando "fleas," as flying columns searched each grid systematically for guerrillas and their suspected supporters. It was like catching "flies in a spider's web," the *Times*'s offi-cial historian and future colonial and Indian secretary Leo Amery put it.[82] Playing with hunting and trapping metaphors, Kitchener even recorded his "weekly bag" of captured Boers. Like a sieve panning for a previously undetectable enemy, or like a "giant mechanical scraper,"[83] Kitchener hoped to "comb out" commando "fleas" and evacuate the population that supported them. Discursively stripped of their humanity, "herds," "flocks," "swarms," and "droves" were enclosed by wire and removed en masse in long marches and open cattle trucks.[84]

With Kitchener's promotion to commander-in-chief in November 1900, the violence, once exemplary, became standard and bureaucratic. To soldiers desensi-tized by many months on the veld, farm burning and forced evictions became routine. And the comfort of general staff headquarters—a venue that facilitated escalating twentieth-century violence—insulated those framing policy from its graphic human costs. Never known for human empathy—Kitchener's favored companion was a tame starling that he kept in a cage[85]—Britain's new commander-in-chief spent more time in an office than he did on the battlefield. And with cold calculation, his troops devastated South Africa. Hoping to starve commandos out, flying columns cleared the landscape, blockhouse-grid by blockhouse-grid, of crops and livestock, most of which were slaughtered, though some were interned in "cat-tle concentration camps."[86] Men captured with arms were sent overseas to POW camps in Bermuda, Ceylon, St. Helena, and India, where Viceroy Curzon, experi-enced with plague segregation and famine relief camps, turned to a new type of internment.[87] Meanwhile, British troops forcibly concentrated women and children in towns and eventually corralled them into suburban camps: "all Boers without exception are targets," Kitchener proclaimed.[88] Included, also, were black Africans, who retained the ability, willingly or otherwise, to support commandos. Kitchener called for the destruction of all African huts and ordered "all natives excepting those found in the Native Reserves" to be removed.[89] Black or white, militants or pacifists, all were caught in sweeping drives. A suspect collectivity rather than individuals guilty or innocent of any formal charge, the inhabitants of the veld, like the colonial poor in India, were treated as a dangerous and indiscriminate mass.

The ultimate goal was to evacuate civilians from the countryside and concentrate them in urban centers. By denuding the country of "everything moveable,"[90] Britain directed its campaign against an entire environment and network of movement. Like Britain's "war against plague"—which also employed "flying columns" to search block-by-block for suspects—military search parties applied the familiar spatial techniques of evacuation and segregation. By removing an amorphous civilian base widely suspected of furnishing insurgents with supplies and intelligence, Kitchener endeavored to "sterilize" the country by denying guerrilla "fleas" the sustenance upon which they "parasitically" depended.[91] Once again, medical and military metaphors intertwined. In Alfred Milner's epidemiological language, the military brought the "guerrilla bands at present *infesting* the country" into gradual submission by placing sympathetic civilians into "quarantine."[92]

"NOTHING BUT FAMINE LIES BEFORE US"

Under Lord Roberts, scorched-earth tactics destroyed more than five hundred homes, rendering thousands destitute and homeless. But a developing refugee crisis worsened under Kitchener, who indiscriminately razed thirty thousand farms and displaced a quarter million civilians. The new commander-in-chief epitomized the grand designs of a colonial power intent on realigning the world (and South Africa in particular) according to the dictates of its own administration. Bolstered by a pre–World War faith in British fiscal and military might, Kitchener expressed a self-assured mastery over nature and a supreme faith in human (or rather British) agency in transforming the colonial world according to a universal rationality. New cultures of military professionalism along with the rise of modern administration—the products of a Victorian "revolution in government"[93]—produced a willingness and capacity to take responsibility for organizing places and peoples on a macro scale.[94] In the process, however, Kitchener's forces created widespread conditions of famine and destitution, replacing a military predicament with a humanitarian catastrophe.

British visions of South Africa as barren and uncultivated betrayed a self-fulfilling prophecy. "Nothing living was left in the country," Kitchener boasted after a year of scorched-earth warfare, and he celebrated the fact that farm burning would "make de Wet pass through a desert."[95] A career of colonial warfare had left the commander-in-chief desensitized to violence and uninterested in its social consequences. "You will not conquer these people until you have starved them out," he maintained.[96] A year later, Alfred Milner also described South Africa as "a desert," readily conceding "the main object of military operations [was] to make it so."[97] Afrikaner statesman Jan Christiaan Smuts was more vivid when he lamented "green and . . . cultivated fields, gardens, and charming houses and farmsteads" transformed into tracts of "withered, barren waste." By the early months of 1901, "all the fields [had] been destroyed" and "the trees of the gardens cut down or pulled up by the roots."[98] Ordinary people experienced the trauma through biblical allusion: displaced from an Edenic paradise, they were afflicted with "war, famine, and disease."[99]

As farmers witnessed the destruction of their crops and livestock, famine loomed large across Britain's newest colonies. Driven from her burned-out farm, where British troops seized seven thousand sheaves of oats, and forced to wander the veld, Mrs. Van den Berg observed her family reduced to "skin and bone—fast shriveling away." Many would starve and die, she feared.[100] Food was also "very scarce" for Mrs. Nienaber, one of the "poorest inhabitants" of Frankfort. After British forces ransacked her farm and requisitioned her vegetable crop, she experienced real famine—when her baby was born "she was so starved that she had fainting fits one after another."[101] Many infants would die, and for Mrs. Vorster, "the pale faces of the starving innocent children" were "too much to dwell upon."[102] For those familiar with emaciated wanderers in famished India, Boer and African civilians must have been a familiar sight.

Echoing the voices of Boer women, the British humanitarian critic Emily Hobhouse warned that "famine hung over the country like a threatening cloud."[103] She was not alone. Milner feared "scarcity and in fact famine . . . [was] inevitable,"[104] while H. G. J. de Lotbinière, an officer and future camp administrator with personal experience in famine-struck India, concurred that with the "country . . . being laid waste . . . there must be a famine in the future if the war continued."[105] The land was "dead and silent, absolutely without life as far as the eye could reach," Hobhouse declared. "No work was going on in the fields," and the land was littered with the "bleached bones" and "carcasses of horses, mules, and cattle."[106] And with a railway heavily employed by military convoys, food could not easily be transported from the coast. In sum, Hobhouse concluded, "nothing but famine lies before us."[107]

Their homes destroyed, their crops seized, and their farms in ashes, many had little choice but to rely on charity. Displaced families with friends and relatives in Cape Colony or Natal sought refuge there, while the privileged traveled overseas to Europe and the Americas. Some even found refuge in India, perhaps to be closer to their husbands or sons in overseas POW camps. Here, the Bombay government complained that refugees from the Transvaal could hardly "be allowed to roam about the streets in Bombay with no ostensible means of subsistence," but neither could they "be supported . . . for an indefinite time at the public expense." Some could rely on private funds, but for others there was "no other way of saving them from starvation" short of sending them, the government warned, "to some famine relief work."[108]

The exodus of refugees ended as travel restrictions, fueled in part by fears of an Afrikaner rebellion in British Cape Colony, prohibited further travel to the coast.[109] Trapped in the interior, the majority of Africans and Afrikaners, helpless and poor, were "obliged to walk for miles in order to seek food [and] shelter."[110] Many were "very poor and needy," the Quaker philanthropist Joshua Rowntree wrote: "weary, sad, grave" and with "a look of destitution imprinted on faces and clothing alike."[111] The Bezuidenhout family occupied stables, barns, outhouses, and other makeshift shelters.[112] Others, the future Pietermaritzburg inmate Elizabeth Neethling lamented, were "left like wild beasts on the veld."[113] In essence, however, Kitchener's tactics amounted to a form of forced urbanization, and the majority left their devastated farms to seek refuge in nearby towns, either on their own accord, or else swept up in British convoys. Here they crowded together in destitute conditions, overburdening existing poor relief mechanisms and causing conflict with long-term (and often pro-British) town dwellers.

In garrison towns, British soldiers distributed rations in hopes of corralling civilians away from roving commandos, while in other cases local philanthropic organizations, often run by Afrikaner notables or the remnants of Boer Republican governments, distributed aid. But there was rarely enough to go around. And with Kitchener's mass clearances, a trickle became a flood. Enfeebled by destitution and in a condition of "squalor and emaciation,"[114] refugees "literally poured in" to centers like Middelburg, which offered "the dumping ground," authorities observed, "of [flying] columns operating all over the Eastern Transvaal."[115] Cities like Bloemfontein swelled to more than twice their peacetime population, leading to severe overcrowding, while tiny Aliwal North, with only eight hundred inhabitants, had to provide for an influx of over two thousand.

Many crowded into private homes previously occupied by British settlers who had fled to Cape Colony upon the outbreak of hostilities. But with a dire housing shortage (compounded by the requisition of the best homes by British officers) others slept rough in the streets or camped at the railway station begging passing soldiers for cloth to cover them. In Potchefstroom and Brandfort, the displaced found shelter in empty hotels, schools, and other buildings, while in Winburg they herded together in an unfinished church. In Johannesburg, many inhabited damp tenements while others occupied the stables and grandstands of the Turffontein racecourse—the future nucleus of a camp.[116] Some appropriated preexisting disciplinary institutions when they found shelter in a vacant jailhouse in Nylstroom or in abandoned Witwatersrand mining compounds at Robinson and Village Deep. At Irene, they lived in wagons on the banks of the Apies River, while in Belfast refugees pitched tents in the public square.[117] Reflecting existing geographies of racial segregation, meanwhile, black Africans congregated in outlying reserves and overcrowded native locations, though others clustered around British army camps desperate for food and work or found their way into cities and towns alongside their Boer counterparts.[118]

Just as racial discourses and dehumanizing rhetoric animated scorched-earth warfare, the colonies' new district commissioners (usually British military officers) in charge of war-torn towns made sense of destitution and disarray through recourse to late-Victorian social and racial terminology. Using coded sanitary language that associated cleanliness with purity and civilization, authorities in occupied towns routinely described congregating Boers as a "dirty, careless, lazy lot," whose sanitary habits were "a disgrace to any European nation."[119] Their wagons and homemade laagers were "models of disorder and usually extremely dirty," the consulting army surgeon Kendal Franks lamented.[120] They "regard all the world a latrine,"[121] another doctor complained, and they were "dirty beyond description." Lacking soap, running water, and basic hygienic amenities, "the majority [had] not had a bath for years," and to the disgust of Mafeking's medical officer, they emitted "filthy secretions" from their noses and eyes.[122]

Dirt, once again, did potent symbolic work, casting wartime refugees as abject colonials rather than proud Europeans. In a period when writers like the Salvation Army general William Booth could "Africanize" the "tribes of savages" living in the "jungles" of east London,[123] the blackened skin of Boer refugees—which required "turpentine . . . to loosen the outer crust of dirt"[124]—further undermined their status as "civilized" Europeans. Congregations of destitute peasants presented "matter out of place," to evoke the anthropologist Mary Douglas's famous cultural definition of "dirt."[125] Sanitary references also meshed with moral and gendered discourse. "Cleanliness [for refugees was] very far removed from Godliness,"[126] Franks observed, and prurient observers derided Boer morals for being "about as clean as their skin."[127] On the ladder of civilization, meanwhile, militaristic refugee women did not conform to domestic British ideals of cleanliness and propriety. Victorian gender norms, feminist historians have pointed out, were themselves markers of racial fitness and civilizational achievement.[128] Moreover, the conviction that many refugees were politically hostile militants in disguise made them doubly undesirable. An ambiguous population—victims and villains, civilized and savage, European and African—they were in special "need of ordering."[129]

As war worsened, refugees endured squalor comparable to Bombay *chawls*. Having recently witnessed plague and famine operations, Lord Hamilton, the secretary of state for India, feared the Boers' "dirty habits" made them especially "liable to epidemics."[130] To many in South Africa, refugees resembled unhygienic Indian coolies in Natal as well as "raw natives" who crowded into rapidly urbanizing British towns like Pietermaritzburg and Port Elizabeth before the war. "Ignorant of town life" and with "indecent habits," they spread "disease, crime and poverty," town dwellers feared.[131] Displaced Africans offered loathsome specters of contagion— part and parcel with South Africa's "sanitation syndrome"[132]—but so did rural Boers who occupied dwellings fit only for "kaffirs or pigs."[133] The refugees carried "diseases of every description,"[134] British observers declared, and their "rooted objection to personal cleanliness"[135] evoked the moral vocabulary of plague operations. At Winburg, refugees brought dysentery and typhoid, and observers warned that "famine fever would break out" and it would be "very contagious."[136] Authorities in prewar Natal and Cape Colony towns evicted unsavory populations to the "regular rows or streets" of segregated suburban locations.[137] A comparable fate awaited wartime refugees, who were destined for camps.

The kindred language of class also influenced British decision makers. As a Colonial Office memo noted, Boer refugees drew natural comparisons with the "dangerous classes" of London slums, who themselves were cast as insurgent forces. Those evacuated from farms were "as a rule, not any better than the mass of our poorer classes," Secretary Chamberlain proclaimed,[138] and most existed "in a very poverty stricken condition."[139] The Quaker observer Allan Rowntree concurred, albeit more sympathetically: "no doubt many of the poor people are dirty and ignorant, but so are thousands of the dwellers of our own country, as has been shown by recent researches conducted by Charles Booth and Seebohm Rowntree."[140] While British social investigators "discovered" poverty in late Victorian Britain and conceived it as a social and moral problem, refugees seemed to embody the many ills of an unhealthy urban life once relocated to towns. The "squalor and dirt" of overcrowded refugee shelters, Kendal Franks maintained, "would equal, if not surpass, some of the residences of the poor in the British Isles, such as Whitechapel and St. Giles."[141]

Smug statements aside, dirt and destitution were less the timeless traits of savagery than the *results* of Britain's "methods of barbarism." Some of the farmsteads British soldiers destroyed (and often looted) contained fine china, libraries, pianos, and other accouterments of prosperity—a point emphasized in pro-Boer accounts, which offered (less influential) counterimages of Afrikaner society as settled, civilized, and respectably middle class.[142] Victims of scorched-earth warfare often had less than twenty minutes to pack their belongings before witnessing their livelihoods lapped in flames. The Van Vuuren family, for example, received a nighttime knock on their door to be told they had only five minutes to evacuate, while another Boer woman noted that "when she tried to save some of her children's clothing, the soldiers threw these back into the flames."[143] The "hitherto wealthy" Mrs. Terblanche likewise complained her family was given twenty minutes to evacuate; another woman, "fine and intelligent-looking," rode in "uncovered cattle trucks littered with stable manure" in a "terrible journey" to Maritzburg.[144] Other middle-class Afrikaners like Mrs. de Kock noted her family was reduced, as a result of the war, to a "mass of suffering humanity."[145]

At the same time, however, many displaced Afrikaners, not to mention their African counterparts, formed an impoverished underclass before the war began. For the majority, wartime dislocation augmented preexisting indigence, transforming rural poverty into urban destitution. Localized crop failures, cattle plague, and locusts swept southern Africa in the years preceding war. A major drought, a local iteration of a globally connected series of environmental disasters, hit in 1896–97, and while resulting dearth did not rival devastation in famine-struck India, conditions were "the most severe in living memory."[146] On the eve of war, the independent Boer Republics thus spent a third of their budgets on poor relief.[147] As Hermann Giliomee has argued, the development of South Africa's "poor white" population was a product of agricultural disaster and population expansion in the 1890s. Deepening poverty continued into the twentieth century as landless "poor whites" and their black African counterparts were squeezed out of an industrializing economy or else transformed into ill-treated laborers.[148] Pauperized by war, Africans and "poor whites" were also victims of longer-term processes of modernization and industrialization that ultimately created what the Boer general and future South African prime minister Jan Christiaan Smuts described as a "dangerous class."[149]

"THE FIRST REFUGEE CONCENTRATED CAMPS"

Though chaotic and impoverished, British-occupied towns in which refugees sought shelter were formidable technologies of war. Surrounded by barbed-wire fences and patrolled by sentries under martial law, they facilitated surveillance and spatial control.[150] As the British commentator Lucy Deane noted, "one [was] hedged about with an elaborate system of 'passes,'" and even trusted British residents required "a 'permit' if . . . out of doors after 9pm, and a 'pass' to go outside the town." The whole country, she continued, was "concentrated apparently along the single Railway-line" and surrounded by "millions and billions of miles of barbed wire."[151] The famous pro-Boer reformer Emily Hobhouse confirmed that refugees in Bloemfontein were "more or less prisoners" who could not "move without passes." Everything was censored, she continued, "spies abound, [and] barbed wire and picquets surround the town."[152]

By channeling rural communities into garrisoned towns—the home ground of British power and the strategic and political centers of a nascent colonial government—Kitchener successfully segregated civilians from roving commandos, denying guerrillas the continued sustenance and support upon which they depended.[153] As they did in previous and subsequent counterinsurgencies, fortified towns facilitated the basic military function of immobilizing suspect civilians and placing them under surveillance. Military success, in other words, did not depend on the organization of camps themselves, and as John Boje points out, scorched-earth warfare had displaced civilians and concentrated them in towns for a full nine months before the first camps were formed.[154] But if the concentration of civilians in urban centers fulfilled Kitchener's essential military objectives, why did Britain take the further step of accommodating concentrated refugees in demarcated campsites? The answer revolves less around the practices of military counterinsurgency than in the politics of humanitarian relief.

Britain approached governance in southern Africa as it did in India: with a fiscal restraint that minimized expenditure on the welfare of suspect colonials. Decades of laissez-faire ideology and stern responses to famine had enshrined such attitudes. Thus, when Colonial Secretary Joseph Chamberlain expressed anxiety about the prevailing "state of scarcity" caused by Kitchener's farm burning and the "real need . . . to prevent famine,"[155] High Commissioner Milner emphasized the grave dangers of "pauperization." It was "highly undesirable to maintain even [the] pacific section of people in idleness," he maintained.[156] Such attitudes intersected with famine relief policies in India, though "poor whites" in pre-war South Africa also had access to settler-colonial welfare arrangements. Only a few years previously, in 1896–97, for example, Cape Colony's British administration had established interim relief works when faced with drought and "cattle plague." In sites "sufficiently concentrated for supervision," Lewis Mansergh's Public Works Department distributed subsistence wages in return for heavy labor—a policy that diverged from the more generous gratuitous charity delivered in the Boer Republics.[157] A "lazy, dirty crowd of so-called men"—mostly unemployed Afrikaners, Italians, and Jews—were thereby domiciled in disused army tents on the Cape Flats, where they labored on road and railway projects.[158]

Now that war had pushed existing social distress to a crisis point, previous experiments in temporary poor relief provided inspiration. Drawing from local and imperial traditions, High Commissioner Milner proposed housing destitute refugees at public relief works where they could labor in return for subsistence rations. "Good opportunity is afforded by the unfinished railways in the Orange River Colony," he continued: earthworks were already in progress and completion of the line would "facilitate policing of [a] troublesome country and be econom[ic] in that way." Such proposals ran into practical difficulties, however. In a state of active war, the military failed to secure ample extramural worksites to make the relief scheme feasible.[159] Yet as Kitchener's columns "dumped down . . . all sorts and conditions of people," social unrest intensified in overcrowded towns. Local authorities were pushed to "their wits' end" trying to maintain order and provide "the barest necessities of life."[160] In modified form, Milner's relief works proposal would be realized in a system of suburban camps, which offered less scope for labor on public works but afforded greater security and logistical infrastructure due to their suburban location.

Among the first recommendations to erect a system of purpose-built camps to confine, shelter, and feed displaced and distressed refugees came from two lesser-known officers in August 1900: Colonel Alfred Edwards and Major Harold Sykes. As district commissioners charged with maintaining order among civilians, these officers were closest to the problems of urban destitution. Though military men, their task, Gert van den Berg notes, was a "purely civic one" and the "main problem" they faced "was the lack of food for the townsfolk." To these officers devolved the almost impossible task of billeting and rationing displaced civilians amid the upheavals of war. In Potchefstroom, Edwards reported a state "bordering on starvation,"[161] and with women looting stores at night, the town was descending into chaos.[162] Riots also threatened in Johannesburg and Heilbron, where food supplies ran out and British authorities were forced to feed the "families of men fighting against us."[163] Having spent much of his career in India, Edwards probably witnessed famine and its ubiquitous camps firsthand. He was also exposed to vivid scenes of civilian suffering at Mafeking a few months previously, where Lord Baden-Powell had erected tents to shelter homeless women and children caught in a seven-month siege.[164] Such arrangements—part of a broader colonial culture of confinement and relief—likely influenced his eventual recommendation to house displaced refugees in formal campsites.

Like his Indian forerunners, Edwards faced the task of disciplining and relieving displaced populations, both desperate and untrustworthy, on a mass and impersonal scale. Camps would accordingly control displaced and suspect populations while enforcing medical and sanitary surveillance and providing rations and shelter in an economic fashion. If British spokesmen animalized the enemy by demarcating a "herd," they invoked pastoral "protection" as the camps' primary motive. The animating goal, for Milner, was to "afford places of refuge . . . to which [civilians] may take themselves [and] their families" for protection and relief.[165] Despite his humanitarian logic, however, Edwards' anti-Boer sentiments "tended toward extremes." While he petitioned the imperial relief officer in Pretoria to ration families loyal to Britain, he was less sympathetic toward enemy civilians, and his "attitudes and actions" were often "harsh."[166] His subordinate Sykes, who claimed to have "arranged the first of the refugee concentrated camps"—a verbal amalgam that reflected the ambiguous nature of these institutions—articulated similar attitudes. In the camps, he noted, the great bulk of inmates, who were "strangers . . . to sanitary regulations," were "better off . . . than ever they were in their lives." But he casually dismissed the "distasteful . . . restrictions" of camp life by noting the "treachery of the women on the farms."[167] Such mindsets encapsulate the Janus-faced nature of camps and account for the frequent interchange of the terms "concentration camp" and "refugee camp" throughout the conflict.[168] As instruments of both military control and humanitarian relief they embodied a double edge of coercion and care characteristic of liberal empire.

Despite the efforts of Edwards and Sykes, it was not until September 1900, when the more influential Lieutenant-General Kelly-Kenny advocated a similar scheme of "refuge camps," as he called them, that the system received official sanction. The Irish Kelly-Kenny, whose family were active proponents of social reform and famine relief in Ireland, was previously assistant adjutant general of Aldershot, Britain's army camp par excellence and the institution through which some hundred thousand British soldiers mobilized on the outbreak of war. It is hardly surprising, then, that the first concentration camps, with their bugle calls and serried rows of bell and

FIGURE 23.

In theory, camps were laid out with "military precision" and every tent "ha[d] its distinguishing letters and numbers." As in India, wartime camps were technologies of legibility—levers to gain knowledge over a new subject population.[10] [Credit: "Barberton Burgher Camp," British Library of Economics and Political Science, Streatfeild/Deane Papers 2/15, Photographs of the Concentration Camps.]

[10] NASA VAB SRC 320, Requisition for sanitary buckets.

marquee tents, resembled army camps accommodating British troops as well as POW camps then in formation in Cape Colony, India, and elsewhere. Despite the military influence, however, Kelly-Kenny insisted that inmates were "not to be prisoners," though they had to "comply with our disciplinary and sanitary orders." At the two camps he proposed in Kroonstad and Bloemfontein, the focus was on "protection and not punishment."[169]

Matters progressed rapidly from here and by March 1901, a network of some forty camps proliferated on the outskirts of inundated towns. Like plague detention centers, the railway offered a central spine to concentrate what one commentator described as the "invertebrate, semi-nomad communities" of the veld.[170] In September 1900, almost a year after the first farm burnings, Roberts prematurely declared the first "refugee camp" in Bloemfontein "a great success."[171] But the formation of camps was an incremental exercise and the main task still awaited: to centralize relief within demarcated boundaries and thus replace haphazard—and far from adequate—public and private charitable efforts with British system and oversight. As Kitchener's forces drove more and more civilians from their farms, this was a process that continued for the next two years.

"ALL PEOPLE WHO WANT RELIEF
SHOULD LIVE IN CAMP"

Whatever their military provenance, wartime camps operated according to long-standing Victorian and imperial principles of social and sanitary control. Fears about evasion and deceit framed policies on the battlefield, but they also extended to social relations in wartorn towns. Milner complained that "a large number of [refugees] . . . were drawing Government supplies by means of misrepresentation."[172] Before camps were in full operation, "many persons [at Kroonstad had likewise] been in receipt of Government rations . . . who have not been entitled to receive them," and "very little discretion ha[d] been formerly exercised in the placing of these people on the ration list."[173] In Orange River Colony, authorities added, refugees preferred "getting all [they] can at Government expense," and would misrepresent themselves in order to receive handouts.[174]

Suspicion was especially directed at "disloyal philanthropic societies" run by local Afrikaner townswomen, as well as supposedly "indiscriminate" relief efforts in the early months of 1900 conducted by outgoing Boer governments.[175] Reciting a traditional mistrust of "native agency," incoming civil authorities depicted the Boers as idle, improvident, and politically impertinent, while complaining that refugees actively defrauded the government. Afrikaner-led relief committees active before camps were fully organized did "far more harm than good"[176] they complained, and the "comforts served out did not go round further than the friends and relations of the committee."[177] One has to be "constantly on the look out for malingerers," civil officials continued, noting refugees had feigned having diarrhea, "evidently [as] a dodge for obtaining a more favoured kind of milk."[178] Another observer warned that refugees "swindle us right and left," lamenting the "hopeless difficulty of finding out genuine cases of want." Soldiers on the veld were not the only ones beset by questions of "legibility." In Johannesburg, for instance, authorities alleged that supposedly destitute refugees begged for clothing in order to sell it for profit.[179] And in a wartime setting, the distribution of relief presented a security threat. Milner noted that without methodical oversight, humanitarian "assistance [might] in some shape or other reach guerrillas and thus prolong the marauding which is the cause of the present destitution."[180]

To the many challenges of wartime destitution, camps offered mechanisms of discriminate, rationalized relief. While Kitchener's web of blockhouses brought clarity to an amorphous landscape, the demarcation of official camps facilitated the social and spatial control of those congregating in towns and cities. The relocation of refugees from crowded and dirty towns to suburban camps was also cast as a health and hygiene measure. The "great deal of sickness" reported in Johannesburg "amongst refugees living in private houses" underscored demands for the "immediate removal of all these people to [camps] where they [would] come under proper sanitary and medical control."[181] Surveillance was another motive. Vredefort Road officials complained that "many refugees who receive rations . . . [were] scattered all around,"[182] and in Heilbron refugees were dispersed throughout the town "adding greatly to the labor of administration" as officials struggled to "supervis[e] the numerous residences."[183] The beleaguered resident magistrate A. G. H. Daller likewise complained that nine hundred refugees in Kroonstad were "practically uncontrolled." In response to scattered disorder, camps "centralize[d] administration, secure[ed] uniformity and . . . possibly save[d] some expense."[184] Such was the logic of concentration.

Looming above all was the colonial exchequer's account book. No less than previously, camps emerged from entrenched anxieties about the "demoralizing effect" of indiscriminate charity. Parallel to Indian famine relief, a primary task was to confine assistance to the truly destitute while denying those with means (some of whom had salvaged reserves of cash before their evacuation). Officials like Alfred Milner searched accordingly for ways to "exclude those . . . [who] were not indigents."[185] Like famine relief works, only the desperate would submit to the vexations of camp life, he believed, while those with means would prefer to reside in town. Consistent with contemporary beliefs that favored limited expenditure on colonial welfare, concentrating relief "in one spot, instead of being scattered about," facilitated "more economical supervision."[186] Such attitudes were changing, partly due to controversy engendered by "starvation diets" and "barbed-wire deterrence" at Indian famine camps. Until Britain's wartime camps engendered their own scandals, however, Milner maintained his "only concern" was "to keep our total expenditure as low as possible."[187]

To this end, officials concentrated relief within demarcated zones according to well-worn workhouse principles. At Kroonstad, "all people who want relief should live in camp," Deputy Administrator Goold-Adams demanded. Refugees who could "well afford to supply themselves with food" were thus denied rations and, with the exception of noted troublemakers, were allowed to live in town. In March 1901, Britain discontinued all relief in Bloemfontein and most other centers, ordering "every person who is unable to support himself [sic] . . . to [a] Refugee Camp."[188] At Pietersburg, "people who were living in town" were moved to camp in June 1901, while in Johannesburg, those who refused to move from town to camp were denied relief accordingly.[189] The superintendent at Standerton likewise confirmed "it would be much better if all Refugees drawing Rations . . . were compelled to live in Camp." As an analog to "residence tests" at Indian famine camps—albeit more haphazard and informal—the policy provided a crude but effective means of restricting relief. As a result, superintendents reported "a considerable diminution in the numbers of those drawing Rations," and a concomitant saving of expense.[190] Once resident in camp, refugees "received prompt relief according to their requirements," and according to Standerton's superintendent, a once disorderly crowd "appear[ed] now quite settled down to camp life."[191] Such was the ideal, if not the reality.

While Kitchener's blockhouse-and-barbed-wire grids functioned as nets, camps filtered those in genuine need from those who could support themselves, and in many centers, "a majority [took] themselves off relief so as to avoid being sent to [the] . . . camps."[192] Security concerns and an impetus to detain rootless populations remained. The provost marshal confined political agitators in camps or prisons under martial law. And yet, the desire to economize at times conflicted with the mandates of control. Many preferred to live in "wretched" and "miserable sheds" in town rather than live in camp,[193] while others voluntarily removed themselves from government ration lists to "evade a closer observation of their actions."[194] At times, the rationalization of relief undercut disciplinary agendas, leaving potentially dangerous agitators free to leave camp. But the decision to permit refugees ineligible for relief to reside in town at their own expense reflects the degree to which camps operated as humanitarian depots and implements of fiscal discipline rather than military technologies alone.

Camps, in sum, were not essential components of Kitchener's military campaign. Rather, they were humanitarian afterthoughts that addressed familiar problems of social control and emergency relief. They only developed when the humanitarian plight—and social and sanitary dangers—posed by refugees congregating in towns became impossible to ignore.[195] War was thus a necessary but not sufficient cause. Like their plague and famine counterparts, camps emerged from prominent cultural attitudes towards the displaced and distressed.

"UNKNOWN IN THE HISTORY OF WAR"?

Britain's "methods of barbarism" registered the totalizing tendencies of war and the discursive denigration of an enemy people. Contemporaries like the Boer general Louis Botha condemned the forced displacement of "helpless and innocent women and children" as a tactic "unknown in the history of civilized warfare."[196] Yet from a military standpoint, Kitchener's tactics were not entirely new. The London evening daily *St. James Gazette* noted Kitchener had merely adopted "the policy of General Valeriano Weyler's 'reconcentration order'" whereby Spanish forces detained Cuba's rural population in a comparable guerrilla context.[197] In the Philippines, American troops under General J. F. Bell likewise experimented with "concentration zones" to detach insurgents from the surrounding population, a campaign that drew inspiration from British and Spanish precedents and from "Indian reservations" on the American frontier.[198] The concentration of civilians thus emerged, at the turn of the century, as a common counterinsurgency tactic, and one that anticipated twentieth-century antiguerrilla actions in Malaya, Kenya, and Vietnam.[199]

But whatever the similarities between Kitchener and Weyler's tactics, British commentators condemned "reconcentration" in Cuba as an expression of Spanish inhumanity. London newspapers sensationally decried the death of 150,000 Cubans, who were forced to erect ad hoc shelters in overcrowded cities, where they perished from malnutrition and disease. But while the South African campaign was just as ruthless, British policy can be distinguished by the subsequent accommodation of forcibly concentrated populations in suburban campsites, which provided emergency rations and shelter in a systematic and economic fashion. British spokesmen represented their camps—audaciously given the circumstances—as acts of humanity that brought women and children under protection and gentlemanly oversight. For British proponents, if not for Afrikaner and African inmates, the provision of camp shelter added a "liberal" guise to counterinsurgency: a putatively humane alternative to the heinous neglect of General Weyler, who simply left Cuban peasants to suffer in overcrowded towns. As War Secretary St. John Brodrick contended, camps represented "the first time in the history of war that . . . one belligerent should make himself responsible for the maintenance of the women and children of the other."[200]

If they were unknown in the history of war, however, camps were already established features of emergency governance in the British Empire. Like their counterparts in plague and famine, wartime concentration camps emerged from deeply held convictions about poverty and poor relief, political economy, sanitation and disease, and the control and classification of mobile and inscrutable populations. At a moment when Britain's "humanitarian zeal" approached the status of "a surrogate religion,"[201] British apologists alluded to "moral decency" and "lawful obligations" to cast the "herding" of refugees into camps as the "humane thing to do."[202] Without the camps, many would "probably have starved" government spokesmen maintained.[203] At the same time, however, familiar problems—exposure, malnutrition, and epidemic diseases—killed inmates by the thousands. For anyone versed in Indian history, the tragedy and scandal that ensued in the months after encampment triggered a shameful sense of déjà vu.

CHAPTER 6 · "Only Matched in Times of
Famine and Plague"

Life and Death in the Concentration Camps

The success and failure of Boer War concentration camps hinged, Alfred Milner
recounted, on the "misfortune [of] . . . trying to combine two contradictory and
incompatible policies: those of "war and peace."[1] The ambiguous nature of the
camps reflected their diverse inmate population, their varied nature over time, and
the extent to which British officialdom was itself a divided entity. In many cases,
efforts to alleviate wartime distress conflicted with the military's ambitions to inflict
it. These tensions mapped onto more general indeterminacies concerning the nature
of wartime camps: Were they to be militarized detention centers or humanitarian
depots? Were their inmates "uncivilized Afrikaner savages" or respectable and
reclaimable Europeans? And were camps tools of conquest or a means to "win the
peace" by introducing to a conquered race the virtues of "British compassion"?

Developed in response to a humanitarian crisis, wartime camps posed many of
the challenges of Indian plague and famine: distributing relief, minimizing expense,
enforcing discipline, and maintaining health among a "mass of suffering humanity."
At the same time, however, South Africa's distinct cultural milieu differentiated Boer
War camps from their Indian forerunners. While British observers denigrated Boer
refugees as degenerate Europeans, they nonetheless distinguished them from Indian
natives and black Africans, who were eventually segregated in a separate system of
camps. In South Africa, meanwhile, local models of settler-colonial welfare and
institutions like mining compounds and public works accommodation inflected
the management of wartime camps, as did military installations. Finally, security

concerns generated a sharper emphasis on political subversion in Boer camps, which concentrated ostensibly neutral and even loyal "refugees"—the "harmless" victims of war—alongside political "undesirables" with evident anti-British sentiments.[2]

"All the world is brought together in the camp," the colonial education minister E. B. Sargant observed,[3] and over the next two years, camps classified a previously inscrutable population, filtering loyal from irreconcilable, white from black, and the deserving from those underserving of relief. Though many assumed the war would only last a few months, lingering hostilities (and resulting camps) permitted more lasting efforts at social engineering. As emergency control in the early months gave way to professional oversight, officials inculcated inmates with British "habits of mind," thereby transforming Afrikaners into "industrious partners" in a modern white South Africa, while consigning black Africans to subservient lives as unskilled laborers. In this, too, Boer camps stood apart. Though Indian famine camps occasionally introduced "healthy youngsters" to "schooling or training of some kind," Indians were marked, especially after the 1857 Rebellion, by an essential colonial difference.[4] The divergent imperial priorities of South Africa (a future white Dominion) and South Asia helped render Boer War concentration camps technologies of inner transformation.

What South Africa's many and diverse inmates did share with their counterparts in India, however, was a tragic and enduring experience with death and disease. Although poor sanitation among refugees congregating in towns offered initial impetus to remove them to camps, substandard planning and official apathy resulted in measles outbreaks and waterborne illnesses like typhoid and dysentery. As in India, camps in South Africa became notorious centers of disease that killed many thousands. And yet, the horrors of modern war bore a dialectical relation to the birth of modern humanitarianism. Ensuing controversy surrounding the camps energized a coherent and lasting tradition of antiwar (and anticamp) activism that offered an early articulation of the destructive nature of modern war. In response to a growing scandal about camp mortality rates, critics like the famed humanitarian Emily Hobhouse echoed the protests of inmates themselves to question, once again, the humanity of concentrating civilians in camps.

"DEALING WITH LARGE BODIES OF MEN"

Whatever its battlefield triumphs, the military proved unequal to the task of caring for destitute refugees. Though accustomed to their own life in barracks, soldiers were inexperienced managing civilians, including large numbers of women and children. Kitchener, for one, was singularly uninterested in administering camps, noting that civil authorities had more time at their disposal and were "better adapted" to "look after . . . arrangements for the comfort of the inmates." "The maintenance of the civilian population," he continued, bore "no reference to military operations," and the camps themselves had "nothing to do with [the] actual prosecution" of war.[5] Having created the displacement and destitution that first generated camps, Kitchener quickly absolved the military of responsibility for managing what he considered to be depots of emergency relief; he delegated matters, instead, to civil authorities.

Among their first actions, the nascent civil governments of Britain's newly annexed colonies launched official bureaucratic departments in February and March 1901, bringing to camp administration official oversight and centralized command. In Bloemfontein, A. G. Trollope became chief superintendent of Orange River Colony camps; his counterpart in Transvaal was W. K. Tucker, a man already active in municipal politics who later gained prominence as the mayor of Johannesburg. Though relatively low ranking, both officials boasted experience "dealing with large bodies of men."[6] As a young officer in India Trollope personally observed famine camps in operation,[7] while Tucker started his career managing enclosed mining compounds on the Rand (and later organized the Klipspruit plague segregation camp).[8] Meanwhile, a variety of subordinate officials adopted similar duties as special civil officers at Indian famine camps. The government favored "mine managers" as ideal superintendents,[9] though some medical officers like Dr. McCulloch at Vryburg had credentials organizing Cape Colony plague camps.[10] Others, however, were architects, merchants, and accountants with little camp experience.

Most superintendents were "thoroughly British in sentiment and . . . by birth," but unlike their counterparts in India, they boasted "an intimate acquaintance with the manners, customs, habits and language of the Boers."[11] Often, however, they lacked organizational acumen. As men presiding over populations dominated by women and children, they articulated a chivalrous language of paternal care. But in the critical words of Emily Hobhouse, they lacked the "womanly resource" necessary to establish comfortable accommodation.[12] At Norvals Pont, Cole Bowen, a superintendent with "marked administrative powers," was "firm, just and kind."[13] But G. F. Esselen at Irene, though "weakly amiable," had "no authority" or "force of character."[14] Others were frequently drunk, suffered from paranoid delusions or were caught molesting female inmates.[15] More troublesome still was the politically suspect Superintendent Wagner at Heilbron, who adorned his office "with portraits of all the leading politicians, generals and traitors of the Boer party." "Nothing more mischievous . . . [or] more calculated to inflame the ill-feeling of the Refugees could be imagined," Trollope complained, and he quickly dismissed him.[16] In the face of limited human and fiscal resources, meanwhile, inmates themselves worked as hospital orderlies, dispensers, and clerks. Echoing familiar concerns about "native agency," prejudice in favor of British administration was evident: according to one report, "want of order in discipline prevails amongst the [Boer] subordinates in camp to a marked degree."[17] As in India, however, camps suffered from—but were necessitated by—a shortage of dependable personnel.

"THE PHYSIOLOGICAL MINIMUM"

For officials and refugees alike, food and shelter were pressing concerns. Until huts could be erected, the army provided used "bell tents" and larger "marquees" for camp hospitals, though "eastern pattern tents," imported from the Indian Ordinance—and sometimes manufactured, incidentally, at "criminal tribe" settlements in South Asia[18]—were more comfortable in hot weather.[19] Rations, likewise, came from army supplies until civil authorities issued their own tenders. Apologists argued rations were "ample to support life" and permitted prudent refugees to "save up . . . supplies for a rainy day."[20] For inmates, however, memories of leaky tents and enduring hunger highlight British shortcomings.

Many entering camps were already suffering from famine and disease. For them, rations were insufficient to maintain health and many deteriorated physically. Logistical challenges were partly to blame. With the surrounding country scorched to ashes, a single rail line, vulnerable to guerrilla raids, was the camps' only lifeline. But whatever the very real challenges of supply, hunger was a function of familiar ideologies. Economy framed the management of camps, which were themselves designed to save expense by confining relief to the truly destitute. In tones that echoed Richard Temple in Bombay, Milner instructed superintendents to observe "the strictest economy."[21] Basic comforts ("strict economy must be exercised in issuing soap";[22] "boys should go barefoot to save expense"[23]) were sacrificed accordingly. In terms of food, likewise, the government directed: "economy is as essential in the management of your camp as the welfare of your charges."[24]

Diets consisted of "mealie meal," a coarse local maize, though in contrast to Indians and black Africans, Boer inmates received tinned and sometimes fresh meat. The more fortunate supplemented their rations with vegetables, vitamins, and other food purchased with wages earned through camp labor.[25] In Standerton and Heidelburg, a dissenting major-general went so far as to supplement rations (against orders) with army supplies; his Irish background made him "keenly attuned to injustice" and he condemned feeding arrangements as "terribly parsimonious."[26] Inmates likewise complained the diet "bears hard on the poor man with no money of his own."[27] Medical inspector Dr. Hime expressed early reservations that rations failed "even [to] supply the physiological minimum of nutriment necessary for the maintenance of health."[28] In statements reminiscent of Dr. Cornish's protests in Madras, meanwhile, J. S. Haldane, a nutritional expert with experience monitoring troop diets at Aldershot,[29] feared rations were "so entirely inadequate" that without extra supplements, "death from sheer starvation (uncomplicated by disease) would probably result within a few months." Mistrusting this analysis, the Colonial Office commissioned a second opinion from Dr. Sidney Martin, a physiologist with expertise in "famine diseases" like typhus and typhoid fever, who only confirmed "the ration might be considered a starvation one."[30] Ration scales increased incrementally over the course of 1901, and soup kitchens opened for children. But the meat—often rotten or full of bone—was hard to cook without stoves or fuel, and sugar was "very impure," prompting menacing rumors that officials had laced it with glass.[31] Many agreed with the Pietermaritzburg inmate Elizabeth Neethling: "for paupers or criminals this might do, but for delicate women and children accustomed to wholesome abundance" the rations were simply "cruel."[32]

Apart from their essentially humane function, rations also fostered discipline. Early distinctions between "A" and "B" rations—which prescribed punitive diets for those with relatives on commando or who did not follow camp regulations— echoed "penal minimums" at Indian famine camps. According to Haldane's calculations, adults on "A" rations received 1,939 calories, while the "B" scale provided only 1,747 calories out of a recommended 2,900.[33] Both rations included meat as well as bread, and were more plentiful than the notorious Temple wage in India, which provided only one pound—approximately 1,500 calories—of grain. Controversial "B" rations were eventually discontinued, but penal diets remained important disciplinary devices for "the idler" and as punishment for dirtiness.[34]

"A CAGE FOR SINGING BIRDS"

As camps organized the destitute and distributed relief, so too did they classify inmates according to perceived security threats. Refugee relief was the primary impetus, but camps nonetheless reflected a wartime ethos of punishment and suspicion. "Our line has been that [the camps] are not penal," War Secretary Brodrick maintained,[35] and Trollope confirmed "these camps are not meant to be prisons."[36] Yet many concurred with Inspector Gostling that "one could get . . . more done by fear than by kindness."[37] Arrangements at plague and famine camps attest that humanitarian motives did not preclude the development of repressive architectures. But war endowed the camps with extra disciplinary layers. As spatial technologies, camps facilitated larger efforts to detain suspects and control the flow of information and supplies. Though the majority were innocent victims, the prevailing belief that inmates were complicit in a partisan war framed their subsequent treatment.

Concentration camps were not the sites of terror and extermination that foreign (and later nationalist Afrikaner) propaganda made them out to be. Many retained open boundaries with adjacent towns: the camp at Vereeniging, for example, was "not enclosed in any way by a barbed-wire or other fence."[38] And when authorities did turn to "double fence[s] of barbed wire," it was ostensibly to "protect" the camp from commando raids as much as to prevent escape.[39] Trollope himself was "averse to having fences with barbed wire,"[40] noting that when "camp limits are defined by conspicuous beacons" rather than fences "there is much less trouble in dealing with the people."[41] Nonetheless, barbed wire rightfully emerged as a symbol of the camps. In areas of active guerrilla resistance officials were "most anxious [for] camp[s to] be enclosed by barbed-wire fencing with entanglements."[42] And while trusted inmates received permits to visit nearby towns, those who proved a "truculent lot"—"more or less uncivilised, ignorant, and bitter"—were "practically prisoners confined inside a barbed-wire fence."[43] In the words of a Vredefort Road inmate, "our camp was a real prison. There were entanglements all around it, and fences and sentries were placed at the entrances."[44]

The camps were important venues of espionage and surveillance, and intelligence agents operating within them identified potential sources of subversion. Regulations prohibited "undesirable behavior," including the singing of patriotic songs, gathering in large meetings, and wearing the political symbols and colors of the Boer republics.[45] Officials reserved the category "undesirable" for outspoken patriots and wives of prominent commandos who "refused to . . . persuade their husbands to surrender."[46] These they distinguished from "*bona fide*" refugees.[47] Kitchener threatened to ship the former "out of the country as . . . dangerous character[s]" and he even suggested permanent banishment to "some island or country . . . Fiji for instance, or . . . Madagascar."[48] Milner and Colonial Secretary Chamberlain dismissed such proposals as "wild talk": one could not simply "get rid of the Boers."[49] And yet, some of the most irreconcilable were indeed shipped overseas.

Civilian concentration camps constituted one node in a larger carceral network that included pass regulations, prisons, and POW camps in Cape Town, Durban, St. Helena, Bermuda, India, and Ceylon. Anxious to transport captured commandos away from southern Africa, a beleaguered War Office petitioned Viceroy Curzon to mobilize India's extensive camp experience and resources to house some 9,000 POWs, mostly at abandoned army barracks like those at Ahmednagar, recently the site of multiple famine camps.[50] Historians have henceforth treated POW and civilian camps as separate entities and have failed to recognize interconnections within Britain's global system of wartime of internment. And yet, the indeterminacy between soldier and civilian that characterized the war made boundaries between these systems porous. The provost marshal transferred POWs deemed politically safe to civilian concentration camps, while any "resident in a refugee camp found committing any act, either by word or deed, tending to prolong the present disturbances" was deported as a POW.[51] In multiple cases, inmates were transferred "up" or "down" Britain's carceral ladder. At Springfontein, for instance, "a dangerous [inmate] continually indulging in seditious talk [and] likely to influence others" presented a "clear case for the POW camps,"[52] while in Heidelburg, military authorities deported thirty men as an "object lesson" to other refugees attempting to escape.[53] Orange River Colony authorities likewise mandated that all men "who may be occupants of a tent from which another man deserts" be shipped to India.[54]

However militant or unfeminine, Boer women were not, on the basis of their sex, reclassified as POWs. Instead, one inmate (and mother of seven) who "had the cheek of wearing the late Free State colors" was removed from Bethulie camp to the nearby jail for two months, while the Bloemfontein lockup incarcerated over one hundred inmates from the nearby camp, "mostly those desperate characters who do not know how to behave themselves," who "insist on wearing the colors forbidden" or who "always complain about food [and] fuel." Among them was an eighty-four-year-old woman and another heavily pregnant. While civilian camps were putatively less punitive than prisons or POW camps, inmates sometimes thought otherwise.[55] Two POWs transferred from Greenpoint "found Refugee Camp life ... very unpleasant" and complained about "small rations" and having to "dig and work as [they] had never done."[56] Whatever the case, international law (the 1899 Hague Convention in particular) protected those incarcerated as POWs; civilian concentration camp inmates, by contrast, had no legal status or safeguards.

Just as camps filtered refugees according to social need, they also functioned as sorting mechanisms to determine the political threat and loyalty of each inmate. As famine operations suggest, security and humanity were not incompatible. Apart

Undesirable Camp.

FIGURE 24.

"The Showyard" camp at Winburg placed undesirables in sheds originally designed for livestock.[11] [Credit: NAUK CO1069/215, Image 105, Undesirable Camp.]

[11] For an image of Kroonstad's "Bird Cage" see Sarah Raal, *The Lady Who Fought: A Young Woman's Account of the Anglo-Boer War* (Plumstead, South Africa: Stormberg, 2000), 89.

from prisons and POW camps, superintendents erected fenced "undesirable wards" at many concentration camps. Enclosed by barbed wire, these centers enforced heavy labor for those "who raise[d] rebellion" and "[could] not hold their tongues from speaking politics."[57] Just as medical officers employed the language of military combat when conducting their "war on plague," intelligence agents invoked the language of epidemiology to portray anti-British sentiment as an *"infection* [that] may spread . . . and become dangerous to the peace and prosperity of South Africa."[58] Given recurring analogies between warfare and disease in the larger history of camps, the medical techniques of segregation and isolation proved only fitting when combatting political subversion. By segregating and, it was hoped, curing deviance, the isolation of undesirables conformed to the "rational" and "scientific" principles of late-Victorian penology.

In Bloemfontein, a "wired-in enclosure" known colloquially as "the Bird Cage" enforced "8 hours [of work] a day with pick and shovel" for "all singing birds."[59] The similar "showyard camp" at Winburg segregated those who "encourage[d] and foster[ed] resistance to rules and regulations," thereby "quarantining" the disaffected and preventing them from infecting those "who only require[d] a little tactful handling to make them reasonably contented."[60] Consisting of corrugated iron sheds surrounded by "a fence of galvanized iron 7 to 8 feet high"[61] and guarded by civil police, the showyard "prevent[ed] communication between people in the town and those in the camp," thereby restricting the flow of bodies and information.[62] The barracks were small and cramped. Formidable perimeter walls obscured any view but the sky.

Most refugees were relatively peaceful, but it was the "troublemakers" who found their way into archives. At Aliwal North, the superintendent "tried kindness and reprimands" but was finally "obliged" to put two women in the undesirables camp, one of whom he had to take out again as her children of one and three years old "could not be pacified." The oldest girl, eighteen years old, "spends her time in shouting the vilest language at those on guard," he reported, "and in yelling the 'Volkslied,'" a patriotic anthem, "in most unmelodious tones till late at night." The girl's mother "evaded the police and handed [her] an axe with which the latter cut the fence and marched out defying the police." The superintendent eventually sentenced the girl to fourteen days in Aliwal jail and placed the mother "in the cage," where she "rav[ed] like a maniac."[63] Ultimately, however, political quarantine was temporary; rehabilitation was the overriding goal. "As a better feeling gains ground" among undesirables, Transvaal's assistant provost marshal instructed, they should "be removed by degrees, without their being told why, into the more desirable camp, where only those loyal and in favor or British Rule should be tolerated."[64]

Ideology was not the only ground for isolation. Superintendents regularly conflated political and social subversion and they cited "imprisonment in a given area surrounded by barbed wire" and "away from the conveniences . . . [of] the camp" as a favored method to "compel the observance of sanitary measures."[65] At Bloemfontein, the superintendent punished the "dirty and lazy" who "refuse[d] to do a little work in helping to keep the camp clean" by "send[ing] 'em into the 8hrs a day gang" at the "Bird Cage."[66] Meanwhile, officials referred to the undesirable ward at Norvals Pont as "Hog's Paradise," for it detained the "extremely dirty" and "verminous."[67]

Social and hygienic discourses also flowed into moral ones, and alleged sexual depravity became the salacious subject of official reports. In response to complaints about "very immoral women" in Bloemfontein camp, for instance, Trollope instructed the superintendent to place such women "in a portion of the camp away from respectable people and caution [them] that if they continue to carry on their immoral practices their rations [would] be cut in half."[68] Casting themselves as paternalistic custodians, superintendents portrayed Boer women as promiscuous, unprincipled deviants. But paternalism often spilled over into prurience, and in one case, soldiers guarding Bloemfontein camp were reprimanded for "looking through a telescope at a man and woman in an unbecoming position." In this case, the respective civil and military authorities agreed to restrict the soldiers' access to camp, though not before reflecting on whether the observed immorality was "free" or "on payment."[69]

In sum, the camps' humanitarian mandates often conflicted with harsh wartime realities. Many expressed reservations about the "wholesale and indiscriminate . . . crowding of women into cages."[70] Such anxieties reflected the contested status of inmates as both victims *and* villains—harmless refugees *and* dangerous suspects. Paradoxically, Trollope commended Bloemfontein's "Bird Cage" to encourage more severe punishments elsewhere, while simultaneously reminding Bloemfontein's more eagerly disciplinarian superintendent that "all persons sent to your camp are supposed to be refugees and treated as such." Adding that the "main duty" of camps was "to house and feed the people and make them comfortable," Trollope's mixed messages reflected a larger conceptual confusion about the nature and purpose of the camps.[71] The dueling missions of "war and peace" were never fully reconciled.

"HAPPIER HARD AT WORK"

The tensions of "war and peace" also inflected work routines. Camp life was patterned around "a system of working squads" that prohibited inmates from "spend[ing] their time in idleness."[72] Security concerns forestalled Milner's original vision of relief labor on road and railway works, while sexual and racial distinctions ordained different arrangements from Indian famine relief works. But camps, nonetheless, presented "a good opportunity [to] make all *bywoners* [poor whites] work and work hard too, which they [apparently] ha[d] not done before the war."[73] Sewing, laundry, sweeping, and cleaning occupied women, while men and teenage boys spent their days "digging, trenching . . . camp cleaning, wood chopping . . . and a dozen other necessary duties."[74] Inducting inmates into a capitalist economy, workers received a nominal wage, and when logistically feasible, authorities paid working fatigues to improve nearby roads and other infrastructure. Like the famine officials he met in India, however, Trollope warned officials to exercise close "personal supervision and satisfy themselves that these men actually do work."[75]

Officials believed inmates would "undoubtedly [be] much happier hard at work than loafing and idling about the camp"—as long as they were "not driven like kaffirs."[76] In a gesture to the Boers' coveted though contested "whiteness," work routines for Afrikaners differed markedly from black African labor regimens. Menial tasks like cleaning latrines awaited native inmates, and when white men were forced to perform "work which is usually done by natives, they [were] at once laughed at and abused by the [camp] women."[77] Though often at variance with Afrikaner attitudes about "kaffir work," British authorities accommodated such sentiments by enforcing a racial division of labor.

As the war continued, and camps became more permanent, officials voiced more edifying discourses of work as a rehabilitating and civilizing influence. This shift mirrored the transition from military to civilian control in early 1901 as the concerns of emergency relief and the dictates of security (paramount in the early months of encampment) gradually gave way to the governmentality necessary to reconcile inmates to British rule. If the Boers were "semi-savage" and "degenerate," officials sensed an essential European core that could be reclaimed under centuries of African grime. Drawing, appropriately, from mining metaphors, they compared the virtues of the Boer to "a rough diamond . . . still hidden from the light . . . because [it has] not yet been cut or polished."[78] Unlike the natives of India, whose indelible difference became a hallmark of colonial rule, and in contrast to South Africa's black population, the Boers presented unique candidates for reform in British eyes. While the "civilizing mission" in its classic formulation is normally associated with the "uplift" of non-Europeans, officials presiding over white Afrikaners implemented it the more vigorously. As conduits of rehabilitation, concentration camps inculcated British modes of thought and behavior in their white inhabitants.

To this end, British officials deemed work an active civilizing force that would transform an agrarian, preindustrial people into productive members of a modern, British South Africa. Camps, according to the historian Elizabeth van Heyningen, were "tools of modernization."[79] Deputy-Administrator H. J. Goold-Adams certainly thought so. He spoke of the opportunity the camps afforded to erode "habits of laziness" and "instill into [the Boers] the great benefit derived from hard work (an unknown quantity among them prior to the war)."[80] Like uprooted urban migrants in industrial Britain, inmates would become modern capitalist subjects. "The Boers will have to work for a living after the war," Trollope added, "and it is highly necessary they should be trained in refugee camps."[81]

By the end of 1901, organized industry had become central to camp life. Apprenticeship in workshops fulfilled the "wish . . . that all boys able to work should learn some trade or other,"[82] even though "a number of young fellows" were "too lazy to work."[83] Carpentry, shoemaking, and blacksmith shops opened not only to perform maintenance work and provide shoes and housing but to train apprentices. In this, they resembled the Salvation Army's industrial schools accommodating criminal classes in both Britain and India.[84] For women and girls, camps offered sewing, knitting, and basket-weaving classes, and Dr. Pratt Yule, the Orange River Colony medical officer of health, even instituted a lecture series and probationary system to give young Boer girls professional training in nursing (though "half-caste" Boer and British girls, or those "entirely English" proved "much more useful as nursing assistants").[85] The refugees "are now learning what will in certain instances be their life work," Pratt Yule concluded, "and there is no reason why the camp hospitals should not become training schools for nurses." The goal was to prepare inmates for membership in a modern, industrial, and white South Africa under British tutelage. Not everyone was optimistic: Heilbron's superintendent predicted an inevitable culture clash between Boer ignorance and the "educated experience" of "Britishers."[86] But reservations aside, the dictates of rehabilitation increasingly inflected camp life.

"A GOLDEN OPPORTUNITY"

Education was another conduit of modernization and Anglicization. Milner was keenly aware that "owing to the prolongation of hostilities large numbers of Boer children [were] wasting . . . the most important period of their lives from an educational point of view."[87] In homage to his grand visions of an English South Africa, the high commissioner dispatched E. B. Sargant, a man with extensive experience working with Whitechapel's "demoralized poor" at London's Toynbee Hall settlement house, to organize education along the lines of British workhouses and "industrial schools." For Sargant, education was a powerful means of social reform—of achieving class harmony through "moral leadership and intellectual guidance."[88] Concentrating a population once scattered across the veld, camps presented a "golden opportunity," he announced, "which will not occur again . . . of teaching every child English"—the language of civilization.[89]

As camps developed, Milner and Sargant seized the opportunity to promote the values and virtues of British imperialism. Anglicization, for both men, was a form of cultural control, but each believed genuinely that the English language and English patterns of thought would benefit inmates. Starting in June 1901, they recruited camp teachers (after careful political vetting) from across the white Dominions (though tellingly, not from Ireland), making sure to choose women who would "conscientiously . . . commend the ideals of the British Empire."[90] The recruits came largely from the "jingo" lower-middle classes and they functioned as "imperial mothers" by disseminating what Eliza Reidi calls "an unsophisticated belief in Britain's righteousness and benevolence."[91] Like English nurses also recruited for camps, these teachers, both "physically strong and attractive," would "by ocular demonstration" present a "favorable impression . . . of true British womanhood."[92]

Controlling the flow of information proved as important inside the camps as it did on the battlefield, though education was impelled by the cultural visions and aspirations of Britain's larger imperial project rather than by military dictates alone. The Colonial Office vetted schoolbooks and lesson plans to propagate pro-British propaganda.[93] More than some crude instrument of wartime publicity, however, schools helped, more subtly, to inculcate "English ways and methods."[94] Confinement in camp, J. H. Corbett of the Transvaal Education Department argued, would replace the "wandering listless habits in which the children are bred on the veld" with the discipline of a settled and civilized life—a familiar goal for supposedly "nomadic" populations across the empire.[95] According to Heilbron's superintendent, camp life would help inmates "conduct themselves in a more civilized manner."[96] To this end, education proved a more sophisticated tool than barbed wire: a governmentality that targeted hearts and minds.

Looking back on the camps' legacy, officials in 1903 noted "the accommodation of many thousands" had "unquestionably raised their level in matters of education, personal cleanliness, and all that goes to build up self-respect."[97] In a statement of Milnerite zeal, the Cape Colony Public Works official Lewis Mansergh noted that by introducing "industrial education" and a "desire for companionship and association," camps had enabled inmates to "hold their own in an industrial community."[98] The camps, officials believed, had transformed primitive ranchers, accustomed to asocial isolation, into future imperial citizens. But while this project encompassed Afrikaner inmates, already "quasi-European," it did not extend to black Africans. Displaced and subsequently concentrated by the same scorched-earth policies as their Afrikaner counterparts, the native camp experience mapped onto existing policies of forced labor and racial exclusion.

"DUTCH SERFDOM AND THE EQUAL RIGHTS OF GREAT BRITAIN"

Authorities cited the "magnanimity of Great Britain" toward the native population as an original justification for war. Black inmates could "appreciate the difference between the serfdom of a Dutch Republic and the equal rights laid down by a Monarchy such as Great Britain," one superintendent remarked. Scorched-earth warfare and forced relocation "runs hard on the surface," he conceded, but "to be fed and sheltered and protected without remuneration amply atones for all."[99] Yet rhetoric rarely matched reality. Per capita, Britain spent less than a third as much on black inmates as Boers, and rations, shelter, and medical care for Africans reflected and perpetuated existing racial inequalities.[100]

Archival records documenting black camps were long ago incinerated—a "whitewashing" of history that fostered public amnesia about the "mutual suffering" of black inmates in the apartheid era.[101] Surviving reports indicate that black and white refugees initially found themselves mixed together in the same canvas camps: the dislocations of war were too messy to maintain pristine racial geographies. At Barberton, for example, "some natives [were] sleeping, eating and drinking in the same tents with the whites." Black servants sometimes accompanied their masters to camp and were sources of pride for families desperate to retain a semblance of their former respectability. British efforts to limit relief to the truly destitute soon militated against such arrangements, however, as did concern about "undue familiarity between white and black inmates."[102] Anyone able to support servants was by definition ineligible for relief, British mindsets maintained. Ever conscious of racial status, meanwhile, Boer refugees of more humble background experienced incarceration alongside natives as a disgrace and humiliation, especially in face of British rhetoric that questioned their claims to "whiteness."

When not actually residing at Boer camps, native refugees congregated in shelters on the edge of formal campsites; sometimes they were "scattered over a large area," though for the purposes of control they were eventually "concentrated in one place" and registered as inmates.[103] As native camps gained administrative structure, a local example—fenced mining compounds at Kimberley and the Rand, themselves modeled on barracks for Indian coolies at Natal sugar plantations—provided direct and conscious prototypes.[104] With their overriding emphasis on economy and their enclosed, self-sufficient nature, African camps "adopted the compound system," one official observed.[105]

As much as they aspired to the exacting discipline of a de Beers compound, however, many African camps remained ad hoc conglomerations constructed of sailcloth, biscuit tins, and "sacks stretched over frameworks of wood."[106] Like Indian famine camps, local materials sufficed. In a surviving report on Edenburg camp, A. G. H. Daller described "slightly built wigwams covered with sacking" reminiscent of "a large gipsy encampment," although "regular streets and intervals [were] . . . observed." There was no school or hospital (one would later be provided) and there was "practically no expense in connection with this settlement save the rations."[107] Social spending on dark-skinned colonials was anathema to Victorian mindsets, and like their counterparts in India, South African officials hoped to make native camps as self-supporting as possible. Camps supplied food, though on an inferior "native scale" that provided similar calories to Boer rations but replaced fresh meat with "Kaffir corn." Mr. Oliphants, a rare literate native, described rations at Honingspruit as inadequate: "we have to work hard all day long," he complained, "but the only food we can get is mealies."[108] Medical attendance was likewise rudimentary,[109] and "with a view to economy," native elders sometimes performed the duty of superintendents,[110] though for substantially less pay than their European counterparts.[111] Voicing a recurring mistrust of "native agency," however, authorities feared the appointment of black officials, like the native headman "Peter" at Brandfort, would come at "the detriment of good order."[112]

As Britain refined its camps by form and function, the familiar process of classification that segregated "undesirables" in separate wards eventually targeted black Africans. In June 1901, the government made arrangements to transport native inmates to an entirely new system of agricultural labor camps under the supervision of Major H. G. J. Lotbinière's Department of Native Refugees.[113] In part, this policy derived from South Africa's "sanitary syndrome." "To a major extent," the "growing fear of disease"—plague among other ailments—compelled the removal of native congregations behind extra fences.[114] Like dirty Afrikaners detained in "Hog's paradise," separate native camps appeased the prejudice of white town-dwellers by removing an "unwholesome" African influence.

A familiar discourse about native demoralization also propelled the move. It was "obviously undesirable that so large a number of natives should be supported by the Government in idleness,"[115] officials concurred, and de Lotbinière voiced a paternalistic concern that "concentration camps near towns [would] surround . . . natives with conditions tending to disorganise them morally and physically."[116] Spanning the Indian Ocean, a pan-imperial ideology emphasized the dangers of pauperizing "natives." Lotbinière noted explicitly that the "lessons of Indian famine camps" had "taught the advisability of keeping natives employed." "If fed for free," he concluded, black Africans would "deteriorate physically and morally." Such preoccupations applied to "semi-savage" "poor whites," but they applied doubly to "the native character."[117]

In reality, black refugees never had the luxury of "idleness." From the outset, they performed "kaffir work" at nearby white camps in return for food.[118] In accordance with new work-or-starve policies, however, their relocation to rural locations on deserted farms permitted a more systematic extraction of labor in a manner resembling government relief works in India and Cape Colony. And while some natives supported guerrilla efforts, Britain normally viewed Africans as either neutral or pro-British. As Kitchener's sweeping drives secured occupation of more and more territory along the railroad, meanwhile, their relocation to rural sites became logistically feasible. By growing their own food, African camps became self-supporting and even turned a profit providing surplus grain to the army and subsidizing Boer camps. As in India, camp authorities maintained ownership of the means of production; in return for labor, inmates received one shilling a day (less than half the wage paid to Boers), which they used to supplement rations. Unsurprisingly, food remained a disciplinary device: overseers withheld rations for unsatisfactory work.[119]

As Witwatersrand mines reopened over the course of 1901, native camps also functioned as labor recruitment depots. Replicating arrangements at criminal tribe camps, which provided workers for the Indian Army, male inmates were drafted for contract work with the British military.[120] Native camps thus reflected larger imperial priorities: they helped the army fill labor shortages, enabling mineworkers in army employ to resume work on the Rand. While Lotbinière's department pursued a paternalistic agenda of protection and relief, its ultimate purpose was to facilitate the exploitation of South Africa's mineral wealth. If white camps inducted inmates into modernity, black camps sheltered natives from its perils, preparing them, instead, for a future of agricultural labor and impermanent work at Transvaal mining compounds.

Like their counterparts in India, officials in charge of native camps directed their governance at bodies rather than souls, providing the nutrition and shelter necessary for a minimal physical subsistence while neglecting inner reform. Lotbinière warned, for example, that education in native camps would both "unsettle the . . . present system of control" and create more inopportune claimants for the franchise.[121] Discipline and punishment were similarly corporal: instead of isolating "undesirables"[122] in reformatory wards, problem natives simply received the lash.[123] For his part, Mr. Oliphants alleged instances of physical abuse, though authorities responded dismissively, noting that many of the natives "have been decidedly insubordinate" and "they . . . deserved all, or even more than they got." Oliphants, they concluded, was "a highly educated native who evidently does not use his advantages in the right direction but is a source of trouble and an annoyance to all who have dealing with him."[124] Ultimately, Britain's promise of native rights and benevolent treatment was chimerical: native camps were preludes to a series of postwar betrayals that ultimately laid the groundwork for apartheid.

"THE PLEASING EFFECT OF REGULAR LINES"

If native segregation was in part a hygienic procedure, Trollope and Tucker viewed the management of camps as an exercise in sanitary uplift. In the process, they espoused a familiar rhetoric about cleanliness and a growing confidence in Western medicine and sanitary science: in terms of cleanliness, Boers were little better than Africans, for they had lost the sanitary "instincts of their [European] forefathers."[125] For medical men eager to uphold the promises of Victorian sanitary reform, camps offered conduits to impose cultural and scientific norms onto "backward" populations. The "unhygienic habits" of inmates, in addition to their suspect politics, were thus occasions for exacting forms of corrective punishment.

Colonial medicine was often a venue, Philip Curtin notes, for expressions of racism and cultural chauvinism.[126] Just as racial depictions of "Afrikaner savages" legitimized scorched-earth warfare, depictions of "dirty Boers" continued in the camps. Much conflict derived from an epidemiological divide between miasmic philosophies of disease—themselves outdated by emergent germ theories—and customary medical practices based on humoral philosophy (prevalent in seventeenth-century Europe to which Boers traced their origins).[127] For spokesmen of an ascendant medical profession steeped in middle-class sensibilities, Boer "home remedies" (like indigenous African healing practices, which they resembled) were recurrent targets of scorn. At Heilbron, Dr. Pratt Yule, a self-described "exponent of European views of hygiene," complained that Boers "smear[ed] floors with cow dung."[128] Meanwhile, Dr. Franks catalogued the Boers' "extraordinary ignorance and prejudice . . . in regard to even the elementary laws of health" with an ethnographic but condescending zeal. A "cow dung bath" was a versatile remedy, he noted, and children suffering from bronchitis were placed in a hollowed-out goat carcass. Many Boer remedies, Franks continued, smacked of superstition:

The tooth of a horse worn on a string round the neck is believed to cure rheumatism. A piece of potato put into each ear, and a necklace made of square pieces of the same, is said to cure earache. Toothache is cured by cutting the finger and toenails of the sufferer off short. These parings are put into a bottle with a lock of his hair and some water. The bottle is then corked and buried, and the toothache disappears.[129]

In other cases a "superstitious fear of the bath" and such "extraordinary [practices] as tying ribbons . . . round ankles and wrists to stay the progress of fevers" became fodder for British doctors.[130] The "lowest classes" in Britain demonstrated similar ignorance, Franks conceded, but the "frequently revolting" methods of Boer medicine were "primitive in the extreme and . . . belong[ed] to the period of the dark ages" rather than the present (British) era of enlightenment and progress.[131] And yet, the specter of a lost European tribe who had degenerated into savagery provoked ardent efforts to "uplift" Boers into a new world of medical modernity.

Having critiqued Boer medicine, proponents upheld sanitary education as an enduring benefit of camp life. In contrast to the perceived dirt and disarray of the Boer Republics, the camps portrayed in official reports emerge as spaces of cleanliness and order. The travelling inspector W. A. Thomson remarked that camps offered "pleasing contrast[s]" to "dirty, untidy, and uncared for" towns.[132] Noting a developing aesthetic of control, A. G. H. Daller relished "the pleasing effect of the regular lines of the tents, the measured intervals, and the chalked perspectives." These were "things which, having no special virtue in themselves, suggest[ed] a spirit of order and cleanliness."[133] Such appearances "reflected great credit on the authorities,"[134] Franks remarked, and by war's end British spokesmen noted with satisfaction that inmates had "learnt much by their sojourn in the camp . . . in the observance of the commoner principles of personal cleanliness and domestic sanitation."[135] But as devastating outbreaks of epidemic disease attest, Franks' self-satisfaction and Daller's cleanly aesthetic were no more than illusions.

"SCENES OF SUFFERING AND SORROW"

Above all, British concentration camps are remembered not for their pristine hygiene but for an enduring tragedy of death and disease. As in India, the concentration of large populations facilitated the rapid spread of epidemics, which threatened the very viability of camps and ultimately derailed larger projects of distributing relief and inculcating habits conducive to industry and governance. Despite the vaunted promise of modern medicine and despite early warnings about "future serious epidemics,"[136] concentration camps were a demographic catastrophe for Africans and Afrikaners: 25,000 Boers and almost as many natives perished out of a total inmate population approaching a quarter million. Based on previous experiences, many expected cholera and smallpox to be the primary killers. But among young children, measles proved most deadly with 6,100 deaths. Typhoid and dysentery (2,400 deaths each) and respiratory ailments (4,200 deaths) were also major killers at camps with impure water supplies and inadequate shelter.[137] Nutritional diseases like *cancrum oris* were also present among children.

Fewer inmates died than in India, but they perished at higher rates. In the darkest months, October and November 1901, the annual death rate approached 40 percent in the Boer camps and was likely as high among Africans. In the worst five months, total deaths surpassed the populations of both Bloemfontein and Pretoria, the

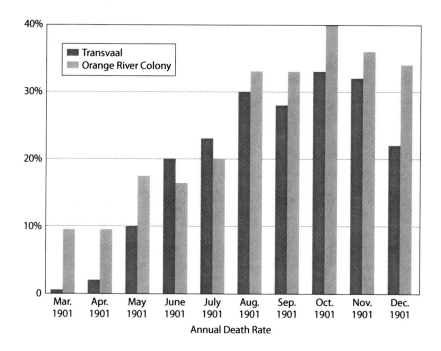

FIGURE 25.

Camp death rates, March 1901–December 1901, at Boer camps in Transvaal and the Orange River Colony. Statistics for Lotbinière's native camps are unavailable, though evidence suggests epidemics peaked later, lasted longer, and were similarly fatal. [Credit: Graph by Bill Nelson.]

former Boer capitals.[138] Statistics fail, however, to convey a full sense of human suffering at a time when funerals and mass graves were recurring motifs of camp life.[139] The emotive words of Reverend A. D. Luckoff, an Afrikaner chaplain at Bethulie camp, provide some insight. After a frantic day searching for milk crates and candle boxes to build coffins, Luckoff described how sorrow and pity had eroded his sense of time and reality: "Four days gone by; but one day is like the other except that on alternate days I take the funerals; for the rest, each day is like preceding morning, noon, and afternoon." In its fragmented and extemporaneous tenor, Luckoff's staccato elegy reveals the desperation of the moment: "one grows so weary of scenes of suffering and sorrow; always red and tear-stained eyes; always Love; helpless, hopeless, impotent, despairing; always face to face with Decay, Change, Death; always the same close, stifling, little tent."[140]

British medical men like Franks and Pratt Yule expressed complacency and contempt as they tried alternately to understate and then to understand the gravity of the situation. Blame fell initially on inmates themselves and the "criminal neglect" of mothers. Female incapacity rather than mismanagement by male decision makers was apparently at fault: "I am considering whether some of the worst cases [of parental delinquency] could not be tried for manslaughter," Kitchener wrote in his typically strident tone.[141] Others suggested the Boers were genetically predisposed to early death. For British officials already steeped in racial worldviews, "heredity play[ed] an important factor" in explaining mortality among the biologically "unfit." Boer mothers were "phlegmatic [and] lazy," and the "stamina of the children at birth [was] not good."[142] Adding a measure of moral opprobrium, Dr. Pratt Yule noted the "frequency of consanguineous marriages among [them] may have some bearing on their apparent susceptibility to infective disease."[143] Again, favorable visions of the Boers as virile Anglo-Saxons were reversed in the concentration camps. With a hint of social Darwinism, a normally sympathetic inspector concluded: "the Boers are not a healthy race." They "have no stamina" and "they inter-marry to a perfectly shocking extent and uncles, nieces, cousins, sister and brother in-laws all live together in a ghastly way."[144]

A more likely explanation, at least for the prevalence of "childhood diseases" like measles, was demographic: camps concentrated high proportions of children (as well as the elderly).[145] Armchair apologists contended that with similar ratios of very young children from very poor families, mortality rates in South Africa could be reproduced in a "theoretical concentration camp" confining select elements of London's poor in Richmond Park.[146] In this vein, Milner and Chamberlain drew from their backgrounds in social reform to highlight perceived similarities between Boer inmates and the metropolitan poor. Marshaling statistics from urban slums, they contextualized camp death rates with those of other unhealthy communities. Officials like Allen McCulloch, the medical officer of Vryburg, confirmed that camp mortality was no worse than the death rate "in mill and manufacturing towns [in] England."[147] Such commentary intersected with larger efforts to understand death and disease in the crowded and concentrated spaces of the nineteenth century. But while some emphasized the quotidian nature of camp mortality, others highlighted the special circumstances of South Africa. In contrast to Europeans, who "enjoy[ed] a certain immunity from measles acquired by the frequency of epidemics at home," Dr. Pratt Yule noted the Boers had "practically lost this immunity . . . by their long sojourn in South Africa." If epidemics were rare in prewar South Africa, they were inevitable outcomes of concentrating previously scattered populations, he maintained.[148]

Whatever the case, the epidemic pitfalls of encampment were entirely foreseeable. Dr. George Turner, a Cape Colony plague officer seconded to Transvaal in 1900, warned early on: "the introduction of disease into these camps . . . would be impossible . . . to escape . . . unless care be exercised."[149] The medical inspector Dr. Whiteside Himes confided similarly that epidemics among populations "long aggregated in camp" had "been recently observed in famine camps in India," and experience at army barracks affirmed "the difficulty of maintaining the health even of troops all in the prime of life."[150] The dangers of concentration were thus well known. From the Indian famines onward, Britain had assembled the expertise, technology, and manpower necessary to predict and prevent such tragedies. The POW camps were a case in point: though the *Manchester Guardian* correspondent Vaughan Nash condemned conditions at Ahmednagar, India, fearing typhoid and cholera would ravage inmates like at nearby famine camps,[151] forethought and planning prevented widespread disease among POWs, who were castigated nonetheless for their "dirty habits" and "liab[ility] to epidemics."[152] Civilian concentration camps, by contrast, failed to secure clean water supplies, quarantine infected populations, or provide the medical treatment and comfortable accommodation necessary to care for displaced noncombatants already weakened by war.

Mortality, in sum, was not inevitable, but a measure of fiscal ideology and political will. The conflicting demands of economy and relief meant that financial constraints often trumped basic medical and sanitary provisions. Early on, Dr. Westerfield at Kimberley feared "the present quite insufficient accommodations for sick women and children" would lead to many deaths if the "present system is persisted in."[153] The carelessness of civil and military officials ("sanitary science [was] *une quantité négligeable*" among Kitchener's forces, Dr. Turner complained[154]) in relocating infected refugees to otherwise healthy camps further amplified mortality: at Heilbron, for example, the "translocation of a large number of refugees from [Kroonstad], a camp in which a very serious epidemic of measles is raging," was "responsible for many deaths."[155] In desperation, the superintendent erected isolation tents to accommodate arrivals, but the careful system of quarantine devised by W. J. Simpson, J. S. Wilkins, and other plague experts in India did not (yet) prevail as a standard policy. Despite claims to the contrary, concentration camps were overcrowded and unhygienic. Army tents designed to billet five often concentrated ten, and they were leaky and damp, leading to pneumonia and other chest ailments. Rations, meanwhile, lacked nutrients. Predictable and avoidable mistakes caused mortality to spike, confounding the camps' humanitarian raison d'être and destroying life rather than saving it.

"ONLY MATCHED IN TIMES OF FAMINE AND PLAGUE"

Like famine and plague camps, wartime concentration camps were controversial institutions, and as mortality mounted, they ignited a political firestorm. Proponents lauded British humanitarian efforts to shelter and ration refugees and they enshrined the provision of modern medicine and sanitation as primary benefits of camp life. Sickness and mortality would have been even worse, the Colonial Office maintained, had refugees been left to starve on the empty veld or in overcrowded towns. But as disease compromised the task of relief, a chorus of criticism once again placed the humanity of camps under scrutiny. Like B. G. Tilak and Romesh Dutt in India, prominent inmates like Elizabeth Neethling protested what they called "extermination camps" to condemn British rule and stoke a nascent Afrikaner nationalism rooted in the politics of "shared suffering." Dismissing as "slanders and untruths" the notion that camps were "act[s] of humanity to save Boer families from starvation," Neethling insisted that what Britain had essentially established were "*punishment* camps." Barbed wire emerged, once again, as a symbol of Victorian empire.[156]

Apart from Neethling, whose writings on the camps became influential in the postwar period, inmates found politically connected advocates in Britain. As it had done in famished India, the Society of Friends followed the camps closely, deputing the former member of parliament and Gladstonian Liberal Joshua Rowntree to South Africa. Women like Ann Francis Taylor (a distant relation of Joseph Taylor who reported on famine camps in India) also travelled to South Africa on behalf of the Quaker relief fund, where they distributed supplies to camp inmates before Military Governor Maxwell discontinued their sometimes-meddlesome services. Above all, however, the humanitarian pacifist, "liberal socialist," and famed antiwar activist Emily Hobhouse emerged as the inmates' primary champion.

The daughter of an Anglican rector, Hobhouse had long harbored an interest in welfare work and social investigation.[157] She gained experience in social matters while ministering to the poor at mining compounds in the United States, and she studied "the dire results of overcrowding and underfeeding" in Britain's industrial cities. Visiting London slums and East End factories, she learned the investigative methodology of the Women's Industrial Council,[158] an organization dedicated to overcoming "masculine indifference to women's interests through social reform methods."[159] With the tenacity fostered by practical experience and with connections in high places (her uncle was a Liberal peer), Hobhouse proved a formidable advocate for Boer women and children—and a thorn in the side of presiding British authorities.

After mobilizing parliamentary support from the likes of future prime minister David Lloyd George and opposition leader Henry Campbell-Bannerman, Hobhouse received permission to visit a handful of camps in the Orange River Colony. In December 1900, she sailed for South Africa (on the same ship as Rowntree), and upon alighting in Cape Town, she traveled inland to launch a firsthand investigative tour. Rumors about the camps were already circulating in Britain, but what Hobhouse found on her month-long visit were conditions "more awful than the wildest imaginings." British camps, she bemoaned, were failing in their humanitarian mission to relieve vulnerable women and children. And as epidemics spread through cold and leaky tents, inmates "were dying like flies of starvation, exposure, and disease."[160] Many met a sudden death, while others—the children she referred to as "faded flowers"—simply withered away.[161]

Upon returning to Britain, Hobhouse launched a fevered publicity campaign that questioned the humanity of the ruling Conservative party in particular and Britain's imperial image more generally. Convinced "the Government . . . would yield only to fear—viz. the fear of public opinion,"[162] she carried the torch of protest with great effect. As symbols of a controversial war, camps became the "stalking horse of the opposition,"[163] War Secretary Brodrick complained, and he noted the difficulty of "keeping up [his] wickets" amid a "storm of criticism."[164] However much the Conservative government portrayed the camps as benevolent refuges, Liberal critics cast them as "prison camps" surrounded by "barbed-wire fences" and "sentries . . . all around."[165] Irish MPs, in particular, criticized the camps as products of a destructive brand of imperial domination, seeing in the Boers a fellow race of white-skinned colonials. Meanwhile, articles such as "Baby Killing in Africa" and "Our Death Camps in South Africa" by yellow-press journalist W. T. Stead sensationally fanned the flames.[166] Conservative organs like the *Times* and *Daily Mail* dismissed Hobhouse and her ilk as hysterical women meddling in public affairs, while casting the Boers as "unnatural women" who involved themselves in military matters and neglected their motherly duties.[167] But as Secretary Chamberlain lamented, "concentration camps had undoubtedly roused deep feeling among people who cannot be classed with the pro-Boers," and "many good people [were] distressed" as a result.[168]

In the end, South African camps garnered even greater controversy in Britain than earlier protests against Indian plague and famine camps, though critics made connections between the two episodes of colonial suffering. During her time in South Africa, Hobhouse witnessed famine firsthand and she deplored the "terrible instances of emaciation among children,"[169] who were "gradually wasting away"

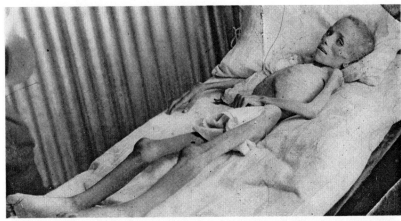

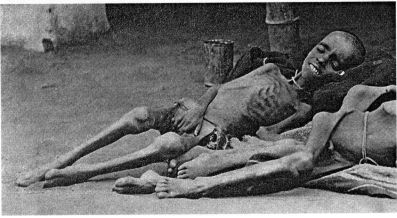

FIGURE 26.

Lizzie van Zyl reaching the final spatial outcome of concentration—the "vanishing point" (above). An anonymous Indian child in a Madras famine camp, 1876–77 (below). Though "atrocity images" of Boer inmates recalled earlier representations of colonial suffering, they elicited more vocal public condemnation. [Credit: wikipedia.org/wiki /Lizzie_van_Zyl#/media/File:LizzieVanZyl.jpg, accessed December 20, 2016; Detail from "Famine in India: five emaciated children, 1876–78." Wellcome Library, V0029718 ICV No. 30199.]

and who reminded her, she added, of the "famine-stricken people of India."[170] Exacerbated (rather than relieved) by poor rations in the camps, many had "simply wast[ed] from improper food," she claimed.[171] Emphasizing death and disease above all, Hobhouse went on to compare mortality rates in South Africa to those prevailing in times of famine and disease. "The full realization of the position dawned on me," she wrote in March 1901: "it was a death rate such as has never been known except in the times of the great plagues."[172]

In her many public lectures and lantern-slide presentations, Hobhouse made dramatic use of the human body in famished form. Among the many images of emaciated children that Hobhouse circulated, the photograph of Lizzie van Zyl, a seven-year-old inmate at Bloemfontein, stands out for its haunting impact.[173] Although Lizzie's skeletal frame (like that of many children in Indian famine camps) was caused by typhoid fever, images of such "walking skeletons" implied a more sinister specter of outright starvation.

To modern viewers, the image immediately recalls a skeletal extreme later realized in the extermination camps of twentieth-century Germany, and the semblance between such images and those taken in Nazi death factories was masterfully exploited by apartheid-era politicians eager to stoke a persecution complex among white Afrikaners.[174] To many contemporaries, however, Lizzie resembled a contemporary specter of colonial suffering: the images emerging from famine relief camps in India. Hobhouse recognized (in ways that historians of the South African camps have not) that mass death from malnutrition and epidemic disease among concentrated inmates was nothing new. Mobilizing analogies between different imperial arenas, she maintained that scenes from the concentration camps could "only be matched by the famine-stricken people of India."[175] And "as in the case of famine-stricken Indian children so widely circulated," she concluded, images like Lizzie's "might be a help in collecting funds."[176] In this way, protest against British relief policy in India coalesced with that in South Africa. The emphasis on emaciated children, meanwhile, anticipated a future of humanitarian protest dominated by outfits like Oxfam and Save the Children.

"THE THIN WHITE VENEER"

It seems only natural that the graphic death of fifty thousand refugees would provoke a scandal. But human suffering does not automatically garner sympathy. In an empire permeated, by some accounts, with violence and abuse, criticism of concentration camps gained traction in unique and unprecedented ways. Exposure, substandard shelter, and bare subsistence diets common at Indian famine camps provoked sympathy in Britain and helped contribute, in James Vernon's words, to the "humanitarian discovery of hunger."[177] Indeed, Colonial Secretary Chamberlain was himself busy distributing private donations for Indian famine relief on the eve of the Anglo-Boer War.[178] But camps in South Africa differed from Indian relief camps not only in the way inmates were governed but also in British responses to them. Critics of Indian camps condemned high mortality, coercive measures, and "barbed-wire deterrence" but their protests never animated the British public like the suffering and death of South Africa.

Differing responses relate, in some degree, to South Africa's military context. In the popular imagination, famine and plague remained "natural disasters" rather than products of British political economy. By contrast, the destitution and displacement that generated Boer War concentration camps were undeniably the result of Britain's controversial scorched-earth warfare. Politicized by the presence of almost half a million British and imperial troops, meanwhile, wartime events in South Africa were sure to attract a keen public following in Britain. And yet, the degree of pity and compassion for enemy civilians engaged in a bitter partisan struggle is remarkable. Why did the plight of Afrikaner inmates, themselves a suspected enemy, warrant a collective outpouring of concern while other cases of imperial suffering generated more muted interest?

Hobhouse effectively mobilized gendered tropes: many inmates were women and children—the ultimate innocents of war—she stressed. But what of black Africans who suffered similar hardships in similar numbers (or inmates at Indian camps, who were also dominated by women and children)? Given that most black Africans remained neutral or even supportive of British efforts during the war, their plight might have laid even greater claim to British compassion than the suffering of their bellicose Boer counterparts. Yet Hobhouse never visited a native camp,[179] and the Aboriginal Protection Society's plea, a full year after the Boer camps became a public issue, to "secure for the natives who are detained no less care and humanity," was too little too late.[180] The profound silence surrounding the plight of African inmates not only foreshadowed later attempts in South Africa to whitewash history and deny the very existence of black camps; it also demonstrated the degree to which compassion was contingent on the politics of race. With "atrocity photos," Hobhouse mobilized a staple of nineteenth-century humanitarianism; and yet, with the Irish famine more than a generation old, few Britons had seen *European* bodies reduced to such dehumanized straits.[181] Visions of white skin stretched over bone had a major psychological impact on Britons more accustomed to the skeletal form in darker-skinned colonials. British audiences could sympathize with Lizzie van Zyl in ways they could not with her anonymous Indian and African counterparts.

At the turn of the nineteenth century, racial hierarchies existed on a finely graded spectrum and representations of the Boers as a semi-African tribe meant their status as white Europeans was never guaranteed. Indeed, representations of the Boers as "nomadic" and "half-savage" had facilitated the dehumanizing process of forced concentration in the first place. And yet, the Boers retained enough of a "thin white veneer,"[182] in the words of Lord Kitchener, to be included as members of a global European civilization and as partners in a future white South Africa. Their conditions of encampment, though better than those of Africans and Indians, appeared especially egregious to "civilized opinion." Beneath the dirt and grime accumulated over centuries of wandering, Britons still recognized the Boers as a people of white, Christian, and European provenance—and one potentially receptive to civilizing agendas that would rehabilitate an ancient but degenerate race. In short, the Boers were "African" enough to be collected into camps, but they were "European" enough for this to be an outrage.

CHAPTER 7 · "A System Steadily Perfected"

Camp Reform and the "New Geniuses from India," 1901–1903

Lucy Deane, a member of the War Office's official investigative committee, wrote that Britain had, in effect, "created out here 33 London slums of the worst description." The "herding" of women and children into camps "where they all died like rats in a hole," she continued, offered "a huge object-lesson to the world in what not to do."[1] These were strong words, especially for a government appointee; but their sentiments were warranted. Despite gradual efforts to normalize administration and make camps more comfortable, the situation in September 1901 was still dire: a general state of disorder, death, and disease prevailed. At Aliwal North, for instance, "soldiers, police, hawkers, refugees, coolies, and niggers seemed to come and go as they pleased;" latrines and cesspools were "scattered around" unhygienically, and the whole camp, one inspector remarked, looked like "a low down Chinese Slum."[2]

Yet just eight months later, in June 1902, High Commissioner Alfred Milner's private secretary John Buchan lauded "the perfection of the management" the camps had attained.[3] After the dark days described by Deane, camps underwent profound and dramatic changes in management and living conditions. The Transvaal Military Governor General Maxwell similarly proclaimed the "organization of the camps [to be] perfected,"[4] and by the end of the war, Britain's colonial administration boasted that "these temporary canvas towns" had attained "the standard of mortality, public health, and even material comfort of the poorer classes in any large European city."[5] This was not just empty rhetoric. After peaking in October and November 1901, mortality dropped dramatically, and by May 1902, death from epidemic disease was largely unknown. Far from a lesson in "what not to do," another official concluded at war's end, the management of camps in the latter months of their existence offered the world "a manual of instruction" for the development of future camps, both in the British Empire and elsewhere.[6] Camps, officials now confirmed, were respectable instruments of colonial welfare and warfare.

Static assessments that paint either grim or agreeable portraits of the camps' best or worst phases have thus far informed politically motivated narratives. But they simplify complex realities and shifting trajectories in a diverse and evolving system. Scholarship remains largely silent about the period after November 1901 when camps underwent substantial reforms, and when the subject is addressed at all, Emily Hobhouse receives outsized credit. Lionized in epic fashion as the savior of the Boer nation (or alternatively, the redeemer of British honor), her criticisms and recommendations led ineluctably, dominant narratives imply, to improved health and well-being. Though Hobhouse and her allies undoubtedly placed camp mortality on the public agenda, the "great woman" approach, while alluring in its tales of personal triumph and adversity, cannot account for the magnitude of change. Fixated on "heroine worship," scholars have largely failed to examine the actual methods by which officials reformed the camps, and they neglect the broader imperial context in which new disciplinary and sanitary regulations were introduced. Developments in the camps cannot be understood through one-dimensional hagiographies, or in the narrow confines of South African history alone. Framed by local and national rather than imperial questions, existing scholarship illuminates the camps' contested significance among different constituencies of modern South Africa—black and white; speakers of English and Afrikaans—but fails to situate the camps within the larger transimperial channels through which British officials (and their critics) operated.[7]

How did high-ranking figures like Alfred Milner and Colonial Secretary Joseph Chamberlain accomplish such remarkable improvements? From what expertise did they draw and what resources did they mobilize? In the quest to reduce mortality and reform camp administration, officials looked for precedents and past practices not only from local models of settler-colonial welfare, but in metropolitan Britain and in the vast expanses of empire. Women from Britain and men with international experience contributed to the process. Looming large were the experiences of metropolitan welfare and the lessons of Indian plague and famine camps, which had delivered emergency discipline and relief according to comparable cultural mindsets and fiscal restraints. From Whitehall to Calcutta, and from the slums of east London to India's mofussil, interimperial exchange and networks of expertise shaped the development and reform of South African concentration camps.

"EVERYTHING MUST BE DONE TO SAVE LIFE"

Despite gradual changes and a casual sense that health and well-being would inevitably improve, mortality continued to rise. Early efforts, starting in March 1901, to requisition more tents and larger hospitals, more doctors and nurses, and more blankets and mattresses had little impact. And while London politicians debated the merits and demerits of encampment, South Africa endured a cold and rainy winter (from June to September 1901), in which pneumonia and a virulent strain of measles killed thousands, complicating the government's public defense of the camps. The controversy approached its climax.

Simply stated, the soaring death rates could not be justified. As Milner confided privately to Chamberlain, "a hundred explanations may be offered and a hundred excuses made, [but] they do not really amount to an adequate defense." By November 1901 it became clear "that the enormous mortality was not merely incidental to the first formation of the camps" but was a direct consequence of forced concentration. And without significant reforms, it "was going to continue."[8] Chamberlain concurred: "It does not seem to me . . . a complete answer to say that the aggregation of people who are specially liable to infectious disease has produced a state of things which is inevitable."[9] Amid growing public scandal surrounding the "methods of barbarism" that generated the camps, mounting death rates prompted a crisis. Senior officials became suddenly introspective as an early emphasis on the "habits of the people" gave way to admissions of British culpability for concentrating people in the first place and then failing to contain disease. The camps scandal had reached its tipping point.

Though relief and rehabilitation first justified the camps, visions of famished inmates dying behind barbed wire challenged Britain's image as a humane imperial power. For Milner and Chamberlain, threatened reputations were clarion calls to action. At times, the high commissioner and colonial secretary complained about the "wholly novel and unusual difficulties" they faced.[10] Camps, another observer pleaded, were "entirely novel" institutions with "which no one . . . had any experience."[11] But such statements were palpably untrue. Britain had led the world in erecting colonial camps and in gaining experience dealing with health, sanitation, and the control of epidemics. Had they looked sooner to the lessons of plague and famine camps, officials might have saved many lives. Instead, the history of South Africa's concentration camps, in their first year of existence, was a tragic story of failing to learn from precedent.

Nonetheless, November 1901 marked a decisive turning point. As familiar excuses rang hollow, earlier efforts to economize relief gave way to urgent statements that "everything must be done to save life"[12] and "expense must not be allowed to stand in the way."[13] "*Coute que coute*, the Concentration Camps must have their requirements satisfied," Milner confirmed.[14] Departing from the fine balancing act between economy and salvation maintained at Indian famine camps, life was now to be "save[d] . . . at all costs."[15] Such statements were familiar: in Bombay, Richard Temple contended the primary purpose of famine camps was to preserve life, and yet resources never materialized. In South Africa, however, with a new conviction that camps were becoming more permanent features of a lasting war—and with the survival of a population of European origin at stake—officials introduced medical and sanitary improvements and built new camps at substantial expense. The total per capita daily expenditure on Boer camps more than doubled, from 8½d in June 1901 to 1s 8½d the following year, though spending on African camps remained unchanged. Meanwhile, authorities invested close to £200,000 in new camps with state-of-the art facilities on the Cape and Natal coasts.[16] Along with money came fresh ideas and expertise as Britain's newest colonies turned to the collective resources of empire for inspiration.

When finally prompted into action, Britain drew critically and self-consciously from a wide array of experience. In the run up to November, W. K. Tucker, the Transvaal's director of camps, complained that many officials were "liable to forget" that they could draw from "all the resources of the Empire" when managing their camps.[17] Following this advice, authorities expanded their horizons and drew from experience gained outside South Africa. Although existing scholarship tends to view the camps in isolation as distinct products of a singular national past, Britain's colonial administration relied heavily on larger histories of controlling and caring for concentrated populations across the empire. Cosmopolitans like Milner and Chamberlain approached governance in South Africa with a global lens, and in the process, they mobilized multiple imperial precedents—both economic and experiential—to remake South African camps.

"ALL THE RESOURCES OF THE EMPIRE"

Before Milner and Chamberlain looked further abroad, the techniques of social investigation and sanitary inspection, honed in metropolitan Britain, offered important reference points. Drawing upon perceived analogies between concentration camps and urban slums—both were inhabited by populations cast as dirty, unhygienic, and socially and racially suspect—the task of controlling the "dangerous classes" of Britain's growing urban concentrations offered much relevant experience. Increasingly, camp authorities envisioned their assignment as an exercise in poor relief and urban governance that echoed earlier attempts to maintain concentrated populations. "Welfare work" was an emerging form of expertise at the turn of the century, and Emily Hobhouse herself recommended the appointment of an investigative committee whose functions would be "similar to those discharged with such excellent effect at home by women guardians of the poor."[18] Middle-class female investigators, Hobhouse emphasized, had the "mother[ly] wit and womanly resource" necessary to guide male superintendents in maintaining health and domestic comfort.[19]

Resisting for too long the notion that the camps needed a major overhaul, the government denied official sanction to philanthropists wishing to follow in Hobhouse's wake. But this glacial intransigence melted over the course of the summer, and in July 1901 the War Office appointed its own Ladies' Concentration Camp Committee to conduct a systematic investigation—and deflect attention, it was hoped, from government failures. Led by Millicent Fawcett, a moderate suffragette known for working within rather than against Victorian gender politics, the committee consisted of six women, three from Britain and three stationed in South Africa, chosen for their pro-war leanings, organizational acumen, and above all, their prominence in issues of public health and social reform. Consisting entirely of women, the committee highlighted the degree to which the government (like Hobhouse herself) considered the concentration camps "a woman's issue" and a matter of poor relief rather than military policy. In this way, authorities offered a social solution—the "uplift" of inmates and the improvement of living conditions—to the outward miseries of camp life.

For political reasons, Hobhouse was denied a spot on the committee (and indeed, the military debarred her from landing in Cape Town upon a return visit: detained aboard her ship under martial law, she experienced a "concentration camp" of a different sort).[20] The chosen members of the committee, however, exhibited the "womanly resource" previously lauded by Hobhouse and they expressed a motherly (if not sisterly) concern for Afrikaner inmates (though like Hobhouse they never visited a native camp). While not a royal *commission*—evidence, Elaine Harrison suggests, that the government did not take its findings seriously[21]—the committee's attentive reports offered valuable recommendations in late 1901, which Milner read carefully and defended to his subordinates.[22] The committee thus represented a significant step on the path to female participation in public life, and its recommendations set a template for future reforms.[23]

Concentration camps and the confined industrial institutions—workhouses, factories, and social housing estates—of urban Britain were clearly linked in British minds. Secretary Brodrick recruited educated middle-class women with backgrounds in social reform and even cited his "own experience as a visiting justice in prisons" as a model for the investigative work to be undertaken.[24] Apart from Fawcett herself, the committee's secretary, Lucy Deane, drew from her experience as a municipal factory inspector in England and Ireland. In private correspondence, she noted she "felt quite at home going from tent to tent," comparing her duties in the camps to "visiting 'workers' at home." By "inspecting water supply, hospital and sanitary arrangements," her tour of the camps felt "for all the world . . . like old days."[25] Deane also had qualifications from the National Health Society as a sanitary inspector and specialist in infant welfare work, complementing the expertise of other members like Dr. Ella Scarlet and Katherine Bereton, who had backgrounds in nursing, sanitation, and children's health.[26] Meanwhile, Dr. Jane Waterston had experience with the Ladies Relief Committee of Cape Town providing for mostly English-speaking war refugees who had fled Transvaal on the outbreak of war and who lived impoverished lives in city tenements. Apart from medical inspections at the leper colony on Robben Island, she had also monitored Cape Colony plague camps earlier in the year.[27] She thereby presided over two separate episodes of encampment in South Africa.

Upon arrival, the committee started its tour in Cape Town—the "view of Table Mountain" made South Africa seem "a country worth fighting for," Fawcett remarked.[28] The ladies visited a variety of institutions—orphanages, industrial schools, labor compounds, and other facilities of confinement and regulation—before embarking on an exhaustive investigation (in a dedicated first-class coach) of some thirty-three concentration camps in Transvaal, Orange River Colony, Cape Colony, and Natal.[29] Though Deane privately condemned the committee's final report as "very white-washy" and "all . . . jam and blarney,"[30] its findings were more strident than the government had hoped for. Eager to denounce the "demoralizing effect" of indiscriminate charity, the committee casually noted that hunger and disease were "part of the price paid for war."[31] And yet, it made substantive and thoroughgoing criticisms that effectively vindicated Hobhouse's earlier stance. Though it waxed eloquent about "criminal negligence" on the part of inmates,[32] the report's findings undermined comforting assertions that high mortality was inevitable among a filthy and uncivilized population. "Blunders have been made,"

Fawcett wrote to Milner, and "in every camp where there has been an exceptionally bad outbreak of disease we think we see causes which more foresight and better organization might have removed."[33]

Among the committee's major recommendations was an improved ration scale (a point more strongly conveyed in private communiqués than in the published report[34]); a reduction in the size of camps to a maximum of three thousand inmates; and the introduction of facilities for disinfecting camp water supplies.[35] Many suggestions were compatible with camp lessons accumulated by Indian officials in the 1890s. Influenced by urban sanitary reform and the insights of Florence Nightingale at Crimean army barracks, the "provision of tanks for boiling all drinking water in camps" was one of the "most urgent recommendation[s]."[36] In addition to more demanding labor regimens (in line with workhouse routines, the committee recommended a compulsory nine-hour workday) and tighter controls over egress and ingress (higher fences and a stricter enforcement of passes), the ladies endorsed a formal system of reporting illness and mandated the compulsory removal of the sick to hospital. Further, the committee recommended regular medical inspections and strict sanitary discipline: bathing, disinfection, and severe punishment "in the interests of inmates" for sanitary infractions.[37] Such reasoning accorded with that of Undersecretary for State Lord Onslow, who articulated a more general attitude: "when a tramp comes into an English workhouse, he has to take a bath." So "why not the same in a concentration camp?"[38]

Metropolitan workhouses offered clear inspiration both for the formation and reform of concentration camps. Inspired by the "workhouse test," the committee criticized the practice, still extant in some districts, of providing rations to refugees living in town, mandating they either move to camp or be cut off from government support entirely. Local institutions also offered guidance. At some of the worst camps the committee ordered a "disinfecting crusade" to perform a thorough weekly cleaning. This was a regimen witnessed firsthand by Dr. Waterston during plague operations, and the committee noted that nothing but measures "similar to those used in Cape Town during the plague could be effectual in dealing with the state of sickness." Tents, bedding, and clothing were to be disinfected with carbolic powder, while "camp police . . . went down the lines of tents, strewing the surface of the ground with chloride of lime."[39]

Ultimately, however, successful camps depended on "the character and capacity of the superintendent." Charged with controlling "some thousands of people wholly unaccustomed to discipline," superintendents required a "personal weight and authority" that was often absent in the junior officers in charge. The Fawcett

Committee recommended replacing superintendents at camps like Aliwal North and Middelburg who were not "firm and strict" enough.[40] Senior figures like A. G. Trollope, chief superintendent in the Orange River Colony—whom the ladies (privately) described as "feeble," "without a chin," and "weak as water"[41]— also received criticism. So too did General Maxwell, the military governor of Pretoria, whom they portrayed as "soft, lazy, and . . . .with no back-bone."[42] In their place, the committee maintained, "a strong man was needed to gradually get control of the camps."[43] With these recommendations in hand, Milner and Chamberlain searched for new personnel to enforce social and sanitary discipline, and reduce mortality rates. The Ladies' Committee lamented the difficulty of obtaining qualified administrators, remarking there had "never been a training school for camp superintendents."[44] But this was not entirely true. When the Colonial Office recruited "strong men" to gain control of the camps, it looked to India.

"INDIAN EXPERIENCE"

In class terms, the Boers were fit subjects for the metropolitan practices of social and sanitary investigation. But Britons also viewed camp inmates with a racial and colonial lens. It was thus only fitting that figures like Milner and Chamberlain drew inspiration from imperial precedents when faced with the care and control of concentrated colonials. Conceiving themselves as actors in a larger transimperial history, they explicitly recognized the "very analogous experience" of Indian plague and famine camps.[45]

The turn to India was perhaps only natural. The Indian Ocean had long been a conduit for the transmission of culture and technology, and in an age of imperial connection, the techno-expertise demanded by new colonies was largely drawn from India. In Thomas Metcalf's words, the British Raj functioned as a "sub-imperial center" that "provided inspiration, precedents, and personnel for colonial administration" to more peripheral regions of empire.[46] By "fruitfully imagining the lessons that could be learned and transferred between differently constituted colonial places," Milner and Chamberlain highlighted the degree to which colonial governance was, in the words of David Lambert and Alan Lester, "a relative and comparative endeavor."[47] But while the turn to India seemed obvious to the Colonial Office, the interchange of ideas, practices, and personnel between different British colonies has thus far eluded historians of the concentration camps, whose work is framed by the political turf wars of contemporary South Africa. Understanding the camps as they developed during the war means following the interimperial thought patterns of British officials themselves and envisioning the camps of South Africa and South Asia as two interconnected episodes of a larger imperial phenomenon.

As colonial secretary, Chamberlain was personally cognizant of Indian famine camps and turned for inspiration to some familiar figures. After the Fawcett Committee's revelations, he sent his private secretary, Lord Onslow, to the nearby though administratively autonomous India Office to interview Sir Thomas Holderness, the newly appointed secretary of the Indian Revenue Department and author of the government of India's official history of the 1896–97 famine.[48] Probing the lessons of Indian camps, Holderness discussed analogous problems of disease and overcrowding and recommended South African officials consult published famine codes on the subject. The next day, Chamberlain's office got busy reading. Holderness also compiled a list of officers with experience at Indian famine and plague camps who were available for further consultation. Of these, James Cleghorn, the recently retired surgeon-general of India and the commanding officer of Bombay's war against plague, traveled to Whitehall from his retirement home in Surrey for an interview. Here, he shared his expertise supervising segregation camps and volunteered to read official reports from South Africa, offering commentary in the margins.[49]

Researchers at the Colonial Office soon realized that in reality plague and famine camps were anything but the orderly bastions of health and well-being that officials in South Africa hoped to assemble. Constrained by even harsher fiscal restrictions than in South Africa, Indian camps were overcrowded, disorganized, and marked by high mortality from exposure and disease. But for the very reason they endured similar (and sometimes more arduous) struggles, Indian camps offered valuable instruction, especially in the control of disease and the discipline of destitute crowds.

Despite obvious differences in context and function, Chamberlain believed Indian and South African camps were similar enough that lessons could be exchanged between them, and he wrote to Milner convincing him that "Indian experience in famine camps" offered a valuable guide.[50] Holderness was at first "doubtful whether . . . Indian experience [would] prove applicable to the S[outh] African problem" and pointed to differences in climate and culture as well as the nature of camp diseases (cholera and smallpox were more prevalent in Indian camps than South Africa's biggest killers, measles and typhoid). Yet his recommendations were broadly applicable. "Judging from . . . Indian experience," Holderness noted, "some of the concentration camps [in South Africa] were too large" and he felt that "better results w[oul]d be ensured by breaking them up." Further, he underscored the need to "guard all sources of water supply." Among other basic lessons, he recommended "segregation [be] resorted to" on the appearance of disease and "close inspection enforced in order to detect cases of illness." Cleghorn concurred. Bombay plague camps demonstrated the supreme importance of "strict discipline" in sanitary matters. "All inmates should be made to keep clean and to observe sanitary regulations," he insisted during his interview at Whitehall.[51] Chamberlain paraphrased many of these observations, noting that earlier practices in India "indicated that the question of a pure water supply is paramount" and that "camps ought not to be too large— not over, say, 5000."[52]

"THE NEW GENIUSES FROM INDIA"

Though the Fawcett Committee made similar recommendations, counsel from prominent experts from India offered additional impetus. Complementing the domestic advice of female social investigators was the cosmopolitan expertise of male professionals, authorized by science and imperial prestige. After interviews with Cleghorn and Holderness, the precedent of plague and famine camps inspired a major reorganization of personnel. Mounting mortality and a fatalistic attitude in South Africa called for new blood and new ideas. From India Chamberlain sought "trained men . . . of high official rank" who were "thoroughly conversant with plague and famine camps."[53] Defensive of his own work, the outgoing chief superintendent A. G. Trollope cited "personal knowledge of some of the famine camps" to note that Indian officials "would not be suitable for controlling Boers, who require different handling to the natives of India."[54] But Milner and Chamberlain disagreed. Whether in India or Africa, the basic technical and sanitary aspects of camp management were broadly analogous.[55] And though "want of local knowledge" was a disadvantage, Indian officers could "adapt themselves to the peculiar conditions obtaining in the Concentration Camps."[56] Indian lessons, they believed, were generally applicable and globally transferrable.

Himself a prominent agent of sanitary reform—he was previously the mayor of Birmingham and founder of the London School of Tropical Medicine in 1899— Chamberlain held colonial medicine in high esteem. He thus telegraphed Viceroy Curzon to recruit camp experts from the Indian Medical Service (IMS) with "technical experience" and a "gift of command" in order to "deal with [the] difficult and unmanageable people" in the concentration camps.[57] With "forethought and science," he hoped Indian experts would enact "expedients for curing or preventing" mortality.[58] Three months later, a cohort of eight Indian officials disembarked at

FIGURE 27.

The "new geniuses from India" as Milner called them: Lieutenant-Colonel Samuel J. Thomson (left) and Colonel James S. Wilkins (right) of the Indian Medical Service (IMS). Trollope and Tucker sought employment in municipal politics. The latter organized the Klipspruit plague segregation camp in Johannesburg in 1903. [Credit: Kent History and Library Center U750/F3; W. T. Pike, *East Anglia in the Twentieth Century: Contemporary Biographies* (Brighton: W. T. Pike, 1912), 235, photo courtesy of the Suffolk Record Office.]

the Natal port of Durban, an act that personally connected two episodes of civilian concentration in the British Empire. The Fawcett Committee's female "intuition" would be backed up by "hard science" and the imprimatur of male "genius." Moreover, the camps would receive an Indian dose of authoritarian management.

Among the chosen officers were individuals well known in the annals of plague and famine. Colonel J. S. Wilkins (IMS), who had gained "large plague experience" in 1896–97 as the special medical officer responsible for inspecting plague camps in

Bombay, became director of the newly created Refugee Camp department in the Orange River Colony. Meanwhile, Lieutenant-Colonel S. J. Thomson (IMS), who had gained "administrative control of both numerous plague and famine camps" as the sanitary commissioner of the North-Western Provinces, qualified for the same post in the Transvaal.[59] Thomson was a dynamic personality with a prolific pen, who left detailed accounts of his experience in multiple camp systems,[60] while Wilkins, though softened in his retirement years as an affable small-town Suffolk mayor, emerges from the archives as an uncompromising disciplinarian.[61] Both were chosen for their success in India, and both started their work in South Africa at close to three times the salary of the officers they replaced.[62] Chamberlain was willing to pay.

Accompanying Wilkins and Thomson was a coterie of subordinate officers, all of whom had "special experience in the management of plague and famine camps."[63] Captain A. F. W. King (IMS) and Captains W. J. W. Brackenbury and W. C. French of the Indian Staff Corps (who had served under Wilkins in Bombay) along with Captain J. C. Robertson (IMS), Lieutenant R. W. Henderson, and C. E. W. Sands of the Indian Police (who served under Thomson[64]) injected military discipline and medical expertise into problem camps as inspectors or superintendents.[65] In this way, Milner and Chamberlain outsourced the management of South Africa's concentration camps, opening a new chapter in a larger imperial story. "There [would] be plenty for . . . [the] superintendents from India . . . to do," the High Commissioner added.[66]

"STRICT DISCIPLINE IN ALL MATTERS"

When they arrived in February 1902, Thomson and Wilkins found many changes already underway. During an early inspection tour, Wilkins noted "there [was] much to be done in the way of sanitation in [the] camps."[67] But much had already improved. The Fawcett Commission's sound recommendations mobilized expertise in related fields of domestic welfare work, while the experience of Dr. Waterston and other health officers like Drs. Turner and McCulloch at Cape Colony plague camps drew from the broader transimperial practices of tropical medical. The impact of "Indian experts" should not be overstated, yet the subcontinent exerted a powerful influence even before Wilkins and Thomson set foot in South Africa. Apart from Holderness and Cleghorn's influence at the Colonial Office, the provisions of Indian famine codes and plague reports inspired new efforts to purify water and segregate the sick. Mortality started a happy and precipitous decline early in the new year.

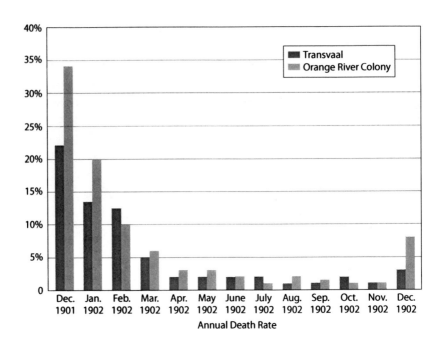

40%

35% ■ Transvaal
     ■ Orange River Colony

30%

25%

20%

15%

10%

5%

0
   Dec. Jan. Feb. Mar. Apr. May June July Aug. Sep. Oct. Nov. Dec.
   1901 1902 1902 1902 1902 1902 1902 1902 1902 1902 1902 1902 1902
                                 Annual Death Rate

FIGURE 28.

Camp death rates, December 1901-December 1902, at Boer camps. Statistics for native camps are unavailable but improvements in mortality were likely less dramatic [Credit: Graph by Bill Nelson.]

Nonetheless, the "new geniuses" and "big guns" from India, as they were infor-mally styled,[68] inaugurated a new phase in the history of the camps. Indian interven-tions unquestionably contributed to overall improvements, Milner believed. The Indian officers "undertook work which . . . was very laborious and difficult," he reported, and "the death-rate of the camps since February shows how satisfactorily they have maintained . . . the camps."[69] Annual mortality stabilized under their tenure from a peak of 40 percent to a much more comfortable annual rate of 2 percent, where it largely stayed until the camps were deconcentrated in late 1902 and early 1903. To a certain degree, the death rate declined after the natural "fade out" of seasonal measles, though Thomson and Wilkins should be credited with preventing additional outbreaks during the South African winter of 1902. Armed with vindicating statistics and bolstered by a new sense of administrative capability, the government claimed by war's end that the "organization of the . . . camps has been steadily perfected."[70]

Camp reform is often equated with a process of "liberalization" and material improvement: the provision of more hospital beds, better latrine accommodation, and arrangements for the increased trucking of supplies. Among Wilkins and Thomson's first acts was to introduce improved ration scales with increased "farinaceous content."[71] According to Thomson, better food and more fuel undoubtedly "improved health and comfort among the inmates." Meanwhile, watertight huts, erected by inmates with support from the Public Works Department, gradually replaced old and leaky tents, first on the high veld, and later throughout the entire camp system. Thomson's project to erect "iron and brick huts . . . 24' by 14'" with windows and "boarded floors" dramatically changed the tented aesthetic of camps in 1902 and prevented further outbreaks of pneumonia.[72] With the more generous economic mindset fostered by Milner, "the Indians" also spent liberally on doctors, medical equipment, and new infrastructure like washhouses, cooking facilities, and water boilers. The management of epidemics also became more systematic and scientific, and in Pretoria, Thomson established a laboratory (equipped with microscopes previously used during plague operations in Cape Town) to identify diseases.[73]

At the same time, however, the disciplinary apparatus of reformed camps exhibited an increasingly coercive edge. In the context of humanitarian reform, South African camps ironically adopted many of the features—barbed-wire fences, armed sentries, and more rigorous systems of punishment—normally associated with the infamous concentration camps of twentieth-century Europe. In the context of sanitation, Wilkins and Thomson revived a coercive ethic first developed in India to police plague and famine victims. Chamberlain declared himself "much impressed by the necessity for strict discipline in all matters relating to health,"[74] and it was precisely this uncompromising stance he hoped to import from India. In the context of famine, Thomson insisted the behavior of "the individual whose habits and customs are opposed to recognized sanitary principles" must be "modified or checked, by force if necessary, so that the health of the surrounding population may not be endangered." That "cherished possession, the liberty of the subject," he continued, must at times be violated, especially in the case of colonial populations who were "as a rule absolute[ly] ignorant" of modern hygiene and who viewed "the slightest innovation . . . with suspicion."[75] What was true of Indians was true of Afrikaners. Death and disarray demanded more rigid medical inspection, more vigorous punishment for sanitary infractions, and fenced isolation wards or "contact camps"—inspirations from plague segregation camps—to arrest disease.

In 1902, the camps witnessed an intensive fence-building campaign. The military had already enclosed some camps with barbed wire, not only to prevent escape but to "protect" refugees from insurgent raids. But new policies carried out by Wilkins and Thomson demarcated enclosed camps as discrete units of sanitary management. Just as concentration camps were wartime adaptations of a technology of colonial "welfare," barbed-wire fences applied a technology of war for the purposes of health and hygiene. The Fawcett Committee advocated that "every camp would benefit by being surrounded by a fence with gates where police or sentries should be posted," but this vision was realized under Thomson and Wilkins's tenure.[76]

By imposing boundaries, fences also enforced existing practices of concentrating relief recipients scattered throughout towns into manageable sites. Camps first emerged to systematize relief, but despite admonitions from the Fawcett Committee, some districts continued to distribute rations, in ad hoc fashion, to destitute town dwellers. In Johannesburg, for example, Thomson condemned "outdoor charity" for "pauperizing the people" and reaffirmed confinement as the organizing principle of colonial welfare. "All recipients of outside relief in Johannesburg must by a certain day hand in their ration tickets or go into the camp," he demanded.[77] Once and for all, fences would compel the destitute to live in camp. Wilkins also condemned the "objectionable practice," still extant in towns like Heilbron, "of keeping families in town." In a South African derivative of the "residence test" at Indian famine camps, lingering cases of "outdoor charity" came to a definite end.[78]

Fences were also important components of medical surveillance. In particular, the Indian practices of mandatory evacuation and segregation became more common. "Indian experience . . . indicate[d] that . . . as soon as a camp becomes unhealthy . . . it must be evacuated,"[79] Chamberlain noted, and after November, superintendents evacuated many unhealthy camps to fresh sites and constructed segregation wards to isolate disease suspects. Impromptu efforts to quarantine measles and other infectious diseases started before Thomson and Wilkins's administration. But when they arrived, the "Indian geniuses" ordered the construction of additional isolation camps, enshrining quarantine as a routine measure of camp administration.[80]

Thomson had often stressed the benefits of segregation but in India he lamented that medical ideals were often impractical.[81] Armed in South Africa, by contrast, with the powers of martial law and the resources of a warfare state, his preferred specifications for quarantine and isolation became reality. In arrangements inspired by Indian plague operations, "all arrivals in camp [were] accommodated in a separate encampment until they [were] pronounced free from infection or contagion by the Medical Officer of the camp." New arrivals were "on no account . . . allowed to enter the Main Camp whilst undergoing this quarantine" and visitors were strictly forbidden "to enter camps set apart for contagious diseases."[82] Like arrangements at India's Khana Junction, Wilkins and Thomson also erected fences to protect water supplies from fouling and barred inmates and visitors from spreading disease by traveling to and from town. Finally, the Indian officers enclosed hospitals with barbed wire and adopted arrangements (and terminology) developed during plague when they constructed "contact camps" and "observation wards." Just as fenced undesirable wards prevented the spread of political subversion, enclosed isolation camps arrested the contagion of measles and other diseases.

"THE TERROR OF THE HOSPITAL"

A stricter regimen of tent-to-tent inspection was also vital to reform. The camp population was "not unlike the more ignorant of the English poor," the Fawcett Committee noted, and it recommended intrusive inspections analogous to those of poor law guardians.[83] Women did much of the work, and relief matrons like Ms. MacBridge at Brandfort, formerly a hospital superintendent in Jamaica and Nigeria,[84] investigated cases of destitution, instructed mothers in the proper care of children, and even inspected inmates' undergarments to ensure they were clean.[85] Most importantly, matrons reported cases of sickness to camp doctors, who removed disease suspects to hospital. With the conviction that "constant vigilance" was necessary to "wage war against the insanitary habits of the people,"[86] meanwhile, officials banned "Boer remedies" as superstitious relics.

As surveillance intensified under Wilkins and Thomson, inmates pushed back in familiar ways. If British doctors derided the Boer pharmacopeia, inmates were equally dubious of British medicine—an understandable position given the tragic outbreak of disease under British management. With echoes of plague suspects in India, many expressed grave fear of camp hospitals, which they considered morgues. Like other preindustrial people, the home was for them the locus of medical care, and despite measurable health improvements enacted by forced hospitalization, some inmates spoke of "murder hospital[s]."[87] In one case, the Harrismith superintendent reported a "child [who] was absolutely terrified at the idea of being removed [to hospital]." "I never remember seeing such a pitiful sight as I saw on the attempted removal," he remarked.[88] As with Indian plague suspects, British doctors complained that Boer inmates had a "rooted objection to sending their children to hospital" and did "all in their power to conceal disease."[89] And since "the conditions of hospital life in the camp" were apparently "much more in favor of the patients than those in the tents," Dr. Pratt Yule could only explain such sentiments as the outgrowth of backward superstition.[90]

In medical matters, however, there was little room for compromise. For British doctors, camp hospitals were more than receptacles of medical science but cultural markers of their own supremacy. Hospitals emerged in the Victorian period as symbols of civilization and modernity—the domain of professional middle-class men disseminating sanitary truths (many of which have now been proven false) according to the dictates of a universal reason. In this context it proved necessary, in the minds of medical men, "to use compulsion" to "save [camp inmates] from themselves."[91] Despite the "terror of the hospital," officials in the months after November 1901 enforced compulsory hospitalization of the sick with increasing rigor and success. Wilkins mandated that any cases of concealment be "severely dealt with."[92] Under the Bombay official's watch, the "Free State Proclamation 4 of 1902" strengthened existing legislation and made superintendents "ex officio JPs" with "summary powers of punishment . . . for breaches of camp sanitary and hospital regulations," enabling them to "commit [offenders] to the nearest public prison."[93] If earlier disorder permitted leniency and toleration, reforms ushered in a new severity.

Above all, Wilkins and Thomson imported the uncompromising ethic of Indian medicine. Though lip service upheld tact and persuasion, they forcibly removed suspect cases to hospital under magisterial powers.[94] The superintendent must be a "strong man" Wilkins contended,[95] with the same power and responsibility as "the officer commanding of a regiment," and he went on to laud the "great powers" of martial law.[96] Thomson noted similarly that "with powers under martial law to insist on [sanitary] orders being carried out," the position of sanitary officials was even stronger in South Africa than under emergency famine and plague legislation. The camps thus afforded "an unusual opportunity" of putting into practice many unfulfilled lessons from India.[97] With no more respect for Boer superstitions than for Hindu folk medicine, Wilkins and Thomson sought to "eradicate the profound belief of these people that a mother's heart is a better guide . . . than the educated experience of a lifetime" of scientific study.[98] As in India, they turned to coercive measures in the paternalistic belief that forced hospitalization was in the best interests of "ignorant" and "uncivilized" inmates.

Whatever its vexations, sanitary reform substantially improved inmates' health. The trauma and desperation of the winter—the "regular tramp of the bearers to morgue tents, and the slowly winding procession every afternoon"—was over at last.[99] But in other ways, inmates experienced medical reforms as unpopular and authoritarian impositions. As in India, intrusive applications of Western epidemiology resulted in substantial pushback: "grave disorder" and a case of assault were even reported at Bethulie owing to a riot by inmates over the forced removal of children to hospital.[100] Meanwhile, rumors spread among a "people naturally suspicious"[101] over the poisoning of children in camp hospitals and corpses being "cut to pieces" by British doctors. In scenes reminiscent of Bombay plague riots, the Indian Medical Service (IMS) officer A. F. W. King faced a rebellion at the Orange River Station camp over post mortem autopsies. One woman assaulted King (and was accordingly handed to military authorities for punishment) while others "congregated at the hospital and stormed into the wards and removed their children."[102] Indian officials may have applied the medical lessons of Indian camps, but the political lessons continued to elude them.

As in India, wild rumors were indicative of more general fear and mistrust, though inmates expressed discontent in more quotidian ways as well. At Irene, for example, they protested the dismissal of Afrikaner nurses and local charitable committees and their replacement with British-approved matrons,[103] while inmates at Vredefort Road complained in writing about authoritarian regulations enforced in March 1902, describing their abode as a "prisoners' camp."[104] With the passage of time, however, most came to terms with Britain's new medical regime, and at festivities organized for Edward VII's coronation in June 1902, many inmates expressed their "appreciation," if we are to believe government accounts, "for the material advantages afforded at no small expense" by British medicine.[105]

"THE PERFECT CAMP"

Camp reform in South Africa reached its pinnacle with the construction of new camps on the Cape and Natal coasts. Following Thomas Holderness's recommendations, Chamberlain endeavored to reduce large inland camps to 5,000 inmates or fewer by opening new campsites.[106] Located close to seaports (East London, King William's Town, and Port Elizabeth in the Cape, and at Merebank and several other sites around Durban in Natal) the camps were unencumbered by problems of supply caused by rail shortages upcountry, though they remained under Transvaal and Orange River Colony jurisdiction and were subject to martial law.[107] These institutions, carefully planned, and constructed by the Public Works Department in consultation with Wilkins and Thomson, were material embodiments of the many camp

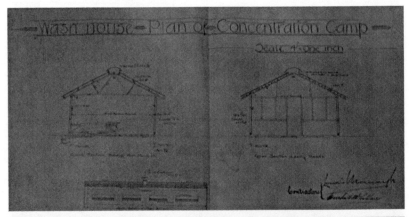

FIGURE 29.
Public Works Department Plans for Wash Houses (above) and construction of
Uitenhage camp close to Port Elizabeth (below). [Credit: NASA KAB M4/52 "Wash
House Plan of Concentration Camp"; NASA KAB AG/452 "Construction work in
operation, Burgher concentration camp, Pannells Mill, Uitenhage, 4 March 1902.]

lessons learned over the course of the nineteenth century. Along the Indian Ocean
coast of South Africa, British officials consummated decades of accumulated experience in the care and control of concentrated humanity. Described by John Buchan
as "perfect" in their management,[108] these camps represented a "blueprint" for the
future.[109]

Earlier camps were results of expediency and emergency conditions. But following Milner's realization early in 1902 that "camps [would] probably be in existence

for the next three years,"[110] the new camps constructed under Wilkins and Thomson's direction embodied the promise of careful and conscious forethought. In Cape Colony, the ubiquitous Lewis Mansergh, the Public Works director previously active erecting plague segregation camps in Cape Town, assumed charge of construction. Described as "a dear good hard-working creature," though one prone to sending "voluminous telegrams" on "endless little matters,"[111] Mansergh approached the coastal camps with attentive and exacting zeal. Consulting with Wilkins and drawing from his own local camp experience, Mansergh incorporated lessons from the nineteenth century's wide array of concentrated institutions. The dimensions of English boarding homes, factories, military barracks, and army hospitals all entered the equation.[112] With mathematical precision, each inmate received four hundred and twenty cubic feet of air space; huts were fifteen feet apart and streets were fifty-eight feet wide.

Arrangements at nearby plague camps on the Cape Peninsula shaped the coastal camps in tangible ways. At Uitenhage, located just outside Port Elizabeth, officials chose "an ideal site for a concentration camp" that was previously recommended for a plague segregation camp (though never actually occupied).[113] Here, Mansergh erected isolation and observation wards "upon lines adopted for similar work in connection with bubonic plague in the Cape Peninsula."[114] Camp morgues, moreover, approximated "similar buildings of this nature erected at the bubonic plague camps," while the sterilization of equipment and clothing employed "a special 'formalin chamber'" previously used "in connection with the suppression of bubonic plague."[115] Latrines, which included bacterial filters and sedimentary chambers for the purification of sewage, likewise fulfilled the demands of modern sanitary science. As illustrated below, the architecture of concentration camps came to approximate Bombay plague camps, organized around a central hospital complex enclosed with barbed wire. Replete with fenced isolation wards for enteric fever and separate hospital blocks for measles, diphtheria, and other ailments, this layout facilitated the careful policing of disease.

The coastal camps undoubtedly provided inmates with greater comfort than their inland predecessors. Mansergh was sometimes guilty of extravagance: still wary of expense, Deputy Administrator Goold-Adams sarcastically derided the "spring mattresses, gold and white dinner service, curtains and carpets" he was apparently furnishing. But when Mansergh replaced leaky tents with "large and airy" huts, he simply fulfilled a recommendation first made by Surgeon Cleghorn, who pointed out that cold tents would harbor measles and pneumonia.[116] Bone china teapots never materialized, but huts at Kabusie boasted "two windows [and] a small kitchen

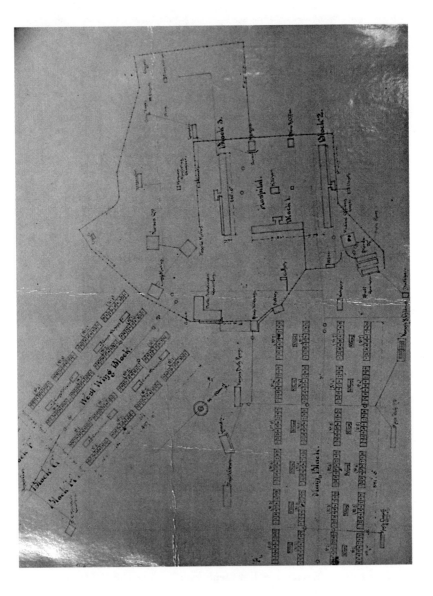

FIGURE 30.

"The Perfect Camp," Amalinda Bluff, East London, Cape Colony. As at the Khana Junction plague segregation camp in India, barbed wire surrounded the hospital and water supply. [Credit: NASA VAB SRC volume 138.]

attached at the back."[117] Meanwhile, the latrine accommodation was "an improved copy of the system obtaining at [nearby] King William's Town"[118] (the shift from the "bucket" to "trench" system here mirrored practices at Indian plague and famine camps.)[119] Economy remained a watchword, however, and many camps made do with used portable huts recycled from military barracks, along with old material from a disused social housing facility.[120] Electric lighting was also deemed an unnecessary expense, despite its potential as a surveillance technology.[121]

If camp sanitation approached "perfection" on the Cape and Natal coasts, so did discipline. Ironically, those camps with the best material living conditions were also those built to more closely supervise the most "irreconcilable" and politically "dangerous" elements from inland camps. Apart from several hundred volunteers willing to relocate to healthier locales, coastal camps mostly accommodated "undesirables and people who [were] giving trouble."[122] The forced relocation to desolate coastal sites, exiled from their upcountry fatherland, was meant as a punitive measure and an object lesson in British power. Moving the "very worst undesirables" (rather than bona fide "refugees") was more politically expedient, authorities also believed. Further, it was hoped the threat of removal would have a good "moral effect" on those remaining, while breaking the chain of local solidarities that kept Boers united against Britons.[123]

The coastal camps achieved new disciplinary refinements adopted from prisons, workhouses, and other concentrated institutions. They thus approximated what Foucault described as "the perfect camp," in which "power would be exercised . . . through exact observation . . . [with] the geometry of the paths, the number and disposition of tents [and] the orientation of their entrances . . . exactly defined."[124] In Benthamite tones, officials in South Africa made statements about the "disposition of space," noting that the "plan of the camp" was the "outcome of considerable thought and attention." Clearly, the built environment would control inmate behavior. The coastal camps, in Mansergh's words, "had the merit of disposing of the quarters of the various officials upon a system which provided for a full oversight of the quarters to be occupied by camp inmates."[125] At both Kabusie and Amalinda Bluff, "considerable care was exercised in the disposition of the buildings," which were "arranged so as to leave an open space . . . about the center of the Camp" where the superintendent—in this case Wilkins's disciple from Bombay, Captain Brackenbury—could occupy a "most central and commanding position."[126] Organized around the hospital, whose personnel maintained close surveillance, rows of uniform huts reproduced an orderly aesthetic, fixing camp populations into legible, geometric, and rationalized spaces. South Africa's coastal camps thereby consummated both the material comfort and more stringent discipline laid out by government officials and their humanitarian critics as a program of reform. In the process, they rendered Boer inmates governable subjects, who, according to Milner, became as easy to manage as "any English crowd."[127]

ANTEBELLUM AFTERLIFE

The war ended, at last, on May 31, 1902, to the considerable relief of Milner and others planning a worst-case scenario in which the war, and the concentration camps, might last another three years. The Peace of Vereeniging was not the end of the camps, however, for they retained a sizeable population into 1903 as depots of relief and rehabilitation. If camps were nothing more than instruments of military strategy as is so often assumed, then their story would indeed have ended in May 1902. But their prominent relief role continued in the months and even years after the war, exemplifying continuities between camps and other relief operations.

In a statement that contradicted earlier wartime representations of a rootless and wandering people, S. J. Thomson noted that inmates, "born, bred, and living all their lives in one locality," displayed an "intense love of home" and were correspondingly eager to return to their farms (apparently British victory had rendered the Boers submissive and domesticated).[128] Facing ongoing expense and the camps' unpopular political associations, the government was equally "anxious to get people back as soon as the military [would] allow."[129] In this context, camps functioned as repatriation depots, accommodating an influx of returning POWs and recently surrendered men, many of whom "had never been subject to camp discipline and gave a considerable amount of trouble."[130] The logistics of return proved more complicated than expected, however. Scorched-earth warfare had devastated the country: green pastures were now barren; and houses and villages were burned. After taking an "oath of allegiance" many returned home for spring sowing in July and August 1902, taking with them a tent and one month's rations.[131] But these, according to Thomson, were a minority—the "well-to-do, the restless, independent, and industrious people" who had their own means of support.[132] In contrast, Wilkins and Thomson detained the majority—those "who [could] not support themselves"[133]— and prevented them from leaving. In October 1902, the camps still contained fifty thousand Boer inmates (the African population at this time is unknown). These were the "lazy" and "indolent": the "poor white" *bywoners* for whom hunger and destitution always loomed.

The last of South Africa's contentious concentration camps finally closed in March 1903. But the underlying humanitarian conditions that first generated them remained. Facing persistent fears about "pauperization" and the pitfalls of outdoor charity in the aftermath of war, Thomson and Wilkins organized a new system of "relief camps" in early 1903, which continued to enforce discipline and provide relief for several years to come. Accommodating the residual camp population and consisting of "tent accommodation, hospitals, medical attendance, [and] schools," these institutions recycled much of the physical infrastructure of existing concentration camps and employed many camp personnel with "experience in disciplinary work."[134] With a system of labor and residence tests—relief applicants lived in camp and worked eight-hour days—inmates performed work on nearby irrigation and railway projects.[135] As in India, the camps distributed wages fixed to the price of grain, which could be deducted for idleness. On the South African veld, Wilkins and Thomson thus reproduced the familiar infrastructure and ideology of Indian famine camps, though they also replicated Milner's unfulfilled 1900 proposal to accommodate wartime refugees on extramural relief works.

Since concentration camps had functioned as relief depots throughout the war, the transition to full-blown relief and repatriation was straightforward. And relief camps were comparatively uncontroversial as well. Emily Hobhouse, permitted back into the country once hostilities had ended, visited the Tweespruit relief camp in 1903 and complained that inmates did not receive a "living wage."[136] But relief work camps did not become a matter of serious public attention, either in Britain or South Africa. Replicating the well-oiled humanitarian and sanitary machinery refined over the course of the war, antebellum camps did not suffer from serious outbreaks of disease like their wartime counterparts. Instead, they offered an inconspicuous denouement to a hotly contested narrative of civilian concentration.

Black Africans also found themselves concentrated in a new system of "camps" (of a sort) as they pursued work at residential mining compounds or else were confined in South Africa's developing system of "locations" in the postwar period. An original justification for British involvement in the war was to protect black Africans from Boer maltreatment. Apartheid did not become South African state policy until 1948, but like plague camps before them, concentration camps laid early groundwork for racial segregation.[137] Speaking of continuities between native concentration camps and later patterns of settlement and segregation, Emelia Molefe, an inmate at Vredefort Road, "thought of the camp as her first experience of 'location' life."[138]

Postwar native locations often recycled the very problems (and solutions) that caused (and resolved) the scandal of concentration camps. Lionel Curtis, a member of Milner's inner circle, voiced a familiar complaint when he emphasized the sanitary menace of natives "scattered beyond the limits of the location."[139] Likewise, Dr. Turner upheld concentration camps (in their reformed incarnation) as models for the sanitary management of locations, which were "almost invariably filthy" and posed epidemiological dangers to European towns.[140] Accommodations for mineworkers at Groenfontein and Vierfontein in 1906 were, for example, "rapidly growing and [were] absolutely without order." But when epidemics broke out, the new superintendent imposed lessons from the concentration camps when he "established barracks and cells" and introduced "strong measures . . . to enforce law and order."[141]

"Camps" of many sorts thus remained integral features of a new imperial landscape. Embittered memories of sacrifice in the camps fomented a martyrdom complex among Afrikaner nationalists and, consequently, the indignant politics of apartheid.[142] Boer inmates quickly forgot that black Africans were also displaced by scorched-earth warfare and concentrated in camps. Instead, they mobilized a singular "paradigm of suffering" in the service of ethnic nationalism.[143] Victims of the camps rapidly became villains: barbed wire, physical segregation, and pass laws—first introduced by Britain as wartime measures—lived on fifty years later in the form of the apartheid security state.[144] Camps begot camps, albeit ones stripped of liberal or humanitarian justifications. Boer War concentration camps were the original sin of South Africa's unpardonable twentieth century.

"A BARBED-WIRE FENCE AROUND THE HOUSE OF COMMONS"

What of the camps' larger legacies in Britain and the world? Camp mortality generated a scandal and a subsequent reform campaign that all but eliminated epidemic disease and made camps safe for their concentrated inhabitants. As was so often the case, however, imperial scandal detracted attention from more quotidian forms of coercion and injustice, while the resolution of scandal served to legitimize the continuation of imperial rule.[145] Enduring images of starving women and children generated widespread sympathy and outrage, but the parameters of dissent did not allow for a more thoroughgoing political critique of the military practices and social policies that generated concentration camps. In the jingoistic atmosphere of war, female philanthropists like Hobhouse, Deane, and Fawcett understandably focused their public attention on the most visible miseries of camp life: the "lack of water," the "bad quality" of the rations, and the "overcrowding of tents."[146] In private the Fawcett committee concurred with Hobhouse: scorched-earth warfare and the forced concentration of civilians was a "mistake which no one but these unpractical ignorant Army men could have committed." Any criticism of the policy that first led to camps, however, was "outside the reference of [the] commission," Deane lamented, and did not appear in the report.[147] Critics and reformers thus addressed the form of the camps, but not the fact of encampment. And by casting their work as strictly humanitarian—Hobhouse insisted the "plucky little body of women who have tried to meet and succor . . . distress" was "non-sectarian and non-political"[148]—their emphasis on the social rather than political manifestations of camps served ironically to deflect attention from the oppressive military practices and underlying cultural prejudices that first generated them.[149]

Parliament likewise oriented protest around living conditions and passed a lily-livered resolution to "alleviate the sufferings and improve the condition of the women and children."[150] But when it came to more substantive debate about the ethics of scorched-earth warfare and mass extrajudicial detention, Liberal leader Henry Campbell-Bannerman complained there was a "barbed-wire fence around the House of Commons."[151] Rallying around practical results, Britain's parliamentary opposition and wider political culture forced the Colonial Office to import experts from India to alleviate mortality, but it failed to generate a sustained ethical and philosophical critique of the military violence and social policies that led to camps. As Timothy Mitchell argues, the resort to "experts" serves to mask political controversy by representing imperial violence and inequality as "technical" problems to be solved via detached and rational science rather than by political reconfiguration.[152] By holding their tongues and ameliorating the death rate instead of condemning the camps outright, critics and reformers ironically helped redeem concentration camps as tenable implements of colonial rule. In an oft-repeated dynamic of British history, the survival of an institution depended on its reform. The implication for British officials was that with the right sanitary precautions and disciplinary provisions, such a thing as a "good" camp was possible. As a consequence, camps were quietly normalized (until World War II at least) as accepted instruments of state power, stamped with humane and liberal marks of legitimacy.

EPILOGUE · Camps Go Global

Lessons, Legacies, and Forgotten Solidarities

> We may . . . stand shoulder to shoulder and see to it that
> the defenseless, the innocent, are respected and pro-
> tected. And that such inhuman institutions as Concentra-
> tion Camps are never resorted to again.
>
> ELIZABETH NEETHLING, inmate at Pietermaritz-
> burg concentration camp, South Africa, 1902

> "Many refugee camps are concentration [camps] . . . they
> are so crowded with people."
>
> POPE FRANCIS, 2017

Writing at the beginning of a still promising twentieth century, S. J. Thomson was
sanguine about the legacy of British camps. As sanitary commissioner of the North-
Western Provinces and outgoing director of Transvaal concentration camps, his
broad experience in India and South Africa not only exposed him to the pitfalls of
large concentration camps but offered "an unusual opportunity of determining
whether it [was] possible to maintain a large body of men, women and children in
large camps, in good health." With proper siting, sanitary provisions, and disciplinary arrangements, he submitted, "the fact was established." Further, Thomson
emphasized, "the lessons learnt in the present instance may . . . prove of interest
and utility should more or less similar circumstances arise in the future." And given
the "varying conditions of existence prevailing in our vast Colonial Empire, it [was]
probable," he concluded, "that such will be the case." Thomson and likeminded
"camp experts" played a pivotal role propagating and to a certain extent exonerating
civilian concentration camps as a legitimate instrument of liberal empire, and they
looked forward to a future in which camps would be included in the humane arsenal
of modern statecraft. In this endeavor, famine, plague, and wartime concentration
camps would offer blueprints for future developments.[1] In their reformed incarnations, the Colonial Office concurred, South African concentration camps were
"deserving of imitation."[2]

For Thomson, the lessons of colonial camps were decidedly medical and humanitarian, and as Brevet-Colonel during World War I, he applied his experience as the

superintendent of Hollymoor military hospital in Birmingham, an institution that supplemented the brick buildings of an existing asylum with familiar rows of army tents to alleviate crowding.[3] To modern readers, however, the term *concentration camp* has entirely different connotations. What were the global legacies of Britain's empire of camps, and how do British practices fit within larger global narratives?

FROM AFRICA TO AUSCHWITZ?

Thomson's, of course, was not the only possible lesson to be gleaned. Four decades later, the Nazi leader Hermann Göring drew a different conclusion. After a heated encounter with the British ambassador Sir Nevile Henderson over Germany's own proliferating empire of camps in 1939, Göring walked to his bookshelf, pulled out the "K" volume of an encyclopedia, and read: "*Konzentrationslager . . .* first used by the British in the South African War."[4] These were sentiments repeated with alacrity by Hitler himself when he declared that concentration camps were English imports, which "we merely read up on . . . in the encyclopedia and then later copied."[5] However mendacious their logic in justifying German crimes by equating them with those of Great Britain, the Nazis only expressed a truism of the time: imperial Britain had "invented" the concentration camp.

Whatever their British origins, the specter of Auschwitz looms inescapably over the history of camps. In her *Origins of Totalitarianism*, Hannah Arendt was among the first to root the maladies of twentieth-century violence in an imperial past. In doing so, she specified British "concentration camps" in South Africa as a forerunner to the ubiquitous camps of totalitarian Germany and the Soviet Union. The Boer camps, Arendt observed, "correspond in many respects to the concentration camps at the beginning of totalitarian rule; they were used for 'suspects' whose offences could not be proved and who could not be sentenced by ordinary processes of law."[6] Yet whatever the phenomenological connections between colonialism and totalitarianism, the path from Africa to Auschwitz was neither obvious nor straightforward. As Robert Gerwarth and Stephan Malinowski remind us, the states with the "longest and ultimately most violent colonial records—France, Britain, the United States, and the Netherlands—remained democracies throughout the twentieth century."[7] To place facile blame on British imperialism for the horrors of Auschwitz and the Gulag, moreover, is to overlook the pivotal and familiar role of events (World War I and World War II), personalities (Hitler, Stalin) and ideologies (fascism, communism). It is also to misread the nature of British camps, which maintained a humanitarian mandate despite the violence and coercion they entailed.

Yet Britain's contribution cannot be dismissed entirely. As a global event in the age of mass media, the South African War helped disseminate the idea of "the camp" on a world-historical stage. Imperial Britain, furthermore, pioneered languages and attitudes later repeated in Europe's "dark century." While scandal simmered in London, camp mortality in India and South Africa riveted a global public. A new and ominous vocabulary quickly developed: the French *camps de concentration*, the Russian *kontsentratsionnyi lager*, and the iconic German *Konzentrationslager* all emerged to describe Britain's wartime camps. German periodicals ran articles like "What Can We Learn from the Boer War,"[8] and of the 358 German-language titles published on the subject, many dealt with camps explicitly.[9] Russians likewise observed events in South Africa, and Leon Trostsky's familiarity with British concentration camps first imported the concept into the Soviet Union.[10] Indian famine camps, moreover, with their heavy labor on public works, may have offered additional inspiration to the Bolsheviks once British consultants disseminated knowledge about them during the 1921 Russian Famine.[11]

As knowledge about British camps achieved global currency, barbed wire, armed sentries, and floodlit barracks became new global icons. If S. J. Thomson portrayed camps as sanitary and humanitarian enclaves, Britain's economic and military rivals, eager to raise the banner of British hypocrisy, portrayed them as sites of violence and terror.[12] Emblematic were illustrations by French artist Jean Veber published in the satirical Paris weekly *L'Assiette au Beurre* and later reprinted in Germany. The Kaiser's air force dropped copies of Veber's images into British trenches in France during World War I,[13] and the edition was reprinted for propaganda purposes in Nazi Germany.[14] The sketches were acts of the imagination more than authentic depictions, though such representations first acquainted the world with stock images that became reality in the 1930s.

British colonial camps desensitized the world to austere aesthetics of suffering and brutality, and they proved especially useful as propaganda tools. British examples loomed large in interwar Europe, and for their own *Konzentrationslager* Nazi officials emphasized resonances with British precedents. Faced with growing international condemnation, the Gestapo suggested "the starving of thousands of innocent women and children in the English concentration camps . . . during the Boer War" might offer effective riposte, while the *Hakenkreuzbanner* journal, in the midst of the Sudetenland crisis, reiterated the "patent" for concentration camps was "entirely English."[15] Such rhetoric climaxed during World War II in Joseph Goebbel's prize-winning film *Ohm Krüger*, which depicted South African concentration camps as instruments of massacre and genocide: the film concludes when a British

LES PROGRÈS DE LA SCIENCE

les prisonniers boërs ont été réunis en de grands etclos où depuis 18 mois ils trouvent le repos et le calme. Un treillage de fer traversé par un courant électrique est la plus saine et la plus sûre des clôtures. Elle permet aux prisonniers de jouir de la vue du dehors et d'avoir ainsi l'illusion de la liberté...

(Rapport officiel au War office.)

FIGURE 31.

A Boer War concentration camp depicted by Jean Veber. The sarcastic caption, quoting the British War Office, reads: "Captured Boers are housed in large enclosures, where they have found quiet and peace for the past 18 months. An electric fence constitutes the healthiest and at the same time safest barrier. This allows the prisoners a clear view, and they thus enjoy the illusion of freedom." [Credit: Sketch by Jean Veber, "Les camps de reconcentration au Transvaal," *L'Assiette au Buerre*, no. 26, September 28, 1901.]

commandant (bearing a striking resemblance to Winston Churchill) massacres women and children inmates.

Goebbels's depiction, of course, was grossly inaccurate. But while it cast claims to British humanity as a sanctimonious ruse, the film mobilized a sense of British righteousness with Machiavellian effect. Filmed a few miles from Berlin's infamous Sachsenhausen *Konzentrationslager*, *Ohm Krüger* audaciously accused imperial Britain of many of the crimes Germany was then committing—a brutal "colonial war" and the forced urbanization of scattered Jewish populations in ghettos and their subsequent concentration in camps (the process resembled, in an extreme and perverse form, the concentration of African and Afrikaner populations in fortified towns and then suburban camps).[16] Living conditions at Nazi camps differed dramatically from those in India and South Africa. And yet, the British example, when effectively manipulated, helped desensitize liberals in Germany and elsewhere to the idea of concentration camps, stamping them with a similitude of legitimacy.

Apart from Nazi publicity, British camps inspired the policies of other empires in tangible ways. Though maligned by Democratic Party critics, the British precedent paved the way, ethically and logistically, for America's own controversial foray into imperial expansion and civilian concentration. Tied to Britain through bonds of language and heritage,[17] the United States sent military attachés to South Africa, who in turn recommended American generals concentrate Filipino insurgents (themselves inspired by Boer tenacity[18]) in "concentration zones" during the Philippine-American War (1899–1902).[19] Meanwhile, Winston Churchill's speech in New York, which cast British camps as humanitarian depots rather than barbed-wire prisons, helped assuage the fears of American liberals still timid about embracing an imperial identity.[20] So too did it inaugurate the future prime minister's own foray into camps: in his later life, Churchill presided over a "pipeline" of detention centers during the Mau Mau Rebellion (1951–54), erecting what Caroline Elkins terms Britain's "imperial gulag" in Kenya.[21] And as global power shifted from Britain across the Atlantic after World War II, a more bellicose America inherited the liberal-imperial mantle of concentration with "strategic hamlets" in Vietnam and the infamous Guantánamo Bay. Whether as strategic instruments of antiterrorism and counterinsurgency or a means to isolate social contagion amid class and racial warfare, camps continued to populate the globe.

Other powers also followed Britain's lead. Through foreign advisors, the translation of reports, and the international transfer of knowledge, concentration camps, as an idea and practice, spread to France, which engaged in its own *camps de regroupement* in Algeria,[22] and even to republican China, which actively appropriated foreign techniques to control dissident groups.[23] And while Hitler's pronouncements about Boer War camps were mostly cynical, British precedents offered direct inspiration, a generation earlier, for imperial Germany's expansion into neighboring South-West Africa in 1904–5.[24] As the *Kaissereich*'s colonial secretary Bernhard Dernburg admitted, "whenever he had had difficulties with a colonial problem, he had found a solution by studying British methods."[25] When Chancellor Bülow ordered "concentration camps for the accommodation and maintenance" of Herero and Namaqua natives. in the aftermath of a brutal colonial war, he accordingly followed the advice of the Rhenish missionary F. Haussleiter, who had personally visited British concentration camps in South Africa and recommended:

the immediate designation of asylums where Herero who participated in the war but not in assassination could find quarter and refuge when laying down their arms . . . To begin with, individual watering places could be designated in which proximity concentration camps would be built.[26]

Far from intended depots of humane relief, however, Germany's colonial *Konzentrationslager* inflicted even more suffering and disease than their British counterparts.[27] S. J. Thomson testified to the possibility of accommodating colonial populations in healthy campsites, but German apathy and racial animus toward African natives meant that sanitary precautions were rarely taken. The result was genocidal in proportion—40 percent of inmates perished from disease and exposure. Again, however, British precedents were relevant: colonial vice-governor Oskar Hintrager absolved Germany of responsibility for notorious mortality at the ominous "Shark Island" *Konzentrationslager* by reminding himself that Britain "had considered it unavoidable to see 20000 [*sic*] women and children die during a very long imprisonment in the concentration camps."[28]

The developing theory and practice of asymmetric warfare, and a building consensus on the efficacy of managing suspect, destitute, and unhygienic populations through mass internment increasingly connected disparate episodes of civilian concentration. But what of Germany's next generation of imperialists: Göring and Himmler? The degree to which concentration camps in the German (and by extension, British) empire inspired Nazi camps intersects with larger debates, kindled by Arendt, concerning connections between colonialism and the violence of World War II.[29] On the one hand, European imperialism (of which Britain's was an exemplary model) assembled many ideas and practices that would inform the Axis's "colonial war" on the Eastern Front. Apart from concentration camps, these included basic ingredients like forced labor, a quest for "living space," a departure from the norms of "civilized war" and a racially coded sanitary language. On the other hand, Germany's African empire was relatively minor, the racism it fostered differed from world-war anti-Semitism, and apart from occasional SS officers with colonial pasts, few sources of institutional continuity bridged colonial and Nazi practices after the Versailles Treaty dismantled Germany's overseas empire.[30]

The imperial contribution, then, did not ordain future practices in any deterministic way. But should it be dismissed entirely? The infamous extermination centers of occupied Poland inhabit another universe from Britain's famine, plague, and wartime concentration camps: mass murder and the terrifying precision with which it was conducted made them exceptional even when compared to their counterparts at Dachau and Buchenwald, or in Stalin's Soviet Union. Early Nazi camps, by contrast, emerged from Western civilization's shared culture of confinement.[31] Like their counterparts in imperial Britain, the first Nazi camps drew inspiration and discursive legitimacy from the workhouse's labor and disciplinary routines.[32] And in the 1930s, political "suspects" and racial enemies were the minority at Nazi camps. Dachau's population was dominated by "beggars, the homeless, petty criminals, and other so-called 'asocials'" well into 1938.[33] The same was true of the Soviet Gulag, which conformed to common paradigms about rehabilitating marginal populations through the discipline of mass labor.[34]

With the outbreak of war, Germany took camps to radical extremes. Yet the process of radicalization depended on familiar languages that demanded the "isolat[ion] [of] the carriers of the bacillus of Bolshevism."[35] Long associated with vermin and plague, the "wandering Jew" was quarantined as a "public health measure." Meanwhile, conditions in overcrowded ghettos and barracks exacerbated the spread of typhus, measles, and other epidemics—major killers at Nazi and British camps alike. As in Britain, however, Nazi camps were invariably depicted as hygienic spaces that isolated "parasites" and euphemistically "cured" the criminal classes.[36] Genocide and ethnic cleansing were only extreme, though logical, results of a cultural and epidemiological impetus to preserve the purity of the social body—an aspiration shared by concentration camps in liberal and illiberal regimes alike. Their three-year genocidal peak notwithstanding, Nazi camps, along with those of Great Britain, can be incorporated within larger transnational histories of confining the mobile, the idle, and the contagious. The seamless post–World War II repurposing of concentration camps for displaced persons and refugees suggests as much; in 1948 the West German Federal Republic even proposed converting Dachau into a labor camp for the "re-education of work-shy elements."[37] As in Britain, camps would live on in postwar Germany. In the words of Herbert Blank, an anti-Nazi imprisoned during World War II, "one should not be put off by the fact that during the Hitler years the term 'camp' was corrupted." That "says everything against Hitler but nothing against camps," which remained valid tools, Blank argued, for converting "the morally ailing . . . back into productive and healthy members of society."[38] In its liberal origins lay the camp's durability.

TOTAL WAR AND CIVILIAN
INTERNMENT

The cultural centrality of the Holocaust, however justified, obscures other manifestations of forced encampment, which drew logistical and ideological succor from Britain. Indeed, Nazi camps are only one chapter in a larger global narrative. Apart from German *Konzentrationslager*, the world wars precipitated a vast network of internment centers concentrating displaced persons and enemy civilians—a process pioneered in South Africa. Until revelations of Nazi crimes ushered in a new euphemistic vocabulary to describe the camps of liberal democracies (reception centers, transit camps, safe zones), these institutions were known simply as "concentration camps" in recognition of their British precedent. In both world wars, the Red Cross used the term "concentration camp" interchangeably with "internment camp," and in World War II American government spokesmen, including President Roosevelt, referred candidly to internment centers for Japanese Americans as "concentration camps."[39]

Contemporaries certainly recognized similarities between British imperial camps and those of World War I. Commenting that she "knew too well what camps could be," Emily Hobhouse conducted an inspection tour at Ruhleben internment camp outside Berlin in 1916. In her estimation, the German camp, a former racetrack much like the camp at Johannesburg fifteen years previously, compared favorably to the camps she visited in South Africa.[40] The unfortunate Wim Hopford, an inmate at Volksrust concentration camp during the Anglo-Boer War who was later interned at Ruhleben as a British subject living in Germany in 1914, likewise found similarities between the two episodes, though he indicated life at Ruhleben was harsher than in South Africa due to "Prussian militarism."[41] From an official perspective, meanwhile, William McDonald, the medical officer of Klerksdorp camp, pointed to his "practical experience of the administration and sanitation" of camps in South Africa when he volunteered to operate what he called "large concentration camps" then developing "in England for prisoners of war, aliens and refugees."[42]

Building on colonial precedents, World War I internment camps emerged out of a culture of confinement shared across the Western world. The Anglo-Boer War did not cause future episodes of concentration in any reductive sense. But it marked an important step in larger global developments: a "guilt by association" logic, pioneered in South Africa, prevailed more and more in the age of "total war," as animosity extended from soldiers to civilians, who were reimagined as members of suspect collectivities. In this way, Britain's nineteenth-century empire of camps contributed to the erosion of earlier cultures of military captivity that had restricted internment solely to armed combatants.[43]

As history repeated itself and Britain turned again to mass concentration in 1915, a familiar figure, Lord Kitchener, now secretary of state for war, presided over a new global network of camps, one that stretched from Britain to the Empire and even to independent Siam, which outsourced camp management to British officials from India—now recognized as experts in the field.[44] Fearing the internment of enemy women and children "savour[ed] too much of concentration camps in the Boer War"—still a controversial subject among "atrocity mongers"[45]—Britain restricted internment in 1915 to adult men. But the growing link between citizenship and nationality, registered early on in South Africa, rendered civilian internment increasingly common throughout the twentieth century. In World War II Britain once again placed women and children in camps, both in Britain and at the Koffiefontein "concentration camp" in South Africa.

Like their imperial predecessors, world-war internment camps proved more than "rational" responses to military predicaments, and in hindsight, Richard Dove maintains, civilian internment "brought little discernible benefit to Britain, but . . . cruelly damaged the lives and livelihoods of those detained."[46] In an age of modern transport and mass population flows, world-war concentration camps rested on familiar prejudices that associated outsiders and immigrants with dirt, disease, and political disloyalty. As in empire, mobility augured danger and medical and humanitarian concerns remained tightly entwined with military rationales. Not only did camps detain covert spies and secret agents but "gypsies without papers" and "impoverished refugees," Matthew Stibbe confirms. Meanwhile, the growing preoccupation with public health and state welfare singled out foreigners as "responsible for the spread of contagious diseases like cholera."[47] Enemy aliens were "suspects on account of birth" and "like symptomless carriers of disease," Alison Bashford and Carolyn Strange observe, they were to be "separated from the general population and closely monitored under the assumption they posed too great a danger to circulate freely."[48]

Racial discourses honed in empire provided additional impetus. In World War I, Britain approached its Ottoman foes with the language of Orientalism: savage and despotic, they were simultaneously bloodthirsty and inept. But the wartime racialization of Germans echoed dehumanizing representations of the Boers, whom Kitchener notably depicted as "savages with a thin white veneer." No longer gentlemanly European adversaries, Germans were uncivilized "barbarians" and "mad brutes" with simian features: as in South Africa, race was deployed as a cultural discourse unattached to biological realities. The "development of an image of the enemy defined by its barbaric tendencies and its failure to conform to British standards of 'civilization' had significant similarities," Zoë Denness confirms, with "discourses which developed regarding the Boer as the 'enemy' during the South African War."[49] Britons understood the war against "the Hun"—a synonym for Germans and for nomadic Asiatic hordes—in the imperial language of "civilization," while Germans, for their part, also regarded the "disorderly, filthy lands and peoples" of Eastern Europe in colonial terms.[50] Coupled with languages of "military necessity" and "national security," such representations served to justify the application, to Europeans themselves, of measures previously consigned to the colonial world. (Again, the concentration of Boers—cast as half-European, half-African—was an early signpost in a larger journey.) World War I, then, was a point of rupture not necessarily because it augured a new "age of extremes" or because it pioneered new methods of violence but because it promoted colonial languages and technologies in the heart of Europe.

Even as camps migrated across Europe, however, they remained phenomena of the global south. Rows of bell tents and army barracks on the Isle of Man formed the principal nucleus for concentrating enemy aliens in Britain.[51] But internment also spread overseas. In South Africa, suspicion extended, once again, to Afrikaners, who maintained cultural and affective ties to Germany during the Great War. Meanwhile, as British mobs ransacked German businesses in South Africa and even threatened to scorch suspect houses to the ground, Britain proposed interning enemy civilians as a "protective measure," thereby echoing similar efforts to reclaim camps as humane technologies during the South African War.[52] Again, however, authorities restricted internment to men out of fear that any broader measures "might be depicted by Germany as another instance of the love of Gr[eat] Britain for shutting up women in concentration camps."[53]

In India, too, world-war internment camps like the one at Ahmednagar, formerly a facility for Boer POWs, concentrated enemy civilians. Here, as elsewhere, Red Cross reports upheld sanitation and organization as exemplary, cementing a notion that Britain's approach was worthy of emulation.[54] Though Vaughan Nash had previously condemned famine and Boer POW camps at Ahmednagar, the World War I facility enacted lessons inherited from the nineteenth century: constructed by the Public Works Department and inspected by Indian Medical Service officers previously conversant with plague and famine camps, it included a quarantine section for plague and cholera suspects and other carriers of infectious disease.[55] Whether in Britain or the empire, efforts to maintain large camps in good health (to echo S. J. Thomson) served to justify British camps vis-à-vis their counterparts in illiberal Russia or Germany, where, the Red Cross confirmed, mortality from disease and malnutrition was much higher.

HIDDEN SOLIDARITIES:
REFUGEE CAMPS

Britain's empire of camps shares a larger history with internment or "concentration camps" in wartime Europe. But as ostensibly humanitarian institutions (that fell lamentably short of their ideals) colonial camps also share a lineage with the refugee camps of the modern world. This, perhaps, is their most relevant contribution, albeit one that demands further research and reflection. As early as the 1880s, British camps provided a fount of international experience in the management of refugees: activists in Austro-Hungary even recruited a British famine expert from India to preside over a congregation of destitute and apparently unsanitary East-European Jews seeking refuge from Russian pogroms.[56] As with civilian internment, however, it was the Great War that proved the pivotal moment for the international proliferation of humanitarian practices honed in empire.

Britons took a leading role in World War I refugee relief, inscribing colonial technologies into a new international order. Once again, Emily Hobhouse was quick to recognize the continuities when she compared the 15,000 homes destroyed in Belgium in 1914 to the 30,000 destroyed in South Africa fifteen years previously, and she contributed her experience to the Women's International Bureau in Amsterdam to help Dutch-speaking refugees (with whom she communicated in rudimentary Afrikaans).[57] Sir Claude Hill, formerly secretary to the governor of Bombay, similarly noted "a close resemblance between the woods in parts of Northeast France in 1918 and the whole province of Gujarat" during the 1899–1900 famine. Both presented a "stark appearance of death," with "villages entirely deserted."[58] In both cases, displaced refugees were accommodated in camps.

Having organized famine relief and Boer POW camps as the Indian viceroy, meanwhile, Lord Curzon presided over new relief camps in 1919 as foreign secretary.[59] As Ottoman troops "laid waste" to Iraq and Asia Minor, "wrecking . . . villages and churches" during the Armenian and Assyrian genocides,[60] Britain established tented "refugee" or "concentration camps," as they were interchangeably known, to accommodate "destitute women and children" at Baqubah and Mosul.[61] Funded by the India Office and initially maintained by the Indian Army, which continued to hone its expertise in the field of humanitarian management, administration devolved in 1919 to civil authorities, who distributed relief to this "ancient" Christian people and enforced labor "on canals, roads, and railway earthworks" to those in a "backward state of civilization." Relief camps and public works enacted familiar protocols pioneered in famished India, while the introduction of

FIGURE 32.
Baqubah "concentration camp" in occupied Iraq, 1919, resembled Boer War
camps in terms of management, underlying motivations, and aesthetic form. Britain
continued to apply the term "concentration camp" to humanitarian relief camps until
World War II. [Credit: "A tent camp for refugees in Baquba in 1919," AGBU Nabur
Library, Paris.]

"efficient sanitary methods" helped stem the tide of cholera, typhus, and measles
epidemics. "Vermin infested" arrivals received a "thorough bathing and disinfection . . . together with their bedding and clothing." Meanwhile, a "barbed-wire
detention section" guarded by the 1/4th Devonshire Regiment (previously active
in the Anglo-Boer War after its transfer from India) confined "malefactors" and
prevented refugees "from wandering all over the country."[62]

Like their predecessors in India and South Africa, refugee camps in the aftermath
of World War I exhibited dynamics of coercion and care characteristic of Britain's
larger imperial culture. In direct and conscious ways, meanwhile, ideas and expertise
were inscribed into what Tehila Sasson calls the emerging "mixed economy" of
international relief administered by state and nongovernmental actors.[63] Like civilian internment camps in World War I, relief efforts in Mesopotamia and elsewhere
drew from accumulated experience in India and Africa. The many pathways through
which international humanitarian actors assimilated British experience are for future
scholars to explore. Clearly, however, international agencies and "imperial careerists" were important sources of transmission as camps reappeared during new
humanitarian crises.

While British camps in Arabia accommodated refugees fleeing genocide, wartime
dislocations spread hunger and disease across Eurasia. The Great Russian famine
of 1921–22 was only matched, contemporaries noted, by those of Victorian India—
and the broad international relief coalition it mobilized helped spread British

methods globally. Recognizing imperial Britain's expertise with famine, international organizations turned for advice to former viceroy Lord Curzon as well as Sir Antony MacDonnell, the veteran secretary of the 1901 Indian Famine Commission. MacDonnell proposed the establishment of relief camps to manage emaciated crowds wandering the Volga valley and threatening the very borders of Eastern Europe. And at Curzon's recommendation, the Russian Famine Relief Fund appointed as its High Commissioner the energetic Indian Medical Service officer Benjamin Robertson, who spent his early career in Bombay inspecting famine relief camps as Wilkins' and Thomson's junior. Guided by the Indian Famine Code, Robertson conducted inspection tours in conjunction with League of Nations representatives to systematize relief and assess the technical infrastructure of Russian camps. "Drawing upon the great fund of his administrative experience in India," the *Daily Telegraph* recorded, Robertson "rendered invaluable service by coordinating the work of various British organizations and making them fit into the limits of one general scheme."[64]

Other British officials also played prominent roles. Recalling personal experience in plague-and-famine-struck India, Sir Claude Hill, formerly the secretary to the governor of Bombay, argued that Russian famine camps would control "aimless wanderers" and enforce hard work among the idle. Hill went on to found the Indian branch of the Red Cross and was promoted in 1921 to director general of the League of Red Cross Societies, where he helped incorporate British camp experience into developing international standards. Many of Hill's insights were eventually adopted by Fridtjof Nansen, leader of international famine relief efforts in Russia and high commissioner of refugees at the League of Nations—a forerunner to the United Nations High Commissioner for Refugees (UNHCR).[65]

If empire was a "laboratory" for new forms of violence that devastated the globe in World War I and after, it also pioneered new methods of humanitarian care and social control. In the wake of decolonization, many ex-colonial officers transitioned to the NGO sector, transferring their expertise to organizations like Save the Children.[66] Oxfam, meanwhile, traces its origins to the Society of Friends, a group that was deeply interested in humanitarian causes at Indian plague and famine camps (the Quaker observer Joseph Taylor recorded much of its work) and in South African concentration camps (as Joshua Rowntree's inspection work attests). In addition to institutional transfers of technical knowledge about discipline and sanitation, however, Britain's empire of camps endowed the world with more general attitudes concerning social and political danger, surveillance of the "other," and the collective management of suspect populations during emergency situations.

A NEW GENEALOGY

The "first camps," Giorgio Agamben reminds us, "were built . . . as spaces controlling refugees," and "the succession of internment camps—concentration camps—extermination camps represents a perfectly real filiation."[67] Agamben's provocative statement points to hidden solidarities between putatively humanitarian enclosures and the repressive practices of wartime Europe. The term *concentration camp* was first coined, after all, to describe military coercion and humanitarian care in South Africa, and contemporaries used the phrase interchangeably with the less ominous *refugee camp*. Indeed, our modern language of concentration camps (repressive) and refugee camps (humane) reifies a dichotomy that did not exist until after World War II.

But while narratives in which refugee camps transform into something more menacing underscore important genealogical connections between different types of camps, they obscure the continued violence directed at refugees in the world today. As putatively humane institutions, refugee camps bear the coercive stamp of their imperial origins, even as memory of their colonial pedigree is repressed or fades away. Especially prevalent in Africa and Asia, the former spaces of empire, refugee camps remain the preferred mechanism to care for and control "unwanted" populations displaced by war, famine, and the unending crises of the modern world. Concealed behind a humanitarian cloak and overshadowed by sensational accounts of Serbian "death camps" and North Korean "gulags,"[68] refugee camps have been quietly normalized as accepted components of global population management. From the "refugee city" at Dadaab in northern Kenya (population 400,000) to Palestinian camps in Jordan; from compounds in Turkey sheltering populations displaced from the Syrian war to exclusionary settlements for stigmatized West African Ebola suspects, we live in a world of camps.

Their putative humanitarian function—political asylum, relief from suffering, protective custody—belies the coercive potential of today's refugee camps. Their inmates, like those at wartime concentration camps, are unusually vulnerable: stripped of basic political rights and legal protections, their continued existence as "bare life" is not assured but depends on the mercy (not always guaranteed) of presiding authorities.[69] Ostensibly humanitarian institutions, camps governed by the UNHCR and other NGOs display a "functional solidarity," in the words of the anthropologist Michel Agier, between "the humanitarian world . . . and the world of police and military ordering." "Rootless" and "superfluous," refugees are "separated off, behind high walls and barriers . . . populating countless camps, kilometers of transit corridors, islands and marine platforms, and enclosures in the middle of deserts." As with British colonial camps, the line between life and death shifts according to fiscal restraints, logistical capacities, and the political interest of the "developed" world.[70]

With potent eloquence, development critics like Agier—and more recently, Pope Francis[71]—expose the hypocrisy of a "humanitarian governance" that continues to detain in camps the most vulnerable as suspects, disease carriers, and dangerous "undesirables." At its best, scholarship on refugees highlights the "commonplaceness" and "multifunctionality" of camps: the degree to which exceptional institutions are now accepted as standard instruments of global governance. Dominated by social scientists and post–World War II analyses, however, this scholarship lacks historical perspective. Modern psychology and totalitarian domination provide one language of critique: many refugee centers "approximate [a] form of 'total institution'" and lead to "suicide, domestic violence, apathy, hopelessness and depression," critics contend.[72] Yet visions summoned by Agier of "massive and depersonalized crowds walking along roads with bundles of clothes on their heads and a child on the back" and "heaped in immense makeshift camps" cry out for comparison with British colonial experiences.[73] Indeed, what Agier unwittingly describes are modern iterations of emaciated famine wanderers and destitute Boer families. In condemning the "disturbing ambiguities of humanitarianism," critics of today's refugee camps turn (when they look to the past at all) to world-war internment or the writings of Arendt and Primo Levi, reactivating the problematic paradigm of Auschwitz. But they fail to account for the provenance of such unsettling similarities in the first place. Refugee and concentration camps are not simply analogous institutions of domination and control, they are two halves of the same whole. With a common ancestor—the enclosures of colonial South Africa and South Asia—and with a shared DNA inherited from an inauspicious imperial birth, they exhibit the twin forces of repression and humanity inherent to liberal empire.

．　　　．　　　．

Having located the origins of civilian concentration in British imperialism, the need for a new genealogy of camps is plain. Future scholarship should commemorate the camps of totalitarian Europe but consider them as exceptional and terrifying perversions of a nonetheless repressive norm. Highlighting common cultural representations concerning social, political, and epidemiological contagion, new narratives should begin with an imperial genesis and continue into the modern era, including civilian concentration from Palestine to Indochina along with the ubiquitous asylum centers and refugee camps that regulate movement and distribute relief in the global South today. So too should they trace the genealogy of Guantánamo Bay, which served as a holding pen—"surrounded by razor barbed wire"—for Haitian refugees suspected of carrying AIDS before its seamless post-9/11 conversion during the infamous "war on terror."[74] The "desultory refugee camps . . . became laboratories," Laleh Khalili confirms, "in which technologies of control, and legal arguments for incarceration, were first tested."[75] In the name of security and development—new twenty-first-century iterations of liberal empire—these camps are imprinted with humane and repressive elements inscribed at their institutional origins as technologies of British imperialism.[76]

Historical amnesia is unfortunate, especially in the case of British camps. By remembering them today, activists will discover relevant contexts for understanding and criticizing contemporary systems of encampment. In this way, a new global narrative—from British India to today—highlights the at times disturbing continuities between liberal empire and new imperial and humanitarian mantras iterated under American global hegemony. Varied and inclusive, such a genealogy provides a useable history for the world's current discontents.

NOTES

INTRODUCTION

1. Testimony of Corrie Brink (née Strauss), quoted in Owen Coetzer, *Fire in the Sky: The Destruction of the Orange Free Statexs* (Weltevreden Park, South Africa: Covos-Day, 2000), 204–5.

2. MSA General Department (Plague), 1899, Vol. 686, No. 559, Establishment in Connection with the Famine.

3. Vaughan Nash, *The Great Famine and Its Causes* (London: Longmans, Green, 1900), 16–21.

4. Mike Davis, *Late Victorian Holocausts: El Nino Famine and the Making of the Third World* (New York: Verso, 2002).

5. Myron Echenberg, *Plague Ports: The Global Urban Impact of Bubonic Plague, 1894–1901* (New York: NYU Press, 2010), 270.

6. Romesh Chunder Dutt, *Economic History of British India*, vol. II (London: Keagan Paul, 1904), 230. David Omissi, "India: Some Perceptions of Race and Empire," in *The Impact of the South African War*, ed. David Omissi and Andrew Thompson (Houndmills: Palgrave, 2002), 218–19.

7. Davis, *Late Victorian Holocausts*.

8. As Ann Laura Stoler points out, "compassion and sympathy are braided through the politics of security." *Carnal Knowledge and Imperial Power: Race and the Intimate in Colonial Rule* (Berkeley: University of California Press, 2002), xiii.

9. Michel Foucault, "Governmentality," in *The Foucault Effect: Studies in Governmentality*, ed. Graham Burchell et al. (Chicago: University of Chicago Press, 1991).

10. According to Foucault, "episteme" refers to an era's distinct "conditions of possibility." It encompasses the arrangements of power and knowledge that make particular worldviews, thoughts, or practices conceivable at any given time. Foucault, *The Order of Things: An Archaeology of the Human Science* (New York: Pantheon Books, 1971).

11. Dominated by military narratives, existing histories incorrectly assume concentration camps were instruments of "scorched-earth warfare" rather than humanitarian responses to it. The standard account is S. B. Spies, *Methods of Barbarism? Roberts and Kitchener and Civilians in the Boer Republics: January 1900–May 1902* (Cape Town: Human & Rousseau, 1977). More recent "revisionism" has questioned prevailing assumptions about camps' coercive military nature, while South Africa's postapartheid academy has sought to excavate the "black" camp experience. Elizabeth van Heyningen, *The Concentration Camps of the Anglo-Boer War: A Social History* (Johannesburg: Jacana Media, 2013) is the most comprehensive revisionist account. Like the scholarship she criticizes, however, van Heyningen does not transcend a national South African framing, even in her helpful literature review, "Costly Mythologies: The Concentration Camps of the South African War in Afrikaner Historiography," *Journal of Southern African Studies* 34, no. 3 (2008). The exchange between Van Heyningen, "'Fools Rush In:' Writing a History of the Concentration Camps of the South African War," *Historia* 55, no. 2 (2010), and Fransjohan Pretorius, "The White Concentration Camps of the Anglo-Boer War: A Debate without End" *Historia* 55, no. 2 (2010) encapsulates political and scholarly disagreements within South African academe.

12. There exists no article or monograph dedicated to famine camps themselves, or to the social attitudes and cultural representations that generated them. Famine camps receive passing mention as components of broader political-economic narratives: B. M. Bhatia, *Famines in India: A Study in Some Aspects of the Economic History of India (1860–1945)* (London: Asia Publishing House, 1963); Hari Shankar Srivastava, *The History of Indian Famines and Development of Famine Policy, 1858–1918* (Agra: Sri Ram Mehra, 1968), and "The Indian Famine of 1876–9," *Journal of Indian History* 44, no. 132 (1966); H. K. Mishra, *Famines and Poverty in India* (New Delhi: Ashish Publishing House, 1992). David Hall-Matthews integrates imperial policy within larger disciplinary and humanitarian practices: "Historical Roots of Famine Relief Paradigms: Ideas on Dependency and Free Trade in India in the 1870s," *Disasters* 20, no. 3 (1996); "Famine Process and Family Policy: A Case Study of Ahmednagar District, Bombay Presidency, India, 1870–84" (D.Phil diss., University of Oxford, 2002). Mike Davis offers a compelling, and sharply critical, account in *Late Victorian Holocausts*. Famine camps feature as occasional components of larger histories of nutrition, the body, and categories of colonial knowledge. David Arnold, "The 'Discovery' of Malnutrition and Diet in Colonial India," *Indian Economic and Social History Review* 31 no. 1 (1994); James Vernon, *Hunger: A Modern History* (Cambridge, MA: Belknap Press of Harvard University Press, 2007).

13. The scant attention dedicated to plague camps contrasts with the rich scholarship on colonial medicine, the social construction of disease, global epidemics, and the intersecting histories of imperial policy and nationalist politics. Relevant work includes Rajnarayan Chandavarkar, "Plague Panic and Epidemic Politics in India, 1896–1914," in *Epidemics and Ideas*, ed. Terence Ranger and Paul Slack (New York: Cambridge University Press, 1992); Echenberg, *Plague Ports*; I. J. Catanach, "Poona Politicians and the Plague," *South Asia* 7, no. 2 (1984); Ira Klein, "Plague, Policy and Popular Unrest in British India," *Modern Asian Studies* 22, no. 4 (1988); Maynard W. Swanson, "The Sanitation Syndrome: Bubonic Plague and Urban Native Policy in the Cape Colony, 1900–1909," in *Segregation and Apartheid in Twentieth-Century South Africa*, ed. William Beinhart and Saul Dubow (London: Routledge, 1995).

14. Iain Smith and Andreas Stucki, "The Colonial Development of Concentration Camps," *Journal of Imperial and Commonwealth History* 39, no. 3 (2011); Sibylle Scheipers, "The Use of Camps in Colonial Warfare," *Journal of Imperial and Commonwealth History* 43, no. 4 (2015); Aidan Forth and Jonas Kreienbaum, "A Shared Malady: Concentration Camps in the British, Spanish, American and German Empires," *Journal of Modern European History* 14, no. 2 (2016).

15. Jonas Kreienbaum, "Guerrilla Wars and Colonial Concentration Camps: The Exceptional Case of German South-West Africa (1904–1908)," *Journal of Namibian Studies: History, Politics, Culture* 11 (2012), 83.

16. Foucault coined the concept "biopolitics" in *History of Sexuality* (New York: Pantheon Books, 1978) and developed it in *The Birth of Biopolitics: Lectures at the College de France, 1978–1979* (New York: Palgrave Macmillan, 2004). For a consideration of "biopolitics" at Indian famine camps, see Anna Clark, "Humanitarianism, Human Rights and Biopolitics in the British Empire, 1890–1902," *Britain and the World* 9, no. 1 (2016).

17. Ann Stoler, "Colony," *Political Concepts: A Critical Lexicon* 1, accessed August 8, 2016, http://www.politicalconcepts.org/issue1/colony/.

18. Giorgio Agamben, *States of Exception* (Chicago: University of Chicago Press, 2005), 5.

19. Partha Chatterjee, *The Nation and its Fragments: Colonial and Postcolonial Histories* (Princeton, NJ: Princeton University Press, 1993).

20. Hannah Arendt noted that in a world that tied human rights to membership in the nation-state, the stateless were essentially stripped of their human status. *Origins of Totalitarianism* (New York: Harcourt, 1968), chapter 9; "We Refugees," in *Altogether Elsewhere: Writers on Exile*, ed. Marc Robinson (Winchester, MA: Faber and Faber, 1994).

21. Antoinette Burton, *The Trouble with Empire: Challenges to Modern British Imperialism* (Oxford: University of Oxford Press, 2015), 2–3, 10.

22. C. A. Bayly, "Knowing the Country: Empire and Information in India," *Modern Asian Studies* 27, no. 1 (1993).

23. Jonathan Hyslop, "The Invention of the Concentration Camp: Cuba, Southern Africa and the Philippines, 1896–1907," *South African Historical Journal* 63, no. 2 (2011).

24. Oliver Macdonagh, "The Nineteenth-Century Revolution in Government: A Reappraisal," in *The Victorian Revolution in Government*, ed. Peter Stansky (New York: New Viewpoints, 1973); Mary Poovey, *Making a Social Body: British Cultural Formation, 1830–64* (Chicago: University of Chicago Press, 1995).

25. James Scott, *Seeing Like a State: How Certain Schemes to Improve the Human Condition Have Failed* (New Haven, CT: Yale University Press, 1998); Clare Anderson, *Legible Bodies: Race, Criminality and Colonialism in South Asia* (Oxford: Berg, 2004).

26. Jon Wilson, *The Domination of Strangers: Modern Governance in Eastern India, 1785–1835* (Basingstoke, UK: Palgrave Macmillan, 2008); James Vernon, *Distant Strangers: How Britain Became Modern* (Berkeley: University of California Press, 2014).

27. Nash, *Great Famine*, 75.

28. MSA Famine Department, 1900, Vol. 172, No. 304, Transvaal Refugees in Bombay.

29. Thomas R. Metcalf, *Imperial Connections: India in the Indian Ocean Arena, 1860–1920* (Berkeley: University of California Press, 2007), 2–7.

30. For intensified interchanges between India and South Africa during the war, see Pradip Kumar Datta, "The Interlocking Worlds of the Anglo-Boer War in South Africa/India," *South African History Journal* 57 (2007); Omissi, "India."

31. For the concept see Robert Gerwarth and Stephen Malinowski, "Hannah Arendt's Ghosts: Reflections on the Disputable Path from Windhoek to Auschwitz," *Central European History* 42, no. 2 (June 2009).

32. David Lambert and Alan Lester, *Colonial Lives Across the British Empire: Imperial Careering in the Long Nineteenth Century* (Cambridge: Cambridge University Press, 2006).

33. Metcalf, *Imperial Connections*; Sugata Bose, *A Hundred Horizons: The Indian Ocean in the Age of Global Empire* (Cambridge, MA: Harvard University Press, 2009).

34. Niall Ferguson, *Empire: The Rise and Demise of the British World Order and the Lessons for Global Power* (New York: Basic Books, 2004).

35. Pankaj Mishra, "Watch This Man," review of *Civilization: The West and the Rest*, by Niall Ferguson, *London Review of Books* 33, no. 21 (2011); Priya Satia, "The Defense of Inhumanity: Air Control in Iraq and the British Idea of Arabia," *American Historical Review* 111 (2006).

36. For these tensions, as they revolved around discourses of difference and similarity, see Thomas R. Metcalf, *Ideologies of the Raj* (New York: Cambridge University Press, 1994).

37. Margery Sabin, *Dissenters and Mavericks: Writings about India in English, 1765–2000* (Oxford: Oxford University Press, 2002), 16.

38. For direct comparison and contrast between British and totalitarian camps, see Aidan Forth, "Britain's Archipelago of Camps: Labor and Detention in a Liberal Empire, 1871–1903," *Kritika: Explorations in Russian and Eurasian History* 16, no. 3 (2015), 651–680.

39. Steven Barnes, *Death and Redemption: The Gulag and the Shaping of Soviet Society* (Princeton, NJ: Princeton University Press, 2011).

40. By some accounts, the entire Soviet century from 1917–89 can be reckoned one long "state of exception." Peter Holquist, "Violent Russia, Deadly Marxism? Russia in the Epoch of Violence, 1905–21," *Kritika* 4 (2003), 651–2.

41. For comparison between British and German imperial cultures that echoes this point vis-á-vis camps, see Isabel Hull, *Absolute Destruction: Military Culture and the Practices of War in Imperial Germany* (Ithaca, NY: Cornell University Press, 2005), 182–96.

42. Colman Hogan and Marta Marin-Domine, eds., *The Camp: Narratives of Internment and Exclusion* (Newcastle: Cambridge Scholars, 2007); Bulent Diken and Carsten Bagge Laustsen, *The Culture of Exception: Sociology Facing the Camp* (London: Routledge, 2005).

43. David Anderson, *Histories of the Hanged: The Dirty War in Kenya and the End of Empire* (New York: W. W. Norton, 2005); Caroline Elkins, *Imperial Reckoning: The Untold Story of Britain's Gulag in Kenya* (New York: Henry Holt, 2005).

44. Michel Agier, *Managing the Undesirables: Refugee Camps and Humanitarian Government* (Cambridge: Polity Press, 2011); Guglielmo Verdirame and Barbara Harrell-Bond, *Rights in Exile: Janus-Faced Humanitarianism* (New York: Berghahn Books, 2005).

45. Arendt, *Origins of Totalitarianism*, 437–60; Wolfgang Sofsky, *The Order of Terror: The Concentration Camp* (Princeton, NJ: Princeton University Press, 1993), 16–27; Giorgio Agamben, *Homo Sacer: Sovereign Power and Bare Life* (Stanford, CA: Stanford University Press, 1998).

46. Mark Mazower, "Violence and the State in the Twentieth Century," *American Historical Review*, 107, no. 4 (2002).

47. Not to mention the wide variety of camps that existed within the German and Soviet Empires. The "new histories" of German concentration camps are now delineating a clear distinction between "extermination camps" like Auschwitz-Birkenau and other concentration camps, which have been conflated for too long. Jane Caplan and Nicholas Waschmann, eds., *Concentration Camps in Nazi Germany: The New Histories* (London: Routledge, 2010).

CHAPTER 1

1. Julie Anne Taylor, *Muslims in Medieval Italy: The Colony at Lucera* (Lanham, MD: Lexington Books, 2005).

2. John H. Elliot, *Empires of the Atlantic World: Britain and Spain in America, 1492–1830* (New Haven, CT: Yale University Press, 2007), 74.

3. Wladyslaw Konopczynski, *Konfederacja barska* (Warsaw: Volumen, 1991), 733–34.

4. Joel Kotek and Pierre Rigoulot, *Le Siècle des Camps* (Paris: JC Lattes, 2000), chapter 1.

5. Vernon, *Distant Strangers*, 22, 25.

6. Eric E. Lampard, "The Urbanizing World," in *The Victorian City: Images and Realities* eds. H. J. Dyos and Michael Wolff (London: Routledge & Kegan Paul, 1973), 8.

7. Harold Platt, *Shock Cities: The Environmental Transformation and Reform of Manchester and Chicago* (Chicago: University of Chicago Press, 2005), 68, 302–3. Victorian "separate spheres" ideology had its correlative in the separation of rich from poor neighborhoods and the functional differentiation of home/work and industrial /commercial/residential areas.

8. The colonization of urban peripheries by temporary "shanty-towns" continues on the outskirts of modern megacities, offering a contemporary iteration of the interplay between camp to city. Mike Davis, *Planet of Slums* (New York: Verso, 2006).

9. G. M. van der Waal, *From Mining Camp to Metropolis: The Buildings of Johannesburg, 1886–1940* (Pretoria: C. van Rensburg Publications of the Human Sciences Research Council, 1987), 8.

10. Organized summer "camping" originated during the U.S. Civil War to "counteract the magnetic quality of army life." Lynn S. Rodney and Phyllis M. Ford, *Camp Administration: Schools, Communities, Organizations* (New York: Ronald Press Company, 1971), 4, 17. The movement received significant stimulus in Britain from the Boy Scouts movement established by Lord Baden-Powell, who himself presided over Boer War concentration camps.

11. Stadiums and amusement parks could be readily converted into concentration camps. The Johannesburg racecourse, for example, became a concentration camp during the Boer War. The Lofthouse amusement park outside Leeds interned enemy aliens in World War I. "Lofthouse-Ruhleben," accessed July 13, 2015, https://lofthousepark. wordpress.com/lofthouse/.

12. NASA TAB PWD 58 5257/02.

13. Philip Curtin, *Disease and Empire: The Health of European Troops in the Conquest of Africa* (New York: Cambridge University Press, 1998), 118–19.

14. Rabinow quoted in Chris Otter, *The Victorian Eye: A Political History of Light and Vision in Britain, 1800–1910.* (Chicago: University of Chicago Press, 2008), 73.

15. Lewis Mumford, *The City in History: Its Origins, Its Transformations, and Its Prospects* (New York: Mariner Books, 1968), 348, 422.

16. Charles Campbell, *The Intolerable Hulks: British Shipboard Confinement, 1776–1857* (Tucson, AZ: Fenestra Books, 2001).

17. Michel Foucault, *Discipline and Punish: The Birth of the Prison* (New York: Pantheon Books, 1977); Michael Ignatieff, *A Just Measure of Pain: The Penitentiary in the Industrial Revolution* (New York: Pantheon Books, 1978).

18. Douglas Hay, *Albion's Fatal Tree: Crime and Society in Eighteenth-Century England* (New York: Pantheon Books, 1976); E. P. Thompson, *Whigs and Hunters: The Origins of the Black Act* (New York: Pantheon Books, 1975).

19. "Vagrancy laws were coercive mechanisms of questionable legality." Julie Kimber, "Poor Laws: A Historiography of Vagrancy in Australia," *History Compass* 11, no. 8 (2013), 541.

20. Ignatieff, *Just Measure of Pain*.

21. Otter, *The Victorian Eye*, 110.

22. For the globalization of prisons, see Frank Dikotter and Ian Brown, eds., *Cultures of Confinement: A History of the Prison in Africa, Asia and Latin America* (Ithaca, NY: Cornell University Press, 2007); Florence Bernault and Janet L. Roitman, eds., *A History of Prisons and Confinement in Africa* (Portsmouth, NH: Heinemann, 2003).

23. Clare Anderson, *Convicts in the India Ocean: Transportation from South Asia to Mauritius* (Basingstoke: Palgrave, 2002), 39.

24. Like many islands in Britain's archipelago of camps, Mauritius boasts an "overlapping, multilayered history," serving as a POW camp (1810–15), penal settlement (1815–53), and then a "vagrant depot" for runaway indentured laborers. Clare Anderson and David Arnold, "Envisioning the Colonial Prison" in *Cultures of Confinement*, ed. Frank Dikotter and Ian Brown, 305–6.

25. Following the Indian Jail Conference (1877), the British Raj "medicalized" the administration of colonial prisons by appointing members of the Indian Medical Service (IMS) as inspectors and superintendents. David Arnold, *Colonizing the Body: State Medicine and Epidemic Disease in Nineteenth-Century India* (Berkeley: University of California Press, 1993), 102–13. Health quickly "became the standard by which the colonial prison administration judged its achievements"; "India: The Contested Prison," 166–67.

26. Clare Anderson, "The Politics of Convict Space: Indian Penal Settlements and the Andaman Islands," in *Isolation: Places and Practices of Exclusion*, ed. Carolyn Strange and Alison Bashford (New York: Routledge, 2003), 41.

27. Marx and Weber quoted in Enzo Traverso, *The Origins of Nazi Violence* (New York: New Press, 2003), 28.

28. E. P. Thompson, "Time, Work-Discipline, and Industrial Capitalism," *Past and Present* 38, no. 1 (1967).

29. Markus Rediker, *The Slave Ship: A Human History* (New York: Viking, 2007). Stanley Elkins offers a stimulating, if controversial, comparison of slave plantations and Nazi concentration camps, *Slavery: A Problem in American Institutional and Intellectual Life* (Chicago: University of Chicago Press, 1959), 103–15.

30. Patrick Joyce, *Rule of Freedom: Liberalism and the Modern City* (New York: Verso, 2003), 73.

31. Shifting work camps in Victorian Britain and its settler colonies also accommodated manual laborers. Michael Morris, "Towards an Archeology of Navvy Huts and Settlements of the Industrial Revolution," *Antiquity* 68 (1994); Peter Davies, "Space and Structure at an Australian Timber Camp," *Historical Archaeology* 39, no. 4 (2005). Generated by "explosive" settler colonization, such camps were especially prevalent in the Anglophone world. James Belich, *Replenishing the Earth: The Settler Revolution and the Rise of the Anglo World* (Oxford: Oxford University Press, 2009), 186, 192, 195, 322.

32. MSA Revenue Department (Famine), 1900, Vol. 19, No. 165, Supply of officers for the supervision of famine relief operations.

33. Clare Anderson, "Convicts and Coolies: Rethinking Indentured Labour in the Nineteenth Century," *Slavery and Abolition* 30, no. 1 (2009); Anderson, *Convicts in the Indian Ocean*, chapter 3.

34. I. R. Phimister, "African Labour Conditions and Health in the South Rhodesian Mining Industry," in *Studies in the History of African Mine Labour in Colonial Zimbabwe*, ed. I. R. Phimister and C. van Onselen (Gwelo, Zimbabwe: Mambo Press, 1978), 104; Charles van Onselen, *Chibaro: African Mine Labour in Southern Rhodesia* (London: Pluto Press, 1976), especially chapter 5–6.

35. Lindsay Weiss, "Exceptional Space: Concentration Camps and Labor Compounds in late Nineteenth-Century South Africa," in *Archaeologies of Internment*, ed. Adrian Myers and Gabriel Moshenska (New York: Springer, 2011), 24.

36. NAUK CO 291/27 No. 5866, Refugee Camps, January 30, 1901.

37. Phimister, "African Labour Conditions and Health," 102.

38. Agier, *Managing the Undesirables*, 66.

39. Alison Bashford and Carolyn Strange, "Asylum-Seekers and National Histories of Detention," *Australian Journal of Politics and History* 48 no. 4, (2002): 509.

40. Geoff Manaugh and Nicola Twilley, "Ebola and the Fiction of Quarantine," *New Yorker*, August 11, 2014.

41. Harriet Deacon, "Patterns of Exclusion on Robben Island, 1654–1992," in *Isolation*, ed. Strange and Bashford; Naomi Paik, "Carceral Quarantine at Guantánamo: Legacies of US Imprisonment of Haitian Refugees." *Radical History Review*, no. 115 (2013).

42. Judy Whitehead, "Bodies Clean and Unclean: Prostitution, Sanitary Legislation, and Respectable Femininity in Colonial North India," *Gender & History* 7, no. 1 (1995): 53.

43. Poovey, *Making a Social Body*.

44. T. Ginouvier quoted in Andre Zysberg, "Galley and Hard Labor Convicts in France (1550–1850), from the Galleys to Hard Labor Camps: Essay on a Long Lasting Penal Institution," in *The Emergence of Carceral Institutions: Prisons, Galleys and Lunatic Asylums, 1550–1900*, ed. Pieter Spierenburg (Rotterdam: Centrum Voor Maatschappij Geschiedenis, Erasmus University, 1984), 119.

45. Problem groups had either to be "devoured" through a process of "making the different similar" or else cordoned off for rehabilitation. Bauman quoted in Dirk Moses, ed., *Genocide and Settler Society: Frontier Violence and Stolen Indigenous Children in Australian History* (New York: Berghahn Books, 2004), 32.

46. For a summary of epidemiological metaphors in Western Europe as they pertained to Jews, see Traverso, *Origins of Nazi Violence*, 101–9.

47. Frantz Fanon, *The Wretched of the Earth* (New York: Grove Press, 1963), 37.

48. Phillippa Levine, *Prostitution, Race & Politics: Policing Venereal Disease in the British Empire* (New York: Routledge, 2003), chapter 11; Douglas M. Peers, "Soldiers, Surgeons and the Campaigns to Combat Sexually Transmitted Diseases in Colonial India, 1805–1860," *Medical History* 42, no. 2 (1998): 153.

49. Richard Coker, "Civil Liberties and the Public Good: Detention of Tuberculosis Patients and the Public Health Act 1984," *Medical History* 45 (2001): 343.

50. Christopher Hamlin, *Public Health and Social Justice in the Age of Chadwick* (New York: Cambridge University Press, 1998).

51. Like plague, cholera was a highly political disease "identified with conquest and foreign rule," and with "disorder" more generally. Arnold, *Colonizing the Body*, 178.

52. IOR/P/5362, North-Western-Provinces Sanitary Proceedings, 1898. For other accounts of pilgrim camps, see S. J. Thomson, *The Silent India, Being Tales and Sketches of the Masses* (London: William Blackwood and Sons, 1913), 207–9; S. J. Thomson, *The Real Indian People* (London: William Blackwood and Sons, 1914), chapter 8.

53. Samuël Coghe, "Population Politics in the Tropics. Demography, Health and Colonial Rule in Portuguese Angola, 1890s-1940s" (PhD diss., European University Institute, 2014).

54. Joyce, *Rule of Freedom*, 73.

55. Mumford, *The City in History*, 362.

56. James Sheehan, *Where Have All the Soldiers Gone? The Transformation of Modern Europe* (Boston: Houghton Mifflin, 2008).

57. Charlie Hailey, *Camps: A Guide to 21st-Century Space* (Cambridge, MA: MIT Press, 2009), 5–6.

58. Gillian Russell, "Theatricality and Military Culture: British Army Camps in the 1770s," *Eighteenth-Century Life* 18, no. 3 (1994); Stuart Mason, "Summer Camps for Soldiers: 1778–1782," *Local Historian* 29, no. 4 (1999).

59. Gordon Bannerman, *Merchants and the Military in Eighteenth-Century Britain* (London: Pickering & Chatto, 2008), 73.

60. Howard N. Cole, *The Story of Aldershot: A History of the Civil and Military Towns* (Aldershot, UK: Gale & Polden, 1951), 25, 109.

61. *Sketches of the Camp at Aldershot* (Farnham, UK: Andrews & Lucy, 1858).

62. Cole, *The Story of Aldershot*, 62.

63. Viceroy Elgin's splendid camp erected while visiting the Nizam's Dominions, for example, consisted of geometric rows of marquee tents similar to those used for hospitals and schools at plague, famine, and concentration camps. IOR/Photo 402(28) Album of views in Western India including Bombay.

64. Maya Jasanoff, *Edge of Empire: Lives, Culture, and Conquest in the East 1750–1850* (New York: Random House, 2005), 122.

65. Arnold, *Colonizing the Body*, 90.

66. Quoted in Levine, *Prostitution, Race and Politics*, 309.

67. Flora A. Steel, *On the Face of the Waters* (New York: Macmillan, 1897), 136.

68. "It is obvious," the 1897 manual *The Health of the British Army in India* maintained, "that order in such a community could be maintained only . . . by investing the Cantonment Magistrate with despotic powers." Levine, *Prostitution, Race, and Politics*, 299.

69. Increasingly, Ann Laura Stoler writes, a "cordon sanitaire surrounded European enclaves, was wrapped around mind and body, around each European man and his home." Stoler, *Carnal Knowledge*, 77.

70. Harold Mytum and Naomi Hall, "Norman Cross: Designing and Operating an Eighteenth-Century British Prisoner of War Camp," in *Prisoners of War: Archaeology, Memory, and Heritage of 19th- and 20th-Century Mass Internment*, ed. Harold Mytum and Gilly Carr (New York: Springer, 2013), 75.

71. David Bell, *The First Total War: Napoleon's Europe and the Birth of Warfare as We Know It* (New York: Houghton Mifflin, 2007).

72. Mytum and Hall, "Norman Cross."

73. Robert S. Davis, "Escape from Andersonville: A Study in Isolation and Imprisonment," *Journal of Military History* 67 (2003): 1067. Eyewitness testimony from Andersonville might be mistaken for the writing of Primo Levi: "One poor boy near cried all night and wished to die and suffer no longer," an inmate wrote. "His body is a mere frame; his hair has fallen out from his head; his scurvy ankles and feet are as large as his waist. I never saw a sight more appalling. Then the awful thought that he is a man, somebody's darling boy, dead, and yet breathing." "National Park Civil War Series: The Prison Camp at Andersonville," accessed September 3, 2014, http://www.nps.gov/history/history/online_books/civil_war_series/5/sec.5.htm.

74. And in both cases, internment narratives fed powerful mythologies of "shared suffering" that animated nationalist politics for decades afterwards. Liz Stanley, *Mourning Becomes . . .: Post/memory and Commemoration of the Concentration Camps of the South African War, 1899–1902* (Manchester: Manchester University Press, 2006); Drew Gilpin Faust, *Republic of Suffering: Death and the American Civil War* (New York: Knopf, 2008).

75. Edward Noyes, "The Contraband Camp at Cairo, Illinois," in *Historical Papers: Selected Proceedings of the Sixth Northern Great Plains History Conference*, ed.

Lysle E. Meyer (Moorehead, MN: Moorehead State College, 1971); Cam Walker, "Corinth: The Story of a Contraband Camp," *Civil War History* 20, no. 1 (1974); Elizabeth Nicholson, Tacy Hadley, and Job Hadley, "A Contraband Camp," *Indiana History Bureau* 1, no. 11/12 (1924).

76. Workhouses were also templates for Nazi concentration camps. Jane Caplan, "Political Detention and the Origin of the Concentration Camps in Nazi Germany, 1933–1935/6," in *Nazism, War and Genocide. Essays in Honour of Jeremy Noakes*, ed. N. Gregor (Exeter, UK: Exeter University Press, 2005); Andreas Gerstrich, "Konzentrationslager: Voraussetzungen und Vorläufer vor der Moderne," in *Welt der Lager zur "Erfolgsgeschichte" einer Institution*, ed. Bettina Greiner and Alan Kramer (Hamburg: Hamburger Edition, 2013).

77. Robert Bucholz and Joseph Ward, *London: A Social and Cultural History* (Cambridge: Cambridge University Press, 2012), 239.

78. Gerard O'Brien, "Workhouse Management in Pre-Famine Ireland," *Proceedings of the Royal Irish Academy*, 86C no. 3 (1986): 125.

79. Charles Dickens, *Oliver Twist, or the Parish Boy's Progress* (London: Richard Bentley, 1838); Charles Kingsley, *The Waterbabies, A Fairy Tale for a Land Baby* (London: Macmillan, 1863).

80. O'Brien, "Workhouse Management," 125.

81. Zygmunt Bauman, *Modernity and the Holocaust* (Ithaca, NY: Cornell University Press, 1989), 18.

82. Pearson quoted in Traverso, *Origins of Nazi Violence*, 31.

83. George Bernard Shaw quoted in Meena Radhakrishna, *Dishonoured by History: "Criminal Tribes" and British Colonial Policy* (Hyderabad: Orient Longman, 2001), 78.

84. William Booth, *In Darkest England and the Way Out* (London: Salvation Army, 1890).

85. Vernon, *Distant Strangers*, 40, 43.

86. Mayhew, quoted in Judith Walkowitz, *City of Dreadful Delight: Narratives of Sexual Danger in Late-Victorian London* (Chicago: University of Chicago Press, 1992), 19. For London social commentators' anthropological mentality, see Deborah Epstein Nord, "The Social Explorer as Anthropologist: Victorian Travelers among the Urban Poor," in *Visions of the Modern City*, ed. William Sharpe and Leonard Wallock (Baltimore: Johns Hopkins University Press, 1987).

87. Quoted in Daniel Pick, *Faces of Degeneration: A European Disorder, c.1848–1918* (New York: Cambridge University Press, 1993), 197, 183.

88. Gareth Stedman Jones, *Outcast London: A Study in the Relationship between Classes in Victorian Society* (Oxford: Clarendon, 1971), 295–96.

89. John Brown, "Charles Booth and Labour Colonies, 1889–1905," *Economic History Review* 30, no. 2 (1977).

90. "To Check the Survival of the Unfit: A New Scheme by the Rev. Osborn Jay, a Militant Bethnal Green Parson, for Sending the Submerged to a Penal Settlement," *The London*, March 12, 1896.

91. W. H. Beveridge quoted in Brown, "Labour Colonies," 356.

92. John Field, "Able Bodies: Work Camps and the Training of the Unemployed in Britain before 1939," in *The Significance of the Historical Perspective in Adult Education Research* (Cambridge: University of Cambridge, Institute of Continuing Education, 2009).

93. Quoted in David A. Reisman, *Alfred Marshall: Progress and Politics* (New York: St. Martin's, 1987), 429.

94. Cole Harris, *Making Native Space: Colonialism, Resistance and Reserves in British Columbia* (Vancouver: University of British Columbia Press, 2002), xxiv.

95. "Indians were seen like the Irish, as nomads not truly settled on the land." Burbank and Cooper, *Empires in World History*, 175.

96. For North American "Indian removals" see Amy Sturgis, *The Trail of Tears and Indian Removal* (Westport, CT: Greenwood Press, 2007); Angela Wilson, "Decolonizing the 1862 Death Marches," *American Indian Quarterly* 28, no. 1&2 (1994); Theda Perdue and Michael D. Green, *Cherokee Removal* (Boston: Bedford St. Martin's, 2004).

97. Benjamin Madley, "From Terror to Genocide: Britain's Tasmanian Penal Colony and Australia's History Wars," *Journal of British Studies* 47 (2008).

98. Samantha Wells, "Labour, Control and Protection: The Kahlin Aboriginal Compound, Darwin, 1911–38," in *Settlement: A History of Australian Aboriginal Housing*, ed. Peter Read (Canberra: Aboriginal Studies, 2000), 64. For the humanitarian origins of Australian aboriginal settlements, see Alan Lester and Fae Dussart, *Colonization and the Origins of Humanitarian Governance: Protecting Aborigines across the Nineteenth-Century British Empire* (New York: Cambridge University Press, 2014), 63–76.

99. Bain Attwood, "Space and Time at Ramahyuck, Victoria, 1863–85," in *Settlement: A History of Australian Aboriginal Housing*, ed. Peter Reed, 44.

100. R. J. Surtees, "The Development of an Indian Reserve Policy in Canada," *Ontario History* 61, no. 2 (1969), 92.

101. Laleh Khalili, *Time in the Shadows: Confinement in Counterinsurgencies* (Stanford, CA: Stanford University Press, 2013), 18.

102. Charles E. Callwell, *Small Wars. Their Principles and Practice*, 3rd ed. (London: Harrison and Sons, 1906).

103. Wells, "Labour, Control and Protection," 67.

104. Henry Schwarz, *Constructing the Criminal Tribe in Colonial India: Acting Like a Thief* (Malden, MA: Wiley-Blackwell, 2010), 82.

105. N. Benjamin and B. B. Mohanty, "Imperial Solution of a Colonial Problem: Bhils of Khandesh up to c. 1850," *Modern Asian Studies* 41, no. 2 (2007): 344.

106. Sandria B. Freitag, "Crime in the Social Order of Colonial North India," *Modern Asian Studies* 25, no. 2 (1991): 232–33.

107. General Charles Hervey and William Sleeman, quoted in Freitag, "Crime in the Social Order," 236.

108. The act, Andrew Major argues, arose out of controversy surrounding the legality of existing tribal settlements. "State and Criminal Tribes in Colonial Punjab: Surveillance, Control and Reclamation of the 'Dangerous Classes,'" *Modern Asian Studies* 33, no. 3 (1999): 668.

109. Salvation Army Archives PWB/4/13, Photocopy of Govt of India, Police Dept., Progs. 19, Series No. 3, March 11, General William Booth to the Secretary of State for India.

110. Rachel Tolen, "Colonizing and Transforming the Criminal Tribesman: The Salvation Army in British India," *American Ethnologist* 18, no. 1 (1991); Meena Radhakrishna, "Surveillance and Settlements under the Criminal Tribes Act in Madras," *Indian Economic & Social History Review* 29, no. 2 (1992): 197; Radhakrishna, *Dishonoured by History*, 74.

111. Technically, criminal tribes were distinct from thugs and dacoits, though in practice a great deal of conflation occurred between them. Freitag, "Crime in the Social Order," n39.

112. Sanjay Nigam, "Disciplining and Policing the 'Criminals by Birth,' Part 1: The Making of a Colonial Stereotype—The Criminal Tribes and Castes of North India," *Indian Economic and Social History Review* 27, no. 2 (1990).

113. David Arnold quoted in Major, "State and Criminal Tribes," 660.

114. "What had begun as a pseudo-scientific way to define criminality while controlling large groups, ended as a bureaucratic shortcut around civil protections." Freitag, "Crime in the Social Order," 260.

115. Major, "State and Criminal Tribes," 657.

116. Booth-Tucker, *Criminocurology; or, The Indian Crim and What to Do With Him* (Simla: Liddell's Printing Works, 1916), 36.

117. NAI Home Department (Judicial), January 1876, Nos. 139–150, Adoption of the necessary measures in order to render Part I of the Criminal Tribes act XXVII of 1871 applicable to the Lower Provinces of Bengal.

118. Benjamin and Mohanty, "Imperial Solution of a Colonial Problem," 347.

119. Freitag, "Crime in the Social Order," 234.

120. E. J. Gunthorpe, *Notes on Criminal Tribes Residing in or Frequenting the Bombay Presidency, Berar and the Central Provinces* (Bombay: 'Times of India' Steam Press, 1882), 3.

121. Freitag, "Crime in the Social Order," 233–34.

122. Gunthorpe, *Notes on Criminal Tribes*, 24.

123. IOR/L/PJ/6/291, File 2250. Colonel Ollivant, Senior Deputy Inspector-General of Police, NWPO to Personal Assistant to Inspector-Gen of Police, NWP, February 27, 1887.

124. Booth-Tucker, quoted in Schwarz, *Constructing the Criminal Tribe*, 88.

125. Salvation Army Archives, PWB/4/13, Photocopy of Govt of India, Police Dept, Progs. 19, Serious No. 3, March 1911, General William Booth, of the Salvation Army to The Secretary of State for India, 12.

126. Gunthorpe, *Notes on Criminal Tribes*, 30, 6.

127. Gilles Deleuze and Felix Guattari, *A Thousand Plateaus: Capitalism and Schizophrenia* (Minneapolis: University of Minnesota Press, 1987), 353. Chess contrasts with the Chinese board-game Go, a contest that involves "arraying oneself in open space, of holding space, of maintaining the possibility of springing up at any point." British spatial tactics amounted to the transformation of a game of Go into a game of chess.

128. NAI Home Department (Judicial), April 1878, Nos. 64–6, "Registration of the Aligarh District under the Criminal Tribes Act, 1871."

129. NAI Legislative Department, November 1871, Nos. 44–127, The Criminal Tribes Act, 1871, memo by Sir DF MacLeod, CB, KCSI.

130. NAI Legislative Department, November 1871, Nos. 44–127, The Criminal Tribes Act, 1871, memo by CP Carmichael, Inspector General of Police to Secretary to Government, NWP, 6 July 1870.

131. Booth-Tucker, *Criminocurology*, 9.

132. Salvation Army Archives PWB/4/13, Photocopy of Govt of India, Police Dept., Progs. 19, Series No. 3, March 11, General William Booth, of the Salvation Army to the Secretary of State for India, 12.

133. Quoted in Major, "State and Criminal Tribes," 676.

134. Quoted in Radhakrishna, *Dishonoured by History*, 89.

135. Benjamin and Mohanty, "Imperial Solution of a Colonial Problem," 361.

136. Major, "State and Criminal Tribes," 671.

137. The term "infest" is common throughout British documents; see in particular Charles Hervey, *Statistics of the Crime of Dacoitie in British Territory and Dependent Native States for the Three Years 1867, 1868 and 1869* (Calcutta: Office of the Superintendent of Government Printing, 1873), 5–21; IOR/V/23/26, No. 124, Report by Major E. R. C. Bradford, General Superintendent of Operations for the Suppression of Thuggee and Dacoity, 2.

138. Sanjay Nigam, "Disciplining and Policing the 'Criminals by Birth,' Part 2: The Development of a Disciplinary System, 1871–1900," *Indian Economic and Society History Review* 27, no. 3 (1990): 266.

139. Booth-Tucker, *Criminocurology*, 32.

140. Radhakrishna, *Dishonoured by History*, 87.

141. NAI Legislative Department, December 1873, Nos. 27–30, Part A, North-Western Provinces Rules under Criminal Tribes Act, 1871: Note from Officiating Inspector-General of Police, NWP, No. 28, August 29 1873.

142. NAI Legislative Department, November 1871, Nos. 44–127, Part A, The Criminal Tribes Act, 1871, P. H. Egerton, Commissioner and Supt, Amritsar Division, 20 Feb. 1869.

143. Quoted in Nigam, "Disciplining and Policing the 'Criminals by Birth,' Part 1," 144. Emphasis in original.

144. Alluding to police persecution condemned by Victor Hugo in *Les Miserables*, Carmichael continued: "What can be harder on a man than that he should, simply because he is a member of a wandering tribe, wander about as it were, with a brand on his brow like Cain?" NAI Legislative Department, November 1871, Nos. 44–127, Part A, The Criminal Tribes Act, 1871, memo by CP Carmichael, Inspector General of Police to Secretary to Government, NWP, 6 July 1870.

145. NAI Home Department (Judicial), January 1876, Nos. 139–150, Adoption of the necessary measures in order to render Part I of the Criminal Tribes act XXVII of 1871 applicable to the Lower Provinces of Bengal.

146. NAI Legislative Department, November 1871, Nos. 44–127, Part A, The Criminal Tribes Act, 1871, Memo by Colonel CJ Showers.

147. Radhakrishna, *Dishonoured by History*, 82.

148. According to J. Monro, NAI Home Department (Judicial), January 1876, Nos. 139–150, Adoption of the necessary measures in order to render Part I of the Criminal Tribes act XXVII of 1871 applicable to the Lower Provinces of Bengal.

149. Freitag, "Crime in the Social Order," 249.

150. Nigam, "Disciplining and Policing the 'Criminals by Birth,' Part 1," 145.

151. Freitag, "Crime in the Social Order," 239, 251, 231.

152. Khalili, *Time in the Shadows*, 3–5.

153. Radhika Singha, *A Despotism of Law: Crime and Justice in Early Colonial India* (New York: Oxford University Press, 1998).

154. NAI Home Department (Judicial), April 1878, Nos. 64–6, Part A, "Registration of the Aligarh District under the Criminal Tribes Act, 1871"; Major, "State and Criminal Tribes," 675.

155. NAI Home Department (Judicial), January 1879, Nos. 59–64, Workings of the Criminal Tribes Act in the North-Western Provinces during 1877.

156. In doing so, they fulfilled a peculiarly colonial dialectic: controlling and reclaiming the "margins" applied both to wild and "marginal" humanity and to the untamed wilderness at the edge of settled society. Steven Barnes notes similar dynamics under the Soviets on the marginal landscapes of Siberia. *Death and Redemption*, chapter 2.

157. Schwarz, *Constructing the Criminal Tribe*, 82; Radhakrishna, "Surveillance and Settlements," 197.

158. NAI Home Department (Judicial), January 1879, Nos. 59–64, Working of the Criminal Tribes Act in the North-Western Provinces during 1877.

159. Schwarz, *Constructing the Criminal Tribe*, 98; Major, "State and Criminal Tribes," 677. Radhakrishna notes "in the Madras Presidency in 1916 alone, over a dozen proposals for new settlements were entertained on the basis of employers' need for labor." Radhakrishna, *Dishonored by History*, 106–7.

160. NAI Legislative Department, November 1871, Nos. 44–127, Part A, The Criminal Tribes Act, 1871, CA Elliott, Esq. Offg. Secy. To Govt. NWP, April 21, 1871.

161. Anderson, "The Politics of Convict Space."

162. Quoted in Radhakrishna, *Dishonoured by History*, 84.

163. A. Aiyappan, *Report on the Socio-Economic Conditions of the Aboriginal Tribes of the Province of Madras* (Madras: Government Press, 1948), 37.

164. For the settlements' many failures see Radhakrishna, "Surveillance and Settlements"; Major, "State and Criminal Tribes," 672.

165. NAI Legislative Department, November 1871, Nos. 44–127, Part A, The Criminal Tribes Act, 1871: Description of the Mughya Domes by Lieut-Col AH Paterson, Insp. Gen. of Police, Lower Provinces.

166. NAUK CO 291/27 No. 5866, Refugee Camps, January 30, 1901.

167. C. 3086-IV, *Report of the Indian Famine Commission. Appendix IV. Replies to Inquiries of Commission* (London: Her Majesty's Stationary Office, 1885), 259.

168. *Sketch of the Medical History of the Native Army of Bombay for the Year 1876* (Bombay: Government Central Press, 1877), 39.

CHAPTER 2

1. J. E. Scott, *In Famine Land: Observations and Experiences in India During the Great Drought of 1899–1900* (London: Harper & Brothers, 1904), 101.

2. "Indian Notes," *The Church Weekly*, August 27, 1897.

3. Scott, *In Famine Land*, 121–2.

4. "Indian Notes," *The Church Weekly*, August 27, 1897.

5. Scott, *In Famine Land*, 122.

6. Nash, *Great Famine*, 7.

7. The government of India recorded the number of relief candidates at public works, but not those specifically accommodated in camps. At the height of the 1899–1901 famine, there were 4.6 million relief workers; many though not all of them lived in camps. In Bombay, where the use of camps was most prevalent, the government counted just under a million on public relief works, most of whom were undoubtedly lodged in camps. Similar numbers pertained to the 1876–77 and 1896–97 famines. Additionally, some 47,000 wanderers were detained in "poorhouse" camps in Bombay Presidency. For full statistics see Cd. 876. *Report of the Indian Famine Commission* (London: Her Majesty's Stationary Office, 1901); *Report on the Famine in the Bombay Presidency, 1899–1902* (Bombay: Government Central Press, 1903), appendices 35–36.

8. Temple, quoted in William Digby, *The Famine Campaign in Southern India: Madras and Bombay Presidencies and Province of Mysore, 1876–1878*, vol. I (London: Longmans, Green, 1878), 373.

9. Dutt, *Economic History*, iv. Modern historians concur: "India was visited more frequently by famines of greater intensity and wider coverage in the colonial epoch as compared with earlier periods." Mohiuddin Alamgir, *Famine in South Asia: Political Economy of Mass Starvation* (Cambridge, MA: Oelgeschlager, Gunn & Hain, 1980), 58.

10. Nash, *Great Famine*, 8.

11. Joseph Taylor, "Famine in India," *Friends' Quarterly Examiner* 34, no. 136 (October 1900), 618.

12. Indian Revenue paid for troops and resources diverted to South Africa and for interning Boer prisoners in POW camps in both India and South Africa. Balasubramanyam Chandramohan, "'Hamlet with the Prince of Denmark Left Out'?: The South African War, Empire and India," in *The South African War Reappraised*, ed. Donal Lowry (Manchester: Manchester University Press, 2000), 156; Omissi, "India: Some Perceptions of Race and Empire," 219.

13. Davis, *Late Victorian Holocausts*, 9. Timothy Mitchell argues that colonial power asserted itself through assumed distinctions between "human" and "nature." *Rule of Experts: Egypt, Techno-Politics, Modernity* (Berkeley, CA: University of California Press, 2002). This invented and self-serving binary helped mask British culpability for famine by depicting it as a "natural" disaster.

14. Nash, *Great Famine*, 8.

15. Amartya Sen, *Poverty and Famines: An Essay on Entitlement and Deprivation* (New York: Oxford University Press, 1981).

16. Native charity was "benevolent but ill-advised," "lavish and undiscriminating." IOR/P/5987, *Bombay Famine Proceedings*, No. 2480 Fortnightly inspection reports of the Sanitary Department; IOR/P/5985, *Bombay Famine Proceedings*, No. 1141, Memo of a tour through famine districts by Mr. Monteath.

17. "Curzon, George Nathaniel, Marquess Curzon of Kedleston (1859–1925)," David Gilmour in *Oxford Dictionary of National Biography*, online edition ed. David Cannadine (Oxford: Oxford University Press, 2004).

18. Quoted in Hall-Matthews, "Famine Process," 192.

19. Humanitarianism, according to Anna Clark, was compatible with the "biopolitical" management and discipline of populations. "Humanitarianism, Human Rights and Biopolitics."

20. Michel Foucault identifies a crucial shift in the eighteenth and nineteenth centuries from the government of territory to that of "things." Rather than simply maintaining sovereignty over a given territory, government transformed into a "plurality of specific aims: . . . ensur[ing] that the greatest possible quantity of wealth is

produced, that the people are provided with sufficient means of subsistence, [and] that the population is enabled to multiply." Foucault, "Governmentality," 91–5.

21. Sanjay Sharma, *Famine, Philanthropy and the Colonial State: North India in the Early Nineteenth Century* (New Delhi: Oxford University Press, 1996), chapter 4.

22. Peter Gray outlines connections between Irish and Indian policy in "Famine and Land in Ireland and India, 1845–1880: James Caird and the Political Economy of Hunger," *Historical Journal* 49, no. 1 (2006).

23. *The Economist*, quoted in Ben Kiernan, "From Irish Famine to Congo Reform: Nineteenth-Century Roots of International Human Rights Law and Activism," in *Confronting Genocide*, ed. R. Provost and Pakhaven (New York: Springer, 2011), 17.

24. *Times*, quoted in Kiernan, "Irish Famine," 20.

25. Temple quoted in Hall-Matthews, "Famine Process," 198.

26. James S. Donnelly Jr., "The Administration of Relief, 1846–7," in *A New History of Ireland, vol. 5, Ireland Under the Union I, 1801–1870*, ed. W. E. Vaughan (Oxford: Clarendon, 1989), 302.

27. Christine Kinealy, *A Death-Dealing Famine: The Great Hunger in Ireland* (Chicago: Pluto, 1997), 66.

28. John Strachey, quoted in Hall-Matthews, "Famine Process," 192.

29. C. 2591 *Report of the Indian Famine Commission, Part I Famine Relief (London:* Her Majesty's Stationary Office, 1880), 31.

30. Thomson, *Real Indian People*, 238–39.

31. Trevleyan quoted in Tehila Sasson and James Vernon, "Practising the British Way of Famine: Technologies of Relief, 1770–1985," *European Review of History* 22, no. 6 (2015): 862.

32. "Temple, Sir Richard, first baronet (1826–1902)," David Steele in *Oxford Dictionary of National Biography*, online ed., ed. David Cannadine (Oxford: Oxford University Press, 2004).

33. Rather than serving Indians impacted by famine, British India's permanent poorhouses sequestered "poor whites" away from public view. In service of white supremacism, natives were not permitted to see destitute Europeans. Ann Laura Stoler, *Carnal Knowledge*, 35, 107; Aravind Ganachari, "'White Man's Embarrassment': European Vagrancy in 19th Century Bombay," *Economic and Political Weekly* 37 no. 25 (2002).

34. Liam Kennedy et al., *Mapping the Great Irish Famine* (Dublin: Four Courts, 1999), 125.

35. Scott, *In Famine Land*, 80.

36. Nash, *Great Famine*, 6.

37. Cd. 876, 14–5; Tehila Sasson, "From Empire to Humanity: The Russian Famine and the Imperial Origins of International Humanitarianism," *Journal of British Studies* 55, no. 3 (July 2016): 525. Nonetheless, wandering was less prevalent in some areas in

1896–1902 due to timelier "village relief." *Report on the Famine in the Central Provinces,* vol. I (Nagpur: Secretariat, 1901), 38.

38. *Report on the Famine in the Bombay Presidency, 1899–1902,* 46.

39. R. A. Dalyell, *Memorandum on the Madras Famine of 1866,* quoted in Alamgir, *Famine in South Asia,* 64.

40. C. 3086-IV, 12.

41. Those who lost the peasant's "ties to the land" and "connection to the soil" were more vulnerable, Hannah Arendt notes, to coercive state powers, and ultimately to incarceration in camps. *Origins of Totalitarianism,* 196–97.

42. C. 3086-IV, 302.

43. David Arnold, *Famine: Social Crisis and Historical Change* (Oxford: Basil Blackwell, 1988), 92; C. 3086-IV, 181.

44. Arnold, *Famine: Social Crisis,* 73–74. Arnold cautions against a view that "people struck by famine are powerless and abject, 'pathetic' . . . in their 'submission' to deprivation." Such depictions render them passively dependent upon the benevolence of the West. But the famished were not "a naked animal on the naked earth," Arnold insists.

45. C. 3086-IV, 239.

46. The "ethnographic subject" was "first and foremost a body," Nicholas Dirks writes, to be "known and controlled through the measurement and interpretation of physical subjects organized in caste and gender categories." "The Crimes of Colonialism: Anthropology and the Textualization of India," *Colonial Subjects: Essays on the Practical History of Anthropology,* ed. Peter Pels and Oscar Salemink (University of Michigan Press, 2000), 173.

47. Nash, *Great Famine,* 39–40.

48. Primo Levi's "Muselmann" formed "an anonymous mass . . . of non-men who march and labor in silence, the divine spark dead within them, already too empty to really suffer." "One hesitates to call them living," Levi continued, "and if I could enclose all the evil of our time in one image, I would choose this: an emaciated man, with head dropped and shoulders curved, on whose face and in whose eyes not a trace of a thought is to be seen." *Survival in Auschwitz* (New York: Simon & Schuster, 1996), 90.

49. Zahid Chaudhary, *Afterimage of Empire: Photography in Nineteenth-Century India* (Minneapolis: University of Minnesota Press, 2012), 186, 176.

50. Rev. C. H. Gill quoted in Scott, *In Famine Land,* 85.

51. Merewether quoted in Davis, *Late Victorian Holocausts,* 154.

52. Cd. 1179 *Papers Regarding the Famine and the Relief Operations in India during 1900–1902* (London: His Majesty's Stationary Office, 1902), 224. Imprudent and improvident, Indian peasants were, Temple noted, "probably more extravagant . . . in their own humble way . . . than any other peasantry with which I am acquainted." Temple Papers, MSS EUR F86/208(a): Minutes of Evidence, 15.

53. S. Ambirajan, "Malthusian Population Theory and Indian Famine Policy in the Nineteenth Century," *Population Studies* 30, no. 1 (1976).

54. According to Colonel Johnson of Mysore. C 3086-IV, 67.

55. Agamben, *Homo Sacer.*

56. William Wordsworth, and Samuel Taylor Coleridge, *Lyrical Ballads with a Few Other Poems* (Bristol: Printed by Biggs and Cottle for T. N. Longman, Paternoster-Row, London, 1798).

57. Scott, *In Famine Land*, 22.

58. For shifting stereotypes of famine refugees, see Jim Masselos, "Migration and Urban Identity: Bombay's Famine Refugees in the Nineteenth Century," in *Bombay: A Metaphor for Modern India*, ed. S. Patel and A. Thorner (Bombay, 1993), 26–27.

59. MSA Revenue Department (Famine), 1897, Vol. 147, No. 4, Relief works sanctioned and other measures adopted to obviate distress.

60. C. 3086-IV, 1.

61. Hall-Matthews, "Historical Roots," 225.

62. *Report on the Famine in the Bombay Presidency 1896–7* (Bombay: Government Central Press, 1898), 18.

63. "Destitute aliens" in a "wretched physical condition" constituted a "constant source of anxiety," officials reported. *Report on the Famine in the Central Provinces*, vol. I, 25.

64. Srivastava, *History of Indian Famines*, 226. In many cases, the military was employed to quell riots and guard trains carrying grain through famine districts. At the height of unrest, Davis asserts, "Social order was preserved only by terror." *Late Victorian Holocausts*, 46, 52.

65. Temple Papers, IOR/F86/183 Report of the Mission to the Famine-Stricken Districts of the Madras Presidency in 1877.

66. *Resolution on the Administration of Famine Relief in the North-Western Provinces and Oudh during 1896 and 1897* (Allahabad: North-Western Provinces and Oudh Government Press, 1897), 59.

67. C. 3086-V, *Report of the Indian Famine Commission. Appendix V. Irrigation as a Protection against Famine* (London: Her Majesty's Stationary Office, 1885), 261.

68. George E. B. Couper, *Sir George Couper and the Famine in the North-West Provinces*, (Calcutta: Statesman Office, 1898), 3.

69. IOR/P/5789, *Bombay Famine Proceedings*, Letter from Political Agent, Mahi Kantha to Secretary of Government, Political Dept., Bombay, 27 Oct. 1899; *Report on the Famine in the Central Provinces*, vol. I, 28.

70. C. 3086-IV, 239.

71. Hall-Matthews, "Famine Process," 224.

72. Pitirim A. Sorokin, *Hunger as a Factor in Human Affairs* (Gainesville: University Presses of Florida, 1975), 234.

73. "Resistance and insecurity characterized the daily life of empire on the ground," Antoinette Burton writes. *Trouble with Empire*, 2–3; Kim Wagner, "'Treading Upon Fires': The 'Mutiny'-Motif and Colonal Anxieties in British India," *Past and Present*, 218 no. 1 (2012).

74. Hunger continued to have revolutionary implications when India's independence movement mobilized famine to political ends. Vernon, *Hunger*, chapter 3.

75. Richard Temple, *Men and Events of My Time in* India (London: J. Murray, 1882), 469.

76. *Report on the Famine in the Central Provinces*, vol. I, 24.

77. "Illegal immigrants" from Native States were liable to deportation, though it was "difficult to discriminate foreigners from permanent residents, the former concealing their domicile from fear of deportation. . . . Only by cross-questioning and catching them out in their statements [could] the truth . . . occasionally [be] ascertained." Cd. 1179, 137.

78. MSA General Department (Plague), 1900, Vol. 952, No. 312, Beggars and Vagrants.

79. To invoke Mary Douglas's symbolic definition of dirt. *Purity and Danger: An Analysis of the Concepts of Pollution and Taboo* (London: Routledge, 1966).

80. MSA Famine Department, 1900, No. 82, Medical supervision of the Famine refugees on the borders of the Cantonment of Nasirabad

81. Cornish quoted in William Digby, *The Famine Campaign in Southern India: Madras and Bombay Presidencies and Province of Mysore, 1876–1878*, vol. II (London: Longmans, Green 1878), 308.

82. MSA General Department (Plague), 1900, Vol. 54, No. 251, Beggars and Vagrants, Measures taken to remove from Bombay.

83. Temple Papers, IOR/F86/208(a): Minutes of Evidence, 56.

84. According to Sir. W. R. Robinson, C. 3086-IV, 306.

85. C. 3086-IV, 305.

86. Temple Papers, IOR/F86/183, Report of the Mission to the Famine-Stricken Districts of the Madras Presidency in 1877.

87. *Report on the Famine in the Central Provinces*, vol. I, 90.

88. Digby, *Famine Campaign*, vol. II, 376.

89. C. 2591, 47.

90. Sorokin, *Hunger*, 227.

91. Temple Papers, IOR/F86/208(a): Minutes of Evidence, 56.

92. IOR/P/5985, *Bombay Famine Proceedings*, No. 1218 Progress of relief operations in the Ahmednagar District.

93. IOR/P/6255, *Bombay Famine Proceedings*, No. 1146, Arrangements for the collection and removal to poorhouses of emaciated wanderers found in and around Ahmedabad.

94. C. 3086-IV, 306.

95. Temple Papers, IOR/F86/183 Report by Col. W. S. Drever, Commissioner of Police.

96. IOR/P/6257, *Bombay Famine Proceedings*, No. 2243, Instructions regarding the opening of camps and relief works for beggars coming to Bombay from Kathiawar.

97. MSA General Department (Plague), 1900, Vol. 952, No. 312, Beggars and Vagrants, Measures taken to remove them from Bombay. This material was filed as a plague matter because authorities used the Epidemic Diseases Act of 1897 to legalize forced detention.

98. Ibid.

99. Temple Papers, IOR/F86/183 Report by Col. W. S. Drever, Commissioner of Police, February 20, 1877.

100. T. W. Holderness, *Peoples & Problems of India* (New York: N. Holt, 1912), 152.

101. Temple Papers, IOR/F86/183, Reply to Temple's Minutes of March 7th and 14th by Dr. Cornish.

102. Digby, *Famine Campaign*, vol. I, 26.

103. Thomson, *Real Indian People*, 113–16.

104. MSS EUR/E171: Press cuttings on the Mysore famine of 1877–78, Letter from S. C. Bayle, Additional Secretary to the Government of India to the Chief Commissioner of Mysore.

105. According to a *Times* correspondent, December 5, 1877, British Library, MSS EUR/E171: Press cuttings on the Mysore famine of 1877–78.

106. MSS EUR/E171: Press cuttings on the Mysore famine of 1877–78, Orders of Collector of North Arcot, Mr. Whiteside.

107. C. 3086-IV, 306.

108. Ibid., 305.

109. MSS EUR/E171: Press cuttings on the Mysore famine of 1877–78, Orders of Collector of North Arcot, Mr. Whiteside.

110. C. 3086-IV, 241.

111. The developing contours of Western political culture, which increasingly relied on the language of "emergency measures" following the age of political revolution, rendered "crisis" a familiar, if unpredictable, feature of Western states. So too did the volatile economic cycles of Victorian capitalism.

112. Localized famines in British India were regular events, a fact hidden by macrolevel colonial statistics, which rendered the 1876–77 and 1896–1901 famines "interruptions of 'normal' processes." B. Murton, "Spatial and Temporal Patterns of Famine in Southern India before the Famine Codes," in *Famine as a Geographical Phenomenon*, ed. Bruce Currey and Graeme Hugo (Boston: D. Reidel, 1984), 71. An identifiably "Western" view of famine as a distinct emergency contrasts with that of famine-afflicted locals, who do not build "definitional firewalls" between famine and general

malnutrition. Davis, *Late-Victorian Holocausts*, 21; Alexander de Waal, *Famine that Kills: Darfur, Sudan, 1984–5* (Oxford: Clarendon, 1989), 6, 10.

113. C. 3086-IV, 342.

114. Temple Papers, MSS EUR F86/208(a): Minutes of Evidence, 47–48.

115. C. 3086-IV, 341; MSA Revenue Department (Famine), 1899, Vol. 33, No. 116, Investiture of certain subordinate judges with First Class Magisterial Powers; *Report on Famine in the Central Provinces*, 54.

116. C. 3086-IV, 22.

117. Temple Papers, MSS EUR F86/208(a): Minutes of Evidence, 56.

118. C. 3086-IV, 181.

119. Temple Papers, MSS EUR F86/208(a): Minutes of Evidence, 56.

120. C. 3086-IV, 240.

121. Temple Papers, MSS EUR F86/208(a): Minutes of Evidence, 56. Cicero's phrase appears in *De Legibus*, book III, part III, sub. VIII. The epigraph of John Locke's *Second Treatise on Government* (London: Printed for Awnsham Churchill, 1690) imprints the maintenance of public health and order (in addition to individual rights and liberty) in the founding document of political liberalism.

122. C. 3086-IV, 181.

123. This was contentious: the District Commissioner noted "it is hardly legal to treat famine-stricken persons . . . as vagabonds loafing about the country with criminal intent." IOR/P/5988, *Bombay Famine Proceedings*, No. 3286, Detention of destitute wanderers in poorhouses in the Nasik District.

124. Carl Schmitt, *The Nomos of the Earth in the International Law of Jus Publicum Europaeum* (New York: Telos, 2006); Agamben, *States of Exception*.

125. Temple Papers, MSS EUR F86/27, Correspondence between Richard Temple and Florence Nightingale. As governor of Bengal in 1873–74, Temple's purchase and gratuitous distribution of grain saved many lives, but criticism of his "wild expenditure"—£6 million—and "indiscriminating outdoor relief" steered him to pursue "strict economy" in 1876–77. Srivastava, *History of Indian Famines*, 125; Davis, *Late Victorian Holocausts*, 37.

126. Temple Papers, MSS EUR F86/27, Correspondence between Richard Temple and Florence Nightingale; Richard Temple, *India in 1880* (London: J. Murray, 1881), 335.

127. Ibid., 336.

128. Temple Papers, MSS EUR F86/27, Correspondence between Richard Temple and Florence Nightingale; Temple, *India in 1880*, 336.

129. James Scott, *The Art of Not Being Governed: An Anarchist History of Upland Southeast Asia* (New Haven, CT: Yale Agrarian Studies Series, 2010).

130. Stedman Jones, *Outcast London*, 14; Booth, *In Darkest England*.

131. Temple Papers, MSS EUR F86/208(a): Minutes of Evidence, 54.

132. Temple, *India in 1880*, 198.

133. Temple Papers, MSS EUR F86/208(a): Minutes of Evidence, 47.

134. For the "high modernist" technologies of "legibility," of which camps formed a part, see James Scott, *Seeing Like a State*. For the Indian context, see Anderson, *Legible Bodies*.

135. C. 3086-IV, 384. In Punjab, circles varied between 6 to 57 square miles each, with populations between 5,000 to 20,000. *Report on the Famine in the Punjab in 1896–7* (Lahore: Punjab Government Press, 1898).

136. Colonel Fraser, chief engineer with the Public Works Department in the North-Western Provinces, described a "famine map" as follows: "Each relief camp [is] shown on the chart by a red circle, with the centre on the line of communication, and within the circle being written villages Nos. o-to-o—the group of which it forms the center." In this way, "the whole country in each district [should be] mapped out" and officials would "know exactly the population we have to deal with and the classes of people to be managed." C. 3086-IV, 95.

137. Ibid., 340.

138. Nash, *Great Famine*, 158.

139. *Report on the Famine in the Bombay Presidency, 1899–1902*, 46.

140. *Report on the Famine in the Bombay Presidency, 1896–7*, 52.

141. In July 1900 46007 wanderers were detained in Bombay Presidency, while 934842 were accommodated on public relief works. Similar numbers obtained in other provinces and in earlier famines. *Report on the Famine in the Bombay Presidency, 1899–1902*, appendices 36, 28.

142. Digby, *Famine Campaign*, vol. I, 349.

143. Ibid., vol. II, 285.

144. Nash, *Great Famine*, 75.

145. Digby, *Famine Campaign*, vol. I, 323, 310.

146. MSA Famine Department, 1902, Vol. 69, No. 222, Notes on inspection by Mr. B. Robertson, CIE, Special Officer.

147. IOR/P/6256, *Bombay Famine Proceedings*, No. 1508, Measures for the restriction of relief to those who are in real need.

148. Temple Papers MSS EUR F86/183 Proceedings of the Madras Revenue Department, March 20 1877, No. 640; C. 3086-IV, 274.

149. Temple, cited in Hall-Matthews, "Famine Process," 223.

150. C. 2591, 60–61.

151. MSS EUR/E171: Press cuttings on the Mysore famine of 1877–78 collected by Col (later Lt-Gen Sir) Richard Hieram Sankey, 95.

152. Ignatieff, *Just Measure of Pain*.

153. IOR/P/5985, *Bombay Famine Proceedings*, No. 1540 Question of enforcing residence on relief works as a condition of relief.

154. Hall-Matthews, "Historical Roots," 220.

155. Figures from Srivastava, "Indian Famine of 1876–9," 883, 886. Total spending for the 1876–8 famine was ₹111.9 million, Srivastava calculates. In 1896–7 it was ₹72.5 million or approximately £4.8 million. There were approximately ₹15 to £1.

156. Temple, quoted in Digby, *Famine Campaign*, vol. I, 373.

157. *Report on the Famine in the Bombay Presidency in 1896–7*, 8.

158. *Report on the Famine in the Bombay Presidency 1899–1902*, 20.

159. T. Higham, *Report on the Management of Famine Relief Works and Notes on Famine Relief Works in Madras, Bombay, Bengal, North-Western Provinces and Oudh, Punjab, and the Central Provinces.* (Simla: Government Central Printing Office, 1897), 16–7.

160. Temple Papers, F86/208(a): Minutes of Evidence, 50.

161. IOR/P/5986, *Bombay Famine Proceedings*, No. 2127, Progress of relief measures in Ahmednagar District.

162. Nash, *Great Famine*, 75.

163. Digby, *Famine Campaign*, Vol. I, 304.

164. Numbers in Bombay in April 1877 were typical: of the approximately 293,000 on relief works, 93,167 were men, 128,076 were women, and 72,212 were children. *Report on the Famine in the Bombay Presidency 1896–7*, cxlix.

165. MSA Famine Department, 1902, Vol. 69, No. 222, Notes on inspection by Mr. B. Robertson.

166. Nash, *Great Famine*, 20. Stone breaking was also unpopular among Public Works officers, for it was difficult to supervise laborers who were "scattered over long distances." *Report on the Famine in the Bombay Presidency 1896–7*, 52.

167. IOR/P/5986, *Bombay Famine Proceedings*, No. 2127, Progress of relief measures in Ahmednagar District.

168. MSA Famine Department, 1901, Vol. 31, No 341, Payment of a grant to the American Marathi Mission at Ahmednagar.

169. There were clear limits to inner reform, however. Colonial governmentality, Sarah Hodges notes, "sought not to organize and reorganize conditions of freedom . . . but instead conditions of unfreedom." Camps thus facilitated obedience and coercion rather than the reform of potential citizen-subjects. "Looting the Lock Hospital in Colonial Madras during the Famine Years of the 1870s," *Social History of Medicine* 18 (2005): 382.

170. Temple Papers, MSS EUR F86/27: Correspondence between Richard Temple and Florence Nightingale.

171. Digby, *Famine Campaign*, vol. II, 4.

172. C. 2591, 42.

173. IOR/P/5985, *Bombay Famine Proceedings*, No. 1141, Memo of a tour through famine districts.

174. Temple Papers, IOR/F86/183, Journal kept by Sir Richard Temple.

175. Mr. Knight, quoted in Couper, *George Couper*, 3.

176. Temple Papers, IOR/F86/183, Reply to Sir Richard Temple's Minutes [by Dr. Cornish], 8.

177. MSA Revenue Department (Famine), 1897, Vol. 140, No. 94, Exaction of a full task in famine relief operations and wages to be paid on famine test works. Emphasis in original.

178. Thomson, *Real Indian People*, 121.

179. C. 3086-IV, 118.

180. Ibid., 216.

181. MSA Revenue Department (Famine), 1900, Vol. 49, No. 71, Orders regarding the restriction of famine relief to what is necessary for the preservation of health and strength.

182. Temple Papers, IOR/F86/183, A Reply to Sir Richard Temple's Minutes [by Dr. Cornish].

183. MSA Famine Department, 1901, Vol. 16, No. 332, Question of subsistence diets and their values. Vernon, *Hunger*, 104–8.

184. David Hall-Matthews, "Inaccurate Conceptions: Disputed Measures of Nutritional Needs and Famine Deaths in Colonial India," *Modern Asian Studies* 42, no. 6 (November 2008): 1194.

185. Nonetheless, camp rations periodically returned to the one pound figure: a sample ration from the North-Western Provinces in 1896 offered adult men a daily diet of just twelve ounces of grain or rice, two ounces of beans or lentils, and small quantities of condiments. MSA Revenue Department (Famine), 1896, Vol. 18, Relief Operations, Orders and Rules issued by the Government of the North-Western Provinces.

186. C. 8812, *Narrative of the Famine in India in 1896–7 by T. W. Holderness* (London: Her Majesty's Stationary Office, 1897), 32.

187. IOR/P/5788, *Bombay Famine Proceedings*, No. 3117, Inspection reports of officers of the Sanitary Department for the fortnight ending 6th July 1900.

188. MSA Revenue Department (Famine), 1900, Vol. 49, No. 71, Orders regarding the restriction of famine relief to what is necessary for the preservation of health and strength.

189. Scott, *In Famine Land*, 193.

190. IOR/P/5986, *Bombay Famine Proceedings*, No. 1948, Report on the condition of persons employed on certain relief works in Sholapur. "Relief has come to be regarded as an obligation on the part of the Government to the people rather than a subject for gratitude on the part of the recipients," a *Times* article (contained in the above file) complained. In response, the collector of Sholapur noted the "ornaments referred to [were] valueless brass armlets and anklets worn by Lambani and Pardi women."

191. IOR/P/5985, *Bombay Famine Proceedings*, No. 1187, High proportion of non-working children on the Kusumbe Relief Camp.

192. Cited in Digby, *Famine Campaign*, vol. II, 324.

193. Officials maintained British administration saved "thousands of little children" from "callous neglect . . . by parents whose natural instincts were weakened by continued scarcity." *Resolution on the Administration of Famine Relief in the North-Western Provinces*, 38.

194. Thomson, *Real Indian People*, 122.

195. Digby, *Famine Campaign*, vol. II, 285.

196. Nash, *Great Famine*, 259.

197. Temple Papers, MSS EUR F86/208(a): Minutes of Evidence, 54.

198. Mr. Weekes in Madras likewise noted that while "distance tests and labour tests and closed camps . . . are baneful in the extreme," any other system of localized outdoor relief required "far more local knowledge" than officials could "possibly possess or acquire." C. 3086-IV, 89.

199. IOR/P/5986, *Bombay Famine Proceedings*, No. 2406. Rules in force in the Jubbulpore Division of the Central Provinces regarding the admission of persons to relief works by tickets.

200. Digby, *Famine Campaign*, vol. II, 287.

201. Temple Papers, MSS Eur, F86/208(a): Minutes of Evidence, 47.

202. Nash, *Great Famine*, 112.

203. MSA Revenue Department (Famine), 1900, Vol. 49, No. 71, Orders regarding the restriction of famine relief to what is necessary for the preservation of health and strength. Native agents, another official charged, "take with both hands—they cheat the Government who pay them, and they take toll from the famishing wretches whose misery they are employed to alleviate." C. 3086-IV, 382.

204. Temple Papers, MSS EUR F86/208(a): Minutes of Evidence, 48.

205. Cd. 876, 16.

206. MSA Famine Department, 1902, Vol. 69, No. 222, Notes on inspection by Mr. B. Robertson.

207. Nash, *Great Famine*, 170, 255.

208. Major General Sir Michael Kennedy, C. 3086-V, 62.

209. Correspondence of Sir James Caird, IOR/H/MISC/796, letter from Viceroy Lytton, 217.

210. Scott, *In Famine Land*, 46.

211. Max Weber, *Sociology of Religion* ed. Talcott Parsons (Boston: Beacon Press, 1922), 90.

212. C. 2591, "Appendix: Dissent on Certain Points from the Report of the Indian Famine Commission," 64–69. Despite Caird and Sullivan's criticisms, the 1880 *Report* largely vindicated the policy of Temple and Lytton. Caird's criticism was likely rooted in personal experience with the flexible approach to famine relief advocated by Sir Robert Peel in the early years of the Irish famine. Grey, "Famine and Land in Ireland and India."

213. C. 3086-IV, 231.

214. Ibid.

215. For Britain's strategic enforcement of caste, see Nicholas Dirks, *Castes of Mind: Colonialism and the Making of Modern India* (Princeton, NJ: Princeton University Press, 2001).

216. Lance Brennan, "The Development of the Indian Famine Codes: Personalities, Politics and Policies," in *Famine as a Geographical Phenomenon* ed. Bruce Currey and Graeme Hugo (Boston: D. Reidel, 1984), 108.

217. Nash, *Great Famine*, 256–57.

218. Davis, *Late Victorian Holocausts*, 41–43.

219. MSA Revenue Department (Famine), 1897, Vol. 46, No. 107, Complaints regarding the insufficiency of the ration prescribed for non-working children.

220. Dutt, *Economic History*, iv.

221. Davis, *Late Victorian Holocausts*, 148.

222. Nash, *Great Famine*, 195.

223. Cd. 876, 23.

224. MSA Famine Department, 1902, Vol. 69, No. 222, Notes on inspection by Mr. B. Robertson.

225. Claude Hill, *India—Stepmother* (London: William Blackwood, 1929), 117.

226. Om Prakash, *Factual Survey Relating to the Employment of Camp Dwellers in the Punjab Relief Camps* (Ludhiana, India: Board of Economic Inquiry, 1950); Amrita Ranyasami, "Systems of Limited Intervention: An Evaluation of the Principles and Practice of Relief Administration in India," *Indian Historical Review* 27 (2000); Sasson and Vernon, "Practising the British Way of Famine," 868.

CHAPTER 3

1. For the Hong Kong-India nexus, see Mary Sutphen, "Not What but Where: Bubonic Plague and the Reception of Germ Theories in Hong Kong and Calcutta, 1894–1897," *Journal of the History of Medicine* 52 (1997).

2. Echenberg, *Plague Ports*, 283–85; Howard Phillips, *Epidemics: The Story of South Africa's Five Most Lethal Human Diseases* (Athens: Ohio University Press, 2012), 44.

3. Extrapolated for periods before camp populations were monitored, it is likely that over 300,000 passed through Bombay camps. Britain did not record India-wide camp populations. Calcutta and areas of eastern India did not resort to segregation camps in large numbers, but camps in major cities like Karachi and Poona rivaled Bombay's numbers. Provincial towns were often evacuated to outlying camps in their entirety, substantially augmenting the numbers. For exact figures and lists of individual camps in Bombay see *Report of the Municipal Commissioner on the Plague in Bombay for the Year Ending 31st May 1899* (Bombay: 'Times of India' Steam Press, 1899), 73–76; *Report of the Municipal Commissioner on the Plague in Bombay for the Year Ending 31st May 1900*

(Bombay: 'Times of India' Steam Press, 1900), 89–92; *Report of the Municipal Commissioner on the Plague in Bombay for the Year Ending 31st May 1901* (Bombay: 'Times of India' Steam Press, 1901), 98–102.

4. William Simpson, *Treatise on Plague Dealing with the Historical, Epidemiological, Clinical, Therapeutic and Preventive Aspects of the Disease* (Cambridge: University of Cambridge Press, 1905), 337–38. Renaissance pest houses were also "shaped by social prejudice," and "by fear as much as pity with regard to the poor." Terence Ranger and Paul Slack, eds., *Epidemics and Ideas: Essays on the Historical Perception of Pestilence* (New York: Cambridge University Press, 1992), 12.

5. Paul Slack, "Responses to Plague in Early Modern Europe," in *In Time of Plague: The History and Social Consequences of Lethal Epidemic Disease*, ed. Arien Mack (New York: New York University Press, 1991), 130.

6. Arnold, *Colonizing the Body*, 191. British governments in London and India routinely opposed the strongly contagionist stance of the Constantinople sanitary conference and other international quarantine regimes. The "English system" of sanitary surveillance at port offered "a unique alterative to quarantine." Krista Maglen, *The English System: Quarantine, Immigration and the Making of a Port Sanitary Zone* (New York: Manchester University Press, 2014), 8.

7. Mark Harrison, *Public Health in British India: Anglo-Indian Preventive Medicine, 1859–1914* (New York: Cambridge University Press, 1994), 123.

8. British-Indian medicine adopted two competing approaches: an "authoritarian paternalist" mode, which remained a minority view after the 1857 Rebellion, and a more pervasive "liberal" conviction that colonial government should not interfere with native health or sanitation. Harrison, *Public Health in British India;* David Arnold, "Touching the Body: Perspectives on the Indian Plague, 1896–1900," *Subaltern Studies* 5 (1987).

9. Cd. 810, *Report of the Indian Plague Commission*, vol. V (1901), 51. Chandarvarkar, "Plague Panic and Epidemic Politics," 203.

10. Rand cited in Chandavarkar, "Plague Panic and Epidemic Politics," 207. "The colonial state," Chandavarkar writes, "would never again orchestrate such a penetrative programme of government, intrude so remorselessly upon the private domain, or attempt to exert such ambitious and extensive measures of social control," 210.

11. Partha Chatterjee, *The Black Hole of Empire: History of a Global Practice of Power* (Princeton, NJ: Princeton University Press, 2012), 119.

12. The Bombay Chamber of Commerce was initially concerned about the "injury to trade likely to result from quarantine," but the city's business lobby supported plague detention camps once the commercial benefits of eliminating plague became clear. MSA Detention and disinfection measures, Bombay, Vol. 366, No. 257.

13. MSA General Department (Plague), 1899, Vol. 617, Views of the various officers regarding the establishment of detention camps.

14. Simpson, *Treatise on Plague*, 382.

15. MSA General Department (Plague), 1899, Vol. 617, Views of the various officers regarding the establishment of detention camps.

16. Ibid.

17. MSA General Department (Plague), 1897, Vol. 70, No. 122, Bubonic Plague Rules for the grant of compensation for articles destroyed.

18. David Arnold, *Science, Technology and Medicine in Colonial India* (New York: Cambridge University Press, 2000), 143.

19. Hill, *India—Stepmother*, 39, 92.

20. Susan Sontag, *AIDS and Its Metaphors* (New York: Farrar, Straus and Giroux, 1988), 9–10.

21. Curtin, *Disease and Empire*.

22. Paul Weindling, quoted in Slack and Ranger, eds., *Epidemics and Ideas*, 14. Military modalities informed nineteenth-century European culture in myriad ways. Sheehan, *Where Have all the Soldiers Gone?*, part 1.

23. The metaphor of war "implements the way particularly dreaded diseases are envisaged as an alien 'other,' as enemies are in modern war." Sontag, *AIDS and Its Metaphors*, 11.

24. Harrison, *Public Health in British India*, 7.

25. MSA General Department (Plague), 1899, Vol. 617, views of the various officers regarding the establishment of Detention Camps.

26. W. F. Gatacre, *Report on the Bubonic Plague by Brigadier-General W. F. Gatacre* (Bombay: 'Times of India' Steam Press, 1897), 207.

27. *Report of the Bombay Plague Committee, Appointed by Government Resolution on the Plague in Bombay, for the Period Extending from the 1st July 1897 to the 30th. April 1898, etc.* (Bombay: 'Times of India' Steam Press, 1898), 62.

28. MSA General Department (Plague), 1899, Vol. 617, Views of the various officers regarding the establishment of detention camps.

29. This was especially true among new recruits and "those who have been studying in England for years." MSA General Department (Plague), 1899, Vol. 535, No. 135, Plague Appointments, English Doctors.

30. Medical officials in India upheld outdated miasmic views longer than their counterparts elsewhere, a stance conditioned by ongoing convictions about "dirty" colonial environs. Germ theory and miasmic views coexisted until 1910, when the latter was finally supplanted. Sutphen, "Not What but Where"; Michael Worboys, *Spreading Germs: Disease Theories and Medical Practice in Britain, 1865–1900* (New York: Cambridge University Press, 2000); I. J. Catanach, "Plague and the Tensions of Empire: India, 1896–1918," in *Imperial Medicine and Indigenous Societies*, ed. David Arnold (Manchester: Manchester University Press, 1988), 162–65.

31. Douglas, *Purity and Danger*.

32. Chandavarkar, "Plague Panic and Epidemic Politics," 211.

33. Hill, *India—Stepmother*, 112.

34. Chandavarkar, "Plague Panic and Epidemic Politics," 211.

35. Sontag, *AIDS and Its Metaphors*, 11. "Victims suggest innocence. And innocence, by the inexorable logic that governs all relational terms, suggests guilt."

36. The terms are common throughout British discourse. The latter appears in MSA General Department (Plague), 1899, Vol. 617, Views of the various officers regarding the establishment of detention camps.

37. Simpson, *Treatise on Plague*, 370.

38. Bombay Health Officer cited in Chandavarkar, "Plague Panic and Epidemic Politics," 235.

39. Simpson, *Treatise on Plague*, 357, 396, 388.

40. J. Spencer Low, "Some Preventive Measures Adopted in the Presidency of Madras During the Late Epidemic of Plague in India," *Transactions of the Epidemiological Society of London* 19 (1899–1900): 70.

41. Cd. 810, *Report of the Indian Plague Commission*, vol. V. (1901), 326.

42. Simpson, *Treatise on Plague*, 357, 366.

43. MSA General Department (Plague), 1899, Vol. 617, Views of the various officers regarding the establishment of detention camps.

44. *Report of the Bombay Plague Committee* (1898), 16.

45. MSA General Department (Plague), 1899, Vol. 617, Views of the various officers regarding the establishment of detention camps.

46. Ibid.

47. MSA General Department (Plague), 1898, Vol. 376, No. 275, Camping arrangements, Bombay.

48. MSA General Department (Plague), 1897, Vol. 153, No. 223/P, Bubonic Plague Observation Measures and Rules, Poona.

49. Echenberg, *Plague Ports*, 50.

50. MSA General Department (Plague), 1898, Vol. 366, No. 257, Detention and disinfection measures, Bombay.

51. MSA General Department (Plague), 1899, Vol. 617, Views of the various officers regarding the establishment of detention camps.

52. Radhakrishna, *Dishonored by History*, 80.

53. MSA General Department (Plague), 1898, Vol. 366, No. 257, Detention and disinfection measures, Bombay.

54. IOR/V24/3651 Annual Report of the Public Health Commissioner with the Government of India.

55. MSA General Department (Plague), 1898, Vol. 441, No. 429, Replies to GR No. 6623/4452 dated November 1897 regarding rules for observation camps.

56. MSA General Department (Plague), 1898, Vol. 366, No. 257, Detention and disinfection measures.

57. Low, "Some Preventive Measures," 61.

58. Cd. 139, *Minutes of Evidence Taken by the Indian Plague Commission with Appendices*, vol. I, (London: Her Majesty's Stationary Office, 1900).

59. Low, "Some Preventive Measures," 75.

60. MSA General Department (Plague), 1897, Vol. 69, Railway disinfection and detention camps.

61. These included purchasing forged inoculation certificates, bribing native officials, and purchasing tickets for stations just outside inspection stations and then crossing check-points by foot. "Others put on new clothes . . . and in other ways made themselves clean and respectable-looking." Low, "Some Preventive Measures," 72, 74.

62. MSA General Department (Plague), 1897, Vol. 153, No. 226/P, Bubonic Plague, Observation Measures and Rules, Central Division.

63. MSA General Department (Plague), 1898, Vol. 366, No. 257, Detention and disinfection measures, Bombay.

64. MSA General Department (Plague), 1899, Vol. 686, No. 559, Establishment in Connection with the Famine.

65. Simpson, *Treatise on Plague*, 381.

66. Gatacre, *Report on the Bubonic Plague*, 208.

67. Cd. 810, 324, 367.

68. MSA General Department (Plague), 1897, Vol. 69, Railway disinfection and detention camps.

69. Cd. 810, 325, 322.

70. Low, "Some Preventive Measures," 64.

71. For Wilkins's published report see Gatacre, *Report on the Bubonic Plague*, 207–18.

72. Hill, *India—Stepmother*, 122.

73. Gatacre, *Report on the Bubonic Plague*, 216.

74. Hill, *India—Stepmother*, 39.

75. Cleghorn quoted in Prashant Kidambi, "'An Infection of Locality': Plague, Pythogenesis and the Poor in Bombay, c. 1896–1905," *Urban History* 31, no. 2 (2004): 258.

76. Gatacre, *Report on the Bubonic Plague*, 211–12.

77. *Report of the Bombay Plague Committee* (1898), 70.

78. Simpson, *Treatise on Plague*, 191.

79. IOR/5362, North-Western-Provinces and Oudh, Sanitary Proceedings, Prog. No. 20 GRC Williams to Impey, January 7, 1898.

80. And they employed "the whole strength of the army." Klein, "Plague, Policy and Popular Unrest," 745.

81. *Report of the Bombay Plague Committee* (1898), 63.

82. Cd. 810, 344.

83. MSA General Department (Plague), 1898, Vol. 376, No. 275, Camping arrangements, Bombay.

84. Bombay's unique circumstances meant "removal to contact camps" was "reserved for cases of extreme overcrowding and . . . very poor patients." Cd. 810, 340.

85. *Report of the Bombay Plague Committee* (1898), 6.

86. Simpson, *Treatise on Plague*, 388.

87. MSA 1900 General Department (Plague), Vol. 952, No. 312, Beggars and Vagrants, Measures taken to remove them from Bombay.

88. Gatacre, *Report on the Bubonic Plague*, 167.

89. Low, "Some Preventive Measures," 69.

90. "Personal Experiences of Plague Officers in India," *British Medical Journal*, July 1, 1899, 25. Holmes, of course, relied on the specialized medical knowledge of his assistant, Dr. Watson.

91. *Report of the Bombay Plague Committee* (1898), 50.

92. NAI Home Department (Public), June 1900, Nos. 291–302, Plague Riot at Cawnpore.

93. MSA General Department (Plague), 1898, Vol. 366, Detention and disinfection measures, Bombay.

94. IOR/P/5362 North-Western Provinces Sanitary Proceedings, No. 6504/490 S. J. Thomson to Secretary to Govt, NWP, December 17, 1897.

95. Low, "Some Preventive Measures," 72.

96. *Report of the Bombay Plague Committee* (1898), 63–64.

97. "The Plague," *British Medical Journal*, May 8, 1897.

98. Gatacre, *Report on the Bubonic Plague*, 210.

99. NAI Home Department (Sanitary): February 1898, Nos. 428–33, North-Western Provinces and Oudh Government Resolution regarding the outbreak of plague at Kankhal in the Hardwar Union Municipality.

100. *Report of the Bombay Plague Committee* (1898), 64.

101. Cd. 810, 323, 321, 333.

102. Simpson, *Treatise on Plague*, 68.

103. Cd. 810, 323.

104. Bucholz and Ward, *London*, 315.

105. The continuing influence of outdated miasmic theories in India and South Africa focused suspicion on "dirty" colonial populations. Fittingly, Australia was the venue for the identification of rat fleas as plague's principle vectors, deflecting attention from human populations. Echenberg, *Plague Ports*, chapter 9.

106. Peter Curson and Kevin McCracken, *Plague in Sydney: The Anatomy of an Epidemic* (Sydney: New South Wales University Press, 1980), 149–50, 174–76.

107. Echenberg, *Plague Ports*, 279.

108. NASA KAB CO 7266 Folio 32c, Port Elizabeth, Bubonic Plague, Quarantine Camps and Stations.

109. "Cape Town Plague Measures," *New York Times*, May 26, 1901.

110. Simpson, *Treatise on Plague*, 396.

111. Elizabeth van Heyningen, "Public Health and Society in Cape Town, 1880–1910" (PhD diss., University of Cape Town, 1989), 292.

112. Simpson, *Treatise on Plague*, 191. British contacts were quarantined in houses, while patients were treated in segregated European hospitals. NASA KAB PWD 2/1/33, Bubonic Plague New Contact Camp Uitvlugt.

113. Cape Town's epidemic killed 207 "whites"; 157 "blacks"; 380 "coloreds"; and 21 "Asiatics." Van Heyningen, "Public Health," 307. The 1904 census counted 77,000 residents, of which roughly half were European.

114. NASA KAB MOH 15/56, Proposed burgher camp at East London.

115. Van Heyningen, "Public Health," 332.

116. Simpson, *Treatise on Plague*, 191.

117. NASA KAB PWD 2/1/32 Cape, Permits to Natives residing at the Eviction Camp, Maitland.

118. Swanson, "The Sanitation Syndrome." Tuberculosis offered further pretext for racialized segregation in the 1920s. Randall M. Packard, *White Plague, Black Labor: Tuberculosis and the Political Economy of Health and Disease in South Africa* (Berkeley: University of California Press, 1989), 194–210.

119. Echenberg, *Plague Ports*, 279.

120. Quoted in Phillips, *Epidemics*, 50.

121. Elizabeth van Heyningen and Lucy Bean, eds., *The Letters of Jane Elizabeth Waterston, 1866–1905* (Cape Town: Van Riebeck Society, 1983), 244.

122. Quoted in Phillips, *Epidemics*, 50.

123. *Cape Times* quoted in van Heyningen, "Public Health," 298.

124. NASA KAB MOH 8, East London Plague Camp, Proposed Alterations. Dr. Montgomery, government plague officer, was instructed to "examine all passengers arriving at and leaving Rosemead Junction . . . .Any person in regard to whom there is the slightest suspicion . . . should be . . . detained."

125. "Cape Town Plague Measures," *New York Times*, May 26, 1901.

126. *South African News* quoted in Echenberg, *Plague Ports*, 286.

127. Dr. Darley Hartley quoted in ibid., 279.

128. Ibid., 285–88.

129. Simpson, *Treatise on Plague*, 389.

130. Carl Nightingale, *Segregation: A Global History of Divided Cities* (Chicago: University of Chicago Press, 2012), 287.

131. Cd. 810, 335, 339, 338.

132. Echenberg, *Plague Ports*, 291–97.

133. *Mahratta*, July 23, 1899, clipping in MSA General Department (Plague), 1899, Vol. 686, No. 559, Establishment in Connection with the Famine.

134. Thomson, *Real Indian People*, 72.

135. Chandavarkar, "Plague Panic," 229.

136. Cd. 810, 335. Corpse inspections were likewise contentious for they violated both Muslim and Hindu rituals; the degree of active ill-feeling depended "very much upon how [they were] done." Cd. 810, 331.

137. MSA General Department (Plague), 1897, Vol. 71, No. 123, Petitions from Mohammedans in Bombay re. Compulsory segregation. Emphasis in the original.

138. George Nathaniel Curzon, "Plague Hospital," in *Lord Curzon through His Writings on Travels and Adventures* (New Delhi: Life Span Publishers and Distributors, 2009), 74.

139. MSA General Department (Plague), 1897, Vol. 71, No. 123, Petitions from Mohamedans in Bombay re. Compulsory segregation.

140. MSA General Department (Plague), 1899, Vol. 686, No. 559, Establishment in Connection with the Famine.

141. Mohandas Gandhi, "The Plague Panic in South Africa," *Times of India*, April 22, 1899.

142. Curzon, "Plague Hospital," 74.

143. NAI Home Department (Public), May 1898, Progs. No. 131–2, Part B, Riots, Plague, dispatch from the Government of Bombay to the Secretary of State regarding in the Bombay City.

144. The riot was triggered by rumors "the filtered water supply [was] being poisoned and of patients being killed in the plague camps." NAI Home Department (Public), June 1900, No. 291–302, Plague Riot at Cawnpore; "Plague Riot in Hindustan, Ten Persons Killed and Segregation Camp Burned at Cawnpore," *New York Times*, April 13, 1900.

145. NAI Home Department (Public), March 1898, Progs. No. 56–7, Part B, Plague Riots Sinnar; "Plague Riots in India, Segregation Camp Burned and the Mob Fired on by Troops," *New York Times*, January 30, 1898.

146. According to Mr. Reade, Charles Rand's replacement as Plague Commissioner in Poona. MSA General Department (Plague), 1899, Vol. 816, No. 975, Notes of the Plague Commissioner while on tour.

147. Cd. 810, 353, 339.

148. Cd. 139, 27.

149. NAI Home Department (Public), June 1900, Nos. 291–302, "Plague Riot at Cawnpore."

150. Gatacre, *Report on the Bubonic Plague*, 211.

151. MSA General Department (Plague), 1900, Vol. 987, No. 231, Particulars regarding the Health and Segregation Camps.

152. *British Medical Journal*, May 3, 1902, 1096.

153. MSA General Department (Plague), 1900, Vol. 987, No. 231, Particulars Regarding the Health and Segregation Camps.

154. *Report of the Bombay Plague Committee* (1898), 84.

155. NASA KAB PWD 2/1/32, Permits to Natives residing at the Eviction Camp, Maitland.

156. Quoted in Echenberg, *Plague Ports*, 71.

157. Hill, *India—Stepmother*, 40.

CHAPTER 4

1. Curzon, "Plague Hospital," 74.

2. Digby, *Famine Campaign*, vol. II, 283.

3. C. 3086-I, *Report of the Indian Famine Commission. Appendix I: Miscellaneous Papers Bearing upon the Condition of the Country and People of India* (London: Her Majesty's Stationary Office, 1881), 223.

4. C. 3086-IV, 219.

5. David Arnold, "Vagrant India: Famine, Poverty and Welfare Under Colonial Rule," in *Cast Out: Vagrancy and Homelessness in Global and Historical Perspective* ed. A.L. Beier and Paul Robert Ocobock (Athens: Ohio University Press, 2008), 120.

6. Temple Papers, IOR/F86/183 Report by Col. W. S. Drever, Commissioner of Police.

7. Solveig Smith, *By Love Compelled: The Story of 100 Years of the Salvation Army in India* (London: Salvationist Publishing, 1981), 73–4; Joseph Taylor, "The Indian Famine," *Friends Quarterly Examiner*, 31(123), July 1897.

8. *Report on the Famine in the Bombay Presidency in 1896–7*, 32.

9. Digby, *Famine Campaign*, vol. II, 288.

10. Temple Papers, IOR/F86/183, Report by Colonel W. S. Drever, Commissioner of Police.

11. C. 8388, *Papers Regarding the Famine and the Relief Operations in India During the Year 1896: with a Copy of the Famine Code for the North-Western Provinces and Oudh* (London: Her Majesty's Stationary Office, 1897), xxix.

12. Temple Papers, IOR/F86/208(a): Minutes of Evidence, 56. See also IOR/P/6257, *Bombay Famine Proceedings*, No. 1870, Expediency of insisting on confinement in poorhouses.

13. IOR/P/5988, *Bombay Famine Proceedings*, No. 3326 Report on the remarks of Mr. T. A. Bailey on Jhalod poorhouse.

14. Digby, *Famine Campaign*, vol. II, 299.

15. C. 8388, xxix.

16. C. 3086-IV, 210.

17. Scott, *In Famine Land*, 120.

18. Dr. Planck, C. 3086-IV, 258.

19. Digby, *Famine Campaign*, vol. II, 288.

20. C. 3086-IV, 271.

21. Surgeon-Major Hewlett noted a coolie would carry "in a basket wooden tickets covered with a distinguishing color—red, blue, yellow . . . [with] red to denote the holder to be taken to hospital as an in-patient, blue as an out-patient, yellow to be fed at the relief kitchen, once, twice, or three times a day." Ibid., 186.

22. Ibid., 268.

23. Ibid., 259.

24. Scott, *In Famine Land*, 118.

25. C. 3086-IV, 266.

26. Dr. Plank in the North-Western Provinces, ibid., 258.

27. Ibid., 259.

28. Ibid., 264.

29. Cd. 205, *Papers Regarding the Famine and the Relief Operations in India During 1899–1900. Vol. I, British Districts* (London: Her Majesty's Stationary Office, 1900), 60.

30. C. 3086-IV, 261.

31. IOR/P/5989, *Bombay Famine Proceedings*, No. 3431, Inspection Reports of Officers of the Sanitary Department.

32. Nash, *Great Famine*, 82.

33. According to Madras Sanitary Inspector Surgeon McNally, C. 3086-IV, 188.

34. MSA Famine Department, 1900, Vol. 63, No. 159, Hutting Accommodation, Question of providing shelter for the labourers on relief works.

35. IOR P/6257, *Bombay Famine Proceedings*, No. 2212, Inspection reports of the Sanitary Department.

36. *Report on the Famine in the Bombay Presidency, 1899–1902*, 22, 29.

37. IOR/P/5985, *Bombay Famine Proceedings*, No. 906, Question of providing shelter.

38. MSA Famine Department, 1900, Vol. 63, No. 159, Hutting Accommodation, Question of providing shelter for the labourers on relief works.

39. MSA Revenue Department (Famine), 1897, Vol. 137, Nos. 60–1, Relief Operations, Orders and rules issued by the Government of the North-Western Provinces, Parts I and II; *Report on the Famine in the Central Provinces*, vol II. (Nagpur: Secretariat Press, 1901), Appendix II.

40. C. 3086-IV, 255.

41. Temple Papers IOR/F86/183, Journal kept by Sir Richard Temple.

42. Digby, *Famine Campaign*, vol. II, 286.

43. Temple Papers IOR/F86/182, Minute upon visiting camps near Madras.

44. C. 3086-IV, 228.

45. Ibid., 234.

46. Temple Papers IOR/F86/183, Proceedings of the Madras Government, Revenue Department, 23 March 1877.

47. IOR/P/5985, *Bombay Famine Proceedings*, No. 1554, Use of coarse Khadi cloth for tents.

48. Temple Papers IOR/F86/183, Proceedings of the Madras Government, Revenue Department, 23 March 1877.

49. IOR/P/5788, *Bombay Famine Proceedings*, No. 3236. Report on the statements made by the District Medical Officer, Sholapur.

50. C. 3086-II, *Report of the Indian Famine Commission. Appendix II. Proceedings of the Commission, and Selected Evidence* (Her Majesty's Stationary Office, 1882), 63.

51. MSA Revenue Department (Famine), 1876–7, Vol. 64, Sanitary Rules to be observed by officers employed on relief operations.

52. IOR/P/6256, *Bombay Famine Proceedings*, No. 1246, Inspection reports of the Sanitary Department.

53. Temple Papers, IOR/F/86/183, Proceedings of the Madras Government, Revenue Department, 23 March 1877.

54. Cd. 9178, *Report of the Indian Famine Commission* (London: Her Majesty's Stationary Office, 1898), 105.

55. MSA Famine Department, 1902, Vol. 69, No. 222, Notes on Inspection by Mr. B. Robertson.

56. *Report on the Famine in Bombay Presidency, 1899–1902*, 29.

57. "The camp should not be a source of danger to the neighboring villages in case cholera or other epidemic disease breaks out amongst the people." C. 3086-IV, 186.

58. MSA Revenue Department (Famine), 1876–7, Vol. 101, Accommodation for Relief Labourers.

59. MSA Revenue Department (Famine), 1897, Vol. 156, No. 114, Permission to provide tents of coarse cloth for sheltering relief workers; IOR/P/5985, *Bombay Famine Proceedings*, No. 1554, Use of coarse Khadi cloth for tents for the people on relief works.

60. MSA Revenue Department (Famine), 1900, Vol. 63, No. 406, Orders regarding hutting arrangements for famine camps.

61. MSA Revenue Department (Famine), 1897, Vol. 147, No. 182, Question regarding the provision of water tight camping accommodation for relief workers.

62. The wish to "save expenditure on hutting, hospital, and other incidental charges," factored into the Indian Famine Commission's 1901 decision to abolish distance and residence tests. Cd. 876, 22.

63. IOR/P/5988, *Bombay Famine Proceedings*, No. 3001, Report on the account of Dr. Klopsch's visits to poorhouses. British authorities responded: "many of the facts in Dr. Klopsch's article are not true, and [are] written with the intent of lauding the poorhouse under the control of his own missionary station." Both Klopsh and the collector of Panch Mahals blamed "native management" for whatever shortcomings existed.

64. Higham, *Report on the Management of Famine Relief*, 3.

65. *Report on the Famine in the Bombay Presidency*, 1896–97, 14. Bombay's sanitary commissioner highlighted the challenge of "distinguishing between actual deaths from *starvation* and deaths from disease accelerated by *privation*." MSA Revenue Department (Famine), 1900, Vol. 7, No. 538, Annual report of the Sanitary Commissioner for the Government of Bombay for the year 1899. Emphasis in original.

66. C. 8812, 46.

67. *Report on the Famine in the Central Provinces*, vol. II, Appendix II, 3–4.

68. Joseph Taylor, "The Famine in India," *Friends Quarterly Examiner* 34, no. 136 (1900): 617–18.

69. *Report on the Famine in the Central Provinces*, vol. II, Appendix II, 3–4.

70. Davis, *Late Victorian Holocausts*, 22.

71. Digby, *Famine Campaign*, vol. II, 307.

72. MSA Revenue Department (Famine), Vol. 5, No. 387, Annual Report of the Sanitary Commissioner for the Government of Bombay for 1900.

73. Joseph Taylor, "The Indian famine," *Friends' Quarterly Examiner* 31, no. 123 (1897): 345.

74. IOR/P/1003 No. 75, Report by Dr. D. D. Cunningham regarding his investigations into the dysentery and diarrhea lately prevalent in Madras.

75. Taylor, "The Indian famine," 345.

76. "The extremely cold winter" of 1899–1900 "combined with crowding in camps" led to measles epidemics. Debhorah Guz, "Population Dynamics of Famine in Nineteenth Century Punjab, 1896–7 and 1899–1900," in *India's Historical Demography: Studies in Famine, Disease and Society*, ed. Tim Dyson (London: Curzon Press), 204.

77. NAUK CO417/335, No. 39407, Blue Book Reports on Refugee Camps.

78. IOR/P/5986, *Bombay Famine Proceedings*, No. 2127, Progress of relief measures in Ahmednagar.

79. C. 3086-I, 223.

80. *Resolution on the Administration of Famine Relief in the North-Western Provinces*, 133. According to Guz, malaria was actually the main killer during famine, though its impact was delayed until the following year. Drought kept malaria under control while people were in camps, but when the monsoon returned, malaria was worse than usual. "Population Dynamics," 204.

81. IOR/P/5986, *Bombay Famine Proceedings*, No. 1984, Report on the progress of relief measures in Ahmednagar.

82. Scott, *In Famine Land*, 103–4.

83. Cd. 876, 61.

84. Nash, *Great Famine*, 180, 80, 181.

85. IOR/P/5986, *Bombay Famine Proceedings*, No. 1990, Outbreak of Cholera in the Devala relief work.

86. IOR/P/5986, *Bombay Famine Proceedings*, No. 2041. Report on the measures taken to check the spread of cholera in the relief camps in Khandesh. The district medical officer noted conditions at Devala were "worse than in any other camp in Western Khandesh." IOR/P/5986, *Bombay Famine Proceedings*, No. 2112, Inspection tours of the officers of the Sanitary Department.

87. IOR/P/5988, *Bombay Famine Proceedings*, No. 3117, Inspection Reports of the Sanitary Department.

88. *Report on the Famine in the Central Provinces*, vol. I, 132.

89. Davis, *Late Victorian Holocausts*, 22. The charge, echoed by Davis, was originally delivered by Elizabeth Whitcombe, "Disease and Mortality in Indian Famines," presentation at a workshop on Famine in India, SOAS, October 1989.

90. Temple Papers IOR/F86/208(a): Minutes of Evidence given before the Indian Famine Commission, 53.

91. Quoted in Digby, *Famine Campaign*, vol. I, 320.

92. IOR/P/6257, *Bombay Famine Proceedings*, No. 3671, Orders of the Government of India on the report of the Famine Commission of 1901.

93. Cd. 876, 22. Although "more efficient . . . organization" might have kept inmates healthier, "much mortality" would have simply been avoided "had gratuitous relief in the villages been less sparingly given." Cd. 876, 68–69.

94. *Report on the Famine in the Bombay Presidency in 1896–7*, 16.

95. Ibid., 16.

96. IOR/P/5985, *Bombay Famine Proceedings*, No. 1051. Sanitary Commissioner for Bombay forwards MO inspection report.

97. MSA Revenue Department (Famine), 1898, No. 2469, dated 23 November 1897, *Resolution on the Administration of Famine Relief in the North-Western Provinces*.

98. *Report on the Famine in the Central Provinces*, vol. I, 4.

99. MSA General Department (Plague), 1899, Vol. 617, Views of the various officers regarding the establishment of Detention Camps.

100. MSA General Department (Plague), 1898, Vol. 441, No. 429, Rules for Observation Camps.

101. Gatacre, *Report on the Bubonic Plague*, 166.

102. *Report of the Municipal Commissioner on the Plague in Bombay* (1899), 71.

103. *Report of the Bombay Plague Committee*, 78.

104. *Report of the Municipal Commissioner on the Plague in Bombay* (1899), 77.

105. MSA General Department (Plague), 1898, Vol. 441, Rules for Observation Camps.

106. MSA General Department (Plague), 1899, Vol. 617, Views of the various officers regarding the establishment of Detention Camps.

107. IOR/P/6255, *Bombay Famine Proceedings*, No. 932, Circulars issued by the Commissioner, ND.

108. "The Plague," *British Medical Journal*, April 10, 1897: 937.

109. Cd. 139, 28.

110. MSA General Department (Plague), 1897, Vol. 152, No. 221/P, Famine establishments transferred for plague duty.

111. For an illustration, see A. G. Butler, "Appendix No. 11 Various Types of Huts and Tents in Common Use," *Official History of the Australian Army Medical Services, 1914–18: Volume II, The Western Front* (Melbourne: Australian War Memorial, 1940), 934.

112. See NASA KAB PWD 2/1/32, Maitland Eviction Camp; NASA KAB PWD 1/2/413, Bubonic Plague East London: Camp Erection and Water Supply.

113. MSA General Department (Plague), 1898, Vol. 246, no, 84, Bubonic Plague Detention and Disinfection Measures, Thana.

114. NASA KAB CO 7266 Folio 32c, Bubonic Plague: Quarantine Camps and Stations.

115. NASA KAB PWD 2/1/32, Construction of Maitland Eviction Camp.

116. NASA KAB MOH 8, East London Plague Camp, West Bank Proposed Alterations.

117. NASA KAB MOH 15/56, Proposed Burgher camp at East London.

118. At least according to Bhikajo Agashe. The medical officer Dr. Jennings described the account as "a deliberate falsehood." MSA General Department (Plague), 1899, Vol. 686, No. 559, Establishment in Connection with the Famine.

119. MSA General Department (Plague), 1897, Vol. 69 Railway disinfection and detention camps.

120. MSA General Department (Plague), 1899, Vol. 617, Views of the various officers regarding the establishment of Detention camps.

121. A sample ration included: 1 lb rice, 1/2 lb wheat, 2 oz ghee, 4 oz dal, and 6 oz vegetables. *Report of the Bombay Plague Committee*, 78. Those with means could purchase additional food from a *bunniah* (shopkeeper) though in 1896–97 and 1899–1901 inmates had to contend with famine prices. The camp master rented cooking utensils, lamps, and other items.

122. Simpson, *Treatise on Plague*, 368.

123. Cd. 810, 336.

124. *Report of the Bombay Plague Committee*, 78.

125. Temple Papers, IOR/F86/183, Report on the Mission to the Famine-Stricken Districts of the Madras Presidency in 1877.

126. MSA General Department (Plague), 1898, Vol. 376, no. 275, Camping Arrangements in Bombay. "The question of caste must be considered even at the cost of a little waste," officials concurred. IOR/P/5989, *Bombay Famine Proceedings* no. 3655, Inspection reports of the Sanitary Department.

127. *Report of the Municipal Commissioner on the Plague in Bombay* (1901); for Parsee philanthropists funding health initiatives see Preeti Chopra, *A Joint Enterprise:*

Indian Elites and the Making of British Bombay (Minneapolis: University of Minnesota Press, 2011), chapter 4.

128. NASA KAB PWD 2/1/33, Bubonic Plague New Contact Camp Uitvlugt.

129. Modern-day refugee camps are likewise nuclei of developing towns. Agier, *Managing the Undesirables*, chapter 7.

130. *Report of the Municipal Commissioner on the Plague in Bombay* (1901), Part I, 101.

131. *Report of the Bombay Plague Committee*, 84.

132. MSA General Department (Plague), Vol. 987, No. 231, Particulars regarding Health and Segregation Camps.

133. See NASA KAB PWD 1/2/415 B540, Ebenezer Road Accommodation Camp.

134. MSA General Department (Plague), 1899, Vol. 735, No. 721, Review of plague in the Surat District.

135. Cd. 810, 345.

136. MSA General Department (Plague), 1900, Vol. 987, No. 231, Particulars regarding Health and Segregation Camps.

137. NASA KAB PWD 1/2/415 B540, Ebenezer Road Accommodation Camp.

138. For street lamps as technologies of self-surveillance and liberal governmentality, see Joyce, *Rule of Freedom*, 109–10; Otter, *The Victorian Eye*.

139. IOR/P/5985, *Bombay Famine Proceedings*, No. 254, Report as to why the numbers on relief works in the Broach District are in excess of other districts.

140. IOR/P/6257, *Bombay Famine Proceedings*, No. 3671. Orders of the Government of India on the report of the Famine Commission of 1901.

141. IOR/P/6257, *Bombay Famine Proceedings*, No. 2266 Report on the Condition of the People and Sanitary Arrangements on Relief Camps in Belgaum District.

142. *Report on the Famine in the Central Provinces*, vol. II, Appendix II, 60.

143. Curtin, *Disease and Empire*, 225–27; Edward Thornhill Luscombe, *Practical Observations on the Means of Preserving the Health of Soldiers in Camp* (Edinburgh: Archibald Constable, 1821).

144. As a member of the Royal Commission on the Sanitary State of the Army in India and a regular correspondent with Richard Temple, Nightingale transferred her insights to the tropics, where military health was a top priority.

145. Arnold, *Colonizing the Body*, 113.

146. NAUK CO447/335 No. 39407, Blue Book Reports on Refugee Camps.

147. Thomson, *Real Indian People*, 111–12.

148. *Famine Relief Code, Bombay Presidency* (Bombay: Government Central Press, 1896), Appendix IV, 55–57.

149. IOR/P/5421, *Sanitary Proceedings Government of India*, Jan–March 1898, 668.

150. Thomson, *Real Indian People*, 112.

151. MSA Revenue Department (Famine), 1896, Vol. 18, Relief Operations, Orders and Rules issued by the Government of the North-Western Provinces.

152. Thomson, *Real Indian People*, 112.

153. MSA Revenue Department (Famine), 1896, Vol. 18, Relief Operations, Orders and Rules issued by the Government of the North-Western Provinces and Oudh.

154. Temple Papers IOR/F86/183, Madras Town Famine Relief 1877, Report by Colonel W. S. Drever

155. *Report on the Famine in the Central Provinces*, vol. III, 60.

156. C. 3086-IV, 188.

157. Thomson, *Sanitary Principles*, 132.

158. MSA Revenue Department (Famine), 1876–7, Vol. 64, Sanitary Rules to be observed by officers employed on relief operations; *Famine Relief Code, Bombay Presidency* (1896), "Appendix IV: Hints for the Information and Guidance of those entrusted with the Management of Famine Camps," 55–57.

159. NASA KAB MOH 426, East London Proposed Plague Camps, 1901.

160. MSA Revenue Department (Famine), 1897, Vol. 136, No. 60, Relief Operations, Orders and rules issued by the Government of the North-Western Provinces.

161. Cd 1179, 325.

162. MSA Revenue Department (Famine), 1876–7, Vol. 64, Sanitary Rules to be observed by officers employed on relief operations; Thomson, *Sanitary Principles*, 117.

163. Cd. 1179, 31.

164. MSA General Department (Plague), 1897, Vol. 153, no. 223/P Bubonic Plague Observation Measures and Rules, Poona.

165. NAUK CO417/335, No. 39407, Blue Book Reports on Refugee Camps.

166. MSA General Department (Plague), 1898, Vol. 376, No. 275, Camping arrangements, Bombay.

167. C. 3086-IV, 45.

168. Ibid., 187.

169. NAUK CO417/335, No. 39407, Blue Book Reports on Refugee Camps.

170. IOR/P/6257, *Bombay Famine Proceedings*, No. 2266, Report on the condition of the people and sanitary arrangements on relief camps; *Report on the Famine in the Central Provinces*, vol. I, 54.

171. *Report on the Famine in the Central Provinces*, vol. II, Appendix II, 17.

172. IOR/P/6255, *Bombay Famine Proceedings*, No. 24, Inspection reports of the Sanitary Department.

173. MSA Revenue Department (Famine), 1897, Vol. 136, No. 60, Orders and rules issued by the Government of the North-Western Provinces and Oudh for the guidance of officers employed on relief works, Part I.

174. IOR/P/5362 *North-Western Provinces Sanitary Proceedings*, 1898, Surgeon-Major Thomson to Commissioner, Allahabad Division, no 6349/360, December 7, 1897.

175. *Report of the Municipal Commissioner on the Plague in Bombay* (1901), 95.

176. The figure extrapolates the 6-month rate of 0.73% recorded at Bombay plague camps. *Report of the Municipal Commissioner on the Plague in Bombay* (1901), 98.

177. *Report on the Famine in the Central Provinces*, vol. II, Appendix II, 17.

178. IOR/P/5987, *Bombay Famine Proceedings*, No. 2480, Fortnightly inspection reports of the Sanitary Department.

179. MSA Famine, 1897, Vol. 159, No. 299, Grant of minimum wages plus the additional daily allowance to all persons segregated.

180. IOR/P/5987, *Bombay Famine Proceedings*, No. 2857, Fortnightly inspection reports of officers of the Sanitary Department for the fortnight ending 8th June 1900.

181. MSA Revenue Department (Famine), 1896, Vol. 18, Relief Operations, Orders and Rules issued by the Government of the North-Western Provinces.

182. *Famine Relief Code, Bombay Presidency 1896*, Appendix IV, 57.

183. Arnold, *Colonizing the Body*, 78.

184. Simpson, *Treatise on Plague*, 66.

185. *Report on the Famine in the Central Provinces*, vol. I, 62.

186. IOR/P/5986, *Bombay Famine Proceedings*, No. 1951, Orders enjoining the strictest attention to all sanitary measures on relief work with a view to arrest outbreaks of cholera.

187. C. 3086-IV, 205.

188. Nash, *Great Famine*, 117.

189. MSA Revenue Department (Famine), 1900, Vol. 12, no. 242, Employment of European Non-Commissioned officers and Native Commissioned and Non-Commissioned officers on famine duty.

190. "Soldiers were told off for famine duty in the Central Provinces and I heard excellent reports of their work," Nash continued. *Great Famine*, 184–85.

191. In the Mysore official Mr. Montcrieff's words. C. 3086-IV, 220.

192. MSA General Department (Plague), 1899, Vol. 537, Plague, Appointments, Military Officers. The quote refers to Captain Lockhard Mure, at Poona.

193. Thomson, *Sanitary Principles*, 2.

194. NAUK CO 417/335 No. 39407, Blue Book Reports on Refugee Camps.

195. Nash, *Great Famine*, 43.

196. IOR/P/5362, North-Western Provinces Sanitary Proceedings, 1898, no. 6504/490, Thomson to Secretary to Govt, NWP, December 17, 1897,

197. MSA General Department (Plague), 1898, Vol. 441, No. 429, Rules for Observation Camps.

198. MSA Revenue Department (Famine), 1897, Vol. 136, No. 60, Relief Operations, Orders and rules issued by the Government of the North-Western Provinces.

199. MSA General Department (Plague), 1898, Vol. 441, No. 429, Rules for Observation Camps.

200. IOR/P/5362, North-Western Provinces Sanitary Proceedings, 1898, Prog. No 165, Nos. 405–412, Secretary to Government NWP to Mr. Sands, Assistant District Superintendent of Police, Haridwar.

201. According to Mr. Wingate in Bombay, C. 3086-IV, 283.

202. MSA General Department (Plague), 1898, Vol. 376, No. 275, Camping arrangements, Bombay.

203. MSA Revenue Department (Famine), 1897, Vol. 63, No. 139, Duties of the officers of the Public Works Department and the Special Civil Officers under the famine code; IOR/P/5985, *Bombay Famine Proceedings*, No. 632, Instructions issued by the Commissioner, ND, for the guidance of Special Civil Officers.

204. MSA Revenue Department (Famine), 1897, Vol. 63, No. 139, Duties of the officers of the Public Works Department and the Special Civil Officers under the famine code.

205. IOR/P/6257, *Bombay Famine Proceedings*, No. 2266, Report on the condition of the people and sanitary arrangements on relief camps.

206. MSA Revenue Department (Famine), 1897, Vol. 136, no. 60, Orders and rules issued by the Government of the North-Western Provinces for the guidance of officers employed on relief works, Part I.

207. C. 8812, 32.

208. Or at the least, the concentration of technical expertise in the hands of a select few enabled "camp experts" to cover up their failures. Mitchell, *Rule of Experts*, chapter 1.

209. Nash, *Great Famine*, 188.

210. MSA Revenue Department (Famine), 1900, Vol. 19, No. 2469, Resolution on the Administration of Famine Relief in the North-Western Provinces.

211. *Report of the Municipal Commission on the Plague in Bombay for the year Ending 31st May 1899* (Part I), 71.

212. Curzon, "Plague Hospital," 74.

213. Nash, *Great Famine*, 81.

CHAPTER 5

1. Streatfeild/Deane Papers 2/11, Transcripts of letters from Lucy Streatfeild to her sister, 31.

2. Spies, *Methods of Barbarism*, and Thomas Pakenham, *The Boer War* (New York: Random House, 1979) are the standard accounts. Though well researched and attentive to detail, these in situ analyses reify camps as instruments of a purely rational military decision-making process and fail to consider similar episodes of civilian concentration outside the purview of counterinsurgency doctrine.

3. Iain Smith, *Origins of the South African War, 1899–1902* (New York: Longman, 1996); Bill Nasson, *The War for South Africa* (Cape Town: Tafelberg, 2010).

4. J. A. Hobson, *Imperialism: A Study* (New York: J. Pott, 1902).

5. John Evelyn Wrench, *Alfred Lord Milner: The Man of No Illusions, 1854–1925* (London: Eyre & Spottiswoode, 1958), chapters 3 and 13–17.

6. While it was ostensibly a "white man's war," the conflict also involved black Africans as messengers, laborers, and scouts. Apart from performing auxiliary roles on both sides, black Africans fought for their own interests, land, and livestock. Peter Warwick, *Black People and the South African War, 1899–1902* (New York: Cambridge University Press, 1983); Bill Nasson, *Abraham Esau's War: A Black South African War in the Cape, 1899–1902* (Cambridge: Cambridge University Press, 2003), chapter 5.

7. Lisle March Phillipps, *With Rimington* (London: Edward Arnold, 1901), 126.

8. Robert Taber, *The War of the Flea: A Study of Guerrilla Warfare Theory and Practice* (New York: Lyle Stuart, 1965).

9. In the words of J. D. Kestell, a chaplain attached to the famed Boer commando general Christiaan de Wet, "we turn to the right and to the left, and our adversary is not able with all his cannon to prevent it. In this way we keep the war going, and increase the expenditure day by day." *Through Shot and Flame* (London: Methuen, 1903), 106.

10. Taber, *War of the Flea*, 29.

11. Pakenham, *Boer War*, 432.

12. Phillipps, *With Rimington*, 212.

13. Saul Dubow, *A Commonwealth of Knowledge: Science, Sensibility, and White South Africa, 1820–2000* (New York: Oxford University Press, 2006), 91–92. "Nodes of British settlement inspired efforts to exert spatial and ideological control over a remade landscape through mechanisms such as architecture, irrigation and tree-planting."

14. Adalbert Sternberg and G.F.R. Henderson, *My Experiences of the Boer War*, (London: Longmans Green, 1901), xx.

15. Phillipps, *With Rimington*, 213

16. Julian Ralph, *An American with Lord Roberts* (New York: F. A. Stokes, 1901), 29.

17. Sternberg, *My Experiences of the Boer War*, 203.

18. Callwell, *Small Wars*, 31.

19. Winston Churchill, *The Boer War: London to Ladysmith via Pretoria* (London: Longmans, Green, 1900), 71.

20. For development of de Wet's legend, see Fransjohan Pretorius, *The Great Escape of the Boer Pimpernel Christiaan de Wet. The Making of a Legend* (Pietermaritzburg: University of Natal Press, 2001).

21. NAUK CO 417/292 No. 32606, Summary of Military Operations, September 19, 1900.

22. Emily Hobhouse, *Emily Hobhouse: Boer War Letters*, ed. Rykie van Reenan (Cape Town: Human and Rousseau, 1920), 106.

23. British discourse on the Boers intersected with nineteenth-century martial race theory that spanned the Indian Ocean. Metcalf, *Imperial Connections*, 71–78.

24. Invisibility augured more drastic measures to come. As Traverso notes of WWI, "With 'an enemy who remained invisible,' warfare became a terrible slaughter carried out amid a 'total absence of hatred.' Very often death was dealt, not by an enemy of flesh and blood, but by an impersonal, cold, alien, hostile machine." *Origins of Nazi Violence*, 83.

25. Kitchener Papers, NAUK PRO 30/57/22, Kitchener to Brodrick, December 20, 1900 Y9; Andre Wessels, ed., *Lord Kitchener and the War in South Africa, 1899–1902* (Sutton Publishing Limited for the Army Records Society, 2006), 76.

26. John Buchan, *The African Colony, Studies in the Reconstruction* (Edinburgh: W. Blackwood and Sons, 1903), 34–35. Conceiving themselves as a "chosen race" and "people of the book," the Boers shared this notion.

27. The old redcoat tactics of visual display were defunct at last, and British troops adopted their namesake khaki uniforms. According to the German general Alfred von Schleiffen, "the modern commander-in-chief is no Napoleon who stands with his brilliant suit on a hill. Even with the best binoculars he would be unlikely to see much, and his white horse would be an easy target." Quoted in Stephen Kern, *The Culture of Time and Space* (Cambridge, MA: Harvard University Press, 1983), 300.

28. Quoted in Spies, *Methods of Barbarism*, 17–18.

29. "Horrors of the Boer War," *New York Times*, August 4, 1901.

30. Kitchener Papers, NAUK PRO 30/57/22, Kitchener to Brodrick, Pretoria, December 20, 1900, Y9.

31. Kitchener Papers, NAUK PRO 30/57/22, Kitchener to Brodrick, April 19, 1901, Y44.

32. Philip Magnus, *Kitchener: Portrait of an Imperialist* (Harmondsworth, UK: Penguin, 1968), 187.

33. "Lord Roberts to General Louis Botha," September 2, 1900, in André Wessels, ed., *Lord Roberts and the War in South Africa, 1899–1902* (Stroud, UK: Sutton Publishing Ltd. for the Army Records Society, 2000), 131.

34. Colonel Rawlinson, quoted in Pakenham, *Boer War*, 534.

35. Quoted in Algernon Methuen, *Peace or War in South Africa* (London: Methuen, 1902), 72.

36. Nasson, *War for South Africa*, 276; see also Sternberg, *My Experiences of the Boer War*, 201–2. In a parliamentary speech, John Ellis, MP, mentioned "I am told that the eyesight of these Boers is of two miles greater radius than that of the British soldiers," *Hansard's Parliamentary Debates*, June 17, 1901, col. 586.

37. Curzon quoted in Wm. Matthew Kennedy, "The Imperialism of Internment: Boer Prisoners of War in India and Civic Reconstruction in Southern Africa, 1899–1905," *Journal of Imperial and Commonwealth History* 44, no. 3 (2016): 11.

38. Kipling quoted in Stowell Kessler, "The Black Concentration Camps of the South African War, 1899–1902" (PhD diss., University of Cape Town, 2003), 41; W.M. Hosek, "The Future of South Africa," *Fortnightly Review*, vol. 67, April 1900, 400.

39. Nasson, *War for South Africa*, 266.

40. Ralph, *An American with Lord Roberts*, 33.

41. Nasson, *War for South Africa*, 266.

42. Quoted in Paula Krebs, *Gender, Race, and the Writing of Empire* (Cambridge: Cambridge University Press, 1999), 117.

43. J. F. C. Fuller, *The Last of the Gentlemen's Wars* (London: Faber and Faber, 1937), 41.

44. Milner quoted in Jennifer Hobhouse Balme, ed., *To Love One's Enemies: The Work and Life of Emily Hobhouse Compiled from Letters and Writings, Newspaper Cuttings and Official Documents* (Cobble Hill, BC: Hobhouse Trust, 1994), 102.

45. Expressing soldierly respect while simultaneously denying the Boers' claim to racial "whiteness," Kitchener added "the South African white," a category apparently restricted to British colonists, "is very inferior to the Boer in . . . [his] capability of standing hardship." Kitchener Papers, NAUK PRO 30/57/22, Kitchener to Brodrick, March 9, 1901, Y131A. The "great question [of the war]," Kitchener continued, "is can they get through the next winter. With any ordinary people I should say it was quite impossible, but with Boers I am doubtful." NAUK PRO 30/57/22, Kitchener to Brodrick, February 23, 1902, Y129.

46. Quoted in Methuen, *Peace or War*, 73.

47. The notion of fixed, biological race existed in tension, in the early twentieth century, with anxiety that Europeans could "degenerate" in colonial environments. Stoler, *Carnal Knowledge*, chapter 4.

48. NAUK CO224/5 No. 1723, Concentration Camp Bloemfontein, December 20, 1901.

49. Alfred Milner, *The Milner Papers, Vol. I, South Africa 1897–1899*, ed. Cecil Headlam (London: Cassell & Company Ltd., 1931), 234. Milner and Buchan perceived a fundamental cleavage between modern Britain and Boer ranchers who remained ignorant of "English constitutionalism" as well as "stray doctrines of the French Revolution, and certain economic maxims from Bentham and Adam Smith." Buchan, *The African Colony*, 47.

50. Buchan, *African Colony*, 69, 56. "The pageantry of the veld was nothing to him," Buchan continued, "and in the amenities of life he scarcely advanced beyond bare physical comfort. He had neither art not literature." Ibid., 69. Buchan returned to the subject in *Greenmantle* (London: Hodder & Sloughton, 1916). For similar representations, see Bill Schwarz, *The White Man's World* (New York: Oxford University Press, 2012), chapter 4.

51. Quoted in George Arthur, *Life of Lord Kitchener*, vol. II (New York: Cosimo, 2007), 12.

52. Quoted in Van Heyningen, *Concentration Camps*, 51.

53. John Boje, *An Imperfect Occupation: Enduring the South African War* (Springfield: University of Illinois Press, 2015), 84.

54. Nasson, *War for South Africa*, 281. The hardy and unflattering image of Afrikaner womanhood, as epitomized by Olive Shreiner's character Tant Sallie in *The Story of an African Farm* (London: Chapman and Hall, 1883), was an influential representation.

55. Kessler, "Black Concentration Camps," 71.

56. For exact timing see Spies, *Methods of Barbarism*; Tony Lucking, "Some Thoughts on the Evolution of Boer War Concentration camps," *Journal of the Society for Army Historical Research* 82 (2004): 155–56.

57. Roberts quoted in Hobhouse Balme, *To Love One's Enemies*, 36.

58. Roberts quoted in Boje, *Imperfect Occupation*, 97.

59. The war might be considered an intermediate stage in a larger global trajectory first charted by Hannah Arendt in which colonies offered "laboratories" for the development of violent practices later unleashed in Europe. *Origins of Totalitarianism*. Devastating tactics against Europeans were not entirely unprecedented, however. To justify British policy the War Office pointed to the Franco-Prussian War and General Sherman's tactics in the American Civil War. NAUK CO417/335, Original Correspondence between the High Commission for South Africa and the War Office: Memorandum on certain points connected with the conduct of hostilities, October 24th, 1901.

60. Circular Memo, No. 29, December 21, 1900, in André Wessels ed., *Lord Kitchener and the War in South Africa, 1899–1902* (Stroud, UK: Sutton Publishing for the Army Record Society, 2006); NAUK CO 105/25, Confidential Correspondence on Martial Law, Treatment of inhabitants of the Transvaal and Orange River Colony (Index No. 66).

61. "Comfortable assumptions of Victorian jurists about freedom from discretionary military power underwent major alteration" during the war. Richard Cosgrove, "The Boer War and the Modernization of British Martial Law," *Military Affairs* 44, no. 3 (1980): 126.

62. NAUK WO 105/18, Telegram from General Hunter, October 1900.

63. NAUK WO 105/28, 94, Ventersburg, feeding women and children.

64. Society of Friends Archives, MS BOX p2/20, 1902, Journal of William Henry Fisher.

65. Kitchener, quoted in Bill Nasson, "Civilians in the Anglo-Boer War," in *Daily Lives of Civilians in Wartime Africa: From Slavery Days to Rwandan Genocide*, ed. John Laban (Westport, CT: Greenwood, 2007), 95.

66. Phillipps, *With Rimington*, 201.

67. NAUK WO 105/23, Telegram of District Commissioner, Heidelberg, September 12, 1900.

68. NAUK CO 417/324 No. 16059, Measures to Put Down Guerrilla Warfare, May 8, 1901.

69. Bell, *The First Total War*.

70. Henri Lefebvre, *The Production of Space* (Cambridge, MA: Blackwell, 1991).

71. Phillipps, *With Rimington*, 117. Awash in inscrutable landscapes, the intelligence agent Lionel James declared himself lost "at sea." *On the Heels of de Wet, by The Intelligence Officer* (London: William Blackwood and Sons, 1902), 75.

72. The Boers, Schreiner continued, "possessed South Africa . . . like no white man has ever possessed it . . . but as the wild beasts and the savages whom they dispossessed had possessed it." As if in warning to would-be invaders, Schreiner considered these "nomadic wanderers" to be virtually "unattackable and impractical to meddle with." Olive Schreiner, "Stray Thoughts on South Africa, by a Returned South African: The Wanderings of the Boer," *Fortnightly Review* 60, no. 356 (1896): 232, 234–35.

73. Buchan, *The African Colony*, 48, 41.

74. Methuen, *Peace or War*, 78.

75. James Beattie, "Recent Themes in the Environmental History of the British Empire," *History Compass* 10 no. 2 (2012): 130.

76. Like Jews, gypsies and other rootless or "mercurial people," the Boers were susceptible to violent efforts to control their movement. As "transients . . . wanderers," and "border crossers," who were, in popular imagery, "wedded to time, [but] not to land," Jews and Boers were both considered "homeless . . . rootless, and 'ancient'" by their settled and sedentary counterparts. Yuri Slezkine, *The Jewish Century* (Princeton, NJ: Princeton University Press, 2004), 8–9, 14, 21.

77. To British soldiers and settlers, the South African veld represented what the cultural theorists Gilles Deleuze and Felix Guattari describe as "smooth space"—an illusive realm they contrast with the "striated order" of modern states. Characterized by "vagabondage, . . . wandering and drifting between regions instead of moving straight ahead between fixed points," the occupant of smooth or "nomad space" could be "distended everywhere." Deleuze and Guattari, paraphrased in Edward Casey, *Fate of Place: A Philosophical History* (Berkeley: University of California Press, 1997), 304–5.

78. Magnus, *Kitchener*, chapter 2.

79. James, *On the Heels of de Wet*, 24.

80. NAUK CO417/295, No. 37723, Probable Distress Relief Works, November 1900, Milner's Diary of Events, November 15, 1900.

81. Magnus, *Kitchener*, 177.

82. L.S. Amery, *Times History of the War in South Africa*, Vol. V, (London: Searle & Rivington, 1900–1909), 403. Similarly, Lieutenant-Colonel R.M. Holden described the blockhouse system as "a complete lace-work or spider's web of wire environment, so interwoven that it is cutter-proof." "The Blockhouse System in South Africa," *Journal of the Royal United Service Institution* 46 no. 1 (1902): 484.

83. According to Rayne Kruger, *Good-bye Dolly Gray: The Story of the Boer War* (Philadelphia: J.B. Lippincott, 1960), 404.

84. The barbed-wire fences of Kitchener's blockhouse grid suggested a ready human application of a technology first developed to herd cattle on the colonial frontier.

Reviel Netz, *Barbed Wire: An Ecology of Modernity* (Middletown, CT: Wesleyan University Press, 2004), parts 1 and 2.

85. "Lord Kitchener's Pet Starling," *Otago Witness*, issue 2710, February 21, 1906, 80.

86. The term "concentration camp" was used to refer to livestock enclosures both during and after the war. See, for example, NASA TAB TAD 57 327/15, Note by HM Webb GVS, December 8, 1909.

87. Kennedy, "Imperialism of Internment"; Stephen Royle, "St Helena as a Boer Prisoner of War Camp, 1900–2: Information from the Alice Stopford Green Papers," *Journal of Historical Geography* 24, no. 1 (1998).

88. Kitchener quoted in Nasson, "Civilians in the Anglo-Boer War," 95.

89. NASA TAB HC 87, Loose report from H. G. J. Lotbinière,

90. Kitchener quoted in *Hansard Parliamentary Debates*, June 17, 1901, col. 585.

91. Nasson notes commando units could "survive parasitically" on supplies and sustenance provided by the civilian population. *War for South Africa*, 220.

92. NAUK CO417/295, No. 35820, Relief to Boer Women and Children. Italics mine.

93. Macdonagh, "The Nineteenth-Century Revolution in Government"; Roy MacLeod, *Government and Expertise: Specialists, Administrators and Professionals, 1860–1919* (Cambridge: Cambridge University Press, 2003).

94. Hyslop, "Invention of the Concentration Camp." For the impact of Britain's Cardwell reforms and professionalizing military command structures in South Africa, see Stephen M. Miller, *Volunteers on the Veld: Britain's Citizen-Soldiers and the South African War, 1899–1902* (Norman: University of Oklahoma Press, 2007), chapter 1.

95. Kitchener Papers, NAUK PRO 30/57/22, Kitchener to Brodrick, February 23, 1902, Y129.

96. Boje, *Imperfect Occupation*, 49.

97. NASA TAB HC 86, File 2, Concentration Camps: Correspondence with Secretary of State.

98. Quoted in Emily Hobhouse, *The Brunt of War and Where It Fell* (London: Methuen, 1902), 21.

99. Many evoked Jeremiah 24:9–10, the epigraph that opens this chapter.

100. Quoted in Emily Hobhouse, *War Without Glamour, or, Women's war experiences written by themselves, 1899–1902* (Bloemfontein: Nasionale Pers Beperk, 1924), 29.

101. Hobhouse, *War Without Glamour*, 11–12.

102. Hobhouse, *War Without Glamour*, 19.

103. Hobhouse quoted in Hobhouse Balme, *To Love One's Enemies*, 243.

104. NAUK CO 417/294 No. 37723, Probable Distress Relief Works, November 1900.

105. NASA TAB HC 87, Report on the workings of the Native Refugee Department.

106. Quoted in Hobhouse Balme, *To Love One's Enemies*, 81.

107. Ibid., 92.

108. MSA Revenue Department (Famine), 1900, Vol. 172, no. 304, Transvaal Refugees in Bombay.

109. Hobhouse complained that the military's refusal to permit Boer women and children to seek shelter in Cape Town forestalled a "sensible plan" that suggested an alternative to herding civilians into camps. Hobhouse Balme, *To Love One's Enemies*, 73.

110. NAUK CO 105/28, letter from Botha to Roberts 15–23 August, 1900.

111. Joshua Rowntree, *The Friend*, 29 March 1902, 196.

112. For Bezuidenhout's testimony, see Elizabeth Neethling, *Should We Forget?* (Cape Town, HAUM, 1903), 90–93.

113. Neethling, *Should We Forget?*, 122.

114. NASA TAB GOV 263 PS 20/01 Vol. XV.

115. NASA TAB MGP 133 15093A/01.

116. Elizabeth van Heyningen, "British Concentration Camps of the South African War," accessed April 15, 2014, http://www2.lib.uct.ac.za/mss/bccd.

117. Van Heyningen, *Concentration Camps*, 116; An early informal camp at Nigel was "a mine site and had a wire enclosure." Kessler, "Black Concentration Camps," 114.

118. Kessler, "Black Concentration Camps," 102.

119. According G. B. Woodroffe, medical officer at Irene. NAUK CO 879/75/3 No. 165, Milner to Chamberlain, forwards report on Transvaal Camps for November by W. K. Tucker.

120. NAUK CO417/335, Copy of Report of the Burgher Camp at Heidelburg, By Dr. Kendal Franks, Hon. Consulting Surgeon to H.B.M.'s Forces, September 7, 1901, 357.

121. NASA VAB SRC Vol. 8 RC2569, Sanitary State of Bloemfontein Camp.

122. NAUK CO 879/75/3, No 165, Milner to Chamberlain, forwards report on Transvaal Camps for November by W. K. Tucker.

123. Booth, *In Darkest England*, 12.

124. According to Rev. F. J. Williams in *The Times*, January 1901. A cutting appears in NAUK WO 32/8008.

125. Douglas, *Purity and Danger*.

126. NAUK CO417/335, Copy of Report of the Burgher Camp at Heidelburg, By Dr. Kendal Franks, Hon. Consulting Surgeon to H.B.M.'s Forces, South Africa. September 7, 1901, 359.

127. Cd. 819. *Reports, &c., on the Working of the Refugee Camps in the Transvaal, Orange River Colony, Cape Colony, and Natal, November 1901* (London: His Majesty's Stationary Office, 1901), 354.

128. Zoë Denness, "Women and Warfare at the Start of the Twentieth Century: The Racialization of the 'Enemy' during the South African War (1899–1902)," *Patterns of Prejudice* 46, no 3–4 (2012): 268–69, 276.

129. In a passage that perfectly describes prevalent British views, the sociologist Philip Smith notes "that which is ambivalent, belonging to no category or sitting on the fence between them, has a high probability of being perceived as dangerous, magical, illegitimate, or in need of ordering." *Punishment and Culture* (Chicago: University of Chicago Press, 2008), 28.

130. Hamilton quoted in Kennedy, "Imperialism of Internment," 7.

131. Gary Baines, "The Origins of Urban Segregation: Local Government and the Residence of Africans in Port Elizabeth, c. 1835–1865," *South African Historical Journal* 22, no. 1 (1990): 77.

132. Swanson, "Sanitation Syndrome."

133. Cd. 893, *Report on the Concentration Camps in South Africa by the Committee of Ladies Appointed by the Secretary of State for War* (London: His Majesty's Stationary Office, 1902), 90.

134. NASA TAB MGP 133 15093A/01.

135. NAUK CO 879/75/3, African, No 165, Transvaal Camp reports forwarded by W. K. Tucker.

136. Hobhouse, *War Without Glamour*, 18.

137. Baines, "Origins of Urban Segregation," 70.

138. NAUK CO879/72/8, Memorandum by Mr. H. W. Just, with letter from Colonial Office to War Office and summary of child mortality and general mortality June to December 1901.

139. Cd. 902, *Further Papers Relating to the Working of the Refugee Camps in South Africa* (London: His Majesty's Stationary Office, 1902), 102.

140. Allan Rowntree, *The Friend*, January 31, 1902, 77.

141. Cd. 819, 216.

142. Hobhouse, *Brunt of War*; Methuen, *Peace or War*, 146–63.

143. Hobhouse, *Brunt of War*, 57.

144. Neethling, *Should We Forget?*, 87, 89.

145. Emily Hobhouse, *War Without Glamour*, 21.

146. Pule Phoofolo, "Epidemics and Revolutions: The Rinderpest Epidemic in Late Nineteenth-Century Southern Africa," *Past & Present* 138, no. 1 (1993): 128.

147. Van Heyningen, *Concentration Camps*, 46.

148. Hermann Giliomee, *Afrikaners: Biography of a People* (Charlottesville: University of Virginia Press, 2010), chapter 10.

149. A former Boer General, Smuts was the Union of South Africa's president when he used the term in 1922. Giliomee, *Afrikaners*, 353.

150. For a description of the fence around the city of Pretoria, see NASA TAB MGP 81 3201/01.

151. Deane/Streatfeild Papers, Streatfeild 2/11 Transcripts of letters from Lucy Streatfeild to her sister, 23, 14.

152. Hobhouse-Balme, *To Love One's Enemies*, 93.

153. Many historians (and contemporaries) argue the camps were militarily counterproductive because they allowed commandos to keep fighting unencumbered by the task of caring for women, children, and the elderly. Botha noted as much when he refused Roberts's somewhat impudent proposal to deposit camp inmates into his care, preferring—extraordinarily and perhaps naively—to trust in British magnanimity to provide for distressed Boer civilians. NAUK CO 105/26 52, Families, burghers, latest phase; Nasson, *War for South Africa*, 242.

154. Boje, *Imperfect Occupation*, 88.

155. Chamberlain cited in van Heyningen, *Concentration Camps*, 70.

156. NAUK CO 417/294 No. 37723, Probable Distress Relief Works, November 1900.

157. As in Indian famines, wartime destitution prompted calls for more permanent colonial welfare infrastructure. Reverend McLure, with a reluctant socialist tinge, spoke of the need for "some permanent organisation . . . to take the place of the . . . [English] poor-law system." Quoted in Elizabeth van Heyningen, "Refugees and Relief in Cape Town, 1899–1902," *Studies in the History of Cape Town* 3 (1980): 71.

158. NASA KAB PWD 2/5/95, Cape Refugee Relief Works, General Correspondence.

159. NAUK CO 417/294 No. 37723, Probable Distress Relief Works, November 1900.

160. NASA TAB MGP 133 15093A/01.

161. Gert van den Bergh, "The Three British Occupations of Potchefstroom during the Anglo-Boer War, 1899–1902," *Scientia Militaria, South African Journal of Military Studies* 37, no. 1 (2009): 98.

162. Van Heyningen, *Concentration Camps*, 47.

163. NAUK WO 108/410, Roberts to Secretary of State for War and High Commissioner, Cape Town, July 2 1900.

164. Spies, *Methods of Barbarism*, 144–45; Fransjohan Pretorius, "The Fate of the Boer Women and Children," in *Scorched Earth*, ed. Fransjohan Pretorius (Cape Town: Human & Rousseau, 2001), 41.

165. Milner to Chamberlain, February 6, 1901, *The Milner Papers, Vol. II*, 197. Edwards further felt the camps would protect peacefully inclined farmers from forced conscription by local commandos. Gert Van den Bergh, "British Scorched Earth and Concentration Camp Policies," *Scientia Militaria: South African Journal of Military Studies* 40, no.2 (2012): 82–84.

166. Van den Bergh, "Three British Occupations," 98.

167. Henry J. Hager, "Horrors of the Boer War," *New York Times*, August 4, 1901.

168. Both critics and proponents used the terms interchangeably, though some inmates maintained they were not refugees but political prisoners. M. van den Berg, for example,

wrote "the enemy hunted us round like dogs and then sought to hide their infamy by saying that we were refugees." Quoted in Hobhouse, *War Without Glamour*, 34.

169. Kelly-Kenny quoted in Spies, *Methods of Barbarism*, 149.

170. "Impressions and Opinions," *Anglo-Saxon Review: A Quarterly Miscellany*, December 7, 1900, 237.

171. Spies, *Methods of Barbarism*, 150.

172. NAUK CO 879/77/1 No. 75, Milner to Chamberlain, March 29, 1902.

173. NASA VAB SRC Vol. 7 RC1911, Report Kroonstad RC, April 1901.

174. NAUK CO 879/77/1 No. 89, Final report for February 1902 from Captain Trollope, 202.

175. Louis Grundlingh, "Another Side to Warfare: Caring for White Destitutes during the Anglo-Boer War (October 1899–May 1900), *New Countree* 45 (1999).

176. Cd. 853, *Further Papers Relating to the Working of the Refugee Camps in the Transvaal, Orange River Colony, and Natal* (London: Her Majesty's Stationary Office, 1901), 31.

177. NAUK CO 417/335 No. 39407, Blue Book Reports on Refugee camps, 178.

178. NAUK CO 879/77/1 No. 89, Final report for February 1902 from Captain Trollope, 202.

179. Cd. 893, 112–13.

180. NAUK CO417/295 No. 35820, Relief to Boer Women and Children, 264.

181. NASA TAB DBC 3, Burgher Camp Johannesburg Letter dated March 11, 1901, from Medical Officer to Superintendent.

182. NASA VAB SRC Vol. 3 RC705, Refugees Camping outside Refugee Camp at Vredefort Road.

183. NASA VAB SRC Vol. 31 RC10324, Report by Dr. Himes.

184. NASA VAB SRC Vol. 5 RC1304, Reports on Kroonstad, Vredefort Road and Brandfort Camps.

185. NAUK CO 879/77/1 No. 75, Milner to Chamberlain, March 29, 1902.

186. Cd. 902, 85.

187. NAUK CO 224/3 No. 2359, Maintenance of Refugees, January 3, 1901.

188. NASA VAB SRC Vol. 2 RC461, Sickness at Kroonstad Camp.

189. Cd. 819, 145.

190. NAUK WO 32/8009, Standerton Camp May Report by acting Supt. Moffat.

191. Cd. 902, 102.

192. Cd. 819, 337.

193. Cd. 893, 91.

194. NASA VAB SRC Vol.7 RC1911, Report Kroonstad Refugee Camp, April 1901.

195. Boje, *Imperfect Occupation*, 88.

196. NAUK WO 105/28 No. 5, Correspondence between Lord Roberts and Louis Botha, September–October 1900.

197. *St. James Gazette* quoted in Hobhouse, *Brunt of War*, 27.

198. Forth and Kreienbaum, "A Shared Malady," 260–61.

199. Smith and Stucki, "The Colonial Development of Concentration Camps"; Forth and Kreienbaum, "A Shared Malady," 266.

200. NASA TAB HC 86 File 6, Ladies Concentration Camp Committee.

201. Gertrude Himmelfarb, "The Age of Philanthropy," *Wilson Quarterly* 21, no. 2 (1997): 52.

202. The *Morning Post*, January 15, 1902, quoted in Nasson, *War for South Africa*, 243.

203. NASA TAB MGP 133 15093A/01.

CHAPTER 6

1. NASA TAB HC 86, draft of a telephone message, November 28, 1901, from Lord Milner to undisclosed recipient.

2. NASA VAB SRC Vol. 138, Item 12. According to the Public Works director, "the status of camp inmates [was] . . . somewhat difficult to define owing to variations in circumstances under which . . . various persons entered the camp."

3. NASA TAB CS 25 3172/01, Sargant to Milner, 14 June 1901.

4. IOR/P/6255, *Bombay Famine Proceedings* No. 1314, Inspection report of the Sanitary Department.

5. NAUK CO 417/323, No. 12352, Refugee Camps, Cost of Maintenance.

6. NAUK CO 291/27, No. 5866 Refugee Camps, January 30, 1901.

7. NASA VAB SRC Vol. 16 RC6316, Discipline in Refugee Camps. Trollope was fluent in Dutch as well as Hindi and Pashtu.

8. Walter Wills, *The Anglo-African Who's Who* (London: L. Upott Gill, 1902), 304; Ken Donaldson, *South African Who's Who* (London: Allen, 1911), 476.

9. NAUK CO 291/27, No. 5866 Refugee Camps, January 30, 1901; NAUK CO 879/77/1 African No. 697. No. 75, Milner to Chamberlain, March 29, 1902.

10. Cd. 893, 167.

11. NAUK CO 879/77/1 African No. 697 No. 75, Milner to Chamberlain, March 29, 1902. Men of "pronounced anti-Boer feelings" were avoided. NAUK CO 291/27, No. 5866 Refugee Camps, January 30, 1901.

12. NAUK WO 32/8061, list of Hobhouse's recommendations and précis of Milner's opinions about them.

13. Hobhouse, *Brunt of the War*, 122.

14. Cd. 893, 120.

15. NASA VAB SRC Vol. 21 RC8040, Desertions from Winburg RC; NASA VAB SRC 4964, Free Railway Pass for Dr. H. S. Reynolds.

16. NASA SRC Vol. 19 RC7253, Report on various RCs by Dr. Hime.

17. NASA VAB SRC Vol. 8 RC2569, Sanitary State of Bloemfontein Camp.

18. Schwarz, *Constructing the Criminal Tribe*, 82.

19. NAUK CO 879/75/3, No. 6, Tents from India. Goold-Adams noted that bell tents issued by the British army "have been found to be by no means well adapted for the housing of Refugee families. They are too small and are besides very hot." NAUK CO 224/7, No. 4537, Concentration Camps, January 10, 1902.

20. NAUK CO224/5 No. 1723, Concentration Camp Bloemfontein, Report by Dr. Kendal Franks.

21. NAUK CO 879/75/3, No. 30, Rules for the Guidance of Refugee Camp Superintendents.

22. NASA VAB SRC Vol. 3 RC533, Trollope's Circular No. 11.

23. NAUK CO 879/77/1, No. 88, letter from Major Anstruther Thomson on inspection of Jo'burg camp.

24. NAUK WO 32/8008, Letter from Goodwin to Maxwell, March 22, 1901.

25. As in India, private traders were invited to camp. "Peyton Brothers" had a monopoly in Transvaal.

26. NASA TAB MGP 207 97/01.

27. NASA VAB SRC Vol. 11 RC3972, Report RC Norvals Pont.

28. NASA VAB SRC Vol. 17 RC6705, Rations issued to Boer Refugees.

29. J. S. Haldane was the brother of future Liberal war secretary R. B. Haldane and father of the famous Communist scientist J. B. S. Haldane. As a pro-Boer activist he solicited the Colonial Office with his calculations. Martin Goodman, *Suffer and Survive: Gas Attacks, Miners' Canaries, Spacesuits and the Bends: The Extreme Life of Dr. J. S. Haldane* (New York: Simon & Schuster, 2007).

30. NAUK CO 879/75/3, No. 79, Memorandum by Dr. J. S. Haldane on the Rations in the Concentration Camps.

31. A. C. Martin addresses these and other rumors in *The Concentration Camps, 1900–1902, Facts, Fables, and Figures* (Cape Town: H. Timmins, 1957) 72–6. A sample of supposedly glass-laced sugar sent to a lab for testing was found to be "very impure" and contained a large amount of fibrous matter. NASA VAB SRC Vol. 15 RC 5657, Report on the analysis of a sample of sugar.

32. Neethling, *Should we Forget?*, 79.

33. NAUK CO 879/75/3, No. 79, Memorandum by Dr. J. S. Haldane on the Rations in the Concentration Camps.

34. Cd. 819, 197, and 199 contain examples of punitive rations being applied after abolition of the official penal scale.

35. Kitchener Papers, NAUK PRO 30/57/22, Brodrick to Kitchener, June 21, 1901, Y64.

36. NASA VAB SRC Vol. 3 RC608, Refugees who are able to support themselves to live in town of Brandfort.

37. NASA VAB SRC Vol. 14 RC5432, Mr W. Gostling granted authority to visit RC Kimberley.

38. NAUK CO417/335, Correspondence to Colonial Office Concerning Refugee Camps, Report by Dr. Kendal Franks.

39. Cd. 819, 160. Following complaints about "immoral conduct" between soldiers and refugees, fences also protected inmates from British troops. NASA VAB SRC Vol. 3 RC520, Refugee Camps to be put out of bounds to all soldiers.

40. NASA VAB SRC Vol. 48, Loose Correspondence, Item 6.

41. Ibid., Item 12.

42. NASA VAB SRC Vol. 10 RC3360, Closing in Refugee Camp in Winburg with wire.

43. NASA VAB SRC Vol. 9 RC3244, Papers concerning interference in camp routine at Vredefort Rd.

44. Coetzer, *Fire in the Sky*, 144.

45. NASA VAB SRC Vol. 8 RC2473, Vredefort Road RC Monthly Report; NASA VAB SRC Vol. 27 RC9416, Inspector Hamilton's Report, Vredefort Road.

46. NASA TAB SOPOW 41 PR/A3828/02.

47. The first chief superintendent of refugee camps in Orange River Colony defined "Bona fide refugees" as "those who have come in from any district (after having signed papers of neutrality) for protection from the enemy, whilst 'all other classes' include those whose . . . immediate relatives are still on commando, dead, or of those who come in through dire poverty, the classification will in a great measure be in [camp superintendents'] hands." NASA VAB CO 2 76/01, Burgher Camps Department Instructions, letters to superintendents.

48. Kitchener Papers, NAUK PRO 30/57/22, Kitchener to Brodrick, June 21, 1901, Y62. In a revisionist rehabilitation, Keith Surridge casts Kitchener as an astute politician who wanted to offer conciliatory peace terms but was prevented from doing so by Milner. Surridge suggests the "Madagascar plan" was simply a provocation rather than a serious suggestion. "The Politics of War: Lord Kitchener and the Settlement of the South African War," in *Writing a Wider War: Rethinking Gender, Race, and Identity in the South African War, 1899–1902*, ed. Gregor Cuthbertson, A. M. Grundlingh, and Mary-Lynn Suttie (Athens: Ohio University Press, 2002), 222–23.

49. Milner Papers, MSS Milner 171, Chamberlain to Milner, January 25, 1901.

50. Kennedy, "The Imperialism of Internment."

51. NASA VAB SRC Vol. 8, RC2607, Notice re conduct of Burghers in Refugee Camps; SRC Vol. 14 RC5431, Men who create disturbances to be sent to POW Camp.

52. NASA VAB SRC Vol. 3 RC678, Telegram from Superintendent of Springfontein camp, March 19, 1901.

53. NASA TAB MGP 123 12760B/01.

54. NAUK CO 879/75/3 No. 176, Encl. 19, Deputy Admin. ORC to Milner.

55. NASA TAB SOPOW 41 PR/A3828/02.

56. NASA TAB PMO 42 PM 2881/01.

57. NASA TAB SOPOW 41 PR/A3828/02.

58. NASA TAB PMO 27 PM 1872/01, Suggestions for General Reorganization of the Boer Refugee Camps. Emphasis mine.

59. NASA VAB SRC Vol. 10 RC3877, Discipline at Refugee Camp Kimberley; NASA VAB SRC Vol. 11 RC3966, Discipline in Bloemfontein Refugee Camp.

60. NASA VAB SRC Vol. 15 RC5998, Report on the Showyard Refugee Camp.

61. Coetzer, *Fire in the Sky*, 146.

62. NASA VAB SRC Vol. 4 RC810, Two camps at Winburg separating desirable refugees from undesirables.

63. NASA VAB SRC Vol. 24 RC8639, Disturbances at Aliwal North RC.

64. NASA TAB PMO 27 PM 1872/01. Examples where inmates are sent to undesirable wards include: NASA VAB SRC Vol. 7 RC1938, SRC Vol. 13 RC4761, SRC Vol. 14 RC5359, SRC Vol. 14 RC5405, SRC Vol. 14 RC5431, SRC Vol. 18 RC6695, SRC Vol. 19 RC7349, SRC Vol. 20 RC7630, SRC Vol. 20 RC7684, SRC Vol. 22 RC8270, SRC Vol. 22 RC8275, SRC Vol. 23 RC8396, SRC Vol. 23 RC8450.

65. NAUK CO417/335, No. 39407, Blue Book Reports on Refugee Camps, "Memorandum on the Concentration Camps. Points Where the Camp Administration seems to have been successful and deserving of imitation."

66. NASA VAB SRC Vol. 11 RC3966, Discipline in Bloemfontein Refugee Camp.

67. Fawcett Papers, 7MGF/E/2 Millicent Fawcett's Diary, II: l. 51—100, August 1901—Sept 1901 [l. 59 dated Aug 23, 1901], 77.

68. NASA VAB SRC Vol. 3 RC520, Refugee Camps to be put out of bounds to all soldiers.

69. NASA VAB SRC Vol. 10 RC3574, Behavior in Camp. Allegations of sexual liaisons between British soldiers and women in the camps were commonplace, though the incidence of rape and sexual violence is unclear.

70. NASA VAB SRC Vol. 21 RC8040, Desertions from Winburg RC.

71. NASA VAB SRC Vol. 11 RC3966, Discipline in Bloemfontein RC.

72. NASA VAB SRC Vol. 15 RC6060, Compulsory Labour in Refugee Camp Vredefort Rd.

73. NASA VAB SRC Vol. 16 RC6558, Sanitary Arrangements at Aliwal North RC.

74. NASA VAB SRC Vol. 15 RC6060, Compulsory Labour in Refugee Camp Vredefort Rd.

75. NASA VAB CO 2 76/01, Burgher Camps Department Instructions.

76. NASA VAB SRC Vol. 14 RC5432, Mr Gostling granted authority to visit Refugee Camp Kimberley.

77. NASA VAB SRC Vol. 20 RC7561, Heilbron Refugee Camp Disturbances.

78. NASA TAB GOV 112 GEN 215/02.

79. By accepting the categories of "modernity" and "progress" at face value, van Heyningen has been accused of replicating British colonial attitudes. Elizabeth van

Heyningen, "A Tool for Modernisation? The Boer Concentration Camps of the South African War, 1900–1902," *South African Journal of Science* 106, no. 5/6 (2010); van Heyningen, "'Fools Rush In.'

80. NASA VAB SRC Vol. 20 RC7561, Heilbron Refugee Camp Disturbances.

81. NASA VAB SRC Vol. 20 RC7563, The Ladies give trouble at Heilbron.

82. NASA VAB SRC Vol. 19 RC7263, Passes for People to live in town, Kimberley.

83. NASA VAB SRC Vol. 19 RC7326, Age of Pupils in Day schools in RCs.

84. Radhakrishna, *Dishonoured by History*, 73–75.

85. NAUK CO 417/335, No. 39407, Blue Books Reports on Refugee Camps, "Memorandum on the Concentration Camps. Points where the camp administration seems to have been successful and deserving of imitation."

86. NASA VAB SRC Vol. 22 RC8215, Refugee Camps Training of Nurses.

87. NASA TAB GOV 103 GEN 36/01; NAUK CO 291/27, No. 9057, Education for Younger Boer Prisoners.

88. Philip Gardner, "'There and Not Seen': E. B. Sargant and Educational Reform, 1884–1905," *History of Education* 33, no. 30 (2004): 614.

89. NASA TAB CS 25 3172/01, Sargant to Milner, June 14, 1901.

90. NASA TAB GOV 11 GEN 53/02.

91. Eliza Reidi, "Teaching Empire: British and Dominions Women Teachers in the South African War Concentration Camps," *English Historical Review* 120, no. 489 (2005): 1344.

92. NAUK CO 879/77/1, No. 12, Tucker's general report for December 1901.

93. While historians think of World War I as inaugurating a world of "modern propaganda," the South African War was an important step in this process; camps might be described as "laboratories of censorship." Paul Zietsman, "The Concentration Camp Schools—Beacons of Light in the Darkness," in *Scorched Earth*, ed. Fransjohan Pretorius (Cape Town: Human & Rousseau, 2001), 90–93.

94. Deane/Streatfeild Papers, Streatfeild 2/9, Letter to Edward Ward at the War Office, September 27, 1901.

95. NAUK CO 291/29, No. 38376, Education Reports, October 11, 1901.

96. Cd. 819, 234.

97. Milner Papers, MSS Milner dep 236, "General Report on Burgher Camps and Burgher Land Settlements on the Transvaal," 228.

98. NASA VAB SRC Vol. 138, Item 17, Report by Lewis Mansergh on Burgher Refugee Camp—Amalinda Bluff, East London, July 18, 1902. British officials believed camps had equipped inmates to live in "larger [more concentrated] centres of population" and had thereby minimized the "dangers to the individual, and possible new problems for the state" that would arise in the "future development" of a modern, industrial South Africa.

99. NASA VAB SRC Vol. 5 RC1121, Report Bloemfontein Native RC.

100. Up until October 1901 Britain spent a monthly average of £52,000 on Trans-

vaal's Boer camps but only £13,250 on native camps, which held almost as many inmates. Cd. 934, *Further Papers Relating to the Working of the Refugee Camps* (London: His Majesty's Stationary Office, 1902), 73–74.

101. The postwar destruction of the Department of Native Refugees' files was likely a matter of archival housekeeping rather than anything more malicious. NASA VAB CO 144 1266/03, Closing of Refugee Camp Department. Surviving documents are scattered throughout other departmental files.

102. Cd. 902, 56.

103. NASA VAB SRC Vol. 5 RC1217, Report on proposed campsite at Thabanachu.

104. Weiss, "Exceptional Space"; Tilman Dedering, "Compounds, Camps, Colonialism," *Journal of Namibian Studies: History, Politics, Culture* 12 (2012); Rob Turrell, "Kimberley's Model Compounds," *Journal of African History* 25 (1984).

105. NAUK CO224/7 No. 25144, Report on Civil Administration since September 1901, 563.

106. NASA VAB SRC Vol. 1 RC182, Drugs to be brought from Messrs Lennon & Co for Native RC Edenburg; Kessler, "Black Concentration Camps," 131.

107. NASA VAB SRC Vol. 5 RC1206, Report on Edenburg and Springfontein Refugee Camps.

108. NASA VAB CO 46 4282/01, Scarcity of food at Native Refugee Camp, Honingspruit.

109. NASA VAB SRC Vol. 4 RC1064, Monthly Report Native Refugee Camp Edenburg. "There is no hospital in camp, only a place of inspection, where sick natives are seen and treated."

110. NASA VAB SRC Vol. 2 RC476, Appointment of Native Supt at Native RC Brandfort.

111. NASA VAB SRC Vol. 1 RC67, Scale of salaries for camp staff. The Head Man "Peter" at Brantford received £60 a year, while European superintendents at native camps typically received £200; superintendents at Boer camps often received £500. NASA VAB SRC Vol. 2 RC323, letter to Supt. Brandfort camp.

112. NASA VAB SRC Vol. 5 RC1359, Appointing white superintendent at Native Camp, Brandfort.

113. Warwick, *Black People and the South African War*, chapter 8.

114. Kessler, "Black Concentration Camps," 115.

115. NAUK CO224/4, No. 37513, Civil Administration ORC.

116. NASA TAB HC 87, Report on the workings of the Native Refugee Department.

117. Stowell Kessler, "The Black and Coloured Concentration Camps," in *Scorched Earth* ed. Fransjohan Pretorius (Cape Town: Human & Rousseau, 2001), 144–45.

118. NASA VAB SRC Vol. 11 RC4173, Employment of Native Servants in RCs.

119. NASA TAB HC 87, Report on the workings of the Native Refugee Department.

120. In this way, they anticipated the exploitation of African labor in refugee camps today. At the Salala refugee camp for internally displaced persons in Liberia, inmates are taken in truckloads to work on rubber plantations owned by the US Firestone company for 50 cents a day. Agier, *Managing the Undesirables*, 57.

121. NASA TAB SNA 28 NA1037/02, Lotbinière to Commissioner for Native Affairs. J. S. Mohlamme, "African Refugee Camps in the Boer Republics," in *Scorched Earth* ed. Fransjohan Pretorius (Cape Town: Human & Rousseau, 2001), 123.

122. Little information exists on politically undesirable natives, though one native inmate at Bethany "used . . . treacherous language" and was "altogether an undesirable type." NASA VAB SRC Vol. 6 RC1499, Undesirable character forwarded by Commandant, Bethany.

123. NASA VAB SRC Vol. 8 RC2724, Medical Report, Aliwal North Native RC.

124. NASA VAB CO 46 4282/01, Scarcity of food at Native Refugee Camp, Honingspruit.

125. According to G. B. Woodroffe, Medical Officer at Irene. NAUK CO 879/75/3, No. 165, Milner to Chamberlain, forwards report on Transvaal Camps for November by W. K. Tucker.

126. Curtin, *Disease and Empire*, 161.

127. Elizabeth van Heyningen, "Women and Disease: The Clash of Medical Cultures in the Concentration Camps of the South African War," in *Writing a Wider War: Rethinking Gender, Race, and Identity in the South African War, 1899–1902*, edited by Greg Cuthbertson, Albert Grundlingh, and Mary-Lynn Suttie (Athens: Ohio University Press, 2002), 186–212; van Heyningen, "Medical History and Afrikaner Society in the Boer Republics at the End of the Nineteenth Century," *Kleio Journal of the Department of History, University of South Africa* 37 (2005).

128. In defense of this practice, Heilbron's superintendent noted the common practice in Africa of smearing floors with cow dung to keep things "clean and tidy." "Conditions which are looked upon by the ordinary Boer as a matter of course," he continued, "do not appear to have prevented him from being healthy and thriving. Consequently, he cannot understand that the non-ventilation of rooms and an ill-swept floor are conducive to sickness and it will take some little time to educate him up to this point." NASA VAB SRC Vol. 13 RC5033, Report on Heilbron camp.

129. NAUK CO224/5 No. 1723, Concentration Camp Bloemfontein, December 20, 1901.

130. NAUK CO 879/75/3, No 165, Milner Reports on Transvaal Camps by W. K. Tucker.

131. NAUK CO224/5, No. 1723, Concentration Camp Bloemfontein.

132. NAUK CO 879/77/1, No. 66, Camp Reports for January 1901 from Transvaal.

133. NASA VAB SRC Vol. 9 RC2894, Mr. Daller's Report on Bloemfontein Refugee Camp.

134. NAUK CO224/5, No. 1723, Concentration Camp Bloemfontein.

135. NASA TAB CT 21 2262/03, General Report on Burgher Camps and Burgher Land Settlements on the Transvaal by Major Leggett, 114; Milner Papers, MSS. Milner dep. 236 Papers relating to land settlement.

136. NASA TAB CS 3 324/01, Telegraph from Dr. Turner, February 1901.

137. Statistics from van Heyningen, *Concentration Camps*, 136–37.

138. In 1900, the estimated population of Bloemfontein was 12,000 and Pretoria was 8,000. The camps recorded 12,639 "white" deaths between August and December 1901; exact figures do not exist for black deaths, but they were likely comparable.

139. A morbid fascination among inmates with "the deathbed" reveals their hopelessness and despondency. Boje, *Imperfect Occupation*, 121–22.

140. A. D. Luckhoff, *Woman's Endurance* (Pretoria: SA News, 1904), entry for October 24.

141. Kitchener Papers, NAUK PRO 30/57/22, Kitchener to Brodrick, July 26, 1901, Y77.

142. NAUK CO 879/75/3, No 165, Milner to Chamberlain, forwards report on Transvaal Camps for November 1901 by W. K. Tucker.

143. NAUK CO224/5, No. 43012, Report by Dr. Pratt Yule, Concentration Camps, November 16, 1901.

144. Deane/Streatfeild Papers 2/11 Transcripts of letters from Lucy Streatfeild to her sister, 106.

145. Bruce Fetter and Stowell Kessler, "Scars from a Childhood Disease: Measles in the Concentration Camps during the Boer War," *Social Science History* 20 no. 4 (1996).

146. NASA TAB HC 61, Clipping from the *Times*.

147. NAUK CO 879/77/1, No. 12, Extract of Tucker's general report for December 1901, 36. Brodrick cited an infant mortality rate of 20% in Manchester and 30% in Russia to suggest camp mortality was nothing unusual. NASA TAB HC 86, File 6, Files on Ladies Concentration Camp Committee.

148. NAUK CO224/5, No. 43012, Report by Dr. Pratt Yule, Concentration Camps, November 16, 1901.

149. NASA TAB CS 4 374/01, Minute on Sanitation by Dr. Turner, February 19, 1901.

150. NASA VAB SRC Vol. 31 RC10324, Report by Dr. Whiteside Himes, 13.

151. Vaughan Nash, "The Boers at Ahmednagar," *London Daily News*, May 2, 1901. For official assessment of the health of Boer POW camps in India, see *Report on the Arrangements Made in India for the Accommodation etc. of Boer Prisoners of War* (Simla: Government Central Printers Office, 1904).

152. According to secretary of state for India Sir George Hamilton. Kennedy, "Imperialism of Internment," 7–8. The lack of young children at POW camps likely prevented the outbreak of childhood diseases like measles.

153. NASA VAB SRC Vol. 7 RC1869, Dr. Westerfield's Protest against conditions at Kimberley RC. Westerfield's superiors deprecated the £735 cost of erecting a requested hospital and largely ignored his protests. For similar warnings, see NASA VAB SRC Vol. 3 RC762, Civilian Doctor required at Norvals Pont; SRC Vol. 6 RC1799, Reports on Spring-fontein, Bethulie, Aliwal North by Mr. Daller; NASA VAB SRC Vol. 8 RC2569, Sanitary State of Bloemfontein Camp; NASA VAB SRC Vol. 3 RC533, Trollope's Circular No. 11.

154. NASA TAB CS 74 2457/02.

155. NASA VAB SRC Vol. 12 RC4569, Movement of Refugees.

156. Neethling, *Should We Forget?*, 45–46.

157. John Fisher, *That Miss Hobhouse* (London: Secker & Warburg, 1971), chapters 1 and 2.

158. Hobhouse, *Boer War Letters*, 15.

159. Ellen Mappen, *Helping Women at Work: The Women's Industrial Council, 1889–1914* (London: Hutchinson Educational, 1985), 12.

160. Hobhouse quoting Mrs. Joubert, *Brunt of War*, 188.

161. Stanley, *Mourning Becomes*, 9.

162. Hobhouse Balme, *To Love One's Enemies*, 224.

163. Kitchener papers, NAUK PRO 30/57/22, Brodrick to Kitchener, June 21, 1901, Y64. Joseph Chamberlain felt rhetoric from the pro-Boer and antiwar segment of the Liberal Party proved "malignant beyond all recent precedent." Milner Papers, MSS Milner 171: Private correspondence between Milner and Chamberlain Chamberlain to Milner, November 4, 1901.

164. Kitchener Papers, NAUK PRO 30/57/22, Brodrick to Kitchener, July 6, 1901, Y70.

165. Lloyd George, *Hansard's Parliamentary Debates*, June 17, 1901, col. 578.

166. W. T. Stead, "Baby-Killing in Africa," *Review of Reviews*, October 1901: 396; "Our Death Camps in South Africa," *Review of Reviews*, vol. 25, January 1902: 8.

167. Krebs, *Gender, Race, and the Writing of Empire*, chapter 3.

168. Milner Papers, MSS Milner 171: Chamberlain to Milner, November 4, 1901.

169. Hobhouse, *Brunt of War*, 189.

170. Ibid., 305–6.

171. Ibid., 189.

172. Hobhouse, *Boer War Letters*, 79. Hobhouse also noted mortality was equal to that "during the worst plague that had occurred within the last century in Europe." Hobhouse Balme, *To Love One's Enemies*, 268.

173. The image was probably taken in November 1900 but not published until June 1901 in *New Age Magazine*. The medical official at Bloemfontein, Dr. Pern, noted he had the photo taken "thinking it might be useful as an instance of what neglect many of the poorer classes of the Boer Refugees treat their children [*sic*]." NASA VAB CO 49 No. 4492/01, Lizzie van Zyl, alleged ill-treatment. Pro-Boer advocates drew different les-

sons, using the photo as evidence of neglect on the part of British authorities. Whatever the case, the photo indicates the prevalence of famine and social devastation caused
by scorched-earth warfare. For further information see Michael Godby, "Confronting
Horror: Emily Hobhouse and the Concentration Camp Photographs of the South African War," *Kronos: 'n Geleentheidspublikasie Van Die Wes-Kaaplandse Instituut Vir
Historiese Navorsing* no. 32 (2006): 42–44.

174. Stanley, *Mourning Becomes*, chapter 6.

175. Hobhouse, *Brunt of War*, 189.

176. NASA VAB SRC Vol. 17 RC6748, Letter by Emily Hobhouse re condition of
children in RCs.

177. Vernon, *Hunger*, chapter 2.

178. Chamberlain Papers, JC 15/438, Canadian aid to Indian famine; and JC
18/7/1, India, 1902–3 Documents.

179. Hobhouse noted, tucked away in an appendix, that she was "unable . . . from
lack of time and strength to investigate the conditions or personally carry relief to the
native camps." *Brunt of War*, 350.

180. NAUK CO 879/77/1 No. 70, Aborigines Protection Society to Colonial
Office, March 24, 1902.

181. The Irish famine presented similar spectacles, though before the age of the
Kodak camera. Hunger and disease during the American Civil War occasioned a similar
production of human skeletons, though memories of the conflict were a generation old.
Faust, *Republic of Suffering*.

182. Kitchener papers, NAUK PRO 30/57/22, Kitchener to Brodrick, June 21,
1901, Y62.

CHAPTER 7

1. Deane/Streatfeild Papers 2/11 Transcripts of letters from Lucy Streatfeild to her
sister, 109–10. Deane underestimated the number of camps.

2. NASA VAB SRC Vol. 14 RC5646, Report Aliwal North RC, Sept 29 1901.

3. NASA TAB SRC Vol. 24 RC8644, Conditions at Coast RCs.

4. NASA TAB GOV 127 GEN/759/02, General Report on Burgher Camps.

5. They had, the official continued, been "placed upon a basis which should probably have required little amendment had [the camps] been called upon to provide for the
lifetime of the inmates." NASA TAB CT 21 2262/03, General Report on Burgher
Camps and Burgher Land Settlements on the Transvaal, 98–99.

6. S. J. Thomson, *The Transvaal Burgher Camps, South Africa* (Allahabad: Pioneer
Press, 1904), 8–9.

7. Even Elizabeth van Heyningen's stimulating critique of existing scholarship
remains entrenched in debates about postapartheid national memory and does not offer
a wider imperial and global framework. "Costly Mythologies."

8. Milner Papers, MSS Milner 171: Private correspondence between Milner and Chamberlain. Milner to Chamberlain, December 7 1901. Milner notes he came to this realization "six weeks or two months ago."

9. Ibid., Chamberlain to Milner, November 4, 1901.

10. Ibid., Milner to Chamblerlain, December 7, 1901.

11. NASA VAB SRC Vol. 31 RC10324, Report by Dr. Himes, Medical Inspector of Refugee Camps in the ORC.

12. NASA VAB SRC Vol. 16 RC6628, Report—Comments on visit of Ladies Commission

13. Cd. 853, 8.

14. NASA TAB HC 86 File 1, Concentration Camps Private Letter File Milner to Goold-Adams, November 19 1901.

15. NAUK CO 879/75/3, No. 30, Secretary to the Orange River Colony Administration to Acting Imperial Secretary, Johannesburg, July 6, 1901, 31.

16. Statistics are calculated from multiple weekly returns submitted by the Department of Refugee Camps and earlier, the Office of the Superintendent of Refugee camps. NAUK CO 224/8, Orange River Colony Despatches No. 51434, Wilkins' Monthly Report for October; NAUK CO 417/362, July 19, 1902; and NAUK CO 879/75/3 No. 188, Milner to Chamberlain, February 7, 1902, contain detailed financial information.

17. Cd. 934, 52.

18. NAUK WO 32/8061, letter from the South African Women and Children Distress Fund to Brodrick on July 1, 1901.

19. Hobhouse Balme, *To Love One's Enemies*, 210.

20. Fisher, *That Miss Hobhouse*, 173–74.

21. Elaine Harrison, "Women Members and Witnesses on British Government Ad Hoc Committees of Inquiry 1850–1930, with Special Reference to Royal Commissions of Inquiry" (PhD diss, London School of Economics and Political Science, 1998), 158.

22. Lucy Deane noted that "of all the people out here . . . [Milner] has shewn the very keenest, most sympathetic interest in our work." Deane/Streatfeild Papers 2/11, Transcripts of letters from Lucy Streatfeild to her sister, 49. In response to Military Governor General Maxwell's complaints about the committee, Milner responded "I make no apology for continuing to worry you about the camps" and noted that recommendations put forth by the Fawcett Committee, "seem to be eminently sensible." NASA TAB HC 86, File 1, Concentration Camps Private Letter File, Milner to Maxwell, November 18, 1901.

23. Krebs, *Gender, Race, and the Writing of Empire*, chapter 3. Harrison disputes this claim, noting the appointment of an all-women's committee was a "cynical response" that "signaled to the military high command in South Africa that the issue was of little importance." Harrison, "Women Members and Witnesses," 163.

24. NASA VAB HC 86, File 6, Files on Ladies Concentration Camp Committee, extracts from Mrs. Fawcett's diary.

25. Deane/Streatfeild Papers 2/11 Transcripts of letters from Lucy Streatfeild to her sister, 5.

26. For information on committee members, see Harrison, "Women Members and Witnesses," 148–64; and Millicent Fawcett, *What I Remember* (New York: G. P. Putnam's Sons, 1925), 153–55.

27. Waterston's life was "devoted to the care of the poor," though Fawcett commented she was "seen as very anti-Boer and is not trusted by the Afrikaner population"; at one point Waterston called Boer inmates "worse than savages and barbarians." Fawcett Papers, 7MGF/E/2 Millicent Fawcett's Diary. For information on Waterston's career see van Heyningen and Bean, eds., *Letters of Jane Elizabeth Waterston*.

28. Fawcett Papers, 7MGF/E/2 Millicent Fawcett's Diary, 25.

29. Ibid., 35–40.

30. Deane/Streatfeild Papers 2/11 Transcripts of letters from Lucy Streatfeild to her sister, 109.

31. Cd. 893, 15.

32. Ibid., 16.

33. NASA TAB HC 86, File 1, Concentration Camps Private Letter File, Fawcett to Milner, November 19, 1901.

34. Deane noted privately "the only thing I have failed over is the Rations, which are in my opinion one of the causes of the death-rate, too scanty and very unsuitable. . . . I have got the amended Rations and I have got it put into the Report but I couldn't get the comment on it made which I wanted." Deane/Streatfeild Papers 2/11, Transcripts of letters from Lucy Streatfeild to her sister, 109.

35. Cd. 893, 19, 12.

36. NAUK CO 417/335, Blue Book Reports on Refugee Camps, 197.

37. Cd. 893, 8–16, 153–60.

38. NAUK CO 179/220, vol. IV, Despatches, Oct–Dec 1901, 98.

39. Cd. 893, 177.

40. Ibid., 7–8.

41. Fawcett Papers, 7MGF/E/2 Millicent Fawcett's Diary, 12–13, 24.

42. Deane/Streatfeild Papers 2/11, Transcripts of letters from Lucy Streatfeild to her sister, 64.

43. Fawcett Papers, 7MGF/E/2 Millicent Fawcett's Diary, 24.

44. Cd. 893, 7.

45. NAUK CO 879/75/3, No. 54. Chamberlain to Milner, November 16, 1901.

46. Metcalf, *Imperial Connections*, 2, 45.

47. Lambert and Lester, *Colonial Lives*, 10–11.

48. C. 8812.

49. NAUK CO 417/335, Blue Book Reports on Refugee Camps.

50. NAUK CO 879/75/3 No. 54, Chamberlain to Milner, November 16, 1901.

51. NAUK CO 417/335, Blue Book Reports on Refugee Camps.

52. NASA TAB HC 86, File 2, Concentration Camps: Correspondence with Secretary of State; reprinted in NAUK CO 879/75/3, No. 54, Mr. Chamberlain to Administrator Lord Milner, November 16, 1901.

53. Ibid.

54. NASA VAB SRC Vol. 16 RC6316, Discipline in Refugee Camps. Trained men as Superintendents from India.

55. Maxwell and Goold-Adams concurred that "men of sufficient calibre" from India were needed for "the difficult post of Superintendent as well as for inspection work." NASA VAB SRC Vol. 48, Loose Correspondence, Item 4, letter from Milner to Goold-Adams, December 18 1901.

56. NAUK CO 417/329, No. 46030, Indian Officers for Concentration Camps.

57. Curzon Papers, MSS EUR F111/171, Tel. No. 412, Sec of State to Viceroy, December 9 1901; NAI Home Department (Medical), April 1902, Progs. No. 111–62, Part B: Deputation of certain officers for duty on Concentration Camps in South Africa.

58. Chamberlain Papers, JC 14/4/2/201, Colonial Affairs, South Africa, 1900–1903, Chamberlain to Milner, November 16.

59. NAUK CO 417/329, No. 46030, Indian Officers for Concentration Camps. IOR/L/MIL/9/405 ff. 225–30 and IOR/L/MIL/9/403 ff. 188–89, 270–75 contain Thomson's and Wilkins's employment records respectively.

60. Thomson's numerous publications included *Sanitary Principles, More Especially as Applied to India* (Calcutta: Brown, 1883); *Transvaal Burgher Camps*; *Silent India*; and *Real Indian People*.

61. *Suffolk County Handbook and Official Directory for 1917* (London, 1917), 445; Suffolk Record Office, EE2/P15/1/2 Borough of Eye, Medical Officer's Report for the Year 1913. See NASA VAB SRC Vol. 25 RC8945, in which Wilkins promotes the creation of a South African Medical Service modeled after the IMS.

62. Wilkins and Thomson received a salary of £2,000 compared to Trollope and Tucker's annual £500 and £700. NAUK CO 879/75/3, No. 130, Chamberlain Milner, January 7, 1902.

63. NAUK CO 417/329, No. 46030, "Indian Officers for Concentration Camps."

64. Thomson, *Transvaal Burgher Camps*, 6.

65. NASA VAB SRC Vol. 19 RC7228, Officers from Indian Govt to take over duties of RCs.

66. NASA VAB SRC Vol. 48, Item 4, Milner to Goold-Adams, December 18, 1901.

67. Wilkins quoted in Hobhouse Balme, *To Love One's Enemies*, 472.

68. NASA TAB HC 86, File 1, Concentration Camps Private Letter File.

69. NAUK CO 879/77/1, No. 173, Milner to Chamberlain, November 29, 1902.

70. Milner Papers, MSS Milner dep. 236, General Report on Burgher Camps and Burgher Land Settlements on the Transvaal by Major Leggett, 98.

71. NASA VAB SRC Vol. 20 RC7763, New rations at Brandfort; NAUK CO 879/77/1 No. 88, Transvaal Monthly Report for February from new General Superintendent Lieut-Col. Samuel Thomson.

72. NAUK CO 879/77/1 No. 88, Transvaal Monthly Report for February from new General Superintendent.

73. NAUK CO 879/77/1 No. 104, letter from Thomson.

74. NASA TAB HC 86, File 2, Concentration Camps: Correspondence with Secretary of State; Chamberlain Papers, JC 14/4/2/203.

75. Thomson, *Sanitary Principles*, 2.

76. Cd. 893, 8.

77. NAUK CO 879/77/1, No. 108, Thomson to Milner.

78. NASA VAB SRC Vol. 24 RC8594, Rations granted to destitute people in town.

79. NASA TAB HC 86, File 2, Concentration Camps: Correspondence with Secretary of State.

80. NAUK CO 879/77/1 No 88, Transvaal Monthly Report for February.

81. Thomson, *Sanitary Principles*, 136–37; Thomson, *Transvaal Burgher Camps*, 8.

82. Cd. 936, *Further Papers Relating to the Working of the Refugee Camps in South Africa* (London: His Majesty's Stationary Office, 1902), 18–19.

83. Cd. 893, 16.

84. NASA VAB SRC Vol. 24 RC8498, Suggestions for Lady Supt of Camps.

85. Cd. 893, 138.

86. Ibid., 15.

87. Elizabeth van Heyningen, "British Doctors versus Boer Women: Clash of Medical Cultures," in *Scorched Earth*, ed. Fransjohan Pretorius (Cape Town: Human & Rousseau, 2001), 193.

88. NASA VAB SRC Vol. 17 RC6922, Refugees Refusing to Report cases of sickness.

89. NAUK CO224/5 No. 43012, Concentration Camps, November 16, 1901.

90. NAUK CO224/3 No. 28862, Refugee Camp Bloemfontein, Report by Dr. Pratt Yule.

91. NAUK CO224/5 No. 1723, Concentration Camp Bloemfontein, December 20, 1901.

92. NASA VAB SRC Vol. 23 RC8374, Report Vredefort Rd. Refugee Camp.

93. NASA TAB LD 24 M1999/01. See also NASA Free State Depot SRC Vol. 24 RC8462, Administering of new camps in the C[ape] C[olony]; SRC Vol. 24 RC8517, Discipline in Refugee Camps; and SRC Vol. 24 RC8639, Disturbances at Aliwal North RC. In the Transvaal, Proclamation 2 of 1902 served a similar purpose for Thomson.

94. NASA VAB SRC Vol. 22 RC8270, Petition for Removal of Senior MO at Orange River RC.

95. NASA Free State Depot SRC Vol. 21 RC8040, Desertions from the Winburg RC.

96. NASA VAB SRC Vol. 22 RC8274, Report on Kimberley RC; SRC Vol. 23 RC8444, Sundried bricks, Bethulie RC.

97. Thomson, *Transvaal Burgher Camps*, 8.

98. NASA VAB SRC Vol. 22 RC8215, Refugee Camps Training of Nurses.

99. Luckhoff, *Woman's Endurance*, Tuesday September 3.

100. NASA VAB SRC Vol. 14 RC5505, Disorder at Bethulie RC.

101. NASA TAB GOV 105 GEN 232/01.

102. NASA VAB SRC Vol. 22 RC8270, Petition for Removal of Senior MO at Orange River RC.

103. NASA TAB HC 86, File 5, Petition from Irene inmates; Henrietta Armstrong, *Camp Diary of Henrietta E. C. Armstrong: Experiences of a Boer Nurse in the Irene Concentration Camp* (Pretoria: Human Sciences Research Council, 1980) complains regularly of the continued concentration of medical authority in the hands of British officials.

104. NASA VAB SRC Vol. 21 RC7828, Extension of Refugee Camp at Vredefort Rd, March 1902.

105. NASA TAB CT 21 2262/03, "General Report on Burgher Camps" by Major Leggett, 101.

106. NAUK CO 879/75/3 No. 54, Chamberlain to Milner, November 16, 1901.

107. NASA VAB SRC Vol. 21 RC8095, Discipline in RCs in Cape Colony.

108. NASA TAB HC 86, File 1, Concentration Camps Private Letter File, Buchan to Wilkins, May 26, 1902.

109. Thomson, *Transvaal Burgher Camps*, 9.

110. NASA VAB SRC Vol. 48, Loose Correspondence, Item 2.

111. NASA TAB HC 86, File 1, Concentration Camps Private Letter File, Goold-Adams to Milner, March 31, 1902.

112. NASA VAB SRC Vol. 138, Item 17, Report by Lewis Mansergh on "Burgher Refugee Camp, Amalinda Bluff, East London, July 18, 1902.

113. Ibid., annex 7.

114. NASA VAB SRC Vol. 28 RC9773, Report on the Uitenhage RC by Mansergh.

115. NASA VAB SRC Vol. 138, Item 17, Report by Lewis Mansergh on "Burgher Refugee Camp, Amalinda Bluff, East London," July 18, 1902.

116. NASA VAB SRC Vol. 24 RC8682, Report on Kabusie RC NAUK CO 417/335, Blue Book Reports on Refugee Camps.

117. NASA VAB SRC Vol. 24 RC8682, Report on Kabusie RC by Dr. Tonkin, Medical Inspector, May 25 1902.

118. NASA VAB SRC Vol. Vol. 22 RC8232, Report on new RC at Kabusi.

119. NAUK CO 417/335, Blue Book Reports on Refugee Camps.

120. NASA VAB SRC Vol. 26 RC9100, Military huts delivered to Kabusie; SRC

Vol. 28 RC9759, Final Report on Kabusie RC; SRC Vol. 28 RC9773, Report on the Uitenhage RC by Mansergh.

121. NASA VAB SRC Vol. 138, Item 13, Remarks about lighting at EL Camp.

122. NASA VAB SRC Vol. 48, Item 15, letter from Wilkins to Supt Buthulie, March 12, 1902.

123. According to the superintendent of Kimberley, "the moral effect" of removal to the coast "would be great; at present many, particularly of the latter, believe and state their belief that British Supremacy is of the most temporary kind, and that very shortly the ascendancy of the SA Republics will be re-established. Let them be moved to distant parts and they would speedily come to recognize that their reinstatement on their properties by force of arms, in a sense favorable to the Boer forces, is most improbable." He added: "It must be borne in mind that intermarriage has joined together very closely in most cases the whole of the inhabitants of every district—and that within reasonable areas the population is virtually only one big family. I consider for our own security in the future that everything possible should be done to break up these communities. . . . If at the cessation of hostilities these people are allowed to swarm back to their farms I do not believe that existence will be possible for the British settler who many find himself either owner or tenant of a farm surrounded by relatives of the dispossessed previous owner." NASA VAB SRC Vol. 16 RC6422, Report on Refugee Camps from Kimberley Supt.

124. Foucault, *Discipline and Punish*, 171.

125. NASA VAB SRC Vol. 138, Item 16, Uitenhage Camp Progress Report, April 5, 1902.

126. NASA VAB SRC Vol. 138, Item 17, Report by Lewis Mansergh on "Burgher Refugee Camp, Amalinda Bluff, East London," July 18, 1902; NASA VAB SRC Vol. 28 RC9759, Final Report on Kabusie RC.

127. NASA VAB SRC Vol. 48, Loose Correspondence.

128. NAUK CO 879/77/1, No. 170, Monthly Report from Thomson, Transvaal, October 22, 1902.

129. NAUK CO 879/75/3, No. 188, Milner to Chamberlain, February 7, 1902.

130. NASA VAB SRC Vol. 33 RC10775, Report on the working of the RCs in the ORC by Wilkins, February 23, 1903.

131. NASA VAB SRC Vol. 24 RC8709, Families leaving RC to return to their farms must sign a document pleading their loyalty to the King.

132. CO 879/77/1 No. 165, letter from Thomson to Buchan.

133. NASA VAB SRC Vol. 25 RC8932, No burgher can leave camp at present who cannot support themselves.

134. NASA VAB SRC Vol. 30 RC10251, Starting of Relief work camps; NASA VAB SRC Vol. 29 RC10007, Tents needed for relief works at Bethulie Kransdaai Relief Camp; Lawrence Richardson, *Lawrence Richardson Selected Correspondence*, ed. Arthur Davey (Cape Town: Van Riebeeck Society, 1977), 90–91, 127–28.

135. NASA VAB DRW 3, Circular Letter No. 1 Instructions to Camp Superintendents Relief Works, ORC.

136. NASA VAB CO 186 4703/03, Visit paid by Miss E. Hobhouse to Tweespruit Relief Works Camp.

137. Weiss, "Exceptional Space," 29.

138. Kessler, "Black Concentration Camps," 74.

139. Nightingale, *Segregation*, 243.

140. NASA TAB CS 74 2457/02.

141. NASA TAB NAB 4 N323/06.

142. For the relationship between a wartime mythology of "shared suffering" and the ideological foundations of apartheid see Stanley, *Mourning Becomes*.

143. Elizabeth van Heyningen, "The Concentration Camps of the South African (Anglo-Boer) War, 1900–1902," *History Compass* 7, no. 1 (2009): 22; Stowell V. Kessler, "The Black and Coloured Concentration Camps of the Anglo-Boer War, 1899–1902: Shifting the Paradigm from Sole Martyrdom to Mutual Suffering," *Historia* 44 no. 1 (1999).

144. Apartheid in 1948 "relied heavily on highly coercive tools bequeathed . . . by earlier generations of government officials." British concentration camps were part of this inheritance. Nightingale, *Segregation*, 233.

145. Nicholas Dirks, *Scandal of Empire: India and the Creation of Imperial Britain* (Cambridge, MA: Belknap Press, 2008).

146. Hobhouse Balme, *To Love One's Enemies*, 163, 259.

147. Deane/Streatfeild Papers 2/11, Transcripts of letters from Lucy Streatfeild to her sister, 109–10.

148. Emily Hobhouse, *Report to the Committee of the South African Distress Fund of a Visit to the Camps of Women and Children in the Cape and Orange River Colonies* (London: Friars Printing Association, 1901), 11. Millicent Fawcett noted similarly "our commission was non-political." Fawcett Papers, 7MGF/E/2 Millicent Fawcett's Diary, 31.

149. They thus turned a "political" problem into a "social one." Conversely, Mrinalini Sinha argues, the tactics of anticolonial protest often involved converting social problems into political ones. *Specters of Mother India: The Global Restructuring of an Empire* (Durham, NC: Duke University Press, 2006).

150. *Hansard's Parliamentary Debates*, June 17, 1901, col. 590.

151. Henry Campbell-Bannerman, *Hansard's Parliamentary Debates*, June 17, 1901, col. 598.

152. Mitchell, *Rule of Experts*.

EPILOGUE

1. Thomson, *Transvaal Burgher Camps*, 8–9.

2. CO417/335, No. 39407, Blue Book Reports on Refugee Camps, "Memorandum

on the Concentration Camps. Points Where the Camp Administration seems to have been successful and deserving of imitation."

3. Fay Crofts, *History of Hollymoor Hospital* (Studley, UK: Brewin Books, 1998), 17–21.

4. Nevile Henderson, *Failure of a Mission: Berlin 1937–1939* (New York: G. P. Putnam's Sons, 1940), 21.

5. Quoted in Paul Moore, "'And What Concentration Camps Those Were!': Foreign Concentration Camps in Nazi Propaganda, 1933–9," *Journal of Contemporary History* 45, no. 3 (2010): 672.

6. Arendt, *Origins of Totalitarianism*, 440.

7. Gerwarth and Malinowski, "Hannah Arendt's Ghosts," 289.

8. Many of these articles were in turn translated and published in English by the *Journal of the Royal United Services Institute*, fostering a cross-fertilization of military ideas. Baron Colmar von der Goltz, "What Can We Learn from the Boer War, translated from the *Deutsche Revue*," *Journal of the Royal United Services Institute* 46, no. 298 (1902); E. Gunter, "A German View of British Tactics in the Boer War, precis from the *Jahrbücher für die Deutsche Armee und Marine*," *Journal of the Royal United Services Institute* 46, no. 292 (1902).

9. Including translated reports by Emily Hobhouse. Nicol Stassen and Ulrich van der Heyden, *German Publications on the Anglo-Boer War* (Pretoria: Protea Book House, 2007).

10. Hyslop, "Invention of the Concentration Camp," 271. For Russian media coverage see Holquist, "Violent Russia, Deadly Marxism?," 635–36.

11. Sasson, "From Empire to Humanity: The Creation of Technologies of Famine Relief, 1880–1922," paper presented at the North American Conference on British Studies, Minneapolis, MN, November 2014.

12. Apart from press condemnation, British camps sparked literary and cultural output in Holland, Germany, and France. Albert Jounet, for example, professed himself an "adversary of English crimes" in "Les Camps de Concentration, Poem vendu de la souscription pour les Boers" (Saint-Raphaël: Chailan, 1902). Most European nations were sympathetic to the Boers and raised donations to benefit Afrikaner inmates in camps.

13. Stanley Appelbaum, *French Satirical Drawings from "L'Assiette au Buerre"* (New York: Dover, 1978), xiv. Veber may have had POW camps in mind when he drew his illustrations, though nothing in the series describes them as such, and readers would have conflated the two institutions.

14. Jean Veber, *L'Assiette au beurre: Les camps de reconcentration au Transvaal* (Bad Saarow: Verlag für militärgeschichte und Deutsches Schrifttum, 1941).

15. Moore, "And What Concentration Camps," 655, 668. Nazi references to British camps are too numerous to catalogue. Even after World War II, German writers

remained preoccupied with British camps, using them to critique the Soviet Gulag while avoiding comparisons with Germany's own recent history. Andrez Kaminski, *Konzentrationslager 1896 bis heute: Eine Analyse* (Stuttgart: Hohlhammer, 1982), 34–38.

16. Hans Steinhoff, dir. *Ohm Krüger*, (Germany, 1941).

17. Paul Kramer, "Empires, Exceptions, and Anglo-Saxons: Race and Rule between the British and United States Empires, 1880–1910" in *The American Colonial State in the Philippines: Global Perspectives*, ed. J. Go and Anne. L. Foster (Durham: Duke University Press, 2003); Frank Schumacher, "Lessons of Empire: The United States, the Quest for Colonial Expertise and the British Example, 1898–1917," in *From Enmity to Friendship. Anglo-American Relations in the 19th and 20th Century*, ed. Ursula Lehmkuhl and Gustav Schmidt (Augsburg: Wissner-Verlag, 2005); Thomas R. Metcalf, "From One Empire to Another: the Influence of the British Raj on American Colonialism in the Philippines," *Ab Imperio* 3 (2012).

18. The Filipino military advisor Juan Villamor read about Boer tactics in Hong Kong newspapers and adopted them in the Philippine-American War. Paul Kramer, *Blood of Government: Race, Empire, the United States, and the Philippines*, (Chapel Hill: University of North Carolina Press, 2006), 131. A small Filipino contingent fought on the Boer side in South Africa. Donal Lowry, "'The World's No Bigger Than a *Kraal*': The South African War and International Opinion in the First Age of Globalization,'" in *The Impact of the South African War*, ed. David Omissi and Andrew Thompson (New York: Palgrave, 2002), 274.

19. S. Slcoum and C. Reichmann, *Reports on Military Operations in South Africa and China* (Washington, DC: Government Printing Office, 1901). Meanwhile, articles like the American military consultant James Chester's "The Great Lesson of the Boer War," *Journal of the Military Service Institution of the United States* 32 (1903) depicted civilian concentration as the natural and legitimate response to guerrilla insurgency.

20. "Mr. Churchill on the War," *New York Herald*, December 9, 1900, quoted in Kramer, *Blood of Government*, 153.

21. Elkins, *Imperial Reckoning*; Anderson, *Histories of the Hanged*.

22. Abderrahman Beggar, "The *camps de regroupement* during the War of Algeria," *The Camp* ed. Colman Hogan and Marta Marin-Domine (Newcastle, UK: Cambridge Scholars, 2007); Khalili, *Time in the Shadows*.

23. Klaus Mühlhahn, "The Dark Side of Globalization: The Concentration Camps in Republican China in Global Perspective," *World History Connected* 6 (2009).

24. Though rivals on a continental stage, relations between European powers in colonial Africa often "embodied . . . connection and cooperation"; information transfers existed not only "between the motherland and the colony, but [between] . . . the colonies of different European empires." Ulrike Lindner, "Imperialism and Globalization: Entanglements and Interactions between the British and German Colonial Empires in Africa Before the First World War," *German Historical Institute London Bulletin* 32, no. 1 (2010): 6–7.

25. Quoted in ibid., 10. Another German spokesman demanded "every civil servant in our protectorate who is appointed to an authoritative position . . . be sent to South Africa first to study the conditions there and to see how things should and should not be done." G. Hartmann, *Deutsch-Südwestafrika im Zusammenhang mit Südafrika* (Berlin, 1899), 12.

26. Haussleiter quoted in Forth and Kreienbaum, "A Shared Malady," 262.

27. Jonas Kreienbaum, *'Ein trauriges Fiasko': Koloniale Konzentrationslager im südlichen Afrika, 1900–1908* (Hamburg: Hamburger Edition, 2015) explores connections between British and German colonial camps at length. German officials were well aware of the dangers of epidemic disease in concentration camps: apart from sensational media reports and British Blue Books transferred to Berlin, the governor of South-West Africa reported his "not very favorable" impression of measles outbreaks when he toured British camps as the German consul to Cape Town. Forth and Kreienbaum, "Shared Malady," 262.

28. Hintrager quoted in Forth and Kreienbaum, "A Shared Malady," 262.

29. Jurgen Zimmerer, "Colonialism and the Holocaust. Towards an Archaeology of Genocide," in *Genocide and Settler Society: Frontier Violence and stolen indigenous children in Australian History* ed. Dirk Moses, (New York: Berghahn Books, 2005); Jurgen Zimmerer, "The Birth of the *Ostland* out of the Spirit of Colonialism: A Postcolonial Perspective on the Nazi Policy of Conquest and Extermination," *Patterns of Prejudice* 39 no. 2 (2005); Casper Erichsen and David Olusoga, *The Kaiser's Holocaust: Germany's Forgotten Genocide and the Colonial Roots of Nazism* (London: Faber and Faber, 2011).

30. Benjamin Madley, "From Africa to Auschwitz: How German South West Africa Incubated Ideas and Methods Adopted and Developed by the Nazis in Eastern Europe," *European History Quarterly* 35, no. 3 (2005), considers the colonial careers of prominent Nazis like Franz Ritter von Epp and Euguen Fischer as well as Hermann Göring's father. Added to these is Fritz Spiesser, a prominent author of colonial novels, who grew up in German South-West Africa and served in the Colonial Affairs Bureau for the Nazi Party. His book *Das Konzentrationslager* (Munich: F. Eher, 1940) argued that more died in British camps than in their Nazi counterparts—a claim in World War II's early stages that was not yet outlandish.

31. The "new histories" of Nazi camps are steering attention toward earlier camps in the 1930s. Nikolaus Wachsmann, "The Dynamics of Destruction: The Development of the Concentration Camps, 1934–1945," in *Concentration Camps in Nazi Germany: The New Histories*, ed. Nikolaus Wachsmann and Jane Caplan (New York: Routledge, 2010); Christian Goeschel and Nikolaus Wachsmann, "Before Auschwitz: The Formation of the Nazi Concentration Camps, 1933–39," *Journal of Contemporary History* 45, no. 3 (2010).

32. Caplan, "Political Detention"; Gerstrich, "Konzentrationslager"; Traverso, *Origins of Nazi Violence.*

33. Goeschel and Wachsmann, "Before Auschwitz, " 524.

34. The Gulag's political prisoners were always a minority amid social outcasts and criminal classes. The iconic depictions of Alexander Solzhenitsyn, while moving and profound, are no more representative of the Gulag than the anguished testimonies of middle-class Afrikaner women like Elizabeth Neethling. For recent insight into the Gulag as an instrument of social reform rather than political terror—scholarship that echoes revisionist work by Elizabeth van Heyningen and Liz Stanley on South Africa—see Barnes, *Death and Redemption*. Continuities between British colonial camps and the Soviet Gulag are also explored by Forth, "Britain's Archipelago of Camps."

35. Quoted in Moore, "And What Concentration Camps," 656.

36. Harold Marcuse, *Legacies of Dachau: The Uses and Abuses of a Concentration Camp, 1933–2001* (Cambridge: Cambridge University Press, 2001), 28–29.

37. Harold Marcuse, "The Afterlife of the Camps," in *Concentration Camps in Nazi Germany: The New Histories*, ed. Jane Kaplan and Nikolaus Wachsmann (New York: Routledge, 2010), 196. For the administration of Nazi concentration camps as displaced persons camps by British officials after World War II, see KZ. Gedenkstätte, *Zwischenräume: displaced persons, Internierte und Flüchtlinge in ehemaligen Konzentrationslagern* (Bremen: Ed. Temmen, 2010), 216–23. Dachau also accommodated refugees from Czechoslovakia after the war and has more recently and controversially offered cheap housing for Afghan migrants fleeing the Taliban. Sophie Hardach, "The refugees housed at Dachau," The Guardian, September 19, 2015, https://www.theguardian.com/world/2015/sep/19/the-refugees-who-live-at-dachau.

38. Quoted in Marcuse, *Legacies of Dachau*, 159.

39. Roger Daniels, "Words Do Matter: A Note on Inappropriate Terminology and the Incarceration of the Japanese Americans," in *Nikkei in the Pacific Northwest: Japanese Americans and Japanese Canadians in the Twentieth Century*, ed. Louis Fiset and Gail Nomura (Seattle: University of Washington Press, 2005).

40. Fisher, *That Miss Hobhouse*, 248–53; John V. Crangle and Joseph O. Baylen, "Emily Hobhouse's Peace Mission, 1916," *Journal of Contemporary History* 14 (1979): 737.

41. Wim Hopford, *Twice Interned: Transvaal 1901–02, Germany 1914–18* (London: John Murray, 1919), 139.

42. NAUK CO 152/342/47, Letter from W. M. McDonald offering his services to the War Office.

43. Matthew Stibbe, "Civilian Internment and Civilian Internees in Europe, 1914–20," *Immigrants & Minorities* 26, no. 1/2 (2008): 51.

44. Panikos Panayi, "Internment in India during the First World War," paper presented at the European Social Science History Conference, April 1, 2016, Valencia, Spain.

45. NAI (Home Department), Political Proceedings, September 1914, No. 395, Telegram from Government of Bombay, No, 997-W.

46. Richard Dove, "'A Matter Which Touches the Good Name of This Country,'" in *"Totally Un-English": Britain's Internment of "Enemy Aliens" in Two World Wars*, ed. Richard Dove (New York: Rodopi, 2006), 12.

47. Matthew Stibbe, *Captivity, Forced Labour and Forced Migration in Europe during the First World War* (London: Routledge, 2013), 52.

48. Bashford and Strange, "Asylum-Seekers," 517.

49. Zoë Denness, "'A Question Which Affects Our Prestige as a Nation': The History of British Civilian Internment, 1899–1945" (PhD diss., University of Birmingham, 2012), 161.

50. Stibbe, *Captivity*, 54.

51. The camp at Frongoch, Wales, meanwhile, interned suspects from the Easter Rebellion in Ireland (1916), an uprising suppressed by a familiar figure: General Maxwell, the former military governor of Pretoria responsible for the administration of concentration camps in South Africa.

52. G. Dorminy, "Pietermaritzburg's Imperial Postscript: Fort Napier from 1910 to 1925," *Natalia* 6, no. 4 (1989): 35–39.

53. Cited in Denness, "'A Question,'" 191.

54. In correspondence with the British government, the International Committee of the Red Cross (ICRC) mentioned "the deplorable conditions in the concentration camps [in South Africa], the amelioration of which is why the Red Cross was founded." Kitchener, however, denied access to the camps by Red Cross representatives. ICRC Archives, Geneva, AAF 8, Files 2–3, Correspondence with Great Britain. For ICRC efforts at World War I camps, see Matthew Stibbe, "Internment of Civilians by Belligerent States and the Response of the International Committee of the Red Cross," *Journal of Contemporary History* 41, no. 1 (2006).

55. F. Thormeyer, Emmanuel Schoch, and Fréd Blanchod, *Rapports de MM. F. Thormeyer, Em. Schoch et le Dr F. Blanchod sur leurs visites aux camps de prisonniers de guerre ottomans et d'internés autrichiens et allemands aux Indes et en Birmanie, février, mars et avril 1917* (Geneva: Georg, 1917).

56. Caroline Shaw, *Britannia's Embrace: Modern Humanitarianism and the Imperial Origins of Refugee Relief* (New York: Oxford University Press, 2015), 214.

57. Crangle and Baylen, "Emily Hobhouse's Peace Mission," 738, 733.

58. Hill, *India—Stepmother*, 116.

59. Lord Curzon, *Hansard's Parliamentary Debates*, December 17, 1919, vol. 38, 288–300.

60. Brigadier-General H.H. Austin, *The Baqubah Refugee Camp: An Account of Work on Behalf of the Persecuted Assyrian Christians* (London: Faith Press, 1920), 9.

61. UNOG Archives, C1531/427/20A/80619/18766/Jacket 3, 1934, Council Committee for the Settlement of the Assyrians of Iraq.

62. Austin, *Baqubah Refugee Camp*, 4, 34, 6, 26, 23, 35, 36.

63. Tehila Sasson, "In the Name of Humanity: Britain and the Rise of Global Humanitarianism" (PhD diss., University of California Berkeley, 2015); Sasson, "From Empire to Humanity: The Russian Famine," 522.

64. Cited in Sasson, "From Empire to Humanity: The Russian Famine," 534.

65. For Hill and Robertson's roles in India see chapters 2–4 of this book. For their careers in Russia see Sasson, "From Empire to Humanity: The Russian Famine," 526, 532–37.

66. Sasson, "In the Name of Humanity," chapter 1.

67. Agamben quoted in Diken and Bagge Laustsen, *Culture of Exception*, 79.

68. Chol-hwan Kang, Pierre Rigoulot and Yair Reiner, *Aquariums of Pyongyang: Ten Years in the North Korean Gulag* (New York: Basic Books, 2005).

69. Hannah Arendt described a twentieth century in which nation-states emerged as guarantors of human rights. The camp—whether for political undesirables or refugees—contained the stateless and displaced: those without rights, who could be readily detained. *Origins of Totalitarianism*, 287.

70. Agier, *Managing the Undesirables*, 5, 1.

71. Cleve R. Wooston Jr., "Pope Francis called refugee centers concentration camps," *Washington Post*, April 23, 2017, https://www.washingtonpost.com/news/acts-of-faith/wp/2017/04/23/pope-francis-called-refugee-centers-concentration-camps-a-jewish-group-says-theres-no-comparison/?utm_term=.c3 bfbb640 b07.

72. Alistair Ager, ed., *Refugees: Perspectives on the Experience of Forced Migration* (New York: Cassell, 1999), 10.

73. Agier, *Managing the Undesirables*, 29.

74. Paik, "Carceral Quarantine," 167. Amy Kaplan, "Where Is Guantánamo?," *American Quarterly* 57, no. 3 (2005).

75. Khalili, *Time in the Shadows*, 77.

76. Vinay Lal, "The Concentration Camp and Development: The Pasts and Future of Genocide," *Patterns of Prejudice* 39, no. 2 (2005).

WORKS CITED

ARCHIVES

Andra Pradesh Archives, Hyderabad

Armenian General Benevolent Union (AGBU) Nabur Library, Paris

Bodleian Library, Oxford
  Milner Papers

British Library, London
  European Manuscripts (MSS EUR)
  India Office Records (IOR)
  Correspondence of Sir James Caird
  Temple Papers
  Curzon Papers

British Library of Political and Economic Science, London School of Economics, London
  Streatfeild/Deane Papers
  Fawcett Papers

International Committee of the Red Cross (ICRC) Archives, Geneva

Kent History and Library Center, Maidstone

League of Nations Archives (UNOG), Geneva

Maharashtra State Archives (MSA), Mumbai
  Revenue Department (Famine)

General Department (Plague)

Famine Department

Mary Evans Picture Library, London

National Archives of India (NAI), Delhi

Home Department

Home Department (Judicial)

Home Department (Public)

Home Department (Medical)

Home Department (Sanitary)

Legislative Department

National Archives of South Africa (NASA) Western Cape Depot (KAB) Cape Town

Colonial Office Files (CO)

Medical Officer of Health (MOH)

Public Works Department (PWD)

National Archives of South Africa (NASA) Orange Free State Depot (VAB) Bloemfontein

Chief Superintendent of Refugee Camps, Orange River Colony (SRC)

Colonial Secretary of the Orange River Colony (CO)

Department of Relief Works (DRW)

National Archives of South Africa (NASA) Transvaal Depot (TAB) Pretoria

Colonial Secretary, Transvaal (CS)

Director of Burgher Camps (DBC)

Secretary of the Governor of the Transvaal and Orange Free State Colonies (GOV)

High Commissioner for South Africa (HC)

Legal Department (LD)

Military Governor, Pretoria (MGP)

Provost-Marshal's Office, Pretoria (PMO)

Secretary for Native Affairs (SNA)

Advisor of Native Affairs (NAB)

Staff Officer, Prisoners of War, Cape Town (SOPOW)

Transvaal Agricultural Department (TAD)

National Archives of the United Kingdom (NAUK)

Colonial Office (CO)

War Office (WO)

Kitchener Papers

Middleton Papers

Royal Geographic Society Picture Library, London

Salvation Army Archives, London

Society of Friends Archives, London

Suffolk Record Office, Ipswich

University of Birmingham, Special Collections, Birmingham

    Chamberlain Papers

War Museum of the Boer Republics, Bloemfontein

Wellcome Library, London

PERIODICALS

Anglo-Saxon Review: A Quarterly Miscellany

L'Assiette au beurre

British Medical Journal

Cape Argus

Cape Times

The Church Weekly

The Economist

Fortnightly Review

The Friend

Friends' Quarterly Examiner

The Graphic

The Guardian

The Illustrated London News

Journal of the Royal United Services Institute

The London

London Daily News

Mahratta

Morning Post

New Age Magazine

New York Herald

The New Yorker

New York Times

Otago Witness

Review of reviews

South African News

St. James Gazette

The Times

The Times of India

The Washington Post

PARLIAMENTARY PAPERS

Cd. 139. *Minutes of Evidence Taken by the Indian Plague Commission with Appendices.* Vol. I. London: Her Majesty's Stationary Office, 1900.

Cd. 205. *Papers Regarding the Famine and the Relief Operations in India During 1899– 1900. Vol. I British Districts.* London: Her Majesty's Stationary Office, 1900.

Cd. 810. *Report of the Indian Plague Commission.* London: Her Majesty's Stationary Office, 1901.

Cd. 819. *Reports, &c., on the Working of the Refugee Camps in the Transvaal, Orange River Colony, Cape Colony, and Natal, November 1901.* London: His Majesty's Stationary Office, 1901.

Cd. 853. *Further Papers Relating to the Working of the Refugee Camps in the Transvaal, Orange River Colony, and Natal.* London: Her Majesty's Stationary Office, 1901.

Cd. 876. *Report of the Indian Famine Commission.* London: Her Majesty's Stationary Office, 1901.

Cd. 893. *Report on the Concentration Camps in South Africa by the Committee of Ladies Appointed by the Secretary of State for War.* London: His Majesty's Stationary Office 1902.

Cd. 902. *Further Papers Relating to the Working of the Refugee Camps in South Africa.* London: His Majesty's Stationary Office, 1902.

Cd. 934. *Further Papers Relating to the Working of the Refugee Camps.* London: His Majesty's Stationary Office, 1902.

Cd. 936. *Further Papers Relating to the Working of the Refugee Camps in South Africa.* London: His Majesty's Stationary Office, 1902.

Cd. 1179. *Papers Regarding the Famine and the Relief Operations in India during 1900– 1902.* London: His Majesty's Stationary Office, 1902.

C. 2591. *Report of the Indian Famine Commission, Part I: Famine Relief.* London: Her Majesty's Stationary Office, 1880.

C. 3086-I. *Report of the Indian Famine Commission. Appendix I. Miscellaneous Papers Bearing upon the Condition of the Country and People of India.* London: Her Majesty's Stationary Office, 1882.

C. 3086-II. *Report of the Indian Famine Commission. Appendix II. Proceedings of the Commission, and Selected Evidence.* London: Her Majesty's Stationary Office, 1882.

C. 3086-IV. *Report of the Indian Famine Commission. Appendix IV. Replies to Inquiries of Commission.* London: Her Majesty's Stationary Office, 1881.

C. 3086-V. *Report of the Indian Famine Commission. Appendix V. Irrigation as a Protection against Famine.* London: Her Majesty's Stationary Office, 1881.

C. 8812. *Narrative of the Famine in India in 1896–7 by T. W. Holderness.* London: Her Majesty's Stationary Office, 1897.

C. 8388. *Papers Regarding the Famine and the Relief Operations in India During the Year 1896: with a Copy of the Famine Code for the North-Western Provinces and Oudh.* London: Her Majesty's Stationary Office, 1897.

Cd. 9178. *Report of the Indian Famine Commission.* London: Her Majesty's Stationary Office, 1898.

Great Britain. *Hansard's Parliamentary Debates.* London: Hansard.

GOVERNMENT REPORTS

Aiyappan, A. *Report on the Socio-Economic Conditions of the Aboriginal Tribes of the Province of Madras.* Madras: Government Press, 1948.

Famine Relief Code, Bombay Presidency, 1896. Bombay: Government Central Press, 1896.

Gatacre, W. F. *Report on the Bubonic Plague in Bombay, by Brigadier-General W. F. Gatacre.* Bombay: Printed at the 'Times of India' Steam Press, 1897.

Gunthorpe, E. J. *Notes on Criminal Tribes Residing in or Frequenting the Bombay Presidency, Berar and the Central Provinces.* Bombay: 'Times of India' Steam Press, 1882.

Report on the Arrangements Made in India for the Accommodation etc. of Boer Prisoners of War. Simla: Government Central Printers Office, 1904.

Report of the Bombay Plague Committee, Appointed by Government Resolution on the Plague in Bombay, for the Period Extending from the 1st July 1897 to the 30th April 1898, etc. Bombay: 'Times of India' Steam Press, 1898.

Report on the Famine in the Bombay Presidency 1896–7. Bombay: Government Central Press, 1898.

Report on the Famine in the Bombay Presidency, 1899–1902. Bombay: Government Central Press, 1903.

Report on the Famine in the Central Provinces in 1899–1900, vols. I, II, III. Nagpur: Secretariat Press, 1901.

Report on the Famine in the Punjab in 1896–7. Lahore: Punjab Government Press, 1898.

Report of the Municipal Commissioner on the Plague in Bombay for the Year Ending 31st May 1899. Bombay: 'Times of India' Steam Press, 1899.

Report of the Municipal Commissioner on the Plague in Bombay for the Year Ending 31ˢᵗ May 1900. Bombay: 'Times of India' Steam Press, 1900.

Report of the Municipal Commissioner on the Plague in Bombay for the Year Ending 31ˢᵗ May 1901. Bombay: 'Times of India' Steam Press, 1901.

Resolution on the Administration of Famine Relief in the North-Western Provinces and Oudh during 1896 and 1897. Allahabad: North-Western Provinces and Oudh Government Press, 1897.

Sketch of the Medical History of the Native Army of Bombay for the Year 1876. Bombay: Government Central Press, 1877.

Slocum. S., and C. Reichmann. *Reports on Military Operations in South Africa and China.* Washington, DC: Government Printing Office, 1901.

PUBLISHED PRIMARY SOURCES

Amery, L. S. *Times History of the War in South Africa.* London: Searle & Rivington, 1900–1909.

Armstrong, Henrietta. *Camp Diary of Henrietta E. C. Armstrong: Experiences of a Boer Nurse in the Irene Concentration Camp.* Pretoria: Human Sciences Research Council, 1980.

Austin, H. H. *The Baqubah Refugee Camp: An Account of Work on Behalf of the Persecuted Assyrian Christians.* London: Faith Press, 1920.

Booth, William. *In Darkest England and the Way Out.* London: Salvation Army, 1890.

Booth-Tucker, Frederick. *Criminocurology; or, The Indian Crim and What to Do With Him.* Simla: Liddell's Printing Works, 1916.

Buchan, John. *The African Colony, Studies in the Reconstruction.* Edinburgh: W. Blackwood and Sons, 1903.

Buchan, John. *Greenmantle.* London: Hodder & Sloughton, 1916.

Callwell, Charles E. *Small Wars: Their Principles and Practice,* 3rd ed. London: Harrison and Sons, 1906.

Chester, James. "The Great Lesson of the Boer War." *Journal of the Military Service Institution of the United States* 32 (1903): 1–7.

Churchill, Winston. *The Boer War: London to Ladysmith via Pretoria.* London: Longmans, Green, 1900.

Couper, George E. B. *Sir George Couper and the Famine in the North-West Provinces.* Calcutta: Statesman Office, 1898.

Creswicke, Louis. *South Africa and the Transvaal War, vol. VI, From the occupation of Pretoria to Mr. Kruger's departure from South Africa, with a summarised account of the guerilla war to March 1901.* Edinburgh: T. C. & E. C. Jack, 1901.

Curzon, George Nathaniel. "Plague Hospital." In *Lord Curzon through His Writings on Travels and Adventures*. New Delhi: Life Span Publishers and Distributors, 2009.

Dickens, Charles. *Oliver Twist, or the Parish Boy's Progress*. London: Richard Bentley, 1838.

Digby, William. *The Famine Campaign in Southern India: Madras and Bombay Presidencies and Province of Mysore, 1876–1878*, volumes I and II. London: Longmans, Green, 1878.

Dutt, Romesh Chunder. *Economic History of British India*, vol. II. London: Keagan Paul, 1904.

Fawcett, Millicent. *What I Remember*. New York: G. P. Putnam's Sons, 1925.

Fuller, J. F. C. *The Last of the Gentlemen's Wars; A Subaltern's Journal of the War in South Africa, 1899–1902*. London: Faber and Faber, 1937.

Gandhi, Mohandas, "The Plague Panic in South Africa." *The Times of India*, April 1899.

Gunter, E. "A German View of British Tactics in the Boer War, precis from the *Jahrbücher für die Deutsche Armee und Marine*." *Journal of the Royal United Services Institute* 46, no. 292 (1902): 801–6.

Hartmann, G. *Deutsch-Südwestafrika im Zusammenhang mit Südafrika*. Berlin, 1899.

Henderson, Nevile. *Failure of a Mission: Berlin 1937–1939*. New York: G. P. Putnam's Sons, 1940.

Hervey, Charles. *Statistics of the Crime of Dacoitie in British Territory and Dependent Native States for the Three Years 1867, 1868 and 1869*. Calcutta: Office of the Superintendent of Government Printing, 1873.

Higham, T., *Report on the Management of Famine Relief Works and Notes on Famine Relief Works in Madras, Bombay, Bengal, North-Western Provinces and Oudh, Punjab, and the Central Provinces*. Simla: Government Central Printing Office, 1897.

Hill, Claude. *India—Stepmother*. London: William Blackwood, 1929.

Hobhouse, Emily. *The Brunt of War and Where It Fell*. London: Methuen, 1902.

Hobhouse, Emily. *Emily Hobhouse: Boer War Letters*. Edited by Rykie Van Reenen. Cape Town: Human and Rousseau, 1920.

Hobhouse, Emily. *Report to the Committee of the South African Distress Fund of a Visit to the Camps of Women and Children in the Cape and Orange River Colonies*. London: Friars Printing Association, 1901.

Hobhouse, Emily. *War Without Glamour, or, Women's War Experiences Written by Themselves, 1899–1902*. Bloemfontein: Nasionale Pers Beperk, 1924.

Hobhouse Balme, Jennifer. *To Love One's Enemies: The Work and Life of Emily Hobhouse Compiled from Letters and Writings, Newspaper Cuttings and Official Documents.* Cobble Hill, BC: Hobhouse Trust, 1994.

Hobson, J. A. *Imperialism: A Study.* New York: J. Pott, 1902.

Holden, R. M. "The Blockhouse System in South Africa." *Journal of the Royal United Service Institution* 46, no. 290 (1902): 479–89.

Holderness, T. W. *Peoples & Problems of India.* New York: N. Holt, 1912.

Hopford, Wim. *Twice Interned: Transvaal 1901–02, Germany 1914–18.* London: John Murray, 1919.

Hosek, W. M. "The Future of South Africa." *Fortnightly Review,* vol. 67, April 1900: 400.

James, Lionel. *On the Heels of de Wet, by The Intelligence Officer.* London: William Blackwood and Sons, 1902.

Jounet, Albert. *Les Camps de Concentration, Poem vendu de la souscription pour les Boers.* Saint-Raphaël: Chailan, 1902.

Kestell, J. D. *Through Shot and Flame.* Johannesburg: African Book Society, 1976.

Kingsley, Charles. *The Waterbabies, A Fairy Tale for a Land Baby.* London: Macmillan, 1863.

Locke, John. *Two Treatises on Government.* London: Printed for Awnsham Churchill, 1690.

Low, J. Spencer. "Some Preventive Measures Adopted in the Presidency of Madras During the Late Epidemic of Plague in India." *Transactions of the Epidemiological Society of London* 19 (1899–1900): 59–86.

Luckhoff, A. D. *Woman's Endurance.* Pretoria: Printed by SA News, 1904.

Luscombe, Edward Thornhill. *Practical Observations on the Means of Preserving the Health of Soldiers in Camp.* Edinburgh: Archibald Constable, 1821.

Methuen, Algernon. *Peace or War in South Africa.* London: Methuen, 1902.

Milner, Alfred. *The Milner Papers, Vol. I, South Africa 1897–1899.* Edited by Cecil Headlam. London: Cassell & Company, 1931.

Nash, Vaughan. *The Great Famine and Its Causes.* London: Longmans, Green, 1900.

Neethling, Elizabeth. *Should We Forget?* Cape Town: HAUM, 1903.

Phillipps, Lisle March. *With Rimington.* London: Edward Arnold, 1901.

Prakash, Om. *Factual Survey Relating to the Employment of Camp Dwellers in the Punjab Relief Camps.* Ludhiana, India: Board of Economic Inquiry, 1950.

Raal, Sarah. *The Lady Who Fought: A Young Woman's Account of the Anglo-Boer War.* Plumstead, South Africa: Stormberg, 2000.

Ralph, Julian. *An American with Lord Roberts.* New York: F. A. Stokes, 1901.

Richardson, Lawrence. *Lawrence Richardson Selected Correspondence*. Edited by Arthur Davey. Cape Town: Van Riebeeck Society, 1977.

Schreiner, Olive. *The Story of an African Farm*. London: Chapman and Hall, 1883.

Schreiner, Olive. "Stray Thoughts on South Africa, by a Returned South African: The Wanderings of the Boer." *Fortnightly Review* 60, no. 356 (1896): 225–56.

Scott, J. E. *In Famine Land: Observations and Experiences in India During the Great Drought of 1899–1900*. London: Harper & Brothers, 1904.

Simpson, William. *Treatise on Plague Dealing with the Historical, Epidemiological, Clinical, Therapeutic and Preventive Aspects of the Disease*. Cambridge: University of Cambridge Press, 1905.

Sketches of the Camp at Aldershot, also Farnham, Waverley Abbey, Moore Park etc. Farnham, UK: Andrews & Lucy, 1858.

Spiesser, Frit. *Das Konzentrationslager*. Munich: F. Eher, 1940.

Stead, W. T. "Baby-Killing in Africa." *Review of Reviews*, October 1901: 396.

Stead, W. T. "Our Death Camps in South Africa." *Review of Reviews*, vol. 25, January 1902: 8.

Steel, Flora A. *On the Face of the Waters: A Tale of the Mutiny*. New York: Macmillan, 1897.

Steinhoff, Hans, dir. *Ohm Krüger*, Germany, 1941.

Sternberg, Adalbert and G. F. R. Henderson. *My Experiences of the Boer War*. London: Longmans, Green, 1901.

Suffolk County Handbook and Official Directory for 1917. London, 1917.

Temple, Richard. *India in 1880*. London: J. Murray, 1881.

Temple, Richard. *Men and Events of My Time in India*. London: J. Murray, 1882.

Thomson, Samuel J. *The Real Indian People*. London: William Blackwood and Sons, 1914.

Thomson, Samuel J. *Sanitary Principles, More Especially as Applied to India*. Calcutta: Brown, 1883.

Thomson, Samuel J. *The Silent India, Being Tales and Sketches of the Masses*. London: William Blackwood and Sons, 1913.

Thomson, Samuel J. *The Transvaal Burgher Camps, South Africa*. Allahabad: Pioneer Press, 1904.

Thormeyer, F., Emmanuel Schoch, and Fréd Blanchod, *Rapports de MM. F. Thormeyer, Em. Schoch et le Dr F. Blanchod sur leurs visites aux camps de prisonniers de guerre ottomans et d'internés autrichiens et allemands aux Indes et en Birmanie, février, mars et avril 1917*. Geneva: Georg, 1917.

"To Check the Survival of the Unfit: A New Scheme by the Rev. Osborn Jay, a Militant Bethnal Green Parson, for Sending the Submerged to a Penal Settlement." *The London*, March 12, 1896.

Veber, Jean, "Les camps de reconcentration au Transvaal," *L'Assiette au Buerre*, no. 26, September 28, 1901.

Veber, Jean, *L'Assiette au beurre: Les camps de reconcentration au Transvaal*. Bad Saarow: Verlag für militärgeschichte und Deutsches Schrifttum, 1941.

Von der Goltz, Colmar. "What Can We Learn from the Boer War, translated from the *Deutsche Revue*." *Journal of the Royal United Services Institute* 46, no. 298 (1902): 1534–39.

Weber, Max. *Sociology of Religion*, edited by Talcott Parsons. Boston: Beacon Press, 1922.

Wordsworth, William, and Samuel Taylor Coleridge. *Lyrical Ballads with a Few Other Poems*. Bristol: Printed by Biggs and Cottle for T. N. Longman, Paternoster-Row, London, 1798.

SECONDARY SOURCES

Agamben, Giorgio. *Homo Sacer: Sovereign Power and Bare Life*. Stanford, CA: Stanford University Press, 1998.

Agamben, Giorgio. *States of Exception*. Chicago: University of Chicago Press, 2005.

Ager, Alistair, ed. *Refugees: Perspectives on the Experience of Forced Migration*. New York: Cassell, 1999.

Agier, Michel. *Managing the Undesirables: Refugee Camps and Humanitarian Government*. Cambridge: Polity Press, 2011.

Alamgir, Mohiuddin. *Famine in South Asia: Political Economy of Mass Starvation*. Cambridge, MA: Oelgeschlager, Gunn & Hain, 1980.

Ambirajan, S. "Malthusian Population Theory and Indian Famine Policy in the Nineteenth Century." *Population Studies* 30 no. 1 (1976): 5–14.

Anderson, Clare. "Convicts and Coolies: Rethinking Indentured Labour in the Nineteenth Century." *Slavery and Abolition* 30 no. 1 (2009): 93–109.

Anderson, Clare. *Convicts in the India Ocean: Transportation from South Asia to Mauritius*. Basingstoke, UK: Palgrave, 2002.

Anderson, Clare. *Legible Bodies: Race, Criminality and Colonialism in South Asia*. Oxford: Berg Publishers, 2004.

Anderson, Clare. "The Politics of Convict Space: Indian Penal Settlements and the Andaman Islands." In *Isolation: Places and Practices of Exclusion*, edited by Carolyn Strange and Alison Bashford, 37–52. New York: Routledge, 2003.

Anderson, Clare, and David Arnold. "Envisioning the Colonial Prison." In *Cultures of Confinement: A History of the Prison in Africa, Asia and Latin America*, edited by Frank Dikotter and Ian Brown, 185–220. Ithaca, NY: Cornell University Press, 2007.

Anderson, David. *Histories of the Hanged: The Dirty War in Kenya and the End of Empire.* New York: W. W. Norton, 2005.

Appelbaum, Stanley. *French Satirical Drawings from "L'Assiette au Buerre:" Selection, Translations, and Text.* New York: Dover, 1978.

Arendt, Hannah. *Origins of Totalitarianism.* New York: Harcourt, 1968.

Arendt, Hannah. "We Refugees." In *Altogether Elsewhere: Writers on Exile* edited by Marc Robinson, 110–19. Winchester, MA: Faber and Faber, 1994.

Arnold, David. *Colonizing the Body: State Medicine and Epidemic Disease in Nineteenth-Century India.* Berkeley: University of California Press, 1993.

Arnold, David. "The 'Discovery' of Malnutrition and Diet in Colonial India." *Indian Economic and Social History Review* 31 (1994): 1–26.

Arnold, David. *Famine: Social Crisis and Historical Change.* Oxford: B. Blackwell, 1988.

Arnold, David. *Science, Technology and Medicine in Colonial India.* New York: Cambridge University Press, 2000.

Arnold, David. "Touching the Body: Perspectives on the Indian Plague, 1896–1900." *Subaltern Studies* 5 (1987): 55–90.

Arnold, David. "Vagrant India: Famine, Poverty and Welfare Under Colonial Rule." In *Cast Out: Vagrancy and Homelessness in Global and Historical Perspective*, edited by A. L. Beier and Paul Robert Ocobock, 117–39. Athens: Ohio University Press, 2008.

Arthur, George. *Life of Lord Kitchener*, vol. II. New York: Cosimo, 2007.

Attwood, Bain. "Space and Time at Ramahyuck, Victoria, 1863–85." In *Settlement: A History of Australian Indigenous Housing*, edited by Peter Reed, 41–54. Canberra: Aboriginal Studies Press, 2000.

Baines, Gary. "The Origins of Urban Segregation: Local Government and the Residence of Africans in Port Elizabeth, c. 1835–1865." *South African Historical Journal* 22, no. 1 (1990): 61–81.

Bannerman, Gordon. *Merchants and the Military in Eighteenth-Century Britain. British Army Contracts and Domestic Supply, 1739–1763.* London: Pickering & Chatto, 2008,

Barnes, Steven. *Death and Redemption: The Gulag and the Shaping of Soviet Society.* Princeton, NJ: Princeton University Press, 2011.

Bashford, Alison, and Carolyn Strange. "Asylum-Seekers and National Histories of Detention." *Australian Journal of Politics and History* 48, no. 4 (2002): 509–27.

Bauman, Zygmunt. *Modernity and the Holocaust.* Ithaca, NY: Cornell University Press, 1989.

Bayly, C. A. "Knowing the Country: Empire and Information in India." *Modern Asian Studies* 27 no. 1 (1993): 3–43.

Beattie, James. "Recent Themes in the Environmental History of the British Empire." *History Compass* 10, no. 2 (2012): 129–39.

Beggar, Abderrahman. "The *camps de regroupement* during the War of Algeria." In *The Camp: Narratives of Internment and Exclusion*, edited by Colman Hogan and Marta Marin-Domine, 154–71. Newcastle, UK: Cambridge Scholars, 2007.

Belich, James. *Replenishing the Earth: The Settler Revolution and the Rise of the Anglo World*. Oxford: Oxford University Press, 2009.

Bell, David. *The First Total War: Napoleon's Europe and the Birth of Warfare as We Know It*. New York: Houghton Mifflin, 2007.

Benjamin, N., and B. B. Mohanty. "Imperial Solution of a Colonial Problem: Bhils of Khandesh up to c. 1850." *Modern Asian Studies* 41, no. 2 (2007): 343–67.

Bernault, Florence, and Janet L. Roitman, eds. *A History of Prisons and Confinement in Africa*. Portsmouth, NH: Heinemann, 2003.

Bhatia, B. M. *Famines in India: A Study in Some Aspects of the Economic History of India (1860–1945)*. London: Asia Publishing House, 1963.

Boje, John. *An Imperfect Occupation: Enduring the South African War*. Springfield: University of Illinois Press, 2015.

Bose, Sugata. *A Hundred Horizons: The Indian Ocean in the Age of Global Empire*. Cambridge, MA: Harvard University Press, 2009.

Brennan, Lance. "The Development of the Indian Famine Codes: Personalities, Politics and Policies." In *Famine as a Geographical Phenomenon*, edited by Bruce Currey and Graeme Hugo, 91–111. Boston: D. Reidel, 1984.

Brown, John. "Charles Booth and Labour Colonies, 1889–1905." *Economic History Review* 30, no. 2 (1977): 349–60.

Bucholz, Robert, and Joseph Ward. *London: A Social and Cultural History*. Cambridge: Cambridge University Press, 2012.

Burton, Antoinette. *The Trouble with Empire: Challenges to Modern British Imperialism*. Oxford: University of Oxford Press, 2015.

Butler, A. G. *Official History of the Australian Army Medical Services in the War of 1914–18: Volume II, The Western Front*. Melbourne: Australian War Memorial, 1940.

Campbell, Charles. *The Intolerable Hulks: British Shipboard Confinement, 1776–1857*. Tucson, AZ: Fenestra Books, 2001.

Caplan, Jane. "Political Detention and the Origin of the Concentration Camps in Nazi Germany, 1933–1935/6." In *Nazism, War and Genocide. Essays in Honour of Jeremy Noakes*, edited by N. Gregor, 22–41. Exeter, UK: University of Exeter Press, 2005.

Caplan, Jane, and Nicholas Waschmann, eds. *Concentration Camps in Nazi Germany: The New Histories*. London: Routledge, 2010.

Casey, Edward S. *The Fate of Place: A Philosophical History*. Berkeley: University of California Press, 1997.

Catanach, I. J. "Plague and the Tension of Empire: India, 1896–1918." In *Imperial Medicine and Indigenous Societies*, edited by David Arnold, 149–71. Manchester: Manchester University Press, 1988.

Catanach, I. J. "Poona Politicians and the Plague." *South Asia* 7, no. 2 (1984): 1–18.

Chandramohan, Balasubramanyam. "'Hamlet with the Prince of Denmark Left Out'?: The South African War, Empire and India." In *The South African War Reappraised*, edited by Donal Lowry, 150–68. Manchester: Manchester University Press, 2000.

Chandavarkar, Rajnarayan. "Plague Panic and Epidemic Politics in India, 1896–1914." In *Epidemics and Ideas: Essays on the Historical Perception of Pestilence*, edited by Terence Ranger and Paul Slack, 203–40. New York: Cambridge University Press, 1992.

Chatterjee, Partha. *The Black Hole of Empire: History of a Global Practice of Power*. Princeton, NJ: Princeton University Press, 2012.

Chatterjee, Partha. *The Nation and Its Fragments: Colonial and Postcolonial Histories*. Princeton, NJ: Princeton University Press, 1993.

Chaudhary, Zahid. *Afterimage of Empire: Photography in Nineteenth-Century India*. Minneapolis: University of Minnesota Press, 2012.

Chopra, Preeti. *A Joint Enterprise: Indian Elites and the Making of British Bombay*. Minneapolis: University of Minnesota Press, 2011.

Clark, Anna. "Humanitarianism, Human Rights and Biopolitics in the British Empire, 1890–1902." *Britain and the World* 9, no. 1 (2016): 96–115.

Coetzer, Nicholas. *Building Apartheid: On Architecture and Order in Imperial Cape Town*. Burlington, VT: Ashgate, 2013.

Coetzer, Owen. *Fire in the Sky: The Destruction of the Orange Free State*. Weltevreden Park, South Africa: Covos-Day Books, 2000.

Coghe, Samuël. "Population Politics in the Tropics. Demography, Health and Colonial Rule in Portuguese Angola, 1890s–1940s." PhD diss., European University Institute, 2014.

Coker, Richard. "Civil Liberties and the Public Good: Detention of Tuberculosis Patients and the Public Health Act 1984." *Medical History* 45 (2001): 341–58.

Cole, Howard Norman. *The Story of Aldershot: A History and Guide to Town and Camp*. Aldershot, UK: Gale & Polden, 1951.

Cosgrove, Richard A. "The Boer War and the Modernization of British Martial Law." *Military Affairs* 44, no. 3 (October 1980): 124–27.

Crangle, John V. and Joseph O. Baylen. "Emily Hobhouse's Peace Mission, 1916." *Journal of Contemporary History* 14 (1979): 731–44.

Crofts, Fay. *History of Hollymoor Hospital*. Studley, UK: Brewin Books, 1998.

Curtin, Philip. *Disease and Empire: The Health of European Troops in the Conquest of Africa*. New York: Cambridge University Press, 1998.

Curson, Peter, and Kevin McCracken. *Plague in Sydney: The Anatomy of an Epidemic*. Sydney: New South Wales University Press, 1980.

Daniels, Roger, "Words Do Matter: A Note on Inappropriate Terminology and the Incarceration of the Japanese Americans." In *Nikkei in the Pacific Northwest: Japanese Americans and Japanese Canadians in the Twentieth Century*, edited by Louis Fiset and Gail Nomura, 183–207. Seattle: University of Washington Press, 2005.

Datta, Pradip Kumar. "The Interlocking Worlds of the Anglo-Boer War in South Africa/India." *South African Historical Journal* 57 (2007): 35–59.

Davies, Peter. "Space and Structure at an Australian Timber Camp." *Historical Archaeology* 39 no. 4 (2005): 59–72.

Davis, Mike. *Late Victorian Holocausts: El Nino Famine and the Making of the Third World*. New York: Verso, 2002.

Davis, Mike. *Planet of Slums*. New York: Verso, 2006.

Davis, Robert S. "Escape from Andersonville: A Study in Isolation and Imprisonment." *Journal of Military History* 67 (2003): 1065–82.

Deacon, Harriet. "Patterns of Exclusion on Robben Island, 1654–1992." In *Isolation: Places and Practices of Exclusion*, edited by Carolyn Strange and Alison Bashford, 152–72. New York: Routledge, 2003.

Dedering, Tilman. "Compounds, Camps, Colonialism." *Journal of Namibian Studies: History, Politics, Culture* 12 (2012): 29–46.

Deleuze, Gilles, and Félix Guattari. *A Thousand Plateaus: Capitalism and Schizophrenia*. Minneapolis: University of Minnesota Press, 1987.

Denness, Zoë. "'A Question Which Affects Our Prestige as a Nation': The History of British Civilian Internment, 1899–1945." PhD diss., University of Birmingham, 2012.

Denness, Zoë. "Women and Warfare at the Start of the Twentieth Century: The Racialization of the 'Enemy' during the South African War (1899–1902)." *Patterns of Prejudice* 46, nos. 3–4 (2012): 255–76.

de Waal, Alexander. *Famine that Kills: Darfur, Sudan, 1984–5*. Oxford: Clarendon, 1989.

Diken, Bulent, and Carsten Bagge Laustsen. *The Culture of Exception: Sociology Facing the Camp*. London: Routledge, 2005.

Dikotter, Frank, and Ian Brown, eds. *Cultures of Confinement: A History of the Prison in Africa, Asia and Latin America*. Ithaca, NY: Cornell University Press, 2007.

Dirks, Nicholas. *Castes of Mind: Colonialism and the Making of Modern India*. Princeton, NJ: Princeton University Press, 2001.

Dirks, Nicholas. "The Crimes of Colonialism: Anthropology and the Textualization of India." In *Colonial Subjects: Essays on the Practical History of Anthropology*, edited by Peter Pels and Oscar Salemink, 153–79. Ann Arbor: University of Michigan Press, 2000.

Dirks, Nicholas. *Scandal of Empire: India and the Creation of Imperial Britain*. Cambridge, MA: Belknap Press of Harvard University Press, 2008.

Donaldson, Kenneth Mackay. *South African Who's Who 1911*. London: Allen, 1911.

Donnelly, James S. Jr. "The Administration of Relief, 1846–7." In *A New History of Ireland, vol. 5, Ireland Under the Union I, 1801–1870*, edited by W. E. Vaughan, 295–306. Oxford: Clarendon, 1989.

Dorminy, G. "Pietermaritzburg's Imperial Postscript: Fort Napier from 1910 to 1925." *Natalia* 6, no. 4 (1989): 30–42.

Douglas, Mary. *Purity and Danger: An Analysis of the Concepts of Pollution and Taboo*. London: Routledge, 1966.

Dove, Richard, "'A Matter Which Touches the Good Name of This Country.'" In *"Totally Un-English": Britain's Internment of "Enemy Aliens" in Two World Wars*, edited by Richard Dove, 11–16. New York: Rodopi, 2005.

Dubow, Saul. *A Commonwealth of Knowledge: Science, Sensibility, and White South Africa, 1820–2000*. New York: Oxford University Press, 2006.

Echenberg, Myron. *Plague Ports: The Global Urban Impact of Bubonic Plague, 1894–1901*. New York: New York University Press, 2010.

Elkins, Caroline. *Imperial Reckoning: The Untold Story of Britain's Gulag in Kenya*. New York: Henry Holt, 2005.

Elkins, Stanley. *Slavery: A Problem in American Institutional and Intellectual Life*. Chicago: University of Chicago Press, 1959.

Elliot, John H. *Empires of the Atlantic World: Britain and Spain in America, 1492–1830*. New Haven, CT: Yale University Press, 2007.

Epstein Nord, Deborah. "The Social Explorer as Anthropologist: Victorian Travelers among the Urban Poor." In *Visions of the Modern City: Essays in History, Art and Literature*, edited by William Sharpe and Leonard Wallock, 122–34. Baltimore: Johns Hopkins University Press, 1987.

Erichsen, Casper, and David Olusoga. *The Kaiser's Holocaust: Germany's Forgotten Genocide and the Colonial Roots of Nazism*. London: Faber and Faber, 2011.

Fanon, Frantz. *The Wretched of the Earth*. New York: Grove Press, 1963.

Faust, Drew Gilpin. *The Republic of Suffering: Death and the American Civil War*. New York: Alfred A. Knopf, 2008.

Ferguson, Niall. *Empire: The Rise and Demise of the British World Order and the Lessons for Global Power*. New York: Basic Books, 2004.

Fetter, Bruce, and Stowell Kessler. "Scars from a Childhood Disease: Measles in the Concentration Camps during the Boer War." *Social Science History* 20, no. 4 (1996): 593–611.

Field, John. "Able Bodies: Work Camps and the Training of the Unemployed in Britain before 1939." In *The Significance of the Historical Perspective in Adult Education Research*. Cambridge: University of Cambridge, Institute of Continuing Education, 2009.

Fisher, John. *That Miss Hobhouse*. London: Secker & Warburg, 1971.

Forth, Aidan. "Britain's Archipelago of Camps: Labor and Detention in a Liberal Empire, 1871–1903." *Kritika: Explorations in Russian and Eurasian History* 16 no. 3 (2015): 651–680.

Forth, Aidan, and Jonas Kreienbaum. "A Shared Malady: Concentration Camps in the British, Spanish, American and German Empires." *Journal of Modern European History* 14, no. 2 (2016): 245–67.

Foucault, Michel. *The Birth of Biopolitics: Lectures at the College de France, 1978–1979*. New York: Palgrave Macmillan, 2004.

Foucault, Michel. *Discipline and Punish: The Birth of the Prison*. New York: Pantheon Books, 1977.

Foucault, Michel. "Governmentality." In *The Foucault Effect: Studies in Governmentality*, edited by Graham Burchell, Colin Gordon, and Peter Miller, 87–104. Chicago: University of Chicago Press, 1991.

Foucault, Michel. *History of Sexuality*. New York: Pantheon Books, 1978.

Foucault, Michel. *The Order of Things: An Archaeology of the Human Science*. New York: Pantheon Books, 1971.

Freitag, Sandria B. "Crime in the Social Order of Colonial North India." *Modern Asian Studies* 25, no. 2 (1991): 227–61.

Ganachari, Aravind. "'White Man's Embarrassment': European Vagrancy in 19th Century Bombay." *Economic and Political Weekly* 37, no. 25 (2002): 2477–86.

Gardner, Philip. "'There and Not Seen': E. B. Sargant and Educational Reform, 1884–1905." *History of Education* 33, no. 6 (2004): 609–35.

Gedenkstätte, KZ. *Zwischenräume: displaced persons, Internierte und Flüchtlinge in ehemaligen Konzentrationslagern, 1945–53*. Bremen: Ed. Temmen, 2010.

Gerstrich, Andreas. "Konzentrationslager: Voraussetzungen und Vorläufer vor der Moderne." In *Welt der Lager zur "Erfolgsgeschichte" einer Institution*, edited by Bettina Greiner and Alan Kramer, 43–61. Hamburg: Hamburger Edition, 2013.

Gerwarth, Robert, and Stephen Malinowski. "Hannah Arendt's Ghosts: Reflections on the Disputable Path from Windhoek to Auschwitz." *Central European History* 42, no. 2 (2009): 279–300.

Giliomee, Hermann. *Afrikaners: Biography of a People*. Charlottesville: University of Virginia Press, 2010.

Gilmour, David. "Curzon, George Nathaniel, Marquess Curzon of Kedleston (1859–1925)." In *Oxford Dictionary of National Biography*, online ed., edited by David Cannadine, January 2011.

Godby, Michael. "Confronting Horror: Emily Hobhouse and the Concentration Camp Photographs of the South African War." *Kronos: 'n Geleentheidspublikasie Van Die Wes-Kaaplandse Instituut Vir Historiese Navorsing* no. 32 (2006): 34–48.

Goeschel, Christian, and Nikolaus Wachsmann, "Before Auschwitz: The Formation of the Nazi Concentration Camps, 1933–39." *Journal of Contemporary History* 45, no. 3 (2010): 515–34.

Goodman, Martin. *Suffer and Survive: Gas Attacks, Miners' Canaries, Spacesuits and the Bends: The Extreme Life of Dr. J. S. Haldane* New York: Simon & Schuster, 2007.

Gray, Peter. "Famine and Land in Ireland and India, 1845–1880: James Caird and the Political Economy of Hunger." *Historical Journal* 49, no. 1 (2006): 193–215.

Grundlingh, A. M. *Dynamics of Treason: Boer Collaboration in the South African War of 1899–1902*. Pretoria: Protea Book House, 2006.

Grundlingh, Louis. "Another Side to Warfare: Caring for White Destitutes during the Anglo-Boer War (October 1899–May 1900)." *New Countree* 35, no. 45 (1999): 137–63.

Guz, Debhorah. "Population Dynamics of Famine in Nineteenth Century Punjab, 1896–7 and 1899–1900." In *India's Historical Demography: Studies in Famine, Disease and Society*, edited by Tim Dyson, 198–221. London: Curzon Press, 1989.

Hailey, Charlie. *Camps: A Guide to 21st-Century Space*. Cambridge, MA: MIT Press, 2009.

Hall-Matthews, David. "Famine Process and Famine Policy: A Case Study of Ahmednagar District, Bombay Presidency, India, 1870–84." D.Phil diss., University of Oxford, 2002.

Hall-Matthews, David. "Historical Roots of Famine Relief Paradigms: Ideas on Dependency and Free Trade in India in the 1870s." *Disasters* 20, no. 3 (1996): 216–30.

Hall-Matthews, David. "Inaccurate Conceptions: Disputed Measures of Nutritional Needs and Famine Deaths in Colonial India." *Modern Asian Studies* 42, no. 6 (2008): 1189–212.

Hamlin, Christopher. *Public Health and Social Justice in the Age of Chadwick*. New York: Cambridge University Press, 1998.

Harris, Cole. *Making Native Space: Resistance and Reserves in British Columbia*. Vancouver: University of British Columbia Press, 2002.

Harrison, Elaine. "Women Members and Witnesses on British Government Ad Hoc Committees of Inquiry 1850–1930, with Special Reference to Royal Commissions of Inquiry." PhD diss, London School of Economics and Political Science, 1998.

Harrison, Mark. *Public Health in British India: Anglo-Indian Preventive Medicine, 1859–1914*. New York: Cambridge University Press, 1994.

Hay, Douglas. *Albion's Fatal Tree: Crime and Society in Eighteenth-Century England*. New York: Pantheon Books, 1976.

Himmelfarb, Gertrude. "The Age of Philanthropy." *Wilson Quarterly* 21, no. 2 (1997): 48–55.

Hodges, Sarah. "Looting the Lock Hospital in Colonial Madras during the Famine Years of the 1870s." *Social History of Medicine* 18, no. 3 (2005): 379–98.

Hogan, Colman, and Marta Marin-Domine, eds. *The Camp: Narratives of Internment and Exclusion*. Newcastle, UK: Cambridge Scholars, 2007.

Holquist, Peter. "Violent Russia, Deadly Marxism? Russia in the Epoch of Violence, 1905–21." *Kritika: Explorations in Russian and Eurasian History* 4, no. 3 (2003): 627–52.

Hull, Isabel. *Absolute Destruction: Military Culture and the Practices of War in Imperial Germany*. Ithaca, NY: Cornell University Press, 2005.

Hyslop, Jonathan. "The Invention of the Concentration Camp: Cuba, Southern Africa and the Philippines, 1896–1907." *South African Historical Journal* 63, no. 2 (2011): 251–76.

Ignatieff, Michael. *A Just Measure of Pain: The Penitentiary in the Industrial Revolution*. New York: Pantheon Books, 1978.

Jasanoff, Maya. *Edge of Empire: Lives, Culture, and Conquest in the East 1750–1850*. New York: Random House, 2005.

Joyce, Patrick. *Rule of Freedom: Liberalism and the Modern City*. New York: Verso, 2003.

Kallaway, Peter, and Patrick Pearson. *Johannesburg: Images and Continuities, A History of Working Class Life through Pictures, 1885–1935*. Braamfontein, South Africa: Ravan Press, 1986.

Kaminski, Andre. *Konzentrationslager 1896 bis heute: Eine Analyse*. Stuttgart: W. Kohlhammer, 1982.

Kang, Chol-hwan, Pierre Rigoulot, and Yair Reiner. *Aquariums of Pyongyang: Ten Years in the North Korean Gulag*. New York: Basic Books, 2005.

Kaplan, Amy. "Where Is Guantánamo?" *American Quarterly* 57, no. 3 (2005): 831–58.

Kennedy, Liam. *Mapping the Great Irish Famine: A Survey of the Famine Decades*. Dublin: Four Courts, 1999.

Kennedy, Wm Matthew. "The Imperialism of Internment: Boer Prisoners of War in India and Civic Reconstruction in Southern Africa, 1899–1905." *Journal of Imperial and Commonwealth History* 44, no. 3 (2016): 423–47.

Kern, Stephen. *The Culture of Time and Space*. Cambridge, MA: Harvard University Press, 1983.

Kessler, Stowell. "The Black and Coloured Concentration Camps." In *Scorched Earth*, edited by Fransjohan Pretorius, 132–53. Cape Town: Human & Rousseau, 2001.

Kessler, Stowell. "The Black and Coloured Concentration Camps of the Anglo-Boer War, 1899–1902: Shifting the Paradigm from Sole Martyrdom to Mutual Suffering." *Historia* 44 no. 1 (1999): 110–47.

Kessler, Stowell. "The Black Concentration Camps of the South African War, 1899–1902." PhD diss., University of Cape Town, 2003.

Khalili, Laleh. *Time in the Shadows: Confinement in Counterinsurgencies*. Stanford, CA: Stanford University Press, 2013.

Kidambi, Prashant. "'An Infection of Locality': Plague, Pythogenesis and the Poor in Bombay, c. 1896–1905." *Urban History* 31, no. 2 (2004): 249–67.

Kiernan, Ben. "From Irish Famine to Congo Reform: Nineteenth-Century Roots of International Human Rights Law and Activism." In *Confronting Genocide*, edited by René Provost and Payam Pakhaven, 13–43. New York: Springer, 2011.

Kimber, Julie. "Poor Laws: A Historiography of Vagrancy in Australia." *History Compass* 11, no. 8 (2013): 537–50.

Kinealy, Christine. *A Death-Dealing Famine: The Great Hunger in Ireland*. Chicago: Pluto, 1997.

Klein, Ira. "Plague, Policy and Popular Unrest in British India." *Modern Asian Studies* 22, no. 4 (1988): 723–55.

Konopczynski, Wladyslaw. *Konfederacja barska*. Warsaw: Volumen, 1991.

Kotek, Joel, and Pierre Rigoulot. *Le Siècle des Camps: détention, concentration, extermination, cent ans de mal radical*. Paris: JC Lattes, 2000.

Kramer, Paul. *Blood of Government: Race, Empire, the United States, & the Philippines*. Chapel Hill: University of North Carolina Press, 2006.

Kramer, Paul. "Empires, Exceptions, and Anglo-Saxons: Race and Rule between the British and United States Empires, 1880–1910." In *The American Colonial State in the Philippines: Global Perspectives*, edited by Julian Go and Anne L. Foster, 43–91. Durham, NC: Duke University Press, 2003.

Krebs, Paula. *Gender, Race, and the Writing of Empire*. Cambridge: Cambridge University Press, 1999.

Kreienbaum, Jonas. "Guerrilla Wars and Colonial Concentration Camps: The Exceptional Case of German South-West Africa (1904–1908)." *Journal of Namibian Studies: History, Politics, Culture* 11 (2012): 85–103.

Kreienbaum, Jonas. *'Ein trauriges Fiasko': Koloniale Konzentrationslager im südlichen Afrika, 1900–1908*. Hamburg: Hamburger Edition, 2015.

Kruger, Rayne. *Good-bye Dolly Gray: The Story of the Boer War*. Philadelphia: J. B. Lippincott, 1960.

Lal, Vinay. "The Concentration Camp and Development: The Pasts and Future of Genocide." *Patterns of Prejudice* 39, no. 2 (2005): 220–43.

Lambert, David, and Alan Lester. *Colonial Lives Across the British Empire: Imperial Careering in the Long Nineteenth Century*. Cambridge: Cambridge University Press, 2006.

Lampard, Eric E. "The Urbanizing World." In *The Victorian City: Images and Realities*, edited by H. J. Dyos and Michael Wolff, 3–57. London: Routledge & Kegan Paul, 1973.

Lefebvre, Henri. *The Production of Space*. Cambridge, MA: Blackwell, 1991.

Lester, Alan, and Fae Dussart. *Colonization and the Origins of Humanitarian Governance: Protecting Aborigines across the Nineteenth-Century British Empire*. New York: Cambridge University Press, 2014.

Levi, Primo. *Survival in Auschwitz: The Nazi Assault on Humanity*. New York: Simon & Schuster, 1996.

Levine, Philippa. *Prostitution, Race & Politics: Policing Venereal Disease in the British Empire*. New York: Routledge, 2003.

Lindner, Ulrike. "Imperialism and Globalization: Entanglements and Interactions between the British and German Colonial Empires in Africa Before the First World War." *German Historical Institute London Bulletin* 32, no. 1 (2010): 4–28.

"Lofthouse-Ruhleben," accessed July 13, 2015, https://lofthousepark.wordpress.com/lofthouse/.

Lowry, Donal. "'The World's No Bigger Than a *Kraal*': The South African War and International Opinion in the First Age of Globalization." In *The Impact of the South African War*, edited by David Omissi and Andrew Thompson, 268–88. New York: Palgrave, 2002.

Lucking, Tony. "Some Thoughts on the Evolution of Boer War Concentration camps." *Journal of the Society for Army Historical Research* 82 (2004): 155–62.

Macdonagh, Oliver. "The Nineteenth-Century Revolution in Government: A Reappraisal." In *The Victorian Revolution: Government and Society in Victoria's Britain*, edited by Peter Stansky, 5–28. New York: New Viewpoints, 1973.

MacLeod, Roy. *Government and Expertise: Specialists, Administrators and Professionals, 1860–1919*. Cambridge: Cambridge University Press, 2003.

Madley, Benjamin. "From Africa to Auschwitz: How German South West Africa Incubated Ideas and Methods Adopted and Developed by the Nazis in Eastern Europe." *European History Quarterly* 35, no. 3 (2005): 429–64.

Madley, Benjamin. "From Terror to Genocide: Britain's Tasmanian Penal Colony and Australia's History Wars." *Journal of British Studies* 47 (2008): 77–106.

Maglen, Krista. *The English System: Quarantine, Immigration and the Making of a Port Sanitary Zone*. New York: Manchester University Press, 2014.

Magnus, Philip. *Kitchener: Portrait of an Imperialist*. Harmondsworth, UK: Penguin, 1968.

Major, Andrew. "State and Criminal Tribes in Colonial Punjab: Surveillance, Control and Reclamation of the 'Dangerous Classes.'" *Modern Asian Studies* 33, no. 3 (1999): 657–88.

Manaugh, Geoff, and Nicola Twilley. "Ebola and the Fiction of Quarantine." *The New Yorker*, August 11, 2014.

Mappen, Ellen. *Helping Women at Work: The Women's Industrial Council, 1889–1914*. London: Hutchinson Educational, 1985.

Marcuse, Harold. "The Afterlife of the Camps." In *Concentration Camps in Nazi Germany: The New Histories*, edited by Jane Kaplan and Nikolaus Wachsmann, 186–211. New York: Routledge, 2010.

Marcuse, Harold. *Legacies of Dachau: The Uses and Abuses of a Concentration Camp, 1933–2001*. Cambridge: Cambridge University Press, 2001.

Martin, A. C. *The Concentration Camps, 1900–1902, Facts, Fables, and Figures*. Cape Town: H. Timmins, 1957.

Mason, A. Stuart. "Summer Camps for Soldiers: 1778–1782." *Local Historian* 29, no. 4 (1999): 212–22.

Masselos, Jim. "Migration and Urban Identity: Bombay's Famine Refugees in the Nineteenth Century." In *Bombay: A Metaphor for Modern India*, edited by Sujata Patel and Alice Thorner, 25–58. New York: Oxford University Press, 1995.

Mazower, Mark. "Review Essay: Violence and the State in the Twentieth Century." *American Historical Review* 107, no. 4 (2002): 1158–78.

Metcalf, Thomas R. "From One Empire to Another: the Influence of the British Raj on American Colonialism in the Philippines." *Ab Imperio* 3 (2012): 25–41.

Metcalf, Thomas R. *Imperial Connections: India in the Indian Ocean Arena, 1860–1920*. Berkeley: University of California Press, 2007.

Metcalf, Thomas R. *Ideologies of the Raj*. New York: Cambridge University Press, 1994.

Miller, Stephen M. *Volunteers on the Veld: Britain's Citizen-Soldiers and the South African War, 1899–1902*. Norman: University of Oklahoma Press, 2007.

Mishra, H. K. *Famines and Poverty in India*. New Delhi: Ashish Publishing House, 1992.

Mishra, Pankaj. "Watch This Man," review of *Civilization: The West and the Rest*, by Niall Ferguson. *London Review of Books* 33 no. 21 (2011): 10–12.

Mitchell, Timothy. *Rule of Experts: Egypt, Techno-Politics, Modernity*. Berkeley: University of California Press, 2002.

Mohlamme, J. S. "African Refugee Camps in the Boer Republics." In *Scorched Earth*, edited by Fransjohan Pretorius, 110–31. Cape Town: Human & Rousseau, 2001.

Moore, Paul. "'And What Concentration Camps Those Were!': Foreign Concentration Camps in Nazi Propaganda, 1933–9." *Journal of Contemporary History* 45, no. 3 (2010): 649–74.

Morris, Michael. "Towards an Archeology of Navvy Huts and Settlements of the Industrial Revolution." *Antiquity* 68 (1994): 573–84.

Moses, Dirk, ed. *Genocide and Settler Society: Frontier Violence and Stolen Indigenous Children in Australian History*. New York: Berghahn Books, 2004.

Mrazek, Rudolf. *Engineers of Happy Land: Technology and Nationalism in a Colony*. Princeton, NJ: Princeton University Press, 2002.

Mühlhahn, Klaus. "The Dark Side of Globalization: The Concentration Camps in Republican China in Global Perspective." *World History Connected* 6 (2009), accessed December 1, 2012.

Mumford, Lewis. *The City in History: Its Origins, Its Transformations, and Its Prospects*. New York: Mariner Books, 1968.

Murton, B. "Spatial and Temporal Patterns of Famine in Southern India before the Famine Codes." In *Famine as a Geographical Phenomenon*, edited by Bruce Currey and Graeme Hugo, 71–90. Boston: D. Reidel, 1984.

Mytum, Harold, and Naomi Hall. "Norman Cross: Designing and Operating an Eighteenth-Century British Prisoner of War Camp." In *Prisoners of War: Archaeology, Memory, and Heritage of 19th- and 20th-Century Mass Internment*, edited by Harold Mytum and Gillian Carr, 75–91. New York: Springer, 2013.

Nasson, Bill. *Abraham Esau's War: A Black South African War in the Cape, 1899–1902*. Cambridge: Cambridge University Press, 2003.

Nasson, Bill. "Civilians in the Anglo-Boer War." In *Daily Lives of Civilians in Wartime Africa: From Slavery Days to Rwandan Genocide*, edited by John Laban, 85–111. Westport, CT: Greenwood, 2007.

Nasson, Bill. *The War for South Africa*. Cape Town: Tafelberg, 2010.

"National Park Civil War Series: The Prison Camp at Andersonville." Accessed November 1, 2014. www.nps.gov/history/history/online_books/civil_war_series /5/sec5.htm.

Netz, Reviel. *Barbed Wire: An Ecology of Modernity*. Middletown, CT: Wesleyan University Press, 2004.

Nicholson, Elizabeth, Tacy Hadley, and Job Hadley. "A Contraband Camp." *Indiana History Bulletin* 1, no. 11/12 (1924): 131–140.

Nigam, Sanjay. "Disciplining and Policing the 'Criminals by Birth,' Part 1: The Making of a Colonial Stereotype—The Criminal Tribes and Castes of North India." *Indian Economic and Social History Review* 27, no. 2 (1990): 131–64.

Nigam, Sanjay, "Disciplining and Policing the 'Criminals by Birth,' Part 2: The Development of a Disciplinary System, 1871–1900." *Indian Economic and Social History Review* 27, no. 3 (1990): 257–87.

Nightingale, Carl. *Segregation: A Global History of Divided Cities*. Chicago: University of Chicago Press, 2012.

Noyes, Edward, "The Contraband Camp at Cairo, Illinois." In *Historical Papers: Selected Proceedings of the Sixth Northern Great Plains History Conference*, edited by Lysle E. Meyer, 203–17. Moorehead, MN: Moorehead State College, 1971.

O'Brien, Gerard. "Workhouse Management in Pre-Famine Ireland." *Proceedings of the Royal Irish Academy. Section C: Archaeology, Celtic Studies, History, Linguistics, Literature* 86C, no. 3 (1986): 113–34.

Omissi, David. "India: Some Perceptions of Race and Empire." In *The Impact of the South African War*, edited by David Omissi and Andrew Thompson, 215–32. New York: Palgrave, 2002.

Otter, Chris. *The Victorian Eye: A Political History of Light and Vision in Britain, 1800–1910*. Chicago: University of Chicago Press, 2008.

Packard, Randall M. *White Plague, Black Labor: Tuberculosis and the Political Economy of Health and Disease in South Africa*. Berkeley: University of California Press, 1989.

Paik, Naomi. "Carceral Quarantine at Guantánamo: Legacies of US Imprisonment of Haitian Refugees." *Radical History Review*, no. 115 (2013): 142–68.

Pakenham, Thomas. *The Boer War*. New York: Random House, 1979.

Panayi, Panikos. "Internment in India during the First World War." Paper presented at the European Social Science History Conference, Valencia, Spain, April 1, 2016.

Peers, Douglas M. "Soldiers, Surgeons and the Campaigns to Combat Sexually Transmitted Diseases in Colonial India, 1805–1860." *Medical History* 42, no. 2 (1998): 137–60.

Perdue, Theda, and Michael D. Green. *Cherokee Removal: A Brief History with Documents*. Boston: Bedford St. Martin's, 1995.

Phillips, Howard. *Epidemics: The Story of South Africa's Five Most Lethal Human Diseases*. Athens: Ohio University Press, 2012.

Phimister, I. R. "African Labour Conditions and Health in the South Rhodesian Mining Industry." In *Studies in the History of African Mine Labour in Colonial Zimbabwe*, edited by I. R. Phimister and C. van Onselen, 102–50. Gwelo, Zimbabwe: Mambo Press, 1978.

Phoofolo, Pule. "Epidemics and Revolutions: The Rinderpest Epidemic in Late Nineteenth-Century Southern Africa." *Past & Present* 138, no. 1 (1993): 112–43.

Pick, Daniel, *Faces of Degeneration: A European Disorder, c.1848–1918*. New York: Cambridge University Press, 1993.

Pike, W. T. *East Anglia in the Twentieth Century: Contemporary Biographies*. Brighton: W. T. Pike, 1912.

Platt, Harold. *Shock Cities: The Environmental Transformation and Reform of Manchester and Chicago*. Chicago: University of Chicago Press, 2005.

Poovey, Mary. *Making a Social Body: British Cultural Formation, 1830–64*. Chicago: University of Chicago Press, 1995.

Pretorius, Fransjohan, "The Fate of the Boer Women and Children." In *Scorched Earth*, edited by Fransjohan Pretorius, 36–59. Cape Town: Human & Rousseau, 2001.

Pretorius, Fransjohan. *The Great Escape of the Boer Pimpernel Christiaan de Wet. The Making of a Legend*. Pietermaritzburg: University of Natal Press, 2001.

Pretorius, Fransjohan. "The White Concentration Camps of the Anglo-Boer War: A Debate without End." *Historia* 55, no. 2 (2010): 34–49.

Radhakrishna, Meena. *Dishonoured by History: "Criminal Tribes" and British Colonial Policy*. Hyderabad: Orient Longman, 2001.

Radhakrishna, Meena. "Surveillance and Settlements under the Criminal Tribes Act in Madras." *Indian Economic & Social History Review* 29, no. 2 (1992): 171–98.

Ranger, Terence, and Paul Slack, eds. *Epidemics and Ideas: Essays on the Historical Perception of Pestilence*. Cambridge: Cambridge University Press, 1992.

Ranyasami, Amrita. "Systems of Limited Intervention: An Evaluation of the Principles and Practice of Relief Administration in India." *Indian Historical Review* 27 (2000): 79–93.

Rediker, Markus. *The Slave Ship: A Human History*. New York: Viking, 2007.

Reidi, Eliza. "Teaching Empire: British and Dominions Women Teachers in the South African War Concentration Camps." *English Historical Review* 120, no. 489 (2005): 1316–47.

Reisman, David A. *Alfred Marshall: Progress and Politics*. New York: St. Martin's, 1987.

Rodney, Lynn S., and Phyllis M. Ford. *Camp Administration: Schools, Communities, Organizations*. New York: Ronald Press Company, 1971.

Royle, Stephen. "St Helena as a Boer Prisoner of War Camp, 1900–2: Information from the Alice Stopford Green Papers." *Journal of Historical Geography* 24, no. 1 (1998): 53–68.

Russell, Gillian. "Theatricality and Military Culture: British Army Camps in the 1770s." *Eighteenth-Century Life* 18, no. 3 (1994): 55–64.

Sabin, Margery. *Dissenters and Mavericks: Writings about India in English, 1765–2000.* Oxford: Oxford University Press, 2002.

Sasson, Tehila. "From Empire to Humanity: The Creation of Technologies of Famine Relief, 1880–1922." Paper presented at the North American Conference on British Studies, Minneapolis, MN, November 7–9, 2014.

Sasson, Tehila. "From Empire to Humanity: The Russian Famine and the Imperial Origins of International Humanitarianism." *Journal of British Studies* 55, no. 3 (2016): 519–37.

Sasson, Tehila. "In the Name of Humanity: Britain and the Rise of Global Humanitarianism." PhD diss., University of California, Berkeley, 2015.

Sasson, Tehila, and James Vernon. "Practising the British Way of Famine: Technologies of Relief, 1770–1985." *European Review of History* 22, no. 6 (2015): 860–72.

Satia, Priya. "The Defense of Inhumanity: Air Control in Iraq and the British Idea of Arabia." *American Historical Review* 111, no. 1 (2006): 16–51.

Scheipers, Sibylle. "The Use of Camps in Colonial Warfare." *Journal of Imperial and Commonwealth History* 43, no. 4 (2015): 678–698.

Schmitt, Carl. *The Nomos of the Earth in the International Law of Jus Publicum Europaeum.* New York: Telos, 2006.

Schumacher, Frank. "Lessons of Empire: The United States, the Quest for Colonial Expertise and the British Example, 1898–1917." In *From Enmity to Friendship. Anglo-American Relations in the 19th and 20th Century*, edited by Ursula Lehmkuhl and Gustav Schmidt, 71–98. Augsburg: Wissner-Verlag, 2005.

Schwarz, Bill. *The White Man's World.* New York: Oxford University Press, 2011.

Schwarz, Henry. *Constructing the Criminal Tribe in Colonial India: Acting Like a Thief.* Malden, MA: Wiley-Blackwell, 2010.

Scott, James. *The Art of Not Being Governed: An Anarchist History of Upland Southeast Asia.* New Haven, CT: Yale Agrarian Studies Series, 2010.

Scott, James. *Seeing Like a State: How Certain Schemes to Improve the Human Condition Have Failed.* New Haven, CT: Yale University Press, 1998.

Sen, Amartya. *Poverty and Famines: An Essay on Entitlement and Deprivation.* New York: Oxford University Press, 1981.

Sharma, Sanjay. *Famine, Philanthropy and the Colonial State: North India in the Early Nineteenth Century.* New Delhi: Oxford University Press, 2001.

Shaw, Caroline. *Britannia's Embrace: Modern Humanitarianism and the Imperial Origins of Refugee Relief*. New York: Oxford University Press, 2015.

Sheehan, James. *Where Have All the Soldiers Gone? The Transformation of Modern Europe*. Boston: Houghton Mifflin, 2008.

Singha, Radhika. *A Despotism of Law: Crime and Justice in Early Colonial India*. New York: Oxford University Press, 1998.

Sinha, Mrinalini. *Specters of Mother India: The Global Restructuring of an Empire*. Durham, NC: Duke University Press, 2006.

Slack, Paul. "Responses to Plague in Early Modern Europe: The Implications of Public Health." In *In Time of Plague: The History and Social Consequences of Lethal Epidemic Disease*, edited by Arien Mack, 111–31. New York: New York University Press, 1991.

Slezkine, Yuri. *The Jewish Century*. Princeton, NJ: Princeton University Press, 2004.

Smith, Iain R. *Origins of the South African War, 1899–1902*. New York: Longman, 1996.

Smith, Iain R., and Andreas Stucki. "The Colonial Development of Concentration Camps." *Journal of Imperial and Commonwealth History* 39, no. 3 (2011): 417–37.

Smith, Philip. *Punishment and Culture*. Chicago: University of Chicago Press, 2008.

Smith, Solveig. *By Love Compelled: The Story of 100 Years of the Salvation Army in India*. London: Salvationist Publishing, 1981.

Sofsky, Wolfgang. *The Order of Terror: The Concentration Camp*. Princeton, NJ: Princeton University Press, 1993.

Sontag, Susan. *AIDS and Its Metaphors*. New York: Farrar, Straus and Giroux, 1988.

Sorokin, Pitirim A. *Hunger as a Factor in Human Affairs*. Gainesville: University Presses of Florida, 1975.

Spies, S. B. *Methods of Barbarism? Roberts and Kitchener and Civilians in the Boer Republics: January 1900–May 1902*. Cape Town: Human & Rousseau, 1977.

Srivastava, Hari Shankar. *The History of Indian Famines and Development of Famine Policy, 1858–1918*. Agra: Sri Ram Mehra, 1968.

Srivastava, Hari Shankar. "The Indian Famine of 1876–9." *Journal of Indian History* 44, no. 132 (1966): 853–86.

Stanley, Liz. *Mourning Becomes . . .: Post/memory and Commemoration of the Concentration Camps of the South African War, 1899–1902*. Manchester: Manchester University Press, 2006.

Stassen, Nicol, and Ulrich van der Heyden. *German Publications on the Anglo-Boer War*. Pretoria: Protea Book House, 2007.

Stedman Jones, Gareth. *Outcast London: A Study in the Relationship between Classes in Victorian Society*. Oxford: Clarendon, 1971.

Steele, David. "Temple, Sir Richard, first baronet (1826–1902)." In *Oxford Dictionary of National Biography*, online ed., edited by David Cannadine. Oxford: Oxford University Press, 2004.

Stibbe, Matthew. *Captivity, Forced Labour and Forced Migration in Europe during the First World War*. London: Routledge, 2013.

Stibbe, Matthew. "Civilian Internment and Civilian Internees in Europe, 1914–20." *Immigrants & Minorities* 26, nos. 1/2 (2008): 49–81.

Stibbe, Matthew. "Internment of Civilians by Belligerent States and the Response of the International Committee of the Red Cross." *Journal of Contemporary History* 41, no. 1 (2006): 5–19.

Stoler, Ann Laura. *Carnal Knowledge and Imperial Power: Race and the Intimate in Colonial Rule*. Berkeley: University of California Press, 2002.

Stoler, Ann Laura. "Colony." *Political Concepts: A Critical Lexicon* 1. Accessed August 8, 2016. http://www.politicalconcepts.org/issue1/colony.

Sturgis, Amy. *The Trail of Tears and Indian Removal*. Westport, CT: Greenwood Press, 2007.

Surridge, Keith. "The Politics of War: Lord Kitchener and the Settlement of the South African War." In *Writing a Wider War: Rethinking Gender, Race, and Identity in the South African War, 1899–1902*, edited by Gregor Cuthbertson, A. M. Grundlingh, and Mary-Lynn Suttie, 213–32. Athens: Ohio University Press, 2002.

Surtees, R. J. "The Development of an Indian Reserve Policy in Canada." *Ontario History* 61, no. 2 (1969): 87–98.

Sutphen, Mary. "Not What but Where: Bubonic Plague and the Reception of Germ Theories in Hong Kong and Calcutta, 1894–1897." *Journal of the History of Medicine and Allied Sciences* 52, no. 1 (1997): 81–113.

Swanson, Maynard W. "The Sanitation Syndrome: Bubonic Plague and Urban Native Policy in the Cape Colony, 1900–1909." In *Segregation and Apartheid in Twentieth-Century South Africa*, edited by William Beinhart and Saul Dubow, 25–42. London: Routledge, 1995.

Taber, Robert. *The War of the Flea: A Study of Guerrilla Warfare Theory and Practice*. New York: Lyle Stuart, 1965.

Taylor, Julie Anne. *Muslims in Medieval Italy: The Colony at Lucera*. Lanham, MD: Lexington Books, 2005.

Thompson, E. P. "Time, Work-Discipline, and Industrial Capitalism." *Past and Present* 38, no. 1 (1967): 56–97.

Thompson, E. P. *Whigs and Hunters: The Origins of the Black Act*. New York: Pantheon, 1975.

Tolen, Rachel. "Colonizing and Transforming the Criminal Tribesman: The Salvation Army in British India." *American Ethnologist* 18, no. 1 (1991): 106–25.

Traverso, Enzo. *The Origins of Nazi Violence*. New York: New Press, 2003.

Turrell, Rob. "Kimberley's Model Compounds." *Journal of African History* 25, no. 1 (1984): 59–75.

Van den Bergh, Gert. "British Scorched Earth and Concentration Camp Policies." *Scientia Militaria: South African Journal of Military Studies* 40, no. 2 (2012): 72–88.

Van den Bergh, Gert. "The Three British Occupations of Potchefstroom during the Anglo-Boer War, 1899–1902." *Scientia Militaria, South African Journal of Military Studies* 37, no. 1 (2009): 95–112.

Van der Waal, G. M. *From Mining Camp to Metropolis: The buildings of Johannesburg, 1886–1940*. Pretoria: C. van Rensburg Publications of the Human Sciences Research Council, 1st edition, 1987.

Van Heyningen, Elizabeth, "British Doctors versus Boer Women: Clash of Medical Cultures." In *Scorched Earth*, edited by Fransjohan Pretorius, 178–97. Cape Town: Human & Rousseau, 2001.

Van Heyningen, Elizabeth. *The Concentration Camps of the Anglo-Boer War: A Social History*. Johannesburg: Jacana Media, 2013.

Van Heyningen, Elizabeth. "The Concentration Camps of the South African (Anglo-Boer) War, 1900–1902." *History Compass* 7 (2009): 22–43.

Van Heyningen, Elizabeth. "Costly Mythologies: The Concentration Camps of the South African War in Afrikaner Historiography." *Journal of Southern African Studies* 34, no. 3 (2008): 495–513.

Van Heyningen, Elizabeth "British Concentration Camps of the South African War." Accessed July 15, 2014. http://www2.lib.uct.ac.za/mss/bccd/.

Van Heyningen, Elizabeth. "'Fools Rush In:' Writing a History of the Concentration Camps of the South African War." *Historia* 55, no. 2 (2010): 12–33.

Van Heyningen, Elizabeth. "Medical History and Afrikaner Society in the Boer Republics at the End of the Nineteenth Century." *Kleio Journal of the Department of History, University of South Africa* 37 (2005): 5–25.

Van Heyningen, Elizabeth, "Public Health and Society in Cape Town, 1880–1910." PhD diss., University of Cape Town, 1989.

Van Heyningen, Elizabeth. "Refugees and Relief in Cape Town, 1899–1902." *Studies in the History of Cape Town* 3 (1980): 64–113.

Van Heyningen, Elizabeth. "A Tool for Modernisation? The Boer Concentration Camps of the South African War, 1900–1902." *South African Journal of Science* 106, no. 5/6 (2010): 58–67.

Van Heyningen, Elizabeth. "Women and Disease: The Clash of Medical Cultures in the Concentration Camps of the South African War." In *Writing a Wider War: Rethinking Gender, Race, and Identity in the South African War, 1899–1902*, edited by Gregor Cuthbertson, Albert Grundlingh, and Mary-Lynn Suttie, 186–212. Athens: Ohio University Press, 2002.

Van Heyningen, Elizabeth, and Lucy Bean, eds. *The Letters of Jane Elizabeth Waterston, 1866–1905*. Cape Town: Van Riebeck Society, 1983.

Van Onselen, Charles. *Chibaro: African Mine Labour in Southern Rhodesia*. London: Pluto, 1976.

Verdirame, Guglielmo, and Barbara Harrell-Bond. *Rights in Exile: Janus-Faced Humanitarianism*. New York: Berghahn Books, 2005.

Vernon, James. *Distant Strangers: How Britain Became Modern*. Berkeley: University of California Press, 2014.

Vernon, James. *Hunger: A Modern History*. Cambridge, MA: Belknap Press of Harvard University Press, 2007.

Wachsmann, Nikolaus. "The Dynamics of Destruction: The Development of the Concentration Camps, 1934–1945." In *Concentration Camps in Nazi Germany: The New Histories*, edited by Nikolaus Wachsmann and Jane Caplan, 17–43. New York: Routledge, 2010.

Wagner, Kim. "'Treading Upon Fires': The 'Mutiny'-Motif and Colonial Anxieties in British India." *Past and Present* 218, no. 1 (2012): 159–97.

Walker, Cam. "Corinth: The Story of a Contraband Camp." *Civil War History* 20, no. 1 (1974): 5–22.

Walkowitz, Judith. *City of Dreadful Delight: Narratives of Sexual Danger in Late-Victorian London*. Chicago: University of Chicago Press, 1992.

Warwick, Peter. *Black People and the South African War, 1899–1902*. New York: Cambridge University Press, 1983.

Weiss, Lindsay, "Exceptional Space: Concentration Camps and Labor Compounds in late Nineteenth-Century South Africa." *Archaeologies of Internment*, edited by Adrian Myers and Gabriel Moshenska, 21–32. New York: Springer, 2011.

Wells, Samantha. "Labour, Control and Protection: The Kahlin Aboriginal Compound, Darwin, 1911–38." In *Settlement: A History of Australian Indigenous Housing*, edited by Peter Read, 64–74. Canberra: Aboriginal Studies, 2000.

Wessels, André, ed. *Lord Roberts and the War in South Africa, 1899–1902*. Stroud, UK: Sutton Publishing for the Army Records Society, 2000.

Wessels, André, ed. *Lord Kitchener and the War in South Africa, 1899–1902*. Stroud, UK: Sutton Publishing for the Army Record Society, 2006.

Whitehead, Judy. "Bodies Clean and Unclean: Prostitution, Sanitary Legislation, and Respectable Femininity in Colonial North India." *Gender & History* 7, no. 1 (1995): 41–63.

Wills, Walter. *The Anglo-African Who's Who and Biographical Sketch-Book*. London: L. Upott Gill, 1902.

Wilson, Angela. "Decolonizing the 1862 Death Marches." *American Indian Quarterly* 28, nos. 1&2 (1994): 185–215.

Wilson, Jon. *The Domination of Strangers: Modern Governance in Eastern India, 1785–1835*. Basingstoke, UK: Palgrave Macmillan, 2008.

Worboys, Michael. *Spreading Germs: Disease Theories and Medical Practice in Britain, 1865–1900*. New York: Cambridge University Press, 2000.

Wrench, John Evelyn. *Alfred Lord Milner: The Man of No Illusions, 1854–1925*. London: Eyre & Spottiswoode, 1958.

Zietsman, Paul. "The Concentration Camp Schools—Beacons of Light in the Darkness." In *Scorched Earth*, edited by Fransjohan Pretorius, 86–109. Cape Town: Human & Rousseau, 2001.

Zimmerer, Jurgen. "The Birth of the *Ostland* out of the Spirit of Colonialism: A Postcolonial Perspective on the Nazi Policy of Conquest and Extermination." *Patterns of Prejudice* 39, no. 2 (2005): 197–219.

Zimmerer, Jurgen. "Colonialism and the Holocaust. Towards an Archaeology of Genocide." In *Genocide and Settler Society: Frontier Violence and Stolen Indigenous Children in Australian History*, edited by Dirk Moses, 49–76. New York: Berghahn Books, 2005.

Zysberg, Andre. "Galley and Hard Labor Convicts in France (1550–1850), from the Galleys to Hard Labor Camps: Essay on a Long Lasting Penal Institution." In *The Emergence of Carceral Institutions: Prisons, Galleys and Lunatic Asylums, 1550–1900*, edited by Pieter Spierenburg. Rotterdam: Centrum Voor Maatschappij Geschiedenis, Erasmus University, 1984.

INDEX

Figures are indicated by page numbers followed by *fig.* and maps are indicated by page numbers followed by *map*.

born criminals: of nomadic tribes, 35–36; preventative detention of, 38–39; spatial relationships of, 36–37

Botha, Louis, 157

Bowen, Cole, 161

Braamfontein camp, 31*fig.*

Brackenbury, W. J. W., 125, 197

Bridewell workhouse, 28

British army camps: Aldershot, 25, 25*fig.*, 152; disciplinary control in, 24; family quarters in, 25*fig.*, 26; functions of, 24; internal geography of, 26; orderliness of, 26; sanitation in, 26–27; social and spatial distancing in, 26

British camps: and Anglo-American political traditions, 13; impact of free press on, 11–12; and liberal politics, 10–11; policing of social deviance in, 11; post-second world war, 12. *See also* encampments; famine camps; plague camps; relief work camps; wartime concentration camps

British empire: Boer War, 129–50; camp expertise of, 186–208, 211, 220, 222, 224; and civilian confinement, 219–20, 226; colonial subjects in, 2; concentration camps in, 130, 213–18; disciplinary repertoires of, 8, 42; disease transmission in, 74; and education, 170; famine policy in, 46–49, 56–60, 66, 73; global crises in, 2–3; and governmentality, 4; and humanitarian relief, 224–25; illiberal history of, 10–11; interimperial connections in, 8–9; and labor discipline, 20, 62–64; legacy of, 9–10, 210–12, 222; medical and moral policing in, 23–24; medical power in, 78–79; migrant workers in, 20; military power in, 78–79; and order, 6–7; public health initiatives in, 23–24; racial discourse in, 220–21; segregation practices in, 15; and social control, 59–60; and spatial control,

59–61; and spread of camp culture, 26, 131, 193–95; threats to profit in, 78

Brodrick, St. John, 157, 164, 181, 191

Buchan, John, 136, 138, 142, 186, 204

Budihal Tank camp, 106

Bülow, Bernhard von, 216

Burnett, C. J., 83

Burnham, Frederick, 134

Burton, Antoinette, 6

Caird, James, 71

Campbell-Bannerman, Henry, 139, 181, 211

camp hospitals, 18, 27, 44, 99, 107–8, 112, 120, 123–24, 126, 162, 170, 188, 201–2

camp management: and discipline, 126–27; and disease, 9, 122; of wartime concentration camps, 186–87

Cape Colony, 21*fig.*, 92, 94, 115, 131, 132*map*, 141, 146, 171, 191

Cape Town: forced removals in, 94; inspection of conditions in, 191; plague in, 75, 92, 192

carceral archipelago of camps, 14, 17–18, 39

Carmichael, C. P., 36, 38

caste boundaries, 71

Chamberlain, Joseph, 72, 148, 150, 164, 178, 181, 184, 187–89, 193–95, 197, 199, 203

Chandvarkar, Rajnarayan, 81, 95

Chatterjee, Partha, 6, 78

Chaudhary, Zahid, 50

children: confinement of, 143; and disease, 110, 178, 181; displacement of, 157; education in British values, 170–71; images of emaciated, 51*fig.*, 182*fig.*, 183; in internment camps, 220; milk and soup kitchens for, 67, 163; in relief work camps, 64–65; starvation of, 181, 182*fig.*, 183; as war victims, 184 cholera, 17, 23, 54, 100, 110–12, 120, 124, 176, 220

Churchill, Winston, 134, 215–16

cities and towns: restructuring of, 99; slum clearance in, 86, 98–99; urban cleansing in, 75*fig.*, 76, 86, 98, 117–18. *See also* inner cities

civilians: coercive military concentration of, 130, 130*fig.*, 144, 156–57; collective punishment of, 139, 141, 143–44; in internment camps, 219–21; support for guerrillas by, 130, 133, 136–39, 141, 144, 146, 150

civil rights: discourse of, 96; suspension of, 37–38, 56

class warfare, 28–31

cleanliness, 81, 114, 147–49, 175

Clean Party, 92

Cleghorn, James, 79, 82–83, 86–87, 91, 120, 122, 125, 127, 194–95, 205

collective punishment, 139, 141, 143–44

colonial populations: authoritarian responses to, 78; control of, 32; "dirty," 81–82, 147–48, 175; displacement of, 32–33; distrust of, 84, 89–90; and fear of camps, 95–96; and fears of contagion, 22–23, 81–83; ingenuity of, 90–92; mobility of, 7; "protective reserves" for, 33; and protests against plague operations, 95; settlements for, 32–33; spatial segregation of, 7, 23; statelessness of, 6; workhouse infrastructure for, 34–35

colonial prisons, 18–19

Colvin, A., 53

common lands, 15

concentration camps: British invention of, 213–16, 225; and colonial expertise, 220, 222; connotation of, 213; depictions of, 218; discourse of, 225; global spread of, 216–17, 221; imitation of, 212–14, 217–18; and military conquest, 28; Nazi, 213–14,

216–19; repurposing of, 218; similarities in, 219. *See also* wartime concentration camps

confinement: of children, 143; and class warfare, 28–29; global culture of, 35; principles of, 19; and regulation of deviance, 18; without trial, 38–39; of women, 38; in workhouses, 28–29

contact camps, 76, 88*fig.*

contagion, 5, 7, 22–3, 30, 37, 40, 52, 74–5, 81–2, 84, 85, 92, 148, 201, 216, 226

contagious disease hospitals, 124

Contagious Diseases Act (1868), 23

contraband camps, 28

coolie depots, 20

Corbett, J. H., 171

Cornish, W. R., 54, 66–67

"criminal classes": calls for removal of, 31; confinement of, 30; and famine, 52–53; surveillance of, 43; in workhouses, 14, 29

criminal tribes: assimilation of, 35–36; banishment of, 40; civil rights of, 38–39; collective punishment of, 38–39; and contagion metaphors, 37; and famine, 53; preventative detention of, 38–39; segregation of, 37; settlement of, 34–35, 38–40

Criminal Tribes Act (1871), 34, 37, 58

criminal tribe settlements: curative labor in, 39–41; disease in, 40–41; factories as, 40; isolation of, 40

Curtin, Philip, 79, 175

Curtis, Lionel, 210

Curzon, George Nathaniel, 47–48, 72, 74, 96–97, 100, 117, 126, 128, 137, 143, 165, 195, 222, 224

Dachau, 218

Dadar Evacuation Camp, 119*fig.*, 122

Daller, A. G. H., 155, 172, 176

"dangerous classes": calls for removal of, 31–32; in camps, 6; in labor camps,

31–32, 42; in the military, 24; in plague camps, 6, 76, 84; vagrancy legislation for, 29

Davis, Mike, 2, 111

Deane, Lucy, 150, 186, 191, 210–11

Deleuze, Gilles, 36

Denness, Zoë, 220

Department of Native Refugees, 173

Dernburg, Bernhard, 216

detention camps: attacks on, 97; comfort of, 116; rations in, 116; rituals of admission in, 114; sanitation in, 117; social and racial distinctions in, 116–17; for suspected plague carriers, 76–77, 114*fig.*

detention centers, 44, 62

Devala camp, 111

De Wet, Christiaan, 134, 135*fig.*, 136, 139, 142, 145

Dhariwal Criminal Tribes Settlement, 40

Digby, William, 61, 64, 66, 68–69, 100, 102–3, 110

discrimination, 84

disease: abandoning camps due to, 124; and camp management, 9, 122; in camps, 100, 109–12, 123–24, 160, 162, 174–79, 183, 188, 192; childhood, 178; and colonial populations, 6; and "dangerous" bodies, 4; and famine, 54; in labor camps, 21; military model of, 79; and quarantine, 22–23; and refugees, 148–49; responses to, 91; and segregation, 23–24; spread of, 3, 9; suspicion of, 1, 5–6; tracking, 90–91; and urbanization, 17. *See also* plague; public health

disease control: scientific, 95; technologies of, 91

disinfection squads, 88

distance test, 63–64, 72

Donnelly, James, 47

dormitory camps, 44, 61–62

Douglas, Mary, 81, 147

Dove, Richard, 220

Dutt, Romesh Chunder, 3, 44, 72, 180

dysentery, 110, 160, 176

eastern pattern tents, 162

East India Company, 44

education: and British values, 170–71; in camps, 170–71, 174

Edwards, Alfred, 151–52

Egerton, P. H., 38

Elgin, Victor Alexander Bruce, 46

Elkins, Caroline, 216

Elliot, C. A., 40

emergency powers, 78–79

encampments: administration of, 160–62; barbed wire in, 103, 114, 164, 166–67, 180; challenges of, 100–101; and civil rights discourse, 96; as contested institutions, 71, 95; contingency plans for, 124; "dangerous classes" in, 6, 14; defining, 12; discipline of, 124–25; epidemics in, 100, 109–10; fences in, 101–3, 124, 126; functions of, 14; genealogy of, 226–27; global spread of, 216–17; and governmentality, 4; hostility towards, 95–96; humanitarian aspects of, 213, 222; imperial precedents for, 193–98, 219; legacy of, 210–11; local context of, 3; management of, 120, 126–27; medical discourse of, 41; military function of, 5, 41; mobile, 106, 107*fig.*; normalization of, 211; and order, 17, 114; origin of, 7; "perfect," 203–5, 206*fig.*, 207–8; physical layout of, 102*fig.*, 103, 107, 109, 122, 205; planning for, 123; post-second world war, 12–13; preventative, 38; and "problem groups," 6; "protective custody" in, 5, 23; quarantine-detention, 22–23; reform in, 186–93, 198–205, 207; regulation in, 115–16; and "rehabilitation," 4; religious violations in, 96;

encampments: administration of *(continued)*
sanitation in, 109–12, 120–26, 128;
shared culture of, 131; shelters in,
115–16; size of, 122–23; standardization of, 101; surveillance of, 125–26;
transformation in, 10; transimperial
narrative of, 8–9; unrest in, 97. *See
also* famine camps; plague camps;
refugee camps; relief work camps;
shelters; wartime concentration
camps
Epidemic Diseases Act (1897), 54, 58, 79
Erukkanchery camp, 106
Esselen, G. F., 161
Ethiopian Famine (1983-85), 73
eugenicist thought, 31
evacuation camps: control of, 118–19;
fences in, 118; medical policing in, 118;
physical layout of, 118, 119*fig.*;
refugees in, 88*fig.*; sanitation in, 76;
and urban cleansing, 76, 86–87, 89,
117–18; voluntary, 98
execution, 18

famine: causes of, 46; fear and anxiety of,
49; in India, 43–44, 45*map*, 46–58;
migration response to, 50; and public
order, 52–53; relief policy, 46–48; and
revenue collection, 48; in Russia,
223–24; social struggle in, 53, 55;
South African, 144–45, 151–52, 162
famine camps: administration of, 58–59;
and caste boundaries, 71; and colonial
expertise, 224; and colonial mobility,
7; colonial populations in, 2–8, 10;
conditions in, 63, 103, 105; construction of, 101; crisis mentality of, 57–58;
criticism of, 71–72; "dangerous
classes" in, 6; death rates in, 109–11,
183; discipline of, 100, 125; disease in,
110–12; establishment of, 55; fences
in, 101–3; and financial strain, 46;
functions of, 44; imperial expertise in,

9; labor in, 3, 43–44, 61–62, 64–66,
103; lessons of, 194–96; and liberal
politics, 11; military function of,
56–57, 125; physical layout of, 102*fig.*,
103; "protective custody" in, 5;
punishment in, 105; quarantine wards
in, 123–24; rations in, 103, 105;
Russian, 224; sanitation in, 100,
109–12, 120, 127; and social control,
59, 70*fig.*; and spatial control, 60–61;
standard operating procedures for,
123–24; surveillance of, 125–26;
suspension of civil rights in, 56–57;
for wanderers, 55–56
famine photographs, 50, 51*fig.*
famine victims: as criminals, 53–54, 58;
danger and unrest of, 52–53; dehumanization of, 50–51; diet for, 67;
dislocation of, 51–54, 60; empathy for,
50–52; forced concentration of, 55–58,
62; images of, 51*fig.*, 182*fig.*; at labor
camps, 66–67; mistrust of, 52–54,
68–69; removal of, 64
famine wanderers: "criminal classes" as,
43, 53; dehumanization of, 50–52;
detention of, 51*fig.*, 55–58, 61–62, 72,
101, 103; nomadic tribes as, 49;
prevention of, 60; removal of, 49;
rights of, 57–58; threat of, 52–54
Fanon, Frantz, 23
farm colonies, 32
Fawcett, Millicent, 190–92, 210
Fawcett Committee, 190–97, 201, 211
fences: British empire, 18, 20, 42, 44; and
displacement, 12; in evacuation camps,
118; and hospitals, 126; labor behind,
103; and medical surveillance,
200–201; and native populations, 173;
and plague detention, 84, 98, 123–24;
and sanitation, 121–22, 200; and
security, 101–3, 107–8, 114; and
segregation, 88*fig.*, 93; and surveillance of population, 59–60; and water

supply, 121, 201; in work camps, 32. *See also* barbed-wire fences

Ferguson, Niall, 9

Field, John, 32

foreigners: segregation of, 93; suspicion of, 14, 54, 220; undeserving, 52

Foucault, Michel, 5, 18

Francis, Pope, 226

Franks, Kendal, 147, 149, 175–76, 178

Freitag, Sandria, 34

French, W. C., 125, 197

Fuller, J. F. C., 137

Gandhi, Mohandas, 96

Gatacre, William F., 89

genocide, 13

germ theory, 80, 85

Gerwarth, Robert, 213

Gibson, Edmund 77

Gilomee, Hermann, 149

Gladstone, Herbert, 30

global pandemics: Asian, 2, 74; Indian, 2, 99; South African, 3. *See also* plague

Goebbels, Joseph, 214–15

Gokuldas Tejpal camp, 115

Goold-Adams, Hamilton, 42, 155, 169, 205

Göring, Hermann, 213

Gostling, A. V., 164

Gray, Henry, 103

Great Bengal Famine (1973), 73

Great Britain: class warfare in, 28–31; factories in, 19; incarceration in, 18; legacy of camps in, 210–12; liberalism of, 37–38, 42; "mass society" of, 17; privatization of common lands in, 15; racism in, 47; responses to plague in, 77; segregation practices in, 14–15; social change in Victorian, 16–17; social dislocation in, 15, 32; urban concentration in, 15–17; "wandering tribes" in, 29–30; workhouses in, 28–30

Great Famine of 1876-77, 40, 45*map*, 46

Great Irish Famine (1845-51), 47

Great Russian Famine of 1921-22, 223

Guantanamo Bay, 216, 227

Guattari, Felix, 36

guerrillas, 140*fig.*; Anglo-Boer War, 133–34, 137, 141–42, 150; and civilian support, 130, 133, 136–39, 144, 146, 150; detention of, 37, 143; and displacement, 94; and evacuations, 5, 130; fear of, 130–31; tactics of, 141; and wandering gangs, 34, 37

guinea worm, 110

Gunthorpe, J. A., 35–36

Habitual Criminals Act (1869), 29, 34

Hadleigh labor colony, 31*fig.*, 32, 39

Haldane, J. S., 163

Hall-Matthews, David, 63

Harrison, Elaine, 190

Harrison, Mark, 79

Haussleiter, F., 217

Heidelburg concentration camp, 25*fig.*

Heilbron, 151, 170–71

Henderson, Nevile, 213

Henderson, R. W., 197

Hewlett, T. G., 107, 122

Higham, Thomas, 64, 109

Hill, Claude, 79, 81, 87, 99, 222, 224

Himes, Whiteside, 179

Hintrager, Oskar, 217

Hobhouse, Emily, 145, 150, 160–61, 180–81, 183–84, 187, 190, 209–11, 219, 222

Hobson, J. A., 131

Holderness, Thomas, 67, 109–10, 120, 123, 127, 194–95, 203

Hollesley Bay camp, 32

Hollymoor military hospital, 213

Holocaust, 219

Hong Kong, 2, 74

Hooper, W. W., 50, 51*fig.*

Hopford, Wim, 219

hospitals: camp, 18, 27, 44, 99, 107–8, 112, 120, 123–24, 126, 162, 170, 188, 201; fear of, 202–3; jail, 85; lock, 54,

191–92; reform and rehabilitation in, 29; and sanitation, 29

workhouse test, 192

World War I: and disease, 223; dislocation of, 223; and famine, 223; internment camps, 219; propaganda in, 214; racial discourse in, 220–21; refugee camps, 222

World War II: anti-Semitism in, 217; and colonialism, 217; concentration camp repurposing after, 218; global power after, 216; internment camps, 219; propaganda in, 214

Younghusband, A. D., 105

Yule, Pratt, 170, 175, 178, 202